PREFACE

The unique collaboration of *Introducing Management* with *The Wall Street Journal Interactive Edition* is a bold step forward in management education. Today's students, in all of their wonderful diversity, are tomorrow's leaders and managers. They are the hope of the 21st century. And just as the workplace in this new century will be vastly different, so too will our teaching and learning environments. While continuing to emphasize the relevance of cultural diversity, ethics and social responsibility, the global economy, and the imperatives of quality and high performance, management educators must step confidently forward. New values and management approaches are appearing; the nature of work and organizations is changing; the age of information is not only with us, it is transforming organizations and our everyday lives.

Introducing Management is designed for this time of transformation. Nowhere are the changes in the world of work and organizations more in evidence, discussed, and examined for significance than in the print and online pages of *The Wall Street Journal*. The integration of this book with access to *The Wall Street Journal Interactive Edition* presents a unique and compelling educational opportunity. It allows the major theories and concepts to be examined in context with practical issues and developments of the day. Each chapter contains a "Management Across Functions" feature keyed to the journal; a *Interactive Journal In Practice* exercise further integrates *The Wall Street Journal Interactive Edition* with chapter content; and both features are further developed for interactive online activities through the book's Web site (www.wiley.com/college/schermerhorn).

Introducing Management is purposefully short, to the point, and organized for ease of use across many different potential applications. It has been developed with the goal of curriculum innovation in mind, and is an excellent fit for integrative, multidisciplinary and project-oriented courses. While presented in one logical framework, chapters can be used in any order of instructional preference. The book is like one of today's high performance organizations—neat, trim, fast and highly capable for the task at hand. For students, it is also straightforward and supportive. The chapter opening study questions, a running margin glossary, and end-of-chapter key terms list and summary orient and assist student readers. And, a comprehensive Web site offers an extensive array of options that allow for course enrichment through the use of career portfolios, critical thinking cases, interactive self-assessment inventories, interactive chapter self-tests, and more.

All management educators face common problems and opportunities when developing courses, working with students, and trying to uphold accreditation standards. This book has been created to support the pursuit of instructional excellence in all such settings. More than ever before, our students have pressing needs as they strive to establish the best possible foundations for life-long learning. They must not only understand the best insights of the disciplines, they must gain exposure to real-world applications and practices, and they must appreciate the dynamic and fast-paced environment of work in an information age and global economy. Our instructional approaches and materials must deliver on all of these dimensions and probably more. *Introducing Management* and its special collaboration with *The Wall Street Journal Interactive Edition* puts into your hands and into those of your students a learning resource that can help meet these needs.

BOOK AT A GLANCE

Introducing Management presents the essentials of management as they apply within the contemporary work environment. In conjunction with *The Wall Street Journal Interactive Edition*, its goal is to introduce management core topics, theories and themes in a manner relevant to the dynamic environment of the new workplace. The subject matter has been carefully chosen to meet AACSB accreditation guidelines while allowing extensive flexibility to fit various course designs and class sizes, including multidisciplinary and integrative curriculum settings. Importantly, this is done by blending the fundamentals of management with special attention to the environment, cultural diversity, globalization, and ethics and social responsibility as paramount concerns of our day.

ORGANIZATION

- The book is organized into four parts Context, Planning and Controlling, Organizing, and Leading.
- Part 1 opens the book with a clear focus on the exciting and dynamic new workplace, environment and information technology, globalization and the importance of ethics and social responsibility.
- Part 2 integrates both planning and controlling as management functions, and includes an all-new treatment of strategic management and entrepreneurship.
- Part 3 covers the essentials of organizing as a management function, with special attention to new developments in organization cultures, designs and work processes.
- Part 4 offers extensive coverage of leadership as a managerial function, including motivation and job design, communication and interpersonal skills, teams and teamwork, and innovation and change leadership.

CONTENT HIGHLIGHTS

Throughout *Introducing Management* every effort is made to bring in the latest thinking and concepts facing managers and organizations today. In addition to core themes of diversity, competitive advantage, quality, globalization, and empowerment, specific coverage includes all of the following topics and more:

multicultural organizations • ethnocentrism • cultural relativism • emotional intelligence • customer-driven organizations • electronic commerce • entrepreneurship • organizational learning • life-long learning • horizontal organizations • cross-functional teams • virtual teams • virtual organizations • process value analysis • re-engineering • work–life balance • strategic human resource planning • performance-based rewards • alternative work arrangements • communication barriers • conflict management • negotiation • teamwork • innovation processes • change leadership • knowledge management

CHAPTER DESIGN

Planning Ahead:

Each chapter begins with a set of *study questions* linked to each of the major subject headings. They serve as learning objectives and create a framework for the chapter summary.

Opening Headline:

The first text in the chapter is introduced with a *Headline* that calls out a key issue or point regarding management today. This is accompanied by a short vignette offering a timely report or example relevant to chapter and to the new workplace of the 21st century.

Embedded Boxes:

In-depth examples are embedded in chapter text to illustrate the important themes of *workforce diversity, ethics and social responsibility, best practices, entrepreneurship and globalization.* Each provides a concise and relevant example without interrupting the flow of the text. The themes of these examples are identified by the following logos:

Workforce Diversity   Entrepreneurship   Best Practices

Ethics and Social Responsibility   Globalization

Manager's Notepads:

Concise lists of helpful hints—the "do's" and "don'ts" of managerial behavior are found in the *Manager's Notepads* included with each chapter. They are designed as useful theory-into-practice summaries, and to assist readers with understanding the action implications of material being studied.

Margin Running Glossary:

Boldfaced key terms from the text are called out and defined in the margin, forming a *running glossary* of the key concepts of the discussion. This turns the margins into a handy study-guide for use in studying chapter content and preparing for examinations.

Margin List Identifiers:

Whenever important lists are introduced in a chapter, *margin list identifiers* are provided as reminders. Like the margin terms, these notes provide a convenient study outline for students.

Chapter Summary:

The end-of-chapter summary is organized according to the study questions in the chapter opening. The summary repeats each study question and offers in concise bullet-list form an overview of key points from that section of the chapter.

List of Key Terms:

The end-of-chapter list of key terms allows the student to double-check familiarity with basic concepts and definitions. Page numbers are included for easy access to the textual reference.

WWW.WILEY.COM/COLLEGE/SCHERMERHORN

The *Introducing Management* Web site features:

- A **Study Guide** for students contains interactive self-tests and Power-Point® outlines for each chapter.
- **Access to** *The Wall Street Journal Interactive Edition*
- **Interactive Journal In Practice** provides students a tutorial on *using* wsj.com for each chapter
- **Interactive Journal Management Across Functions**
- **Interactive Journal Online Cases**
- **The Wall Street Journal Reading Room**
- Access to Wiley's **Business Extra** featuring an archive of articles from *The Wall Street Journal*, FAST COMPANY magazine articles, and more.
- **Interactive Self-Assessments**
- The **Career Assessment Portfolio** provides templates for students to build a resume and a career portfolio that documents, in electronic form, their academic and personal accomplishments for external review. This resource can help them frame and summarize personal credentials for potential internship sources and full-time employers. The Career Advancement Portfolio can be easily maintained and updated for purposes of outcome assessment within a course or program of study, as well as for the student's personal and career development.
- **Instructor's Resources** including teaching tips for using Interactive Journal In Practice feature and answers for the discussion questions; answers for the Interactive Journal Online Case discussion questions; and downloads for the PowerPoint® Slides, Instructor's Manual; Test Bank; and Computerized Test Bank.

INSTRUCTIONAL SUPPORT PACKAGE

The **Instructor's Resource Guide,** prepared by William L. Gardner of the University of Mississippi, is a unique, comprehensive guide to building a system of customized instruction. The manual offers helpful teaching ideas, advice on course development, sample assignments, and chapter-by-chapter text highlights, learning objectives, lecture outlines, class exercises, lecture notes, and more. The Instructor's Resource Guide is available in print, for downloading from the password protected Schermerhorn Web site, and on the Instructor's CD-ROM.

The **Test Bank,** prepared by Michael K. McCuddy of Valparaiso University, includes multiple choice, true-false, and essay questions. The answers for the multiple choice and True/False questions include the text page reference and the pedagogical element being tested. The test bank also tells the instructor whether a particular question is factual or applied in nature. The Test Bank is available in print, on the Instructor's CD-ROM, in Brownstone Research Group's Diploma testing software, and can be downloaded from the password protected Schermerhorn Web site.

Diploma, Brownstone Research Group's highlyacclaimed assessment software for instructors, is available to adopters and combines flexible test-creation features with a comprehensive grade book for easy administration and tracking of paper quizzes, network-based tests, and Internet exams.

PowerPoint® Slides are available for use in class and in management training programs. Full-color slides feature all of the key text figures and John Schermerhorn's class-tested collection. In addition, Cheryl Wyrick of California State Polytechnic University-Pomona, has provided a set of slides for each chapter containing lecture outlines, concepts, and diagrams. The slides are available for downloading on the password-protected Schermerhorn Web site and on the Instructor's CD-ROM.

The **Instructor's CD-ROM** includes a compilation of the electronic files for the instructor's manual, test bank, computerized test bank, and Power-Point® presentations.

Wiley's Management Video Library Series offers selections from the highly respected business news program, *Nightly Business Report (NBR)*. This comprehensive video package ties directly to the core topics of the text and brings to life real-world examples of managers in practice. Each of the segments is approximately three to seven minutes long and can be used to introduce topics to the students, enhance lecture material, and provide real-world context for related concepts.

PACKAGES FOR CUSTOMER VALUE

The FAST COMPANY *Handbook of the Business Revolution,* sponsored by John Wiley & Sons, Inc., provides six insightful articles reprised from past issues of the magazine about the changing landscape of leadership, work, and careers. These thought-provoking articles are sure to challenge, stimulate, and inspire your students. The *Handbook of the Business Revolution* can be packaged with *Introducing Management,* for a nominal fee by using this special set ISBN 0-471-37622-1. Contents in this handbook are:

Leadership
- Everything I Thought I Knew About Leadership Was Wrong
- At VeriFone It's a Dog's Life (and they love it!)

Work
- It Doesn't Take a Wizard to Build a Better Boss
- The Seven Sins of Deadly Meetings

Careers
- How Do You Know When It's Time to Go?
- How to Get a Piece of the Action

Take Note! is a collection of lecture outlines, figures, and art from the PowerPoint® Slides that illustrate key concepts in the text. These figures appear on each page with space for student note-taking. *Take Note!* can be packaged with *Introducing Management*, for a nominal fee by using this special set ISBN 0-471-37665-5.

ACKNOWLEDGMENTS

Introducing Management was initiated and completed with the support of editor Brent Gordon and a great team at John Wiley & Sons. Special appreciation is due Joe Heider (Executive Publisher), Susan Elbe (Publisher), Jessica Garcia (Marketing Manager), Kelly Tavares (Senior Production Editor), Harry Nolan (Senior Designer), Cynthia Rhoads (Supplements Editor), and Cynthia Snyder (Editorial Assistant). The extraordinary efforts of David Kear (Media Editor) in providing the best in Web support were indispensable for a true 21st-century product. Bill Gardner provided top-quality instructor's resource materials, Michael McCuddy prepared the substantial test bank, and Cheryl Wyrick has provided a comprehensive set of PowerPoint® Slides and *Take Note!* for each text chapter. A special thanks goes to Michael Albert of San Francisco State University for reviewing and providing thoughtful suggestions for the *Take Note!* supplement. Thank you everyone for your investment in this project.

Table of Contents

Chapter 3   Globalization and International Management   36

Opener: *Live and Work in a Global Village*

Chapter 4   Ethical Behavior and Social Responsibility   54

Opener: *Make this World a Better Place*

PART 2   PLANNING AND CONTROLLING

Chapter 5   Planning—To Set Direction   70

*Opener: **Know What You Want to Accomplish***

PART 3 ORGANIZING

Chapter 8 Organizing — To Create Structures **123**

Opener: Structures Must Support Objectives and Strategies

Chapter 9 Organizational Culture and Design **138**

Opener: Design for Integration and Empowerment

Chapter 10 Human Resource Systems   **152**

Opener: Make People Your Top Priority

PART 4 LEADING

Chapter 15   Innovation and Change Leadership   243

*Opener: **Innovation = Competitive Advantage***

MODULE

Chapter One

Management Today

PLANNING AHEAD—
Chapter 1 Study Questions

- How is the workplace changing?
- Who are managers and what do they do?
- What is the management process?
- What are the challenges ahead?

SMART PEOPLE CREATE THEIR OWN FUTURES

THE 21ST CENTURY IS HERE. In the new workplace everyone must respond and adapt to a rapidly changing society with constantly shifting demands and opportunities. Learning and speed are in; habit and complacency are out. That's all part of the theme driving the popular magazine *Fast Company* and its mission to be a "handbook of the business revolution." While noting that it is hard to comprehend the new world of work at the very time that it is being rapidly created, *Fast Company* reports the importance of these core understandings for anyone who seeks career success today. Organizations are rapidly changing; the nature of work itself is changing; the global economy is driven by innovation and technology; even the concept of success, personal and organizational, is evolving. These developments, say the editors, affect us all and offer both "unparalleled opportunity and unprecedented uncertainty." And in this age of continuous challenge, a compelling message must be heard—smart people and smart companies create their own futures![1]

Yes, we live and work in a challenging environment of great opportunity and dramatic uncertainty. Personal and organizational success must be forged in workplaces that are being reinvented with the themes of participation, empowerment, involvement, teamwork, flexibility, self-management, and more. Careers must be redefined in terms of flexibility, free agency, skill portfolios, entrepreneurship, and others. And importantly, all of this is accompanied by continuing calls for higher performance from organizations and the people who make them run. Society today demands nothing less than the best from all its institutions.

Organizational leaders everywhere know that success in challenging times requires extraordinary commitments to operating efficiency, technology utilization, product quality, and customer satisfaction. Importantly, they also understand that organizations must build credibility by excelling continuously on performance criteria that include concerns for innovativeness, employee development, and social responsibility as well as measures of profitability and investment value. As Johnson & Johnson CEO Ralph S. Larsen says, "Reputations reflect behavior you exhibit day in and day out through a hundred small things. The way you manage your reputation is by always thinking and trying to do the right thing every day." [2]

THE NEW WORKPLACE

General Electric's CEO Jack Welch is viewed by some as one of the great corporate leaders of our time. He heads a multinational enterprise with 275,000+ employees operating in over 100 countries. He does so using the analogy of the local grocery store. According to Welch: "If the customer isn't satisfied, if the stuff is getting stale, if the shelf isn't right, or if the offerings aren't right, it's the same thing. You manage it like a small organization. You don't get hung up on zeros." Welch also recognizes that success builds from the talents of people. "We have to get everybody in the organization involved," Welch says. "If you do that right, the best ideas rise to the top." [3]

In his leadership style and practices, Jack Welch demonstrates an important aspect of progressive organizations today. People—what they know, what they learn, and what they do with it—are the ultimate foundations of organizational performance. They represent an *intellectual capital* of talents, knowledge and experience that is indispensable in creating long-term success.[4] The ultimate elegance of the new workplace may well be its ability to combine the talents of many people, sometimes thousands of them, to achieve unique and significant high performance results.

Among those that have built reputations and long-term success from such understanding is the innovative furniture maker Herman Miller Corporation. Respect for the talents and rights of its employees is a rule of thumb at the firm, whose core values include the statement, "Our greatest assets as a corporation are the gifts, talents and abilities of our employee-owners. . . . When we as a corporation invest in developing people, we are investing in our future." Managers report regularly to workers on the firm's profits and productivity. A special incentive plan gives workers a share in financial gains from the productivity improvements they suggest. Former CEO Max DePree says, "At Herman Miller, we talk about the difference between being successful and being exceptional. Being successful is meeting goals in a good way—being exceptional is reaching your potential."[5]

WHAT IS AN ORGANIZATION?

An **organization,** from the large corporation to the local convenience store, is a collection of people working together to achieve a common purpose. In so doing, the members are able to accomplish tasks that are far beyond the reach of anyone acting alone. The *purpose* of any organization is to produce goods and/or services that satisfy the needs of customers. This ability to contribute something useful to society is what justifies its existence. Indeed, a clear sense of purpose that is tied to "quality products" and "customer satisfaction" is increasingly viewed as a source of organizational strength and performance advantage. At Medtronics, the large Minnesota-based medical products company, for example, employees are noted for innovation and commitment to a mission with a clear and singular mission—helping sick people get well. The sense of corporate purpose clearly centers attention on a goal that is easily shared: improving the health and well-being of those who use the company's products.

> ● An **organization** is a collection of people working together in a division of labor to achieve a common purpose.

Organizations are **open systems** that interact with their environments in the continual process of transforming resource inputs into product outputs in the form of finished goods and/or services. As shown in *Figure 1.1*, the external environment is a source of both resources and customer feedback, and can have a significant impact on operations and outcomes. Feedback from the environment tells an organization how well it is meeting the needs of customers and society at large. If customers don't buy or use the organization's products, it won't be able to operate or stay in business over the long run. In this sense, the customer truly reigns supreme. For example, the ultimate test for Medtronic and its corporate purpose rests with the marketplace: Once someone uses a Medtronic product, the question becomes "Will they do so again . . . and will they recommend that others do the same?"

> ● An **open system** transforms resource inputs from the environment into product outputs.

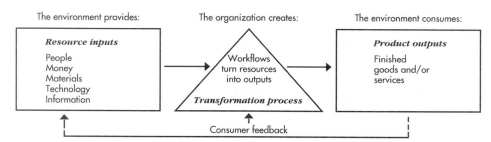

Figure 1.1   Organizations as open systems.

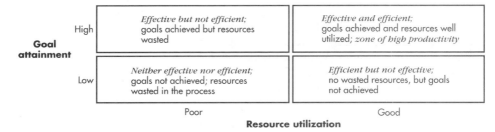

Figure 1.2   Productivity and organizational performance.

PRODUCTIVITY AND ORGANIZATIONAL PERFORMANCE

Organizations perform well when resources are well utilized and customers are well served. The notion of *value-added* is very important in this context. If operations add value to the original cost of resource inputs, then (1) a business organization can earn a profit—that is, sell a product for more than the cost of making it (e.g., fast-food restaurant meals), or (2) a nonprofit organization can add wealth to society—that is, provide a public service that is worth more than its cost (e.g., fire protection in a community). To achieve such ends, all of an organization's resources must be well utilized in the right ways and at the right times to create high-quality products at minimum cost. This is measured as **productivity,** the quantity and quality of work performance, with resource utilization taken into account. *Figure 1.2* describes productivity in two dimensions of organizational performance—effectiveness and efficiency.

● **Productivity** is the quantity and quality of work performance, with resource utilization taken into account.

Performance effectiveness is a measure of task output or goal accomplishment. This is a direct line to ultimate customer service and satisfaction. If you are working in the manufacturing area of a computer firm, for example, performance effectiveness may mean that you meet a daily production target in terms of the quantity and quality of keyboards assembled. By so doing, you allow the company as a whole to maintain its production schedule and meet customer demands for timely delivery and high-quality products.

● **Performance effectiveness** is an output measure of task or goal accomplishment.

Performance efficiency is a measure of the resource cost associated with goal accomplishment. It is a measure of outputs realized compared to inputs consumed. Cost of labor is a common efficiency measure. Others include equipment utilization, facilities maintenance, and returns on capital investment. In the example of computer assembly again, the most efficient production is that accomplished at a minimum cost in materials and labor. If you were producing fewer computer keyboards in a day than you were capable of, this would contribute to inefficiency in organizational performance. Similarly, poor quality in the form of mistakes or wasted materials would also be inefficient work that would raise costs for the organization.

● **Performance efficiency** is a measure of the resource cost associated with goal accomplishment.

CHANGING NATURE OF ORGANIZATIONS

Perhaps no productivity theme is stronger today than the issue of quality. Indeed, there has been a revolution of sorts among modern-day consumers. They are unrelenting in their demand for quality products and services. Organizations that fail to deliver quality and/or do not listen to the needs of customers will be left struggling in highly competitive environments. The term **total quality management (TQM)** refers to operating with an organization-wide commitment to continuous improvement and meeting customer needs completely. The quality commitment is a recognized hallmark of organizational excellence.

Although the emphasis on quality and customer service continues to push organizations in new directions, other transitions are also evident. Right from the beginning of this book it is important to recognize that progressive organizations increasingly display features that differ substantially from past traditions. Prominent trends in the changing nature of organizations include:[6]

- *Command-and-control is out*—traditional hierarchical structures and approaches are proving too costly and cumbersome to meet today's competitive pressures.

- *Information technology is in*—computers and information technology continue to change the way work is done and the ways organizations operate.

- *Teams are in*—less vertical and more horizontal organizations are leveraging talent by using teamwork to strategic advantage.

- *Empowerment is in*—a growing premium on knowledge, talents, and commitment creates participatory and high involvement work settings.

- *New worker expectations are in*—the new generation of workers seeks more informality, performance-driven rewards, less emphasis on status and more work-life balance.

> ● **Total quality management (TQM)** is managing with an organizationwide commitment to continuous work improvement, product quality, and meeting customer needs completely.

> ←———
> Trends in organizations

MANAGERS AND THE NEW WORKPLACE

This book is about managers and the people who work in our new, exciting, and highly demanding workplace. A **manager** is someone in an organization who is responsible for the work performance of one or more other persons. Serving in positions with a wide variety of titles (such as supervisor, team leader, division head, administrator, vice president, and so on), they mobilize people and resources to accomplish the work of organizations and their subunits. When we talk about managers, whether at the level of team leader or senior executive, the focus will always be on a shared managerial responsibility—to ensure the accomplishment of high-performance results through the efforts of many people. This is accomplished through **management**—the process of planning, organizing, leading, and controlling the use of resources to accomplish performance goals. As stated by management theorist Henry Mintzberg, being a manager in this sense is a most important job:

> "No job is more vital to our society than that of the manager. It is the manager who determines whether our social institutions serve us well or whether they squander our talents and resources."[7]

> ● A **manager** is a person who is responsible for the work performance of one or more other persons.

> ● **Management** is the process of planning, organizing, leading, and controlling the use of resources to accomplish performance goals.

WHO ARE THE MANAGERS?

● **Top managers** are responsible for the performance of the organization as a whole or of one of its major parts.

In the traditional organizational pyramid, **top managers,** such as CEO Ralph Larsen of Johnson & Johnson, ensure that major performance objectives are established and accomplished in accordance with the organization's purpose. Common job titles at this level are chief executive officer, chief operating officer, president, and vice president. These senior managers or executives are responsible for the performance of an organization as a whole or for one of its significant parts. They pay special attention to the external environment, are alert to potential long-run problems and opportunities, and develop appropriate ways of dealing with them. The best top managers are future-oriented strategic thinkers who make many decisions under highly competitive and uncertain conditions.

● **Middle managers** report to top managers and oversee the work of large departments or divisions.

Middle managers are in charge of relatively large departments or divisions consisting of several smaller work units. Examples are clinic directors in hospitals; deans in universities; and division managers, plant managers, and branch sales managers in businesses. They report to top managers and develop and implement action plans consistent with higher level objectives. They should also be team oriented and able to work well with peers to help coordinate activities across the organization. Especially today, middle managers are assuming new responsibilities for implementing complex projects that require the participation of persons from different parts of organizations.

● **Team leaders** or **supervisors** are formally in charge of teams or work units.

A first job in management typically occurs as an assignment as **team leader** or **supervisor**—someone in charge of a smaller work unit composed of nonmanagerial workers. Even though most people enter the workforce as technical specialists, sooner or later they advance to positions of initial managerial responsibility. Job titles at this level vary greatly but include such designations as department head, group leader, and unit manager. These managers ensure that their work teams or units meet performance objectives that are consistent with the plans of middle and top management. *Manager's Notepad 1.1* offers advice on the performance responsibilities of team leaders and supervisors.[8]

ACCOUNTABILITY AND MANAGERIAL PERFORMANCE

The nature of managerial work is always evolving as organizations change and develop with time. A *Wall Street Journal* report describes the transition this way: "Not so long ago they may have supervised 10 people sitting outside their offices. Today they must win the support of scores more—employees of different backgrounds, job titles, and even cultures . . . these new managers are expected to be skilled at organizing complex subjects, solving problems, communicating ideas, and making swift decisions."[9] And in this context, all managers must face and master a common problem: They must set the conditions through which individuals and groups contribute to organizational productivity. Furthermore, they must do so while being held "accountable" for results achieved. Formally defined, **accountability** is the requirement of one person to answer back to higher authority and show results achieved for assigned duties. Every manager's daily challenge is to fulfill a performance accountability for results achieved by a team or work unit. To do so, however, they depend on the accomplishments of the members to make this performance possible. Truly effective managers fulfill this accountability while utilizing organizational re-

● **Accountability** is the requirement to show performance results to a supervisor.

> **MANAGER'S NOTEPAD 1.1**
>
> ### NINE RESPONSIBILITIES OF TEAM LEADERS AND SUPERVISORS
>
> 1. Plan meetings and work schedules.
> 2. Clarify goals and tasks and gather ideas for improvement.
> 3. Appraise performance and counsel team members.
> 4. Recommend pay increases and new assignments.
> 5. Recruit, train, and develop team members.
> 6. Encourage high performance and teamwork.
> 7. Inform team members about goals and expectations.
> 8. Inform higher levels of team needs and accomplishments.
> 9. Coordinate with other teams and support their work efforts.

sources in ways that result in *both* high-performance outcomes *and* high levels of satisfaction for the workers.

Quality of Work Life

With respect to satisfaction, the term **quality of work life (QWL)** is frequently used as an indicator of the overall quality of human experiences in the workplace. The QWL concept expresses a true respect for people at work—an important theme that will be addressed in many ways throughout this book. Practically speaking, a high quality of work life is one that offers the individual such things as fair pay, safe working conditions, respect for talents, opportunities to learn and use new skills, room to grow and progress in a career, protection of individual rights, and pride in the work itself and in the organization. Part of any manager's accountability is to achieve high-performance outcomes while maintaining the quality of work life. Simply put, in the new workplace productivity and a high-quality work life can and should go hand in hand.

- **Quality of work life (QWL)** is the overall quality of human experiences in the workplace.

Valuing Diversity

Closely associated with the quality of work life concept is another aspect of managerial accountability—valuing diversity.[10] The term **workforce diversity** describes demographic differences among members of the workforce, principally differences in age, gender, race, national origin, and physical characteristics. Today's workforce is increasingly diverse not only in demographics, but also in cultural traditions and lifestyles. This presents both a challenge in terms of required employer support and an opportunity with respect to potential performance gains.[11]

- **Workforce diversity** describes demographic differences (age, gender, race and ethnicity, and able-bodiedness) among members of the workforce.

Managers are supposed to value diversity and help everyone work to their full potential. But what does this really mean? A female vice president at Avon answers the question this way: "consciously creating an environment where *everyone* has an equal shot at contributing, participating, and most of all advancing."[12]

Valuing diversity may be easier to express in concept than to accomplish in practice. A diversity team assembled at Boston Edison, for example, includes a member committed to contributing his experiences as an African-American, gay, and HIV positive individual. He says: "This has not been an easy transition for any of us. What I am trying to get across, to my team of colleagues, is that I am a human being and I want to be respected for my talents and intelligence." [13]

Diversity barriers in organizations can exist as **prejudice** involving negative, irrational attitudes of some members toward people different from themselves. It can also take the form of **discrimination** that disadvantages such persons by denying them the full benefits of organizational membership. And it can result in what some call the **glass ceiling effect**—the existence of an invisible screen that prevents disfavored persons or minorities from rising above a certain level of organizational responsibility. [14]

- **Prejudice** is the display of negative, irrational attitudes toward people different from one's self.

- **Discrimination** denys some people the full benefits of organizational membership.

- The **glass ceiling effect** is an invisible barrier that limits career advancement of minorities.

CHANGING NATURE OF MANAGERIAL WORK

Among the many changes affecting managerial work today, the concept of the "upside-down pyramid" is one of the most symbolic. As described in *Figure 1.3*, this new way of looking at organizations puts operating workers at the top of the pyramid. They are supported in their work efforts by managers located below. The managers are there to help workers serve customer needs. Everyone in the upside-down pyramid becomes a value-added worker—someone who does things that create eventual value for best serving the customers.

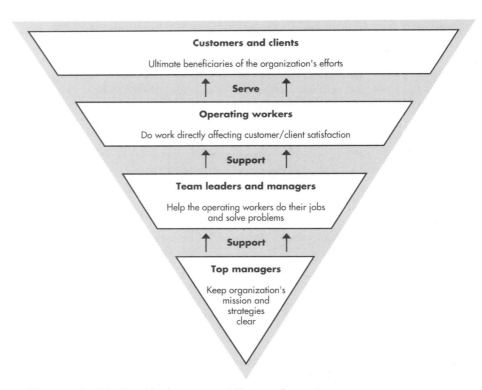

Figure 1.3   The "upside-down-pyramid" view of organizations.

The implications of this new perspective are dramatic for day-to-day work in all settings. We are entering a time when the best managers are known more for "helping" and "supporting" than for "directing" and "order-giving." Even in this age of high technology, people and their talents are critical building blocks of organizational success. Jobs in the new workplace put more emphasis on teamwork, and people move from project to project as their skills and expertise are applicable. Increasingly, even the title of "manager" is often replaced in organization charts by "coordinator," "coach," or "team leader."

THE MANAGEMENT PROCESS

If productivity in the form of performance effectiveness and performance efficiency is a measure of organizational success, "management" is what managers do to achieve it.

FUNCTIONS OF MANAGEMENT

Success in management requires a capacity to recognize problems and opportunities in daily events, make good decisions, and take appropriate action. The management process of fulfilling this responsibility involves the four functions described in *Figure 1.4* as: planning, organizing, leading, and controlling.

Planning

Planning is the process of setting performance objectives and determining what actions should be taken to accomplish them. Through planning, a manager identifies desired work results and identifies the means to achieve them. Take, for example, an Ernst & Young initiative to better meet the needs of its

● **Planning** is the process of setting objectives and determining what should be done to accomplish them.

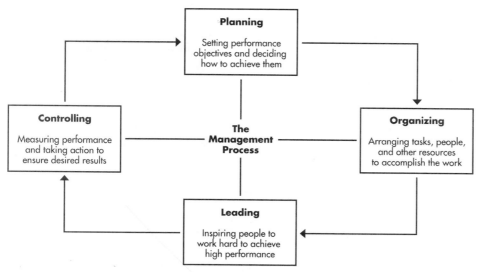

Figure 1.4   Four functions of management.

female professionals.[15] Top management grew concerned about the firm's retention rates and criticism in a report by Catalyst, a research group focusing on corporate women. Chairman Philip A. Laskaway responded by setting a planning objective to reduce turnover rates that were running some 22 percent per year and costing the firm $150,000 per job to hire and train new staff.

Organizing

● **Organizing** is the process of assigning tasks, allocating resources, and arranging activities to implement plans.

Organizing is the process of assigning tasks, allocating resources, and arranging and coordinating the activities of individuals and groups to implement plans. Through organizing, managers turn plans into actions by defining jobs, assigning personnel, and supporting them with technology and other resources. Continuing with the Ernst & Young example, Laskaway created a new Office of Retention for the company and hired Deborah K. Holmes as director to head it. As problems were identified in various locations, Holmes convened special task forces to tackle them and recommend location-specific solutions.

Leading

● **Leading** is the process of arousing enthusiasm and directing efforts toward organizational goals.

Leading is the process of arousing people's enthusiasm to work hard to fulfill plans and accomplish objectives. Through leading, managers build commitments, encourage activities that support goals, and influence others to do their best work on the organization's behalf. At Ernst & Young, Holmes identified a core issue—work at the firm was extremely intense and women often felt strain because their spouses also worked. She became a champion for improved work-life balance and pursued it through the special task forces. Although she admits that "there's no silver bullet" in the form of a universal solution, new initiatives included "call-free holidays" where professionals do not check voice mail or e-mail on weekends and holidays and "travel sanity" that limits staffers' travel to four days a week so they can get home for weekends.

Controlling

● **Controlling** is the process of measuring performance and taking action to ensure desired results.

Controlling is the process of measuring work performance, comparing results to objectives, and taking corrective action as needed. Through controlling, managers maintain active contact with people in the course of their work, gather and interpret reports on performance, and use this information to plan constructive action and change. At Ernst & Young, Chairman Laskaway and Director Holmes knew what the retention rates were when they started this program, and they measured for improvements as the program progressed. In one location the retention rates improved from 70 percent to 81 percent. Holmes believes that small positive steps will lead to lasting and significant change. The goal of improved work-life balance will continue to be pursued, and retention rates will be used as indicators of performance accomplishments.

MANAGERIAL ACTIVITIES AND ROLES

Although the management process may seem straightforward, things are more complicated than they appear at first glance. In his classic book, *The Nature of*

≡Browser≡

Go to: http://www.wiley.com/college/schermerhorn

 THE WALL STREET JOURNAL.
WILEY

IN PRACTICE

Welcome to *the Wall Street Journal Interactive Edition*! The purchase of this text allows you four months of access to exciting business news as it happens. The Interactive Journal brings Introduction to Management alive with practical situations and applications.

In order for you to experience the full power of this combination, the Interactive Journal is keyed to interact with specific sections of the text. Each section is unique, and at the end of the experience, you will have a full and complete understanding of how the Interactive Journal works to inform and condition you for the future.

TAKE A TOUR

When you enter the Interactive Journal, the Front Section is laid out similarly to the newspaper edition of The Wall Street Journal. The left of your computer screen contains the menu system that allows you to navigate the site. Click on the five major subsections:

1. **Front Section**
2. **Marketplace**
3. **Money and Investing**
4. **Tech Center** and
5. **Sports.**

Navigation buttons are always available to return you to the Front Section.

One particularly useful tool is the Search engine internal to the Interactive Journal. Under **"Journal Atlas,"** there is a **SEARCH** link that allows you to look for relevant news articles from the last 30 days in the Interactive Journal, Barrons and Dow Jones Online. Try it now to look for interesting business executives or news items that interest you. When you are finished, return to the Front Section.

Chapter 1, The Dynamic New Workplace, recognizes the speed of change in the new, electronic age. Business executives are under increasing pressure to stay current of new technologies, processes, and events.

One area where this speed is evident is the rise of e-business on the Web. No one has taken greater advantage of this opportunity than Dell Computers, located at http://www.dell.com.

Dell pioneered the use of the Internet to design, cus-

tomize, and order computer equipment online. It now sells over $14 million/day off of its Web site.

DELIVERABLE

Compare Dell's site to Gateway http://www.gateway.com and Compaq, http://www.compaq.com. Under the **"Journal Atlas,"** click on **"Business Index"** to see if there are any articles in today's Interactive Journal edition on any of the three firms.

Using the Interactive Journal search engine, search for articles on the three computer manufacturers and any information on e-business.

DISCUSSION QUESTIONS:

1. Some business pundits are calling the Web the biggest change in business since the Industrial Revolution. Do you agree or disagree?
2. What advantages does getting the Wall Street Journal online allow users? The publisher?
3. Will being online encourage you to make greater use of The Wall Street Journal?

 *Note: The underscored words/phrases in the Interactive Journal feature indicate Internet links provided in the online versions. See the *Introducing Management* Web site at www.wiley.com/college/schermerhorn.

Managerial Work, Henry Mintzberg offers this observation on the daily activities of corporate chief executives:

> There was no break in the pace of activity during office hours. The mail, . . . telephone calls, . . . and meetings . . . accounted for almost every minute from the moment these executives entered their offices in the morning until they departed in the evenings.[16]

Today we would have to add ever-present e-mail to Mintzberg's list of executive preoccupations.[17] Mintzberg is also careful to note that the manager's day is unrelenting in intensity and pace. The managers he observed had little free time because unexpected problems and continuing requests for meetings consumed almost all the time that became available. And importantly, he points out that the responsibility of executive work was all-encompassing in the continual pressure it placed on improving performance results. Says Mintzberg,

> The manager can never be free to forget the job, and never has the pleasure of knowing, even temporarily, that there is nothing else to do. . . . Managers always carry the nagging suspicion that they might be able to contribute just a little bit more. Hence they assume an unrelenting pace in their work.[18]

Clearly, managerial work is busy, demanding, and stressful not just for chief executives but for managers at all levels of responsibility in any work setting. A summary of research on the nature of managerial work offers this important reminder:

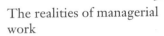
The realities of managerial work

- Managers work long hours.
- Managers work at an intense pace.
- Managers work at fragmented and varied tasks.
- Managers work with many communication media.
- Managers work largely through interpersonal relationships.[19]

In trying to systematically describe the nature of managerial work and the demands it places on those who do it, Mintzberg offers the set of 10 roles depicted in *Figure 1.5*. The roles managers must be prepared to perform fall into three categories.[20] A manager's *interpersonal roles* involve interactions with persons inside and outside the work unit. The *informational roles* involve the giving, receiving, and analyzing of information. The *decisional roles* involve using information to make decisions to solve problems or address opportunities.

Interpersonal roles	**Informational roles**	**Decisional roles**
How a manager interacts with other people • Figurehead • Leader • Liaison	How a manager exchanges and processes information • Monitor • Disseminator • Spokesperson	How a manager uses information in decision making • Entrepreneur • Disturbance handler • Resource allocator • Negotiator

Figure 1.5 Ten managerial roles.

MANAGERIAL AGENDAS AND NETWORKS

The following description provides a glimpse of an effective general manager (or GM) in action. It portrays two activities that the author, John Kotter, considers critical to a general manager's success in mastering daily challenges—agenda setting and networking.

> On his way to a meeting, a GM bumped into a staff member who did not report to him. Using this opportunity, in a two-minute conversation he: (a) asked two questions and received the information he needed; (b) reinforced their good relationship by sincerely complimenting the staff member on something he had recently done; and (c) got the staff member to agree to do something that the GM needed done.[21]

Through *agenda setting*, good managers develop action priorities for their jobs that include goals and plans that span long and short time frames. These agendas are usually incomplete and loosely connected in the beginning but become more specific as the manager utilizes information that is continually gleaned from many different sources. The agendas are kept always in mind and are "played out" whenever an opportunity arises, as in the GM's unanticipated hallway meeting.

Good managers implement their agendas by working with a variety of people inside and outside the organization. In this example, the GM was getting things done with the help of a staff member who did not report directly to him. This is made possible by *networking*—the process of building and maintaining positive relationships with people whose help may be needed to implement one's work agendas. Networks are indispensable to managerial success in today's complex work environments, and the best managers devote much time and effort to network development.

MANAGERIAL SKILLS AND COMPETENCIES

A *skill* is an ability to translate knowledge into action that results in desired performance. Many skills are required to master the challenging nature of managerial work, and the most important ones allow managers to help others be highly productive. Robert L. Katz classified the essential skills of managers into three categories: technical, human, and conceptual.[22] Although all three skills are essential for managers, *Figure 1.6* shows that their relative importance tends to vary by level of managerial responsibility.

A **technical skill** is the ability to use a special proficiency or expertise to perform particular tasks. Accountants, engineers, market researchers, and computer scientists, for example, possess technical skills. These are initially acquired through formal education and are further developed by training and job experience. Technical skills are most important at lower levels of management.

The ability to work well in cooperation with other persons is a **human skill.** It emerges in the workplace as a spirit of trust, enthusiasm, and genuine involvement in interpersonal relationships. A manager with good human skills will have a high degree of self-awareness and a capacity to understand or empathize with the emotions and feelings of others. Given the highly interpersonal nature of managerial work, such skills are critical for all managers. They are consistently important across the managerial levels.

● A **technical skill** is the ability to use a special proficiency or expertise in one's work.

● A **human skill** is the ability to work well in cooperation with other people.

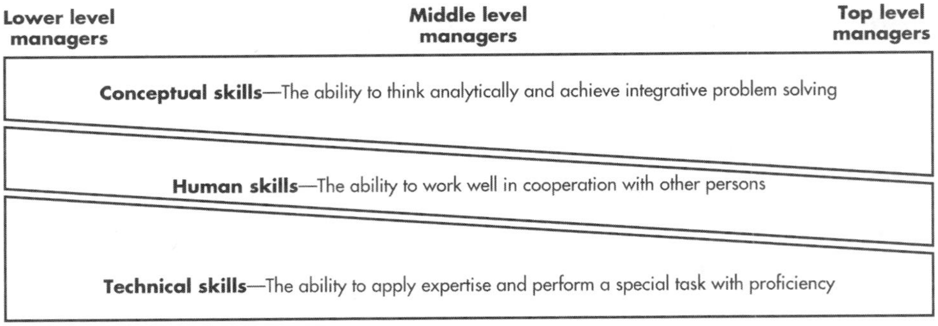

Lower level managers	Middle level managers	Top level managers

Conceptual skills—The ability to think analytically and achieve integrative problem solving

Human skills—The ability to work well in cooperation with other persons

Technical skills—The ability to apply expertise and perform a special task with proficiency

Figure 1.6 Essential managerial skills.

All good managers ultimately have the ability to view situations broadly and to solve problems to the benefit of everyone concerned. This ability to think analytically is a **conceptual skill.** It involves the capacity to break down problems into smaller parts, to see the relations between the parts, and to recognize the implications of any one problem for others. As managers assume ever-higher responsibilities in organizations, they must deal with more ambiguous problems that have longer term consequences. Conceptual skills gain in relative importance for higher management levels.

Business and management educators are increasingly focused on helping people acquire *managerial competencies*—skills or personal characteristics that

● A **conceptual skill** is the ability to think analytically and solve complex problems.

MANAGER'S NOTEPAD 1.2

PERSONAL COMPETENCIES FOR MANAGERIAL SUCCESS

- *Leadership:* Ability to influence others to perform tasks.
- *Self-objectivity:* Ability to evaluate oneself realistically.
- *Analytic thinking:* Ability to interpret and explain patterns in information.
- *Behavioral flexibility:* Ability to modify personal behavior to reach a goal.
- *Oral communication:* Ability to express ideas clearly in oral presentations.
- *Written communication:* Ability to express one's ideas clearly in writing.
- *Personal impact:* Ability to create a good impression and instill confidence.
- *Resistance to stress:* Ability to perform under stressful conditions.
- *Tolerance for uncertainty:* Ability to perform in ambiguous situations.

contribute to high performance in a management job.[23] A number of these competencies are identified in *Manager's Notepad 1.2*. You can use this notepad as a checklist, noting specific personal strengths and weaknesses. This self-assessment offers a starting point or further developing your career readiness.

THE CHALLENGES AHEAD

Just what are the challenges ahead? The facts are clear, but they deserve to be pointed out again and again. Those who want to succeed in the 21st-century workplace must reach for the heights of personal competency and accomplishment. They must be self-starters and leaders who find continuing ways to add value to employers even as the environment continues to change. They must be willing, as J&J CEO Larsen said, to "do the right things" everyday. Importantly, they must be willing to continuously learn from experience to remain as capable in the future as they are in the present.

THE 21ST CENTURY WORK ENVIRONMENT

There are many ways to describe what lies ahead for people at work and for the organizations they support. All have significant career implications. Consider, for example, this capsule description of major themes in this book. Together they introduce the management challenges already evident in the emerging 21st century work environment.

- *Globalization*—The global economy is a reality and we are all touched by it. The processes of business innovation, production and service delivery increasingly span the globe.[24] Corporate leaders and government leaders alike know that economic competitiveness is now a challenge of worldwide scope.

- *Technology*—This is the age of information technology and electronic networking.[25] Our work and non-work lives are full of bar codes, automatic tellers, electronic mail, e-commerce, Internet resources, and more . . . always more. The availability and ease of transferring information is affecting organizations as work environments and even the very nature of business itself.

- *Knowledge*—In the information age, knowledge and knowledge workers increasingly drive organizations. They are, says management consultant Peter Drucker, the principal resources of a competitive society.[26] Because knowledge constantly makes itself obsolete, the pressure is on everyone to learn and continually apply new knowledge to problems and opportunities.

- *People*—The forces of diversity are challenging organizations and their members to deal positively with differences.[27] Pressures remain on social institutions from education to government to business to revise outdated human resource policies and operations. Those who rise to the challenge will find that valuing diversity creates strategic opportunity, even in difficult and highly competitive labor markets.

Management Across Functions

INFORMATION SYSTEMS

Information Systems Drive e-Commerce

On its first day of trading on the Nasdaq Stock Market, shares of eToys, Inc., shot up almost 400%. The market value of the firm ended up 35% greater than its well-established but more traditional rival Toys " " Us, Inc. This e-commerce success story exemplifies the strategic opportunity of a high-tech and Web-based business plan. CEO Toby Lenk says: "We pioneered a new channel and that about it, from the ground up, from a new perspective." But there is more to the company than advanced computers and information systems. Customers come first at eToys, and top-rated customer service is always top priority. The firm's easy-to-use Web site was specifically designed to make new users immediately comfortable with online shopping. Speed is also paramount. eToys moves constantly at "Web speed" as it reinvents and transforms itself for ever-new opportunities. As its competitors stick with traditional business strategies, eToys has forged ahead into books, music, videos, software and even baby products. And according to Lenk it will continue to do so to keep ahead of the competition. "We fully intend to be a moving target;" he says, "If we stand still, we'll get shot." [29]

- *Change*—We have left times of stability and entered times of dramatic and continuous change. Values, cultures, and societies are changing along with organizations, and they are changing quickly. They have no choice. Our world moves extraordinarily fast. The high-performance premium is earned not only by being able to do the right things, but by doing them faster than the competition.[28]

In this context and especially in a society where knowledge workers are increasingly important, new managers must be well educated. And, they must continue that education throughout their careers. Success in turbulent times comes only through continuous learning. It comes only to those who are unrelenting in efforts to develop, refine, and maintain job-relevant skills and competencies.

The question that must, of course, be asked and sincerely answered at this point is—"Are you ready?"

CAREER READINESS IMPERATIVES

British educator and consultant Charles Handy calls our turbulent times "the age of unreason." [30] It is an era of high-performance expectations where change is a way of life. It demands new organizational and individual responses in the relentless quest for high performance. Everywhere *new* workers are expected to use *new* ways to achieve high productivity under *new* and dynamic conditions. They are expected to become involved, participate fully, demonstrate creativity, and find self-fulfillment in their work. They are expected to be team players who understand the needs and goals of the total organization and who use new technologies to their full advantage.

The typical career of the 21st century won't be uniformly full-time and limited to a single large employer. It is more likely to unfold opportunistically and involve several employment options over time. Skills must be portable and of value to more than one possible employer; these skills must be carefully maintained and upgraded over time. One career consultant describes this scenario with the analogy of a surfer: "You're always moving. You can expect to fall into the water any number of times, and you have to get back up to catch the next wave." [31]

Handy's advice in meeting the career challenge is straight on. Start now. Don't delay. Build for yourself and then diligently maintain a "portfolio of skills" that are always up-to-date and valuable to potential employers.

While still a student at Ohio University, Ronald Larimer developed a very professional online *Career Advancement Portfolio*.[32] It includes a resume documenting his leadership activities in student affairs, student work providing computer support for an instructor, and summer work experience. The portfolio also includes examples of Ron's skills at computer programming, use of spreadsheet and database software, writing skills, and even a sample PowerPoint presentation. Using his electronic career portfolio as the lead, Ron obtained a summer internship between his junior and senior years. His portfolio is also helping him achieve his choice of jobs after graduation.

Why not build your own *Career Advancement Portfolio?* Visit our website for full details and an easy-to-use on-line template!

Visit our website at www.wiley.com/college/schermerhorn to build your own Career Advancement Portfolio

SUMMARY

How Is the Workplace Changing?

- Organizations operate collections of people working together to achieve a common purpose.
- As open systems, organizations interact with their environments in the process of transforming resource inputs into product outputs.
- Organizations seek productivity in the quantity and quality of work performance, with resource utilization taken into account.
- In today's dynamic environment, organizations are adopting new forms and practices to meet the challenges of new technology, intense competition, and demanding customers.
- Present trends in organizations emphasize information utilization empowerment, teams and respect for new worker expectations.

Who Are Managers and What Do They Do?

- Managers facilitate work accomplishments by people in organizations.
- Top managers concentrate on long-term concerns; middle managers help coordinate activities across the organization; team leaders and supervisors focus on group or work-unit objectives.

- The manager's challenge is to fulfill performance accountability while being dependent on team members or subordinates to do the required work.
- Managers must respect the quality of work life and value diversity in supporting the work efforts and experiences of others.
- The focus of managerial work in increasingly on "coaching" and "supporting" others rather than simply "directing" and "order-giving."

What Is the Management Process?

- The management process consists of the four functions of planning, organizing, leading, and controlling.
- Managerial work is intense and stressful and places a great emphasis on the ability to perform well in interpersonal, informational, and decision-making roles.
- Effective managers create and maintain interpersonal networks that facilitate the accomplishment of task agendas.
- Managers must develop and maintain essential technical, human, and conceptual skills to succeed in a dynamic environment.

What Are the Challenges Ahead?

- Today's turbulent environment challenges managers and organizations in complex and demanding ways.
- Information and technological change are modifying organizations and bringing added emphasis on knowledge and knowledge workers.
- Everyone in today's work force must commit to continuous learning and life-long personal development.
- Careers today require "portfolios" of skills that are continually developed and well communicated to potential employers.

KEY TERMS

Accountabilityt (p. 7)
Conceptual skill (p. 13)
Controlling (p. 10)
Discrimination (p. 7)
Glass ceiling (p. 7)
Human skill (p. 12)
Leading (p. 10)
Management (p. 5)
Manager (p. 5)
Middle managers (p. 5)

Open system (p. 3)
Organization (p. 2)
Organizing (p. 10)
Performance effectiveness (p. 4)
Performance efficiency (p. 4)
Planning (p. 9)
Prejudice (p. 7)
Productivity (p. 3)

Quality of work life (QWL) (p. 7)
Team leaders or supervisors (p. 6)
Technical skill (p. 12)
Top managers (p. 5)
Total quality management (TQM) (p. 4)
Workforce diversity (p. 7)

SELF-TEST

Take the interactive Self-Test for this chapter on the Schermerhorn Web Site

Chapter Two

Environment and Information Technology

PLANNING AHEAD—
Chapter 2 Study Questions

- What is the environment of organizations?
- What is a customer-driven organization?
- How does information technology benefit organizations?
- Why is organizational learning important?

LEARNING IN A VIRTUAL WORLD

TECHNOLOGY EMPOWERS PEOPLE. IT is also changing the nature of college education and corporate training. Distance learning is gaining a strategic foothold as new computer technologies become mainstays of instructional support. At Duke's Fuqua School of Business, executives from different countries complete their executive MBA program through computer-mediated distance learning programs combined with intensive residency periods. The new Western Governors University is a university without walls; the new Florida Gulf Coast University expects to serve 25 percent of its students through distance learning; and technology-driven distance learning is a core strategy of the University of Phoenix and the Instituto Technologío y de Estudios Superiores de Monterrey, Mexico. And in the corporate sector, companies like AT&T are offering more and more of their training programs through the Internet.[1] Other examples of new directions in virtual education abound.

Just as computers and information technologies have changed education and learning processes, they are also dramatically and continually changing the nature of work and organizations themselves. The key is information and the way it flows and is utilized by people in organizations. *More* information about *more* things is being made available to *more* people in organizations *more* quickly than ever before. One of the most important concepts to understand in this regard is **intellectual capital,** which is defined as the collective brainpower or shared knowledge of a workforce.[2]

● **Intellectual capital** is the collective brainpower or shared knowledge of a workforce.

In this era of information, knowledge is an irreplaceable resource, and the goal should always be to grow and create intellectual capital. This is especially true in the global economy, which has been described by Peter Drucker as one in which "the productivity of knowledge and knowledge workers" will become the decisive competitive factor.[3] IBM's CEO Louis V. Gerstner, Jr., puts the challenge this way: "We believe very strongly that the age-old levers of competition—labor, capital, and land, are being supplemented by knowledge, and that most successful companies in the future will be those that learn how to exploit knowledge—knowledge about customer behavior, markets, economies, technology—faster than their competitors."[4]

EXTERNAL ENVIRONMENTS OF ORGANIZATIONS

Once a benchmark for science fiction writers, the dawning of the 21st century presents new demands on organizations and their managers. Success will be achieved in a world of intense competition, continued globalization of markets and business activities, and even more rapid technological change. No organization can hesitate or rest on past laurels in our uncertain world. The future belongs to those who can create and maintain "competitive advantage" in complex and dynamic environments.

WHAT IS COMPETITIVE ADVANTAGE?

● A **competitive advantage** allows an organization to deal with market and environmental forces better than its competitors.

Management attention on the environments of organizations is focused increasingly on the concept of **competitive advantage.**[5] This is the utilization of a *core competency* that clearly sets an organization apart from its competitors and gives it an advantage over them in the marketplace. An organization may achieve competitive advantage in many ways, including through products, pricing, customer service, cost efficiency, and quality, among other aspects of operating excellence. But regardless of how the advantage is achieved, the key result is the same—an ability to consistently do something of high value that one's competitors cannot replicate or do as well.

Managing organizations for competitive advantage in challenging environments may well be the critical theme of the day. Corporate leaders and senior executives in all organizations must understand that competitive advantage can only be achieved by continuously scanning the environment and then adapting operations based on what is learned.

Consider the success story of John Sortino. He started the Vermont Teddy Bear Company by selling teddy bears from his car in Burlington. Since then the firm has grown into a substantial local employer, winner of the prestigious Heritage of New England Award, and the largest Teddy Bear maker in North America. The firm's products are backed with lifetime and no-questions-asked guarantees. In building the company, Sortino recognized that success in a demanding environment would come to those who promote their products truthfully and operate with a commitment to exceptional quality. His vision was on target. Vermont Teddy Bears can now be bought worldwide off the Internet.[6]

THE GENERAL ENVIRONMENT

The **general environment** consists of all the background conditions in the external environment of an organization. This portion of the environment forms a situational context for managerial decision making. The major external environmental issues of our day include factors such as the following:

- *Economic conditions*—general state of the economy in terms of inflation, income levels, gross domestic product, unemployment, and related indicators of economic health.

- *Social-cultural conditions*—general state of prevailing social values on such matters as human rights and the natural environment, trends in education and related social institutions, as well as demographic patterns.

- *Legal-political conditions*—general state of the prevailing philosophy and objectives of the political party or parties running the government, as well as laws and government regulations.

- *Technological conditions*—general state of the development and availability of technology in the environment, including scientific advancements.

- *Natural environment conditions*—general state of nature and conditions of the natural or physical environment, including levels of public concern expressed through environmentalism.

What is in the general environment?

Differences in these and related general environment factors are especially noticeable when organizations operate internationally.[7] External conditions vary significantly from one country and culture to the next. Managers of successful international operations understand these differences and help their organizations make the operating adjustments needed to perform within them. The pharmaceutical giant Merck, for example, derives half or more of its business from overseas operations. In a drive to further increase its market share, the firm has entered into cooperative agreements with European companies, conducted research with European partners, and worked with European governments on legal matters.

- The **general environment** consists of cultural, economic, legal-political, and educational conditions.

THE SPECIFIC ENVIRONMENT

The **specific environment** consists of the actual organizations, groups, and persons with whom an organization must interact in order to survive and prosper. These are environmental elements of direct consequence to the organization as it

- The **specific environment** consists of the actual organizations and persons with whom an organization interacts.

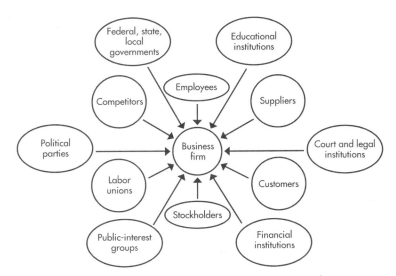

Figure 2.1   Multiple stakeholders in the environment of organizations.

operates on a day-to-day basis. The specific environment is often described in terms of **stakeholders**—the persons, groups, and institutions who are affected in one way or another by the organization's performance. *Figure 2.1* shows multiple stakeholders as they may exist in the external environment of a typical business firm.

Sometimes called the *task environment*, the specific environment and the stakeholders are distinct for each organization. They can also change over time according to the company's unique customer base, operating needs, and circumstances. Managers must be alert to spot these changes and deal with them in ways that create opportunities for competitive advantage. For example, a dynamic environment means opportunity for the automobile racing industry. Racing entrepreneurs like O. Burton Smith of Speedway Motor Sports, NASCAR drivers like Jeff Gordon, and thousands of fans are turning the racing business into big business indeed. When the stock cars are running at Smith's $140 million Texas Motor Speedway, some 185,000 fans may be in attendance.

Important stakeholders common to the specific environment of most organizations include:

- *Customers*—specific consumer or client groups, individuals, and organizations that purchase the organization's goods and/or use its services.
- *Suppliers*—specific providers of the human, information, and financial resources and raw materials needed by the organization to operate.
- *Competitors*—specific organizations that offer the same or similar goods and services to the same consumer or client groups.
- *Regulators*—specific government agencies and representatives, at the local, state, and national levels, that enforce laws and regulations affecting the organization's operations.

● **Stakeholders** are the persons, groups, and institutions directly affected by an organization's performance.

What is in the general environment?

CUSTOMER-DRIVEN ORGANIZATIONS

Question: What's your job?
Answer: I run the cash register and sack groceries.
Question: But isn't it your job to serve the customer?
Answer: I guess, but it's not in my job description.[8]

This conversation illustrates what often becomes the missing link in the quest for total quality and competitive advantage: customer service. Contrast this conversation with the experience of a customer of the Vermont Teddy Bear Company, who called to report that her new mailorder teddy bear had a problem. The company responded promptly, she said, and arranged to have the bear picked up and replaced. She wrote the firm to say "thank you for the great service and courtesy you gave me." [9]

WHAT DO CUSTOMERS WANT?

Customers put today's organizations to a very stiff test. They demand value-pricing for high-quality goods and services; anything less is unacceptable. A *Harvard Business Review* survey reports that American business leaders rank customer service and product quality as the first and second most important goals in the success of their organizations, respectively.[10] In a survey by the market research firm Michelson & Associates, poor service and product dissatisfaction were also ranked #1 and #2 as reasons why customers stop shopping at a particular retail store.[11]

Just imagine if every customer or client contact with an organization was positive. Not only would they return again as members of a loyal customer base, but they would also tell others and expand the size of that base. In order to achieve such results organizations must find out what customers want and then give it to them. Typically, this means goods and services that are high in quality and low in cost, meet their needs, and require only short waiting times.

INTERNAL AND EXTERNAL CUSTOMERS

Figure 2.2 expands the open-systems view of organizations introduced in Chapter 1 to now depict the complex internal environment of the organization. The various parts of the organization exist as subsystems that are linked to one another in the process of daily operations. The notion of customer service applies to relationships among these internal components as well as to the organization's external relationships.

External customers are the ones we normally think of. They purchase the goods or services produced. **Internal customers,** by contrast, are found within the organization. They are the individuals and groups who use or otherwise depend on quality results of others' work in order to do their own jobs well. For example, Hewlett-Packard employees work as both customers and suppliers. To

● An **external customer** is the customer or client who buys or uses the organization's goods and/or services.

● An **internal customer** is someone who uses or depends on the work of another person or group within the organization.

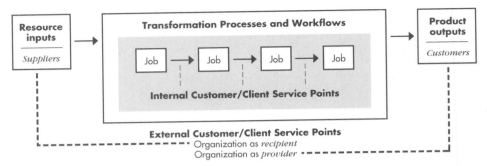

Figure 2.2 The importance of external and internal customers.

someone assembling circuit boards, her supplier is the person making chips and her customer is the person who puts the boards into finished components. They are expected to work together to make sure everyone has the quality materials needed to pass a quality product on to the next workstation.

CUSTOMERS AND QUALITY OPERATIONS

● **Operations management** studies how organizations transform resource inputs into product and service outputs.

The branch of management theory specifically concerned with the activities and decisions through which organizations transform resource inputs into finished goods or services is **operations management.** *Figure 2.3* offers a customer-driven model of operations. The process begins with attention being directed toward the needs of customers: "What do they want? Where do they want it? When do they want it?" Given answers to these questions, resources can be mobilized and actions taken to meet customer expectations. This is the area of "value-added" activity, where people, technology, resources, and structures combine to accomplish the work of the organization.[12] But as noted in this figure, these value-added efforts should be guided by very specific operations objectives that reflect customer interests—low-cost, on-time delivery, and high-quality.

Total quality management introduced in Chapter 1 is now a way of life in world-class firms.[13] The competitive demands of a global economy are an important force in this race toward total quality operations. Quality standards set by the International Standards Organization (ISO) in Geneva, Switzerland, have been adopted by many countries. Businesses that want to compete as

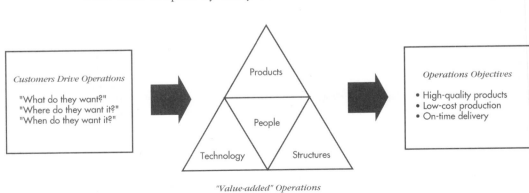

Figure 2.3 A customer-driven view of organizations.

"world-class companies" are increasingly expected to have **ISO 9000 certification** at various levels. This certification, granted only after a rigorous assessment by outside auditors, provides customers with assurance that a set of solid quality standards and processes are in place.

In the United States, the Malcolm Baldrige National Quality Awards were established to benchmark excellence in quality achievements. Competitors for the awards must show true commitments to total quality operations, such as:

- Top executives incorporate quality values into day-to-day management.
- The organization works with suppliers to improve the quality of their goods and/or services.
- The organization trains workers in quality techniques and implements systems that ensure high-quality products.
- The organization's products are as good as or better than those of its competitors.
- The organization meets customers' needs and wants and gets customer satisfaction ratings equal to or better than those of competitors.
- The organization's quality system yields concrete results such as increased market share and lower product-cycle times.[14]

● **ISO 9000 certification** is granted by the International Standards Organization to indicate conformance with a rigorous set of quality standards.

Quality essentials for the Baldrige National Quality Awards

MANAGER'S NOTEPAD 2.1

DEMING'S 14 POINTS TO QUALITY

1. Create a consistency of purpose to innovate; put resources into research and education, maintaining equipment and new production aids.
2. Learn a new philosophy of quality to improve every system.
3. Require statistical evidence of process control.
4. Require statistical evidence of control in purchasing, and deal with fewer suppliers.
5. Use statistical methods to isolate the sources of trouble.
6. Institute modern on-the-job training.
7. Improve supervision to develop inspired leaders.
8. Drive out fear and instill learning.
9. Break down barriers between departments.
10. Eliminate numerical goals and slogans.
11. Constantly revamp work methods.
12. Institute massive training for employees in statistical methods.
13. Retrain people in new skills.
14. Create a structure that pushes everyday on the prior points.

QUALITY AND CONTINUOUS IMPROVEMENT

● **Continuous improvement** involves always searching for new ways to improve operations quality and performance.

Employee involvement and participation in the search for quality solutions is an important aspect of the TQM process. It is closely tied to the emphasis on **continuous improvement**—always looking for new ways to improve upon current performance. A basic philosophy of total quality management is that one can never be satisfied; something always can and should be improved upon—continuous improvement must be a way of life. Consider *cycle time*—the elapsed time between receipt of an order and delivery of the finished product. The quality objective here is to find ways to serve customer needs more quickly. Time, in all respects, is critical to competitive advantage. Banks, for example, should try to keep cycle times to a minimum in loan departments. After all, the quicker a bank can process mortgage loan applications the more likely it will keep customers away from competitors.

The work of W. Edwards Deming is a useful benchmark for a total quality commitment to continuous improvement. His principles are straightforward: tally defects, analyze and trace them to the source, make corrections, and keep a record of what happens afterward.[15] Deming's path to quality follows the basic proposition that the cause of a quality problem may be some component of the production and operations processes, like an employee or a machine, or it may be internal to the system itself. If it is caused by an employee, that person should be retrained or replaced. Similarly, a faulty machine should be adjusted or replaced. If the cause lies within the system, blaming an employee only causes frustration. Instead, the system must be analyzed and constructively changed. A comprehensive, rigorous, and learning-based approach underlies Deming's 14 points to quality as summarized in *Manager's Notepad 2.1.*

INFORMATION TECHNOLOGY UTILIZATION

● In a **networked economy** commerce is increasingly Internet based.

Organizations and their customers are increasingly influenced by the emergence of what is called a **networked economy**—one where all aspects of commerce are increasingly Internet-based. In this new environment, information technology (or "IT") plays a commanding and ever-expanding role. As the electronic interface among an organization's suppliers, employees, and customers, IT utilization can be a major source of competitive advantage for those progressive enough to embrace its great potential.

ELECTRONIC OFFICES AND ELECTRONIC COMMERCE

The future is now when it comes to the rapidly evolving state of computer and information technologies. Organizations are changing as the new technologies exert their influence. Information departments or centers are appearing on organization charts. The number and variety of information career fields is rapidly expanding. Job titles such as Chief Information Officer and Chief Knowledge Officer are appearing in the senior ranks of organizations. All of this, and more, is characteristic of the great opportunities of our new age of information.

THE WALL STREET JOURNAL.

WILEY

IN PRACTICE

In the last 20 years, the impact of information technology on the general business environment has been monumental. While this new technology has generated outstanding opportunities, it also introduces tremendous levels of turbulence into previously stable industry settings.

Online news is available from a number of sources, including the Interactive Journal, CNN (http://cnn.com), financial news at CNNFN (http://cnnfn.com), USA Today (http://usatoday.com), and the New York Times (http://www.nytimes.com).

The Interactive Journal recognizes the importance of emerging technologies with its **TECH CENTER** headings. Click on this section to discover the latest moves and countermoves made by leading technology firms. **TECH CENTER** maintains its own search engine, located at the bottom of the page that looks exclusively for technology news.

Company Profiles, located in the left-hand menu list, provide an in-depth look at various high-technology companies, including Dell Computer, Amazon.com, and eBay. Insightful information, including major company executives and strategies, helps to present each firm as an interesting case study. Each profile includes Web links to the Interactive Journal **Briefing Books,** a concise compilation of statistics and information on each firm. In addition, each Profile includes links to Interactive Journal articles from the last several years that cover the firm.

Under the **Resources:** heading in the left-hand menu, click on **Special Reports** and view several of them for content. The Interactive Journal compiles a series of articles that take an in-depth look at an emerging topic.

Interactive Journal also manages e-mail discussions on a variety of topics. These can be accessed from the **TECH CENTER** under

TECH VOICES

near the bottom of the page.

Click on one of the discussions that interests you. You can participate in the conferencing by entering your information at the bottom of the page. Look over some of the comments and be prepared to offer your insights in class.

DELIVERABLE:

Select any technology firm listed under the **Company Profiles** listing. Discuss its use and dependence on information technology in the conduct of the firm's business activities. Provide a timeline of its recent activities, with an emphasis on its place in the future of technology.

Answer the question: Will this firm be around in 2010? Support your decision with specific facts from the Interactive Journal.

DISCUSSION QUESTIONS:

1. What effect has technology had on the delivery of higher education in the last 10 years?

2. How has technology increased or decreased the level of turbulence many firms face in their industries? Discuss specific examples.

3. What advantages does having the WSJ online provide for you as an information consumer?

 *Note: The underscored words/phrases in the Interactive Journal feature indicate Internet links provided in the online versions. See the *Introducing Management* Web site at www.wiley.com/college/schermerhorn.

A good example of the everyday impact of information technology on work is the *electronic office*. This term refers to the use of computers and related technologies to electronically facilitate operations in an office environment. What was once a future possibility is now an everyday reality: People work at "smart" stations supported by computers that allow sophisticated voice, image, text, and other data-handling operations. Voice messaging utilizes the voice recognition capabilities of computers to take dictation, answer the telephone, and relay messages. Databases are easily accessed to prepare and analyze reports. Documents drafted via word processing are stored for later retrieval and/or sent via electronic mail or facsimile transmission to other persons. Meeting notes are jotted in palm-held electronic diaries and up-loaded into computer files. Computer conferencing and videoconferencing are commonplace, as people work in teams convened over great distances—even around the world—without meeting personally face to face.

But there is more to IT utilization than the electronic office itself. Indeed, the very nature of business is being transformed in the networked economy. If you want to buy a book today, it may be easier to purchase it off the Internet than from your local bookstore. That's not good news for the local retailer, but it accounts for the success of Amazon.com, the pioneer virtual bookstore. Amazon.com is a great example of one of the hottest new business developments of our time—**electronic commerce.** Called *e-business* by many, this is a business form in which commercial transactions take place through the use of advanced IT, including special telecommunications and computer mediation.[16] Simply put, e-business is done online rather than face to face. One of the companies most interested in supporting such developments, of course, is IBM. It describes the steps in developing e-business as follows:[17]

- ● **Electronic commerce** or *e-business* uses information technology to support online commercial transactions.

→ Steps in developing e-business

Step 1 in e-business—establishing a Web site and then using the site to publish information electronically.

Step 2 in e-business—advancing the Web site to "self-service" status, where customers can do things like check their account status or trace the location of a package for delivery.

Step 3 in e-business—further advancing the Web site to allow "transactions," including the buying and selling of merchandise and managing resource supply and product distribution chains.

"Discover books you'll love at Amazon.com" reads the brochure that arrives with the gift book from your friend. The book comes by priority mail, was ordered online, paid for by credit card, and shipped immediately. The package is even gift wrapped and carries a personal note from the gift giver—entered via computer, of course. The firm invites you to shop in their bookstore anytime you want day or night, 365 days a year. After all, the bookstore is online. It is e-business with a capital "E." Traditional booksellers are finding it tough to compete against a company that advertises: "Your next book is only a click away." Amazon.com has established a new level and form of competition in electronic commerce. What began as an online bookstore is now rapidly expanding into other product and service lines—including toys, cards, electronics, and auctions.

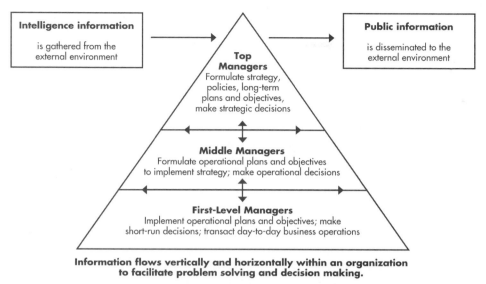

Intelligence information

is gathered from the external environment

Public information

is disseminated to the external environment

Top Managers
Formulate strategy, policies, long-term plans and objectives, make strategic decisions

Middle Managers
Formulate operational plans and objectives to implement strategy; make operational decisions

First-Level Managers
Implement operational plans and objectives; make short-run decisions; transact day-to-day business operations

Information flows vertically and horizontally within an organization to facilitate problem solving and decision making.

Figure 2.4   External and internal information needs of organizations.

INFORMATION NEEDS OF ORGANIZATIONS

The foundations of e-commerce and the electronic office rest with *information*, or data made useful for decision making. With today's technologies, the external and internal information needs of organizations as described in *Figure 2.4* are better served than ever before.

Information in the external environment must be accessed and used to successfully manage the organization/environment relationship. This *intelligence information* is needed to deal effectively with such outside parties as competitors, government agencies, creditors, suppliers, and stockholders. As Peter Drucker says about the information age, "a winning strategy will require information about events and conditions outside the institution." He goes on to add that organizations must have "rigorous methods for gathering and analyzing outside information." [18] In addition to gathering intelligence information, organizations also provide to the external environment many types of *public information*. This serves a variety of purposes ranging from image building to product advertising to financial reporting for taxes.

Within organizations, people need vast amounts of information to make decisions and solve problems in their daily work. Higher-level managers tend to emphasize information utilization in strategic planning, whereas middle and lower managers focus more on operational considerations involving the implementation of these plans. All workers engage in gathering, storing, sharing, and utilizing information to solve operating problems in order to meet the needs of internal and external customers.

INFORMATION SYSTEMS AND NETWORKS

Organizations that best harness IT to meet the needs just described are well positioned for competitive advantage. People in any work setting, large

● **Management information systems** use IT to collect, organize, and distribute data for use in decision making.

or small, must have available to them the right information at the right time and in the right place if they are to perform effectively. This is made possible by information systems that collect, organize, and distribute data in such a way that they become meaningful as information. **Management information systems,** or MIS, are specifically designed to use IT to meet the information needs of managers as they make a variety of decisions on a day-to-day basis.

The chief information officer or CIO is typically responsible for all aspects of computer, information, and telecommunications systems and their utilization. But everyone is important as a client or end user of information systems. The task is always to utilize information systems to make good decisions, to master the IT requirements of complex projects, and more generally to continuously utilize IT well for enhanced productivity. As you look ahead, keep in mind the advice in *Manager's Notepad 2.2.*

● **Intranets** are computer networks that allow persons within an organization to share databases and communicate electronically.

Central to organizational information systems today is the integration of computers and software into *networks* that allow users to easily transfer and share information through computer-to-computer linkages. **Intranets** are networks of computers with special software that allow persons working in various locations for the same organization to share databases and communicate electronically. The goal is to promote more integration across the organization and improve operations efficiency and quality. At Ford, for example, more than 120,000 workstations scattered in company offices around the world are linked by an intranet. Moreover, using a technology called the Concentric Network, Ford integrates voice, data, and video in a single network that allows employees to share information and work together in real time. In terms of competitive edge, the firm reports that the time between the point at which a new car is ordered and delivered is down to 15 days. The firm wants to build and sell most of its vehicles "on demand." [19]

A related trend in IT utilization is the emergence of fully integrated *enterprisewide networks* that move information quickly and accurately from one point to another within an organization. For example, a field salesperson may pass on a customer's suggestion for a product modification via electronic mail. This mail arrives at the computer used by a product designer at company headquarters. After creating a computer-assisted design for the product, the designer

---

MANAGER'S NOTEPAD 2.2

AVOIDING COMMON INFORMATION SYSTEMS MISTAKES

● Don't assume that more information is always better.
● Don't assume that computers eliminate human judgment.
● Don't assume that the newest technology is always best.
● Don't assume that nothing ever goes wrong with computers.
● Don't assume that everyone understands how the system works.

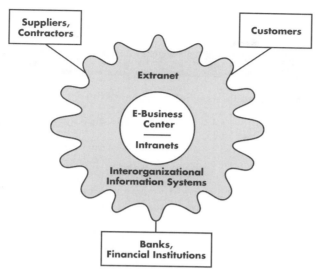

Figure 2.5   How e-businesses work through intranets and interorganizational information systems.

passes it on simultaneously to engineering, manufacturing, finance, and marketing experts for their preliminary analysis. Working as a computer-mediated team, everyone including the field salesperson may then further consider the design and agree on its business potential.

Another important IT application lies with the relationship between an organization and its environment—specifically in respect to dealings with suppliers and customers. **Extranets** are computer networks that use the public Internet to allow communication between the organization and elements in its external environment. These *interorganizational information systems* are the foundation for the fast-paced developments occurring in electronic commerce. They electronically link the organization with its suppliers and/or customers to move and share documents such as purchase orders, bills, receipt confirmations, and even payments for services rendered. An example is provided in *Figure 2.5*.

● **Extranets** are computer networks that use the public Internet for communication between the organization and its environment.

ORGANIZATIONAL LEARNING

In the complex, dynamic and high technology environment described in this chapter, organizational leaders must understand that the old ways of managing aren't good enough anymore. This is an age of continuing social and organizational transformations.[20] Intellectual capital is at a premium, and knowledge workers, the people whose intellects create value in organizations, are critical assets. The only way that any organization can stay truly competitive in the 21st century environment is to combine the best understandings of the past be with new thinking. Along with IT utilization, organizational learning and knowledge management are the challenges of the day.

Management Across Functions

SALES AND MARKETING

Knowledge Sharing Fuels a Sales Organization

It may not be easy to get employees to share knowledge with one another. But if you can pull it off, the sky's the limit in terms of performance gains. Take the experience of Buckman Laboratories, Inc., a closely held chemical company in Memphis, Tennessee. The firm is a leader in knowledge management and uses information technology to support an in-house network of 54 computer discussion groups. Most groups focus on the firm's products and how to improve them to gain customers and keep them satisfied. Salespersons share tips worldwide on how to close client deals and they communicate with research and manufacturing personnel to solve special sales problems. Questions get answered quickly and customers notice the improvements in service time. Says one: "One of the reasons they have business around here is they are faster than the competition. I'm not aware that their competitors can pool the whole brainpower of the organization." When Robert Buckman set out to remake his company, that was the goal. Through hard work, top information technology, and a willingness to empower his staff to communicate directly with one another, he's largely succeeded. And even though the industry remains competitive, his emphasis on knowledge management continues. "I don't think we'd be a player today if we hadn't done those things," he says.[23]

WHAT IS A LEARNING ORGANIZATION?

"Learning," says British Petroleum's (BP) CEO John Browne, "is at the heart of a company's ability to adapt to a rapidly changing environment." He goes on to add, "In order to generate extraordinary value for its shareholders, a company must learn better than its competitors and apply that knowledge throughout its businesses faster and more widely than they do."[21] Like other progressive organizations today, BP is striving to build the foundations of a true **learning organization.** This is an organization that "by virtue of people, values, and systems is able to continuously change and improve its performance based upon the lessons of experience."[22]

● A **learning organization** is able to continuously change and improve based on the lessons of experience.

There is no doubt that organizations and workers of all types today must continually adapt to new situations if they are to survive and prosper over the long run—this is a reality of the new workplace. Consultant Peter Senge, author of the popular book *The Fifth Discipline*, identifies the following core ingredients of learning organizations:[24]

Ingredients of learning organizations

1. *Mental models*—everyone sets aside old ways of thinking.
2. *Personal mastery*—everyone becomes self-aware and open to others.
3. *Systems thinking*—everyone learns how the whole organization works.

4. *Shared vision*—everyone understands and agrees to a plan of action.

5. *Team learning*—everyone works together to accomplish the plan.

Senge's concept of the learning organization places high value on developing the ability to learn and then make that learning continuously available to all organizational members. BP's CEO Browne says that organizations can learn from many sources. They can learn from their own experience. They can learn from the experiences of their contractors, suppliers, partners, and customers. And they can learn from firms in unrelated businesses.[25] All of this, of course, depends on a willingness to seek out learning opportunities from these sources and to make information sharing an expected and valued work behavior. In addressing the challenges of competing in a global economy, for example, General Electric's CEO Jack Welch says, "The aim in a global business is to get the best ideas from everywhere. . . . Our culture is designed around making a hero out of those who translate ideas from one place to another, who help somebody else."[26]

KNOWLEDGE MANAGEMENT

Consistent with the opportunities of information technology and an emphasis on organizational learning, a new term is earning a significant place in management theory and practice. The concept of **knowledge management** is used to describe the processes through which organizations develop, organize, and share knowledge to achieve competitive advantage.[27] The significance of knowledge management as a strategic and integrating force in organizations is represented by the emergence of a new executive job title—*Chief Knowledge Officer*, or CKO. This position of CKO is responsible for energizing learning processes and making sure that an organization's portfolio of intellectual assets and pool of knowledge are well managed and continually enhanced. Furthermore, the intellectual assets include such things as patents, intellectual property rights, trade secrets, and special processes and methods, as well as the accumulated knowledge and understanding of the entire workforce. For example, John Peetz, chief knowledge officer at Ernst & Young, considers knowledge management critical. "It's one of four core processes—sell work, do work, manage people, and manage knowledge." His responsibilities include communicating the importance of sharing knowledge, initiating and supporting projects to distribute knowledge, and managing the firm's technological infrastructure.[28]

● **Knowledge management** encompasses the processes utilizing organizational knowledge to achieve competitive advantage.

SUMMARY

What Is the External Environment of Organizations?

● Competitive advantage and distinctive competency can only be achieved by organizations that deal successfully with dynamic and complex environments.

● The external environment of organizations consists of both general and specific components.

- The general environment includes background conditions that influence the organization, including economic, socio-cultural, legal-political, technological, and natural environment conditions.
- The specific environment consists of the actual organizations, groups, and persons an organization deals with; these include suppliers, customers, competitors, regulators, and pressure groups.

What Is A Customer-Driven Organization?

- Any organization must develop and maintain a base of loyal customers or clients, and a customer-driven organization recognizes customer service and product quality as foundations of competitive advantage.
- Customer service is a core ingredient of total quality operations, and it includes concerns for both internal customers and external customers.
- To compete in the global economy, organizations are increasingly expected to meet ISO 9000 certification standards of quality.
- Total quality management involves making a strategic objective of the organization and supporting it by continuous improvement efforts.

How Does Information Technology Benefit Organizations?

- Continuing advances in computers and information technology bring many opportunities for improving the workplace through better information utilization.
- Today's "electronic" offices with E-mail, voice messaging, and networked computer systems are changing the nature of office work.
- A major and rapidly growing force in the economy are e-businesses, which engage in electronic commerce through the Internet.
- A management information system, or MIS, collects, organizes, stores, and distributes data in a way that meets the information needs of managers.
- Intranets are computer networks that allow persons within an organization to share databases and communicate electronically.
- Extranets are computer networks using the public Internet for communication between the organization and its environment.

Why Is Organizational Learning Important?

- The old ways of management aren't good enough anymore; an age of transformation demands that the best of the past must be combined with new thinking for organizations to be competitive in the 21st century.
- A learning organization is one in which people, values, and systems support continuous change and improvement based upon the lessons of experience.
- Knowledge management is the process of capturing, developing and utilizing the knowledge of an organization to achieve competitive advantage.

KEY TERMS

Competitive advantage (p. 20)

Continuous improvement (p. 26)

Electronic commerce (p. 28)

External customer (p. 23)

Extranets (p. 31)

General environment (p. 21)

ISO 9000 certification (p. 25)

Intellectual capital (p. 20)

Internal customer (p. 23)

Intranets (p. 30)

Knowledge management (p. 33)

Learning organization (p. 32)

Management information systems (p. 30)

Networked economy (p. 26)

Operations management (p. 24)

Specific environment (p. 21)

Stakeholders (p. 22)

SELF-TEST Take the interactive Self-Test for this chapter on the Schermerhorn Web Site

Chapter Three

Globalization and International Management

LIVE AND WORK IN A GLOBAL VILLAGE

THERE IS NO DOUBT about it. We live in an international community. Led by CNN, network television brings on-the-spot news from around the world into our homes, 24 hours a day. Newspapers from around the world can be read from the Internet at the touch of a keyboard on your desktop PC. It is easy to stay informed as reporters tell us the latest on the economies of Asia, strife in Kosovo, and political developments in the nations of Africa, among many examples. The far corners of the globe are more directly accessible than ever before. It is possible to board a plane in Minneapolis and fly nonstop to Beijing; it is sometimes less expensive to fly from Columbus, Ohio, to London than to Albany, New York. Colleges and universities offer an increasing variety of study abroad programs. E-mail links us to friends and work partners around the world and at low cost. We live in a global village and we work in a global economy.

The global village isn't just for tourists and travelers. It's for all of us, and we must recognize the emergence and implications of a global workplace.[1] It is already difficult to buy a car that is really "made in America," since so many components are manu-factured in other countries. The gas station with the green-and-white BP logo is operated by British Petroleum; the familiar Shell station is brought to you courtesy of Royal-Dutch/Shell. And did you know that the majority of McDonald's sales are now coming from outside of the United States and that some of its most profitable restaurants are located in places like Moscow, Budapest, Beijing, and elsewhere? Astute business investors know all this and more. They buy and sell only with awareness of the latest financial news from Hong Kong, London, Tokyo, New York, Johannesburg, and other of the world's financial centers. And in this time of high technology they don't even have to leave home to do it—the latest information is readily available on the Internet.

As the world shrinks, and as the operations of organizations large and small increasingly span national boundaries, new tests of managerial skills and viewpoints are emerging. Today's business leaders must think and act globally in the quest for competitive advantage. Procter & Gamble, for example, pursues a global strategy with a presence in more than 70 countries. Coke and Pepsi compete aggressively for the markets of China, India, and other nations. Like many other companies, they actively pursue international business opportunities in search of:

- *Profits:* Global operations offer expanded profit potential.
- *Customers:* Global operations offer new markets to sell products.
- *Suppliers:* Global operations offer access to needed raw materials.
- *Capital:* Global operations offer access to financial resources.
- *Labor:* Global operations offer access to lower labor costs.

← Reasons for engaging in international business

PROCESSES OF GLOBALIZATION

This is the age of **globalization** and the worldwide interdependence of resource supplies, product markets, and business competition.[2] The significance of the global economy is described by scholar and consultant Rosabeth Moss Kanter as "one of the most powerful and pervasive influences on nations, businesses, workplaces, communities, and lives."[3] Success in meeting its challenges will be earned by a new breed of manager who is informed about international developments, transnational in outlook, competent in working with people from different cultures, and always aware of regional developments in a changing world.

● **Globalization** is the worldwide interdependence of resource supplies, product markets, and business competition.

THE NEW EUROPE

Europe is a good example of continuing political and economic developments in regionalization. The **European Union (EU)** is a grouping of 15 countries that have agreed to support mutual economic growth by removing barriers that previously limited cross-border trade and business development. Expectations are that the EU will expand to include at least 25 members in the near future.

● The **European Union (EU)** is a political and economic alliance of European countries.

At present, only Switzerland and Norway from Western Europe remain outside the group. At least a dozen countries, including several new republics of the former Soviet Union, have applied to join or expressed interest in joining.

As an economic union, the EU has created a global force to be reckoned with. Members are linked through favorable trade and customs laws to facilitate the free flow of workers, goods and services, and investments across national boundaries. Businesses in each member country have access to a market larger than the United States and Japan combined. Among the important developments is the advent of a new common currency—the "Euro," that is part of Europe's march into the 21st century. Although there is still political and economic risk to Europe's economic and monetary union, the expected benefits include higher productivity, lower inflation, and steady growth.

Importantly, there is a lot more to Europe than the EU alone. New political and economic opportunities are transforming businesses throughout the region. It wasn't too long ago, for example, that workers at Petofi Printing & Packaging Co., a formerly state-owned cardboard box and container maker in Kecskemet, Hungary, drank beer at work and didn't worry too much about making containers in the wrong colors and sizes. Today it's a different story in the newly privatized Petofi Printing & Packaging Co. New machinery and worker incentives have replaced communist-era machines and labor practices. Petofi now has a quality assurance lab checking on its suppliers and has won quality awards from the World Packaging Organization. It achieved ISO 9000 certification and is competing well against Western rivals who have difficulty meeting its cost-plus-quality advantages.[4]

THE AMERICAS

● **NAFTA** is the **North American Free Trade Agreement** linking Canada, the United States, and Mexico in a regional economic alliance.

The United States, Canada, and Mexico have joined together in the **North American Free Trade Agreement,** or **NAFTA.** This agreement largely frees the flow of goods and services, workers, and investments within a region that has more potential consumers than its European rival, the EU. Getting approval of NAFTA from all three governments was not easy. Whereas Canadian firms worried about domination by U.S. manufacturers, American politicians were concerned about the potential loss of jobs to Mexico. Whereas Mexicans feared that free trade would bring a further intrusion of U.S. culture and values into their country, Americans complained that Mexican businesses did not operate by the same social standards as they did—particularly with respect to environmental protection and the use of child labor.

● *Maquiladoras* are foreign manufacturing plants that operate in Mexico with special privileges.

Often at issue in NAFTA controversies are the operations of *maquiladoras,* foreign manufacturing plants allowed to operate in Mexico with special privileges in return for employing Mexican labor.[5] They import materials, components, and equipment duty free, locally assemble finished products, and then export them with duty paid only on the "value added" in Mexico. Reports indicate that *maquiladoras* are flourishing, gaining in productivity, and creating jobs. Critics accuse them of exploiting the availability of lower cost Mexican labor and giving away jobs that would otherwise go to Americans. At issue here is *protectionism,* the desire to protect domestic workers and industries from foreign competition.

Optimism regarding business and economic potential extends throughout Central and South America as well. Many countries of the region are cutting tariffs, updating their economic policies, and welcoming foreign investors. Chile is being discussed as the next NAFTA partner, and other countries may soon follow. Some are even seeking the creation of a Free Trade Area of the Americas (FTAA), a proposed free trade zone that would stretch from Point Barrow, Alaska, all the way to Tierra del Fuego, Chile. Other pieces of this potential pan-American economic union are already in place.[6] The MERCOSUR agreement links Bolivia, Brazil, Paraguay, Uruguay, and Argentina; the Andean Pact links Venezuela, Colombia, Ecuador, Peru, and Bolivia; and the Caribbean Community, CARICOM, is also becoming a significant economic linkage.

ASIA AND THE PACIFIC RIM

Although the region's recent financial problems have taken some of the luster off, Asia must be respected for what *Fortune* magazine has called a "megamarket." The region is not only still growing as a power in the world economy, but it has already achieved superpower status.[7] Japanese companies account for a large majority of *Fortune*'s "Pac Rim 150"—an annual listing of the largest Asian firms. Sprinkled among the list can be found a number of emerging world-class competitors from other Asian countries: Samsung (South Korea), Sime-Darby (Malaysia), and Siam Cement (Thailand), to name just three.

Wherever you travel or do business in the Asian region, "opportunity" is the watchword of the day. Member countries of the **Asia-Pacific Economic Cooperation (APEC)** forum represent a third of the global marketplace, and rank as the world's top market for cars and telecommunications equipment. It is not just low-cost labor that attracts businesses to Asia; the growing availability of highly skilled "brainpower" is increasingly high on its list of advantages. India, for example, with a growing economy and the second largest population in the world, is gaining a world-class reputation for its software industry.

China commands well-deserved attention as the world's largest single-country marketplace. Its importance in the global economy will surely increase in the future. But China's relations with the global economy also remain complicated by human rights concerns and poor protection of foreign copyrights and intellectual property, among other issues. Executives at Salient Systems, an Ohio manufacturer of railway weighting systems, have already recognized the potential and the complications. They are working with China's Ministry of Railways on a $4 million project, and they expect a long-term market for their products. But they've also had to learn how to protect their intellectual capital and manage the financial details. Says Chief Financial Officer Sharron Harrison, "in China, the language barrier and the great distance are extremely difficult."[8]

● **APEC, Asia-Pacific Economic Cooperation,** is a platform for regional economic alliances among Asian and Pacific Rim countries.

AFRICA

Look at the map in *Figure 3.1* and consider how Africa beckons international business. On the discouraging side, the rates of economic growth in sub-Saharan Africa are among the lowest in the world, many parts of the region suffer from terrible problems of poverty and the ravishment of a continuing AIDS epidemic, and the need for sustained assistance from the industrialized countries is

Figure 3.1 Africa, continent of opportunity.

well established. Yet, a report on the foreign investment environment of Africa concludes that the region's contextual problems are manageable.[9] "In fact, they should be viewed as opportunities," says Harvard professor James A. Austin, one of the report's co-authors. He adds: "If a company has the managerial and organizational capabilities to deal with the region's unique business challenges, then it will be able to enter a promising market."[10] Post-apartheid South Africa, in particular, has benefited from political revival. It is experiencing economic recovery and attracting outside investors. Coca-Cola is one firm that is responding to the opportunity, projecting 15 percent growth rates as part of its regional business plan. CEO M. Douglas Ivester says: "We see an Africa more directly accountable for its own destiny than it has for centuries."[11]

ENVIRONMENT OF INTERNATIONAL BUSINESS

● An **international business** conducts commercial transactions across national boundaries.

The **international businesses** that conduct for-profit transactions of goods and services across national boundaries are the foundations of world trade. They are the engines for moving raw materials, finished products, and specialized services from one country to another in the global economy. International businesses of all types and sizes are found in the form shown in *Figure 3.2*.

FORMS OF INTERNATIONAL BUSINESS

● In **global sourcing** materials or components are purchased abroad for assembly at home into a final product.

A common first step into international business is **global sourcing**, the process of manufacturing and/or purchasing components around the world and then assembling them into a final product. This is an international division of labor in which activities are performed in countries where they can be done well at the lowest cost. Global sourcing for cars assembled in the United States, for exam-

Figure 3.2   Five common forms of international business—from market entry to direct investment strategies.

ple, may mean purchasing windshields, instrument panels, seats, and fuel tanks from Mexico as well as electronics for antilock braking systems from Germany.

A second form of international business involves **exporting**, selling locally-made products in foreign markets, and/or **importing**, buying foreign-made products and selling them in domestic markets. Governments often look to export industries, large and small, as one way to correct trade imbalances.

By entering into a **licensing agreement** a foreign firm pays a fee for the rights to make or sell another company's products. This international business approach typically grants access to a unique manufacturing technology, special patent, or trademark rights held by the licensor. **Franchising** is a form of licensing in which the licensee buys the complete "package" of support needed to open a particular business, such as a McDonald's restaurant.

To establish a direct investment presence in a foreign country, many firms enter into **joint ventures** or co-ownership arrangements for business operations. This is done by equity purchases and/or direct investments by a foreign partner in a local operation, or by the creation of a new business by a foreign and local partner. International joint ventures are "strategic alliances" that help participants to gain things through cooperation that otherwise would be difficult to achieve independently. In return for its investment in a local operation, for example, the outside or foreign partner often gains new markets and the assistance of a local partner who understands them. In return for its investment, the local partner often gains new technology as well as opportunities for its employees to learn new skills by working in joint operations. *Manager's Notepad 3.1* offers a checklist for choosing joint venture partners.[12]

A **wholly owned subsidiary** is a local operation completely owned and controlled by a foreign firm. When making such investments, foreign firms are clearly taking a business risk. They must be confident that they possess the expertise needed to manage and conduct business affairs successfully in the new environment.

- In **exporting** local products are sold abroad.

- **Importing** is the process of acquiring products abroad and selling them in domestic markets.

- A **licensing agreement** occurs when a firm pays a fee for the rights to make or sell another company's products.

- **Franchising** provides the complete "package" of support needed to open a particular business.

- A **joint venture** establishes operations in a foreign country through joint ownership with local partners.

- A **wholly owned subsidiary** is a local operation completely owned by a foreign firm.

MULTINATIONAL CORPORATIONS

While many companies may engage in international business, a true **multinational corporation** (or **MNC**) has extensive operations in more than one foreign country. Premier MNCs found in annual *Fortune, Business Week,* and *Wall Street Journal* listings of the world's largest firms include General Electric, Exxon, and AT&T from the United States; Nippon Telegraph & Telephone, Mitsubishi Bank, and Toyota Motor of Japan; and Royal Dutch/Shell of the Netherlands and Great Britain.[13] Also important on the world scene are *multinational*

- A **multinational corporation (MNC)** is a business firm with extensive international operations in more than one foreign country.

MANAGER'S NOTEPAD 3.1

CHECKLIST FOR JOINT VENTURES

- Choose a partner familiar with your firm's major business.
- Choose a partner with a strong local workforce.
- Choose a partner with future expansion possibilities.
- Choose a partner with a strong local market and products.
- Choose a partner with shared interests in customer needs.
- Choose a partner with good profit potential.
- Choose a partner in sound financial standing.

organizations (MNOs)—like the International Red Cross, the United Nations, and the World Bank, whose nonprofit missions and operations span the globe.

Many of the world's MNC's are becoming increasingly "borderless" in business strategy and practice. As the global economy grows more competitive, multinationals are acting more like **transnational corporations** that operate globally without being identified with one national "home." [14] Executives with transnationals view the entire world as the domain for acquiring resources, locating production facilities, marketing goods and services, and for enhancing brand image.

● A **transnational corporation** is an MNC that operates worldwide on a borderless basis.

Among the American automakers, Ford Motor Company is moving in a transnational direction. The pathway to the future, say Ford executives, is borderless management and a global mindset. Even with its long history of international involvement—Henry Ford had a sales branch in France by 1908 and a manufacturing facility in England by 1911—the company is still learning how to master the challenges of global operations. The company is globalizing product development, purchasing, sales, and manufacturing. Multifunctional teams staffed from around the world develop new cars and trucks as the firm strives to become a true global company.

COMPLICATIONS OF GLOBAL OPERATIONS

Both the global corporations and the countries that "host" their foreign operations should mutually benefit from any business relationship. The potential host-country benefits include larger tax bases, increased employment opportunities, technology transfers, the introduction of new industries, and the development of local resources. *Figure 3.3* shows, however, that things can and sometimes do go wrong in MNC-host country relationships. Host countries can feel exploited. For example, they may complain that MNCs extract excessive profits, dominate the local economy, interfere with the local government, do not respect local customs and laws, fail to help domestic firms develop, hire the most talented of local personnel, and do not transfer their most advanced technologies.

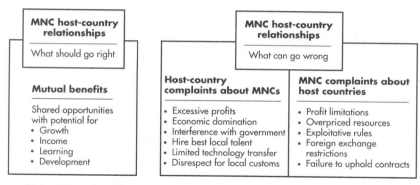

Figure 3.3 What should go right and what can go wrong in MNC-host country relationships.

Of course, executives of MNCs sometimes feel exploited as well. They may face host government restrictions making it difficult to take profits out of a country or to obtain needed raw materials. The protection of intellectual property is a concern for some manufacturers, and managing relationships with foreign government agencies can be very complicated. Consider, for example, what happened when Quicksilver Enterprises, a California maker of ultra-light airplanes, licensed a Brazilian distributor to build and sell the planes in that country. Six months after the Brazilians learned how to build, fly, and fix the planes, royalty payments to Quicksilver stopped. The Brazilian company claimed it had changed the design and created a new plane. Quicksilver took a loss of over $100,000.

MNCs may also encounter difficulties in the country where their headquarters are located. Even as many MNCs try to operate more transnationally, home-country governments and citizens tend to identify them with local and national interests. Corporate decision makers are likely to be engaged by government and community leaders in debates about a firm's domestic social responsibilities. Typical home-country criticisms of MNCs include complaints about transferring jobs out of the country, shifting capital investments abroad, and engaging in corrupt practices in foreign settings. Often this point is missed until its implications hit a local community. The town of Shelby, North Carolina, knows just how cut-throat the global economy can be. The announcement that Kemet Electronics would lay off some 500 local employees and shift their jobs to Mexico hurt. One employee commented: "I worked all this time to get what I've got, and now it's gone. I thought I had found security."[15]

ETHICAL ISSUES IN INTERNATIONAL BUSINESS

The ethical aspects of global business deserve special attention. In 1977, the Foreign Corrupt Practices Act made it illegal for American firms to engage in a variety of corrupt practices overseas, including giving bribes and excessive commissions to foreign officials in return for business favors. This law specifically bans payoffs to foreign officials to obtain or keep business, provides punishments for executives who know about or are involved in such activities, and requires detailed accounting records for international business transactions. Critics complain that the law doesn't recognize the "reality" of international business, placing American companies at a disadvantage because they can't engage in what locals may regard as "standard business practice."

Another concern in the global business arena is "sweatshop" operations, that employ local labor at low wages and often in poor working conditions. Firms that follow the world's low-cost labor supplies to countries like the Philippines, Sri Lanka, and Vietnam, increasingly face activist criticisms when their labor practices violate external standards. The use of child labor is a highly visible and controversial issue in this regard. Initiatives to eliminate child labor include an effort by "Rugmark" to discourage purchases of handmade carpets that do not carry its label. Complaints about child labor and other disputable human resource practices are common in the context of outsourcing contracts by multinational corporations. Nike, for example, has been the target of such criticism. However, it was recently praised in the business and popular press for releasing on its Website the names of contractors making sports equipment under its label for various universities. The company's mission statement says: "Nike will share responsibility with our manufacturing partners to continually improve the workplace for any worker manufacturing Nike products." By releasing the list of 42 manufacturers in 11 countries, Nike was publicly standing behind this commitment in the full scope of its worldwide operations.[16]

Yet another ethical issue in international business relates to global concerns for environmental protection. Not only is the world's citizenry worried about disasters, such as the pollution aftermath of the Gulf War, but more generally it expects global corporations to always respect the natural environment and pursue safe industrial practices. Industrial pollution of cities, hazardous waste, depletion of the rain forest and other natural resources, and related concerns are now worldwide issues. As global corporate citizens, MNCs are expected to uphold high standards in dealing with them—whenever and wherever they operate.

CULTURE AND GLOBAL DIVERSITY

● **Culture** is a shared set of beliefs, values, and patterns of behavior common to a group of people.

Culture is the shared set of beliefs, values, and patterns of behavior common to a group of people. Anyone who has visited another country knows that cultural differences exist. The business and managerial implications of these differences must be understood. An American exporter, for example, once went to see a Saudi Arabian official. He sat in the office with crossed legs and the sole of his shoe exposed—an unintentional sign of disrespect in the local culture. He passed documents to the host using his left hand, which Muslims consider unclean, and he refused to accept coffee when it was offered, suggesting criticism of the Saudi's hospitality. The price for these cultural miscues was the loss of a $10 million contract to a Korean better versed in Arab ways.

● **Ethnocentrism** is the tendency to consider one's culture as superior to all others.

Local customs vary in too many ways for most of us to become true experts in the many cultures of our diverse world. Yet there are things we can do to respect differences, successfully conduct business abroad, and minimize culture shock. Importantly, **ethnocentrism,** or the tendency to view one's culture as superior to others, must be avoided. The basic building blocks of cultural awareness, as suggested in *Manager's Notepad 3.2,* are self-awareness, respect, and sensitivity.[17]

Browser

Go to: http://www.wiley.com/college/schermerhorn

 THE WALL STREET JOURNAL.

WILEY

IN PRACTICE

The globalization of the business community is a fact of doing business in the 21st century. Mangers must increasingly communicate with far-flung operations in a variety of international settings. Local information is no longer good enough, as global situations, including political, economic, and financial events, can have an impact on local decisions.

WORLD-WIDE ▶

The Interactive Journal commits significant resources to this international setting, primarily with its **Worldwide** section. Located on the right side of the **Front Page** section, Worldwide concentrates on global events that impact businesses around the world. Worldwide offers specific focus pieces on **Europe, Asia,** and the **Americas.** These areas are accessed in the left-hand menu window under the **Worldwide** heading.

In the **Europe** and **Asia** sections, near the bottom of the page, are additional links to

COUNTRY NEWS ⎯⎯

news stories from specific countries. **COUNTRY NEWS** supports a drop-down-box listing recent articles.

A collection of business articles is contained in a section of **Special Reports,** which can be accessed from the left-hand menu near the bottom, under **Resources.** Locate any series involved in discussions of global business conditions.

CHAPTER 3:

Globalization and International Management emphasizes the importance of 21st century managers taking a world-view of business topics. Click on the **Asia** and **Europe** links under the Worldwide heading in order to see breaking news from those particular areas of the world.

In the left-hand menu, under **Other wsj.com Sites,** click on the **Travel** link. Articles involving travel throughout the world are provided in this section.

Choose a particular area of the world, and see what articles are relevant.

Under **Travel Center,** there is a link to **City Guides.** Travel information is provided, including sightseeing, shopping, and lodging.

DELIVERABLE:

Pick either Asia or Europe and provide a one-page synopsis of three major headlines of the day. Include a 2–3 sentence description of each newsworthy event. Then choose to focus on a particular country in the region by choosing **Country News.** Once again, provide a short synopsis of the top three stories from that list.

DISCUSSION QUESTIONS:

1. How important is the new European Union to the United States in regard to trade?

2. What effect has NAFTA had on trade in North America?

3. How involved do you believe you will be in International business?

 *Note: The underscored words/phrases in the Interactive Journal feature indicate Internet links provided in the online versions. See the *Introducing Management* Web site at www.wiley.com/college/schermerhorn.

MANAGER'S NOTEPAD 3.2

STAGES IN ADJUSTING TO A NEW CULTURE

- *Confusion:* First contacts with the new culture leave you anxious, uncomfortable, and in need of information and advice.
- *Small victories:* Continued interactions bring some "successes," and your confidence grows in handling daily affairs.
- *The honeymoon:* A time of wonderment, cultural immersion, and infatuation, with local things viewed most positively by you.
- *Irritation and anger:* A time when "negatives" overtake "positives," and the new culture becomes a target of criticism.
- *Reality:* A time of rebalancing; you are able to enjoy the new culture while recognizing its less desirable elements.

SILENT LANGUAGES OF CULTURE

● **Culture shock** is the confusion and discomfort a person experiences when in an unfamiliar culture.

A traveler's first impressions when abroad are often of differences in dress, spoken language, and physical setting. In addition, however, differences in what some call the "silent languages" of culture are also present—including differences in use of space, time orientation, and the like.[18] Any and all cultural differences can be exhilarating and interesting. They can also contribute to **culture shock** that appears in the form of confusion and disorientation. Learning to recognize cultural differences, both the obvious and the "silent" ones, is a good first step toward success in cross-cultural competency.[19]

Use of Language

It is not only the language itself that can vary across cultures; the way a language is used for communication is also a variable. Anthropologist Edward T. Hall[20] describes *low-context cultures* whose members are very explicit in using the spoken and written word. In places like Canada, Germany, and United States, words tend to convey the message. In *high-context cultures*, by contrast, words convey only part of the message. The rest is interpreted from the "context" that may include body language, the physical setting, and past relationships—all of which add meaning to what is being said. Hall describes Asian and Middle Eastern cultures as typically high context, while most Western cultures are considered low context. British Airways, for example, learned that even meals served and the dinner plates used were communicating with its international customers. When surveyed by BA, Japanese customers commented that BA's food was "not bad for Westerners." But, they also pointed out that the white china dishes were similar to those used in Japanese hospitals and prisons. "The futher away from our Western culture we go, the less satisfied our customers are," said one BA marketing manager.

Use of Space

Proxemics is the study of how space is used to communicate. And, the use of space is known to vary among the world's cultures.[21] Arabs and many Latin Americans, for example, prefer to communicate at much closer distances than is standard in American practice. Misunderstandings are possible if one person moves back as another moves forward to close the interpersonal distance between them. Some cultures of the world also value space differently than others. Americans tend to value large *and* private office space. The Japanese are highly efficient in using space and even executive offices are likely to be shared in major corporations.

Time Orientation

The way people perceive and deal with time orientation also varies across cultures. The anthropologist Hall describes **monochronic cultures** in which people tend to do one thing at a time, such as schedule a meeting and give the visitor one's undivided attention for the allotted time.[22] This is standard American business practice. In **polychronic cultures,** by contrast, time is used to accomplish many different things at once. The American visitor to an Egyptian client may be frustrated by continued interruptions as people flow in and out of the office and various transactions are made.

● In a **monochronic culture** people tend to do one thing at a time.

● In a **polychronic culture** time is used to accomplish many different things at once.

Religion

Religion is a source of ethical and moral teaching. It is also another cultural variable with implications that may extend to business practices. At a minimum, the traveler and businessperson should be sensitive to the rituals, holy days, and other expectations associated with religions in foreign countries. When working with Muslims, for example, it should be remembered that the Islamic holy month of Ramadan is a dawn-to-dusk time of fasting. Similarly, Islamic banks operate within guidelines set forth in the holy *Koran* and therefore charge no interest. Nike executives know first-hand the influence of such Islamic religious traditions. The firm once ran into problems when a design for one of its training shoes was misinterpreted. The mark was supposed to resemble "flames" but in its visual presentation resembled the word *Allah* as written in Arabic. Some called for a boycott of Nike products and the design was quickly changed.

Role of Contracts

Cultures vary in their use of contracts and agreements. In the United States a contract is viewed as a final and binding statement of agreements. In other parts of the world, including the People's Republic of China, it may be viewed as more of a starting point. Once in place, the contract is expected to continue to emerge and be modified as the parties work together over time. In the United States, contracts are expected to be in writing; requesting a written agreement from an Indonesian Muslim who has given his "word" may be quite disrespectful.

VALUES AND NATIONAL CULTURES

The work of Geert Hofstede, scholar and management consultant, offers a popular framework for understanding value differences across national cultures. *Figure 3.4* shows how selected countries rank on the five dimensions Hofstede now uses:[23]

Hofstede's dimensions of national cultures

- *Power distance:* The degree to which a society accepts the unequal distribution of power in organizations.
- *Uncertainty avoidance:* The degree to which a society tolerates risk and situational uncertainties.
- *Individualism–collectivism:* The degree to which a society emphasizes individual self-interests versus the collective values of groups.
- *Masculinity–femininity:* The degree to which a society emphasizes assertiveness and material concerns versus greater concern for human relationships and feelings.
- *Time orientation:* The degree to which a society emphasizes short-term considerations versus greater long-term concern for the future.

Hofstede's framework is a useful starting point for examining the managerial implications of cultural differences. For example, workers from high power–distance cultures, such as Singapore, can be expected to show great respect to people in authority. In high uncertainty–avoidance cultures, employment practices that increase job security are likely to be favored. In highly individualistic societies (the United States ranked as the most individualistic country in Hofstede's sample), workers may be expected to emphasize

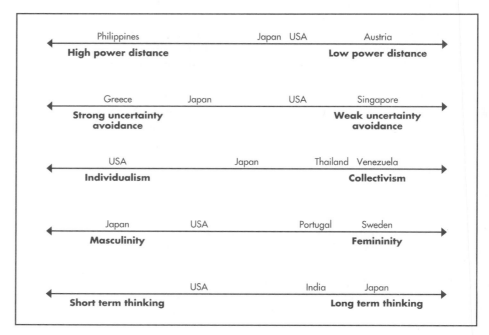

Figure 3.4   How countries compare on Hofstede's dimensions of national culture.

self-interests more than group loyalty. Outsiders may find that the workplace in more masculine societies, such as Japan, displays more rigid gender stereotypes.[24] And the corporate strategies of businesses in more long-term cultures are likely to be just that—more long-term oriented.

ESSENTIALS OF CROSS-CULTURAL UNDERSTANDING

Another researcher and consultant, Fons Trompenaars, approaches cross-cultural understanding in a way that integrates some of the notions of popular and national cultures just discussed. He focuses attention on systematic differences in the ways relationships are handled among people, attitudes toward time, and attitudes toward the environment.[25] By better understanding patterns of differences in these areas, he suggests we can improve our cross-cultural work effectiveness.

Trompenaars identifies five ways in which people differ culturally in how they handle relationships with one another.

- *Universalism vs. particularism:* The degree to which a culture emphasizes rules and consistency in relationships, or accepts flexibility and the bending of rules to fit circumstances.
- *Individualism vs. collectivism:* The degree to which a culture emphasizes individual freedoms and responsibilities in relationships, or focuses more on group interests and consensus.
- *Neutral vs. affective:* The degree to which a culture emphasizes objectivity and reserved detachment in relationships, or allows more emotionality and expressed feelings.
- *Specific vs. diffuse:* The degree to which a culture emphasizes focused and in-depth relationships, or displays broader and more superficial ones.
- *Achievement vs. prescription:* The degree to which a culture emphasizes earned or performance-based status, or status based on social standing and nonperformance factors.

According to Trompenaars, attitudes toward time differ in the relative emphasis given to the present versus the past and future. In cultures that take a *sequential view*, time is considered a continuous and passing series of events. This somewhat casual view of time may be represented by a circle and the notion that time is recycling, in the sense that a moment passed will return again. In cultures that take a *synchronic view*, by contrast, time takes on a greater sense of urgency. It is more linear, with an interrelated past, present, and future. Pressures to resolve problems quickly so that time won't be "lost" are more likely in synchronic than sequential cultures.

Finally, Trompenaars recognizes that cultures vary in their approach to the environment. In cultures that are *inner-directed*, people tend to view themselves as quite separate from nature. They are likely to consider the environment as something to be controlled or used for personal advantage. In cultures that are *outer-directed*, people tend to view themselves as part of nature. They are more likely to try and blend with or go along with the environment than to try to control it.

MANAGEMENT ACROSS CULTURES

Competition and the global economy have given rise to the *global manager*—someone comfortable with cultural diversity, quick to find opportunities in unfamiliar settings, and able to marshal economic, social, technological, and other forces for the benefit of the organization. Says Robin Willett, Group Deputy Chairman of Willett Systems, Ltd. of the United Kingdom: "Our aim has always been to be a truly global company, not simply an exporter. We work very hard at developing and maintaining an international mindset that is shared by everyone—from senior management to staff." [26] Global managers, simply put, apply the management functions successfully across national and cultural borders.

When Compaq Computers merged with Digital Equipment Corporation, it took over Digital's subsidiary and joint venture operations in Southeast Asia. The firm's "Borderless Asean" strategy involves developing business partnerships with software companies, information technology consultants, and marketing agencies. Warehousing for the region is outsourced to a Singaporean firm with operations in neighboring countries. In the dynamic and complex environment of the Asia-Pacific Basin, the company seeks business expansion through integration with the regional economy. [27]

ARE MANAGEMENT THEORIES UNIVERSAL?

● **Comparative management** is the study of how management practices differ systematically from one country and/or culture to the next.

For quite some time, management practices in North America and Western Europe were used as models around the world. Now the search for management insights has taken on a worldwide focus. The field of **comparative management** studies how management practices systematically vary among countries and cultures. An important question to be raised and answered in the process is—"Are management theories universal?"

Geert Hofstede, whose framework for understanding national cultures was introduced earlier, believes that management theories should not be applied universally. [28] He worries that many are ethnocentric and fail to take proper account of cultural differences. As an example, he argues that the American emphasis on *participation* in leadership reflects the culture's moderate stance on power distance. National cultures with lower scores, such as Sweden and Israel, are characterized by even more democratic leadership initiatives. France and some Asian countries with higher power-distance scores seem less concerned with participative leadership.

Hofstede also points out that the motivation theories of American scholars emphasize individual performance. He considers this viewpoint consistent with the high individualism found in Anglo-American cultures predominate in the United States, Canada, and the United Kingdom. Where values are more collectivist the theories may be less applicable as motivation is linked more to group affiliations. Even a common value, such as the desire for increased humanization of work, may lead in different management directions among cultures. Until recently, the United States pioneered in broadening jobs to enrich them for *individual* workers. Elsewhere in the world, such as in Sweden, the emphasis was on broadening jobs for *groups* of workers.

Management Across Functions

MANUFACTURING

Global Sourcing in Manufacturing

Victoria's Secret has learned the secret of manufacturing from a global base. If you visit the Slimline, Ltd., plant in Sri Lanka, you'll find over 1400 workers and very progressive management. The firm is a leading supplier to Victoria's Secret and is a sought-after local employer. It uses top-of-the-line technology for manufacturing and information systems. A new $4 million computer system links the firm with U.S. retailers. Management practices are state-of-the-art as well. You'll find not only high technology, but also a Japanese inventory control approach, emphasis on quality, plenty of team-building and teamwork, good pay, and an egalitarian management style. The firm is committed to employee safety and comfort, and there is even a new gym with exercise machines and a trainer. Managing Director Dian Gomes regularly has team meetings with employees. He says: "You have to make this place fun to work at." One worker says: "We feel this is our company." [30]

Similar cautions are in order regarding Japanese management practices, which have also attracted great interest over the years. Researchers, for example, have characterized Japanese management along the following lines.[29]

- *Lifetime employment*—with both the organization and the individual expected to grow and mature together over time.
- *Job rotation and broad career experience*—allowing workers to gain broad experiences, not just specialized skills.
- *Information sharing*—including information on performance objectives and accomplishments as well as on proposed activities and problems.
- *Group decisions*—spreading responsibility for results and creating a team feeling.
- *Quality emphasis*—with everyone expected to produce high-quality work and to help others to do the same.

Japanese management practices

But as interesting and provocative as these ideas may be, the lessons of Japanese management practices aren't easy to translate.[31] Today we recognize that not all Japanese organizations operate strictly in this manner, that changes in Japanese society are putting pressures on these practices, and that the practices themselves have important cultural roots. While others can still learn and benefit from the insights, any transfers of traditional Japanese management practices must be made in full awareness of significant cultural differences (such as described by Hofstede) and the need for appropriate adaptation to new settings.

The best approach to comparative management is an alert, open, inquiring, and always cautious one. It is important to identify both the potential merits of management practices found in other countries *and* the ways cultural variables may affect their success or failure when applied elsewhere. We can and should be looking for new ideas to stimulate change and innovation. But we should hesitate to accept any practice, no matter how well it appears to work somewhere else, as a universal prescription to action. Indeed, the goal of comparative management studies is not to provide definitive answers. Rather, it is to help develop creative and critical thinking about the way managers around the world do things and about whether or not they can and should be doing them better.

GLOBAL ORGANIZATIONAL LEARNING

In the dynamic and ever-expanding global economy, cultural awareness is helping to facilitate more informed transfers of management and organizational practices. We live at a fortunate time when managers around the world are realizing they have much to share with and learn from one another. The notion of "global organizational learning" is timely and relevant. This point is evident in the following words of Kenichi Ohmae, noted Japanese management consultant and author of *The Borderless World:*

> Companies can learn from one another, particularly from other excellent companies, both at home and abroad. The industrialized world is becoming increasingly homogeneous in terms of customer needs and social infrastructure, and only truly excellent companies can compete effectively in the global marketplace.[31]

We do have a lot to learn from one another. But it must be learned with full appreciation of the constraints and opportunities of different national cultures and environments. Like the American management practices before them, Japanese approaches and those from other cultures must be studied and adapted for local use very carefully. This applies to the way management is practiced in Mexico, Korea, Indonesia, Hungary, or any other part of the world. As Hofstede states, "Disregard of other cultures is a luxury only the strong can afford. . . . [The] consequent increase in cultural awareness represents an intellectual and spiritual gain.[32]

SUMMARY

What Are the Processes of Globalization?

- The processes of globalization are making the diverse countries of the world increasingly interdependent regarding resource supplies, product markets, and business competition.
- The global economy is now strongly influenced by regional developments that involve growing economic integration in Europe, the Americas, and Asia, and the economic emergence of Africa.

What Is the Environment of International Business?

- Five forms of international business are global sourcing, exporting and importing, licensing and franchising, joint ventures, and wholly owned subsidiaries.
- Global operations are influenced by important environmental differences among the economic, legal-political, and educational systems of countries.
- A multinational corporation, or MNC, is a business with extensive operations in more than one foreign country.

- MNCs offer potential benefits to host countries in broader tax bases, new technologies, and employment opportunities. MNCs can also disadvantage host countries if they interfere in local government, extract excessive profits, and dominate the local economy.

How Does Culture Create Global Diversity?

- Management and global operations are affected by the dimensions of popular culture, including—language, use of space, time orientation, religion, and the nature of contracts.

- Management and global operations are affected by differences in national cultures, including Hofstede's dimensions of power distance, uncertainty avoidance, individualism–collectivism, masculinity–femininity, and time orientation.

- Differences among the world's cultures may be understood in respect to how people handle relationships with one another, their attitudes toward time, and their attitudes toward the environment.

How Do Management Practices Transfer Across Cultures?

- The management process must be used appropriately and applied with sensitivity to local cultures and situations.

- The field of comparative management studies how management is practiced around the world and how management ideas are transferred from one country or culture to the next.

- Cultural values and management practices should be consistent with one another; practices that are successful in one culture may work less well in others.

- The concept of global management learning has much to offer as the "borderless" world begins to emerge and as the management practices of diverse countries and cultures become more visible.

KEY TERMS

Asia Pacific Economic Corporation (APEC) (p. 39)

Comparative management (p. 50)

Culture (p. 44)

Culture shock (p. 46)

Ethnocentrism (p. 44)

European Union (EU) (p. 37)

Exporting (p. 41)

Franchising (p. 41)

Globalization (p. 37)

Global sourcing (p. 40)

Importing (p. 41)

International business (p. 40)

Joint venture (p. 41)

Licensing agreement (p. 41)

Maquiladora (p. 38)

Monochronic cultures (p. 47)

Multinational corporation (p. 41)

North American Free Trade Agreement (NAFTA) (p. 38)

Polychronic cultures (p. 47)

Transnational corporation (p. 42)

Wholly owned subsidiary (p. 41)

SELF-TEST   Take the interactive Self-Test for this chapter on the Schermerhorn Web Site

Chapter Four

Ethical Behavior and Social Responsibility

PLANNING AHEAD—
Chapter 4 Study Questions

- What is ethical behavior?
- How do ethical dilemmas complicate the workplace?
- How can high ethical standards be maintained?
- What is corporate social responsibility?

MAKE THIS WORLD A BETTER PLACE

THE GOOD NEWS IS that more and more organizations are adding a new job title—Vice President of the Environment—to their executive suites. These senior managers work on everything from a company's recycling program to long-term corporate environmental policies. Global warming, global sustainability, and environmental protection are all on the agenda as organizations pursue what some call "the greening of the bottom line." [1] The goal of "Taking Better Care of Our World" has been prominent at Quad/Graphics since the firm's founding, and reflects a commitment to minimizing the company's environmental impacts. And at Du Pont, line managers are evaluated annually on how well they manage their environmental responsibilities. Vice president Paul Tebo says, "Our attitude is corporate environmentalism as a long-term cost saver for the company." [2]

Not all reports from the corporate world are always as positive as the opening examples. The cost of unethical and criminal acts by U.S. workers, for example, is estimated at over $400 billion a year.[3] Clearly, it is time to get serious about the moral aspects and social implications of decision making in organizations. In anyone's career and in any organizational setting, the ultimate task must be considered to be more than simply meeting performance expectations. Performance goals must always be achieved through ethical and socially responsible action. The following reminder from Desmond Tutu, archbishop of Capetown, South Africa, is applicable to managers everywhere.

> You are powerful people. You can make this world a better place where business decisions and methods take account of right and wrong as well as profitability. . . . You must take a stand on important issues: the environment and ecology, affirmative action, sexual harassment, racism and sexism, the arms race, poverty, the obligations of the affluent West to its less-well-off sisters and brothers elsewhere.[4]

WHAT IS ETHICAL BEHAVIOR?

"Ethics" are moral principles that set standards of good or bad, or right or wrong, in one's conduct and thereby guides the behavior of a person or group.[5] They help people make choices among alternative courses of action. **Ethical behavior** is what is accepted to be "good" and "right" as opposed to "bad" or "wrong" in the context of the governing moral code. Is it truly ethical, for example, for an employee to take longer than necessary to do a job? To make personal telephone calls on company time? To call in sick to take a day off for leisure? To fail to report rule violations by a co-worker?

- **Ethical behavior** is accepted as "right" or "good" in the context of a governing moral code.

None of these acts is strictly illegal, but many people would consider one or more of them to be unethical. Indeed, most ethical problems arise when people are asked to do or find themselves about to do something that violates their personal conscience. For some of them, if the act is legal they proceed with confidence. For others, however, the ethical test goes beyond the legality of the act alone. The issue extends to personal **values**—the underlying beliefs and attitudes that help determine individual behavior. To the extent that values vary among people, we can expect different interpretations of what behavior is ethical or unethical in a given situation.

- **Values** are broad beliefs about what is or is not appropriate behavior.

Values drive the natural products firm Tom's of Maine. Founded by Tom Chappell and his wife Kate, the company was described by the Council of Economic Priorities as one of the "saints of social responsibility." Tom's products cost more, but for the extra price customers get the satisfaction of knowing they support a company whose products don't pollute the environment. Tom says, "I believe we have been able to expand upon the historical point of view that business is just for making money to a broader view that business is about doing good for others in the process of getting financial gain." At Tom's of Maine the mission statement says, "we do not need to sacrifice our responsibility to society, the environment, our community, or our coworkers to be profitable or successful."[6]

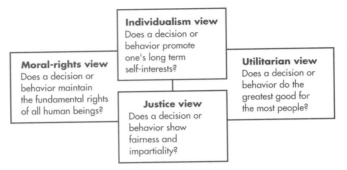

Figure 4.1 Four views of ethical behavior.

ALTERNATIVE VIEWS OF ETHICAL BEHAVIOR

● The **utilitarian view** considers ethical behavior as that which delivers the greatest good to the greatest number of people.

Figure 4.1 shows four alternative views of ethical behavior.[7] The **utilitarian view** considers ethical behavior as that which delivers the greatest good to the greatest number of people. Founded in the work of 19th-century philosopher John Stuart Mill, this is a results-oriented point of view that tries to assess the moral implications of decisions in terms of their consequences. Business decision makers, for example, are inclined to use profits, efficiency, and other performance criteria to judge what is best for the most people. A manager may make a utilitarian decision to cut 30 percent of a plant's workforce in order to keep the plant profitable and save jobs for the remaining 70 percent.

● The **individualism view** considers ethical behavior as that which advances long-term self-interests.

The **individualism view** of ethical behavior is based on the belief that one's primary commitment is to the advancement of long-term self-interests. If self-interests are pursued from a long-term view, the argument goes, such things as lying and cheating for short-term gain should not be tolerated. If one person does it, everyone will do it, and no one's long-term interests will be served. The individualism view is supposed to promote honesty and integrity. But in business practice it may result in a *pecuniary ethic*, described by one observer as the tendency to "push the law to its outer limits" and "run roughshod over other individuals to achieve one's objectives."[8]

● The **moral-rights view** considers ethical behavior as that which respects and protects fundamental rights.

Ethical behavior under a **moral-rights view** is that which respects and protects the fundamental rights of people. From the teachings of John Locke and Thomas Jefferson, for example, the rights of all people to life, liberty, and fair treatment under the law are considered inviolate. In organizations today, this concept extends to ensuring that employee rights such as the following are always protected: right to privacy, due process, free speech, free consent, health and safety, and freedom of conscience.

● The **justice view** considers ethical behavior as that which treats people impartially and fairly according to guiding rules and standards.

The **justice view** of moral behavior is based on the belief that ethical decisions treat people impartially and fairly according to guiding rules and standards. This approach evaluates the ethical aspects of any decision on the basis of whether it is "equitable" for everyone affected. In terms of *procedural justice*, policies and rules are fairly administered. For example, does a sexual harassment charge levied against a senior executive receive the same full hearing as one made against a shop-level supervisor? In terms of *distributive justice*, people are treated the same regardless of individual characteristics based on ethnicity, race, gender, age, or other particularistic criteria. For example, does a woman with the same qualifications and experience as a man receive the same consideration for promotion?

CULTURAL ISSUES IN ETHICAL BEHAVIOR

The influence of culture on ethical behavior is increasingly at issue as businesses and individuals travel the world. Levi CEO Robert Haas says that addressing ethical dilemmas as a corporate executive "becomes even more difficult when you overlay the complexities of different cultures and values systems that exist throughout the world."[9]

Those who believe that behavior in foreign settings should be guided by the classic rule of "When in Rome do as the Romans do" reflect the position of **cultural relativism.**[10] This is the notion that there is no one right way to behave and that ethical behavior is always determined by its cultural context. When it comes to international business, for example, an American executive guided by rules of cultural relativism would argue that the use of child labor is okay if it is consistent with local laws and customs. *Figure 4.2*, however, contrasts this position with an absolutist alternative suggesting that if a behavior or practice is not okay in one's home environment it shouldn't be acceptable anywhere else. In other words, ethical standards are more universal in nature and should apply absolutely across cultures and national boundaries. Critics of the absolutism approach claim that it is a form of *ethical imperialism*, or the attempt to externally impose one's ethical standards on others.

Business ethicist Thomas Donaldson discusses the debate between cultural relativism and absolutism. Although there is no simple answer, he finds fault with both extremes. He argues instead that certain fundamental rights and ethical standards can be universally preserved while values and traditions of a given culture are respected.[11] The core values or "hyper-norms" that should transcend cultural boundaries focus on human dignity, basic rights, and good citizenship. They are shown in *Manager's Notepad 4.1*. With a commitment to core values that create a transcultural ethical umbrella, Donaldson believes international business behaviors can still be tailored to local and regional cultural contexts. In the case of child labor, for example, the American executive might ensure that any children working in a factory under contract to his or her business would be provided schooling as well as employment.

● **Cultural relativism** suggests there is no one right way to behave; ethical behavior is determined by its cultural context.

Cultural relativism	Absolutism
No culture's ethics are superior. The values and practices of the local setting determine what is right or wrong.	Certain absolute truths apply everywhere. Universal values transcend cultures in determining what is right or wrong.
When in Rome, do as the Romans do.	*Don't do anything you wouldn't do at home.*

Figure 4.2 The extremes of cultural relativism and absolutism. *Source:* Developed from Thomas Donaldson, "Values in Tension: Ethics Away from Home," *Harvard Business Review*, Vol. 74 (September–October 1996), pp. 48–62.

MANAGER'S NOTEPAD 4.1

HOW COMPANIES CAN RESPECT CORE OR UNIVERSAL
VALUES

Respect for human dignity
- Create corporate culture that values employees, customers, and suppliers.
- Keep a safe workplace.
- Produce safe products and services.

Respect for basic rights
- Protect rights of employees, customers, and communities.
- Avoid anything that threatens safety, health, education, living standards.

Be good citizens
- Support social institutions, including economic and educational systems.
- Work with local government and institutions to protect environment.

ETHICS IN THE WORKPLACE

The real test of ethics is when a situation is encountered that challenges personal ethical beliefs and standards. The burden is put on the individual to make good choices in difficult circumstances. An engineering manager speaking from experience sums it up this way: "I define an unethical situation as one in which I have to do something I don't feel good about." [12]

WHAT IS AN ETHICAL DILEMMA?

- An **ethical dilemma** is a situation with a potential course of action that, although offering potential benefit or gain, is also unethical.

An **ethical dilemma** is a situation that requires a choice regarding a possible course of action that, although offering the potential for personal or organizational benefit or both, may be considered unethical. It is a situation in which action must be taken but for which there is no clear consensus on what is "right" and "wrong."

In a survey of *Harvard Business Review* subscribers, most of the ethical dilemmas reported by managers involved conflicts with superiors, customers, and subordinates. [13] The most frequent issues involved dishonesty in advertising and in communications with top management, clients, and government agencies. Problems dealing with special gifts, entertainment, and kickbacks were also reported. Significantly, the managers' bosses were singled out as sometimes pressuring their subordinates to engage in unethical activities. These included requests to support incorrect viewpoints, sign false documents, overlook the boss's wrongdoings, and do business with the boss's friends.

While you consider the potential difficulties of these situations, here is a short case to test yourself. It was originally presented to this same sample of managers. What would you do?

The Case of the Foreign Payment: The minister of a foreign nation asks you to pay a $200,000 consulting fee. In return for the money, the minister promises special assistance in obtaining a $100 million contract that would produce at least a $5 million profit for your company. The contract will probably go to a foreign competitor if not won by you.

Among the *Harvard Business Review* subscribers responding to this case, 42 percent said they would refuse to pay; 22 percent would pay but consider it unethical; 36 percent would pay and consider it ethical in the foreign context.

RATIONALIZATIONS FOR UNETHICAL BEHAVIOR

Why might otherwise reasonable people act unethically? Think back to the earlier examples and to those from your experiences. Consider the possibility of being asked to place a bid for a business contract using insider information, paying bribes to obtain foreign business, falsifying expense account bills, and so on. "Why," you should be asking, "do people do things like this?" In fact, at least four common rationalizations may be used to justify misconduct in these and other ethical dilemmas.[14]

- Convincing yourself that the behavior is not really illegal.
- Convincing yourself that the behavior is really in everyone's best interests.
- Convincing yourself that nobody will ever find out what you've done.
- Convincing yourself that the organization will "protect" you.

Four ways of thinking about unethical behavior

After doing something that might be considered unethical, a rationalizer says, *"It's not really illegal."* This expresses a mistaken belief that one's behavior is acceptable, especially in ambiguous conditions. When dealing with "shady" or "borderline" situations in which you are having a hard time precisely defining right from wrong, the advice is quite simple. When in doubt about a decision to be made or an action to be taken, don't do it.

Another common statement by a rationalizer is: *"It's in everyone's best interests."* This response involves the mistaken belief that because someone can be found to benefit from the behavior, the behavior is also in the individual's or the organization's best interests. Overcoming this rationalization depends in part on the ability to look beyond short-run results to address longer term implications. It also requires looking beyond results in general to the ways in which they are obtained.

Sometimes rationalizers tell themselves, *"No one will ever know about it."* They mistakenly believe that a questionable behavior is really "safe" and will never be found out or made public. Unless it is discovered, the argument implies, no wrong was really committed. Lack of accountability, unrealistic pressures to perform, and a boss who prefers "not to know" can all reinforce such thinking. In this case, the best deterrent is to make sure that everyone knows that wrongdoing will be punished whenever it is discovered.

Finally, rationalizers may proceed with a questionable action because of a mistaken belief that *"the organization will stand behind me."* This is misperceived loyalty. The individual believes that the organization's best interests stand above all others. In return, the individual believes that top managers will condone the behavior and protect the individual from harm. Again, the advice is straightforward: loyalty to the organization is not an acceptable excuse for misconduct.

FACTORS INFLUENCING ETHICAL BEHAVIOR

It is almost too easy to confront ethical dilemmas from the safety of a textbook or a college classroom. In practice, people are often challenged to choose ethical courses of action in situations that arise unexpectedly. The pressures to respond or act may be contradictory and great. It is helpful to understand the factors influencing ethical behavior as shown in *Figure 4.3.*

The Person

Family influences, religious values, personal standards, and personal needs, financial and otherwise, will help determine a person's ethical conduct in any given circumstance. Managers who lack a strong and consistent set of personal ethics will find that their decisions vary from situation to situation as they strive to maximize self-interests. Those who operate with strong *ethical frameworks*, personal rules or strategies for ethical decision making, will be more consistent and confident since choices are made against a stable set of ethical standards.

Consider, for example, how personal values can help one meet even the most difficult of tests. After his apparel factory burned down, many people said that Aaron Feurstein was crazy when he kept some 1,000 workers on the payroll. Today Malden Mills of Lawrence, Massachusetts, is back in business producing Polartec and Polarfleece knits. And owner, president, and CEO Feurstein couldn't be prouder. He paid his jobless employees over $15 million during the several months it took to rebuild the plant. Now he is reaping the

Figure 4.3 Factors influencing ethical behavior at work—the person, organization, and environment.

gains of a loyal workforce dedicated to their customers. Feurstein calls his decision just "common sense." [15]

The Organization

The organization is another source of important influences on ethics in the workplace. Earlier, we noted how supervisors can affect employee behavior. Just exactly what a supervisor requests, and which actions are rewarded or punished, can certainly affect an individual's decisions and actions. The expectations and reinforcement provided by peers and group norms are likely to have a similar impact. Formal policy statements and written rules, although they cannot guarantee results, are also very important in establishing an ethical climate for the organization as a whole. They support and reinforce the organizational culture, which can have a strong influence on members' ethical behavior.

The Environment

Organizations operate in external environments composed of competitors, government laws and regulations, and social norms and values, among other influences. Laws interpret social values to define appropriate behaviors for organizations and their members; regulations help governments monitor these behaviors and keep them within acceptable standards. The climate of competition in an industry also sets a standard of behavior for those who hope to prosper within it. Sometimes the pressures of competition contribute further to the ethical dilemmas of managers. Former American Airlines president Robert Crandall once telephoned Howard Putnam, then president of now-defunct Braniff Airlines. Both companies were suffering from money-losing competition on routes from their home base of Dallas. A portion of their conversation follows. [16]

Putnam: Do you have a suggestion for me?
Crandall: Yes. . . .   Raise your fares 20 percent. I'll raise mine the next morning.
Putnam: Robert, we —
Crandall: You'll make more money and I will, too.
Putnam: We can't talk about pricing.
Crandall: Oh, Howard. We can talk about anything we want to talk about.

The U.S. Justice Department disagreed. It alleged that Crandall's suggestion of a 20 percent fare increase amounted to an illegal attempt to monopolize airline routes. The suit was later settled when Crandall agreed to curtail future discussions with competitors about fares.

Outside groups and stakeholder organizations can also influence the ethical environment. In respect to workers' rights around the world, for example, the Council on Economic Priorities is part of an initiative called Social Accountability 8000, or SA8000. It proposes labor standards and a certification system to show that firms do not use child or forced labor, do offer safe working conditions, do pay sufficient wages for workers' basic needs, do respect rights to organize, and do not regularly require more than 48-hour workweeks.

Browser

Go to: http://www.wiley.com/college/schermerhorn

THE WALL STREET JOURNAL.

WILEY

IN PRACTICE

Ethical behavior among business professionals is an arguable topic. While many businesses contend that they act in an ethical manner, many people still consider most businesses unethical in nature, overpowered by the profit motive.

Lately, businesses have begun to recognize how ethics and social responsibility can pay off in increased profits and a more loyal customer base. Recently, many firms have adopted codes of ethics as formal, organizational documents.

Examine some formal codes of ethics at the following Internet sites:

Business Ethics Resources on the WWW http://www.ethics.ubc.ca/resources/business/.

Tom's of Maine's mission, including employee volunteerism http://www.romsofmaine.com/mission/.

Click on the **Marketplace** heading. In the left-hand menu box you will find **Law** under the **In This Section** heading. Click on it and inspect which articles have an ethical emphasis. The chapter identifies the legal component present in most ethical situations.

Now click on the **wsj.com** "logo" and it will take you to the **Contents** of this day's journal. You can click on any of the links to take you to a specific section of the Interactive Journal.

Locate **Page One Columns** in the left-hand column and you will notice that each day of the week has a different focus: Monday is **The Outlook,** Tuesday is **Work Week,** etc. This feature provides quick news items on each topic. Click on several of them to view the contents of this week.

Return to **Contents** and look for **Marketplace Columns** in the second column. Many of these articles are directly related to social responsibility on the job. Once again, the focus of these articles changes every day.

The **Contents** feature of the Interactive Journal supports an easy way to navigate the Web site. You can always return to this section by clicking on the **wsj.com logo.**

An additional Web site can be found at the National Whistleblower Center http://www.whistleblowers.org/index.html.

DELIVERABLES:

Attempt to identify articles on ethical and social responsibility behavior from a specific region of the world. Discuss how these behaviors differ from the United States. Be prepared to link the discussion back to the four "views" of ethical behavior discussed in the chapter.

DISCUSSION QUESTIONS:

1. Discuss how the four alternative "views" of ethics provided in the chapter can be applied to the real world.

2. Discuss an ethical situation you located in the Interactive Journal and how it might be handled differently in the United States.

3. How do you intend to deal with "ethical dilemmas" as described in the chapter?

*Note: The underscored words/phrases in the Interactive Journal feature indicate Internet links provided in the online versions. See the *Introducing Management* Web site at www.wiley.com/college/schermerhorn.

MAINTAINING HIGH ETHICAL STANDARDS

There are a variety of methods for maintaining ethical practices in workplace affairs. Each can play an important role in advancing any organization's commitment to high ethical standards.

ETHICS TRAINING

Ethics training, in the form of structured programs to help participants understand the ethical aspects of decision making, can help people incorporate high ethical standards into their daily behaviors. But, it is important to keep the purpose of ethics training in perspective. An executive at Chemical Bank put it this way: "We aren't teaching people right from wrong—we assume they know that. We aren't giving people moral courage to do what is right—they should be able to do that anyhow. We focus on dilemmas." [17] Many of these dilemmas arise as a result of the time pressures of decisions. Most ethics training is designed to help people deal with ethical issues while under pressure and to avoid the four common rationalizations for unethical behavior that were discussed earlier.

> ● **Ethics training** helps people better understand the ethical aspects of decision making.

Manager's Notepad 4.2 presents a seven-step checklist for making ethical decisions when confronting an ethical dilemma. It offers a convenient reminder that the decision making process includes responsibility for double-checking a decision before taking action. The key issue in the checklist may well be Step 6, which confronts the decision maker with the *mirror test*—the risk of public disclosure of your action and your willingness to bear it. [18] This is perhaps the strongest way of all to test whether a decision is consistent with one's personal ethical standards.

WHISTLEBLOWING

Agnes Connolly pressed her employer to report two toxic chemical accidents, as she believed the law required; Dave Jones reported that his company was using unqualified suppliers in the construction of a nuclear power plant; Margaret Newsham revealed that her firm was allowing workers to do personal business while on government contracts; Herman Cohen charged that the ASPCA in New York was mistreating animals; Barry Adams complained that his hospital followed unsafe practices. [19] They were **whistleblowers,** persons who expose the misdeeds of others in organizations in order to preserve ethical standards and protect against wasteful, harmful, or illegal acts. Unfortunately, in spite of good intentions they all were fired from their jobs.

> ● A **whistleblower** exposes the misdeeds of others in organizations.

It is no secret that whistleblowers face the risks of impaired career progress and other forms of organizational retaliation, up to and including termination. [20] Today, federal and state laws increasingly offer them some defense against "retaliatory discharge." But legal protection can still be inadequate. Laws vary from state to state, and federal laws mainly protect government workers. [21] Even with legal protection, potential whistleblowers can face organizational barriers that include—*strict chain of command* that makes it hard to

MANAGER'S NOTEPAD 4.2

CHECKLIST FOR MAKING ETHICAL DECISIONS

Step 1. Recognize the ethical dilemma.
Step 2. Get the facts.
Step 3. Identify your options.
Step 4. Test each option: Is it legal? Is it right? Is it beneficial?
Step 5. Decide which option to follow.
Step 6. Double-check your decision by asking two questions:
    "How would I feel if my family found out about my decision?"
    "How would I feel about this if my decision were printed in the local newspaper?"
Step 7. Take action.

bypass the boss; *strong work group identities* that encourage loyalty and self-censorship; and *ambiguous priorities* that make it hard to distinguish right from wrong. In the attempt to remove these and other blocks to the exposure of unethical behaviors, some organizations have formally appointed staff members to serve as "ethics advisors." Others have convened *moral quality circles* to help create shared commitments for everyone to work at their ethical best.[22]

MANAGEMENT SUPPORT

Senior managers have the power to shape an organization's policies and set its moral tone. They can and should serve as models of appropriate ethical behavior for the entire organization. Not only must their day-to-day behavior be the example of high ethical conduct, but top managers must also communicate similar expectations throughout the organization . . . and reinforce positive results. The same responsibility extends to all managers in a position to influence the ethical behavior of the people who work for and with them. Every manager becomes an ethical role model, and care must be taken to do so in a positive and informed manner.

The important supervisory act of setting goals and communicating performance expectations is a good case in point. A surprising 64 percent and 238 executives in one study, for example, reported feeling under pressure to compromise personal standards to achieve company goals. A *Fortune* survey also reports that 34 percent of its respondents felt a company president can create an ethical climate by setting *reasonable* goals "so that subordinates are not pressured into unethical actions."[23] Clearly, a supervisor may unknowingly encourage unethical practices by exerting *too* much pressure for the accomplishment of goals that are *too* difficult.

FORMAL CODES OF ETHICS

Formal **codes of ethics** are official written guidelines on how to behave in situations susceptible to the creation of ethical dilemmas. They are found in organizations and in professions such as engineering, medicine, law, and public accounting. In the professions, ethical codes try to ensure that individual behavior is consistent with the historical and shared norms of the professional group. In organizations, codes of ethical conduct identify expected behaviors in terms of general citizenship, the avoidance of illegal or improper acts in one's work, and good relationships with customers. Items frequently addressed include workforce diversity, bribes and kickbacks, political contributions, the honesty of books or records, customer–supplier relationships, and the confidentiality of corporate information.

● A **code of ethics** is a written document that states values and ethical standards intended to guide the behavior of employees.

Although interest in codes of ethical conduct is growing, it must be remembered that the codes have limits; they cannot cover all situations, and they cannot guarantee universal ethical conduct. The value of any formal code of ethics still rests on the underlying human resource foundations of the organization—its managers and other employees. There is no replacement for effective hiring practices that staff the organization with honest and moral people. And there is no replacement for the leadership of committed managers who are willing to set the examples and act as ethical role models to ensure desired results.

CORPORATE SOCIAL RESPONSIBILITY

Concerns for ethical behavior cannot be limited to individuals alone. They must also apply and be examined at the level of the organization. In Chapter 2, the environment of a business firm was described as a network of other organizations and institutions with which it must interact. In this context, **corporate social responsibility** is defined as an obligation of the organization to act in ways that serve both its own interests and the interests of its many external *stakeholders*—individuals and groups who are affected in one way or another by the behavior of an organization. The leadership beliefs that guide socially responsible organizational practices are described as:[24]

● **Corporate social responsibility** is the obligation of an organization to act in ways that serve the interests of its stakeholders.

← Beliefs guiding socially responsible practices

- The belief that people do their best in healthy work environments that permit job involvement, respect for contributions, and a good balance of work and family life.

- The belief that organizations function best over the long run when located in healthy communities with high qualities of life.

- The belief that organizations realize performance gains and efficiencies when they treat the natural environment with respect.

- The belief that organizations must be managed and led for long-term success.

- The belief that the reputation of an organization must be protected to ensure consumer and stakeholder support.

SOCIAL RESPONSIBILITY AND PERFORMANCE

There is little doubt that the public at large now expects businesses and other organizations to act with genuine social responsibility. Stakeholder expectations that organizations integrate social responsibility into their core values and daily activities are increasingly well voiced. Going back to the earlier example of Tom's of Maine, founders Tom and Kate Chappell clearly state: "The company remains committed to environmental and social responsibility while developing a product line with the highest quality natural ingredients."[25]

On the research side, the argument that acting with a commitment to social responsibly will negatively affect the "bottom line" is hard to defend. There is increasing evidence that high performance in social responsibility can be associated with strong financial performance and, at worst, has no adverse financial impact. There seems little reason to believe that businesses cannot serve the public good and a broad pool of stakeholders as well as advance the financial interests of their shareholders. Indeed, recent evidence suggests the existence of a *virtuous circle* in which corporate social responsibility leads to improved financial performance for the firm and this in turn leads to more socially responsible actions in the future.[26]

SOCIAL RESPONSIBILITY IN ACTION

There are many action domains in which social responsibility can be pursued by business firms and other organizations. These include concerns for ecology and environmental quality, truth in lending and consumer protection, and aid to education. They also include direct service to community needs, positive

 Management Across Functions

BUSINESS LAW

Directors Go For Global Ethics Codes

The legal environment of business and management is dynamic and significant for its influence on corporate decision making. This environment is especially challenging in the context of globalization where firms are increasingly multinational and where operations span cultural and national boundaries. Company directors worldwide are setting new standards for their employees' ethical conduct in global business. The Conference Board surveyed 122 firms in 22 countries to examine their ethical standards. Boards of Directors in 78% report that they are setting such standards and establishing global business ethics codes. This is up from 41% in 1991 and 21% in 1987. Self-regulation by businesses of their employees' behaviors is preferred to the costly alternatives of government regulation and legal suits. By being proactive in setting internal corporate ethical standards for ethical conduct around the world, businesses also serve diversity goals and increase respect for alternative cultures. However, regional differences in laws and customs require expert advice and continued monitoring of the global ethical codes.[28]

employment practices, positive diversity practices, progressive labor relations and employee assistance, and general corporate philanthropy, among other possibilities. A **social audit** can be used at regular intervals to report on and systematically assess an organization's resource commitments and action accomplishments in these and other areas.

    Any such assessment of corporate social performance might include these four criteria: (1) Is the organization's *economic responsibility* met? (2) Is the organization's *legal responsibility* met? (3) Is the organization's *ethical responsibility* met? (4) Is the organization's *discretionary responsibility* met?[27] As you move down the list, the criteria progress toward ever-greater demonstrations of socially responsible activities. An organization is meeting its economic responsibility when it earns a profit through the provision of goods and services desired by customers. Legal responsibility is fulfilled when an organization operates within the law and according to the requirements of various external regulations. An organization meets its ethical responsibility when its actions voluntarily conform not only to legal expectations but also to the broader values and moral expectations of society. The highest level of social performance comes through the satisfaction of an organization's discretionary responsibility. Here, the organization voluntarily moves beyond basic economic, legal, and ethical expectations to provide leadership in advancing the well-being of individuals, communities, and society as a whole.

> ● A **social audit** is a systematic assessment of an organization's accomplishments in areas of social responsibility.

Levi Strauss was the first U.S. multinational to establish strict guidelines for the treatment of workers and for the environmental impacts of foreign plants making its products. A team of company inspectors makes routine visits to more than contract factories abroad. They look for health and safety hazards, the use of child labor, and wage standards, among other concerns. The firm halted contracts in Burma over human rights concerns, and it paid for the education of a Bangladesh contractor's underage employees. It operates with specific guidelines for business partner and country selection in international business.[29]

SOCIAL RESPONSIBILITY AND THE LEGAL ENVIRONMENT

Governments will often pass laws and establish regulating agencies to ensure that organizations act responsibly. You know these agencies best by their acronyms: FAA (Federal Aviation Administration), EPA (Environmental Protection Agency), OSHA (Occupational Safety and Health Administration), and FDA (Food and Drug Administration), among many others.

    Business executives often complain that many laws and regulations are overly burdensome. Small business owners, in particular, express concerns that regulations raise costs by creating the need for increased paperwork and staff to maintain compliance and by diverting managerial attention from important productivity concerns. In reality, the legal environment is both complex and constantly changing. Many themes already discussed as being key areas of social responsibility are backed by major laws. Managers must stay informed about new and pending laws as well as existing ones. As a reminder of the positive side of legislation, consider those examples of how the U.S. government takes an active role in regulating business affairs.

- *Occupational safety and health*—the Occupational Safety and Health Act of 1970 firmly established that the federal government was concerned about worker health and safety on the job.
- *Fair labor practices*—the Equal Employment Opportunity Act of 1972 and many following regulations are designed to eliminate discrimination in labor practices based on race, gender, age, national origin, and marital status.
- *Consumer protection*—the Consumer Product Safety Act of 1972 gives government authority to examine and force a business to withdraw from selling any product that it feels is hazardous to the consumer.
- *Environmental Protection*—the Air Pollution Control Act of 1962 was the first in a series designed to eliminate careless pollution of the air, water, and land.

As public demands grow for organizations to be accountable for ethical and social performance as well as economic performance, the manager stands once again in the middle. It is the manager whose decisions affect "quality-of-life" outcomes in the critical boundaries between people and organizations and between organizations and their environments. Today's workers and managers, as well as tomorrow's, must accept personal responsibility for doing the "right" things. Broad social and moral criteria must be used to examine the interests of multiple organizational stakeholders in a dynamic and complex environment. Decisions must always be made and problems solved with ethical considerations standing side by side with high-performance objectives, be they individual, group, or organizational.

SUMMARY

What Is Ethical Behavior?

- Ethical behavior is that which is accepted as "good" or "right" as opposed to "bad" or "wrong."
- Simply because an action is *not illegal* does not necessarily make it ethical in a given situation.
- Because values vary, the question of "What is ethical behavior?" may be answered differently by different people.
- Four ways of thinking about ethical behavior are the utilitarian, individualism, moral-rights, and justice views.
- Cultural relativism reflects the viewpoint that no culture is ethically superior to any other.

How Do Ethical Dilemmas Complicate the Workplace?

- When managers act ethically, they can have a positive impact on other people in the workplace *and* on the social good performed by their organizations.
- An ethical dilemma occurs when someone must decide whether or not to pursue a course of action that, although offering the potential for personal or organizational benefit or both, may be considered potentially unethical.

- Managers report that their ethical dilemmas often involve conflicts with superiors, customers, and subordinates over such matters as dishonesty in advertising and communications as well as pressure from their bosses to do unethical things.

- Common rationalizations for unethical behavior include believing the behavior is not illegal, is in everyone's best interests, will never be noticed, or will be supported by the organization.

How Can High Ethical Standards Be Maintained?

- Ethics training in the form of courses and training programs helps people better deal with ethical dilemmas in the workplace.

- Whistleblowers expose the unethical acts of others in organizations, even while facing career risks for doing so.

- Top management sets an ethical tone for the organization as a whole, and all managers are responsible for acting as positive models of appropriate ethical behavior.

- Written codes of ethical conduct formally state an organization's expectations of its employees regarding ethical conduct in workplace affairs.

What Is Corporate Social Responsibility?

- Corporate social responsibility is an obligation of the organization to act in ways that serve both its own interests and the interests of its many external publics, often called stakeholders.

- Criteria for evaluating corporate social performance include economic, legal, ethical, and discretionary responsibilities.

- Government agencies are charged with monitoring and ensuring compliance with the mandates of law.

- Managers must be well informed about existing and pending legislation in a variety of social responsibility areas, including environmental protection and other quality-of-life concerns.

- All decisions made and actions taken in every workplace should allow performance accountability to be met by high ethical standards and socially responsible means.

KEY TERMS

Code of ethics (p. 65)	Ethical dilemma (p. 58)	Social audit (p. 66)
Corporate social responsibility (p. 65)	Ethics training (p. 63)	Utilitarian view (p. 56)
Cultural relativism (p. 57)	Individualism view (p. 56)	Values (p. 55)
Ethical behavior (p. 55)	Justice view (p. 56)	Whistleblower (p. 63)
	Moral-rights view (p. 56)	

SELF-TEST  Take the interactive Self-Test for this chapter on the Schermerhorn Web Site

Chapter Five

Planning—To Set Direction

PLANNING AHEAD—
Chapter 5 Study Questions

- How does planning work?
- What types of plans are used by managers?
- How does planning utilize decision making?
- What planning tools and techniques are available?

KNOW WHAT YOU WANT TO ACCOMPLISH

CEO T. J. Rodgers of Cypress Semiconductor Corp. is known for meticulous planning and careful control. Cypress employees work with clear and quantified performance goals, which they typically set by themselves—it's important to Rodgers that the goals are "self-imposed." The goals are entered into an organizationwide computer database. Anyone in the company can review another person's goals, even those of Rodgers. On most days, there are thousands of goals on the system, each with expected dates of accomplishment. During weekly progress reviews, goals may be redefined and any needed corrective action taken. A monthly report summarizes accomplishments for everyone in the company. Says Rodgers—"We want people to decide what they are going to do, why it makes sense, how important it is, and when they will complete it." [1]

Management involves looking ahead, deciding what needs to be accomplished, and then helping people take the actions needed today in order to best meet the challenges of the future. The management system used by T. J. Rodgers is very high on performance accountability. There is no doubt that Cypress employees are expected to achieve consistent high performance results. But the system is also designed to identify problems before they interfere with performance. Rogers says: "Managers monitor the goals, look for problems, and expect people who fall behind to ask for help before they lose control of or damage a major project." [2]

HOW PLANNING WORKS

The process of management involves planning, organizing, leading, and controlling. The first of these functions, **planning,** is a process of deciding exactly what one wants to accomplish and how to best go about it. As described in *Figure 5.1*, planning creates a solid platform for the entire management process. It sets the stage for further managerial efforts at *organizing*—allocating and arranging resources to accomplish essential tasks; *leading*—guiding the efforts of human resources to ensure high levels of task accomplishment; and *controlling*—monitoring task accomplishments and taking necessary corrective action. In today's demanding environments, it is essential to always stay one step ahead of the competition. Planning helps organizations to become better and better at what they are doing and to stay action oriented. An Eaton Corporation annual report, for example, once stated: "Planning at Eaton means taking the hard decisions before events force them upon you, and anticipating the future needs of the market before the demand asserts itself."

● **Planning** is the process of setting objectives and determining what should be done to accomplish them.

THE PLANNING PROCESS

Planning focuses on **objectives**—the specific results or desired outcomes. The planning process is a systematic framework for setting performance objectives and deciding how to achieve them. It results in the creation and implementation of a *plan*, or statement of action steps to be taken in order to

● **Objectives** are specific results that one wishes to achieve.

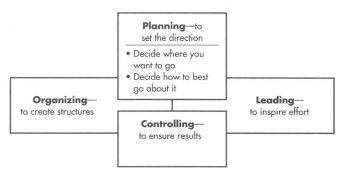

Figure 5.1   The role of planning in the management process.

accomplish the objectives. The recommended steps in systematic approach to planning include:

Five steps in the planning process

Step 1. Define your objectives. Identify desired outcomes or results in very specific ways. Know where you want to go; be specific enough that you will know you have arrived when you get there or know how far off the mark you are at various points along the way.

Step 2. Determine where you stand vis-à-vis objectives. Evaluate current accomplishments relative to the desired results. Know where you stand in reaching the objectives; know what strengths work in your favor and what weaknesses may hold you back.

Step 3. Develop premises regarding future conditions. Try to anticipate future events. Generate alternative "scenarios" for what may happen; identify for each scenario things that may help or hinder progress toward achieving your objectives.

Step 4. Analyze possible action alternatives, choose the best among them, and decide how to implement. List and carefully evaluate the possible actions that may be taken. Choose the alternative(s) most likely to accomplish your objectives; describe step by step what must be done to follow the chosen course of action.

Step 5. Implement the plan and evaluate results. Take action and carefully measure your progress toward objectives. Do what the plan requires; evaluate results; take corrective action and revise plans as needed.

In the complex setting of the modern workplace, however, these planning steps must not be thought of as something done only by outside consultants or staff experts. And, it is not something managers should do while working alone in quiet rooms, free from distractions, and at scheduled times. Rather, planning must become a part of everyday work routines. It must be an ongoing activity that is continuously done in an otherwise hectic and demanding work setting.[3] And as this chapter will also describe, the best planning is always done with the participation and involvement of the people whose work efforts are required if the objectives are to be achieved. For example, Lynn Mercer achieved success as a plant manager for Lucent Technologies by making and implementing plans quickly. She focused on creating a mission from the top and allowing workers to develop the methods. Says Mercer: "If I give you the end game, you can find your way there."[4]

BENEFITS OF PLANNING

Organizations face pressures from many sources. Externally, these include the forces of competition, increased government regulations, ever more complex technologies, the uncertainties of a global economy, and the sheer cost of investments in labor, capital, and other supporting resources. Internally, they include the quest for operating efficiencies, new structures and work arrangements, greater diversity in the workforce, and related managerial challenges. Planning in such circumstances offers a number of benefits and important advantages for the performance of organizations and for the careers of those who work in them.

At Aetna U.S. Healthcare, planning for satisfied employees results in satisfied customers. Realizing that good customer relations are keys to success, company executives have made staff development a key planning objective. Training for new employees includes classroom instruction and supervised on-the-job experience. After training, another planning objective is activated: to increase efficiency by promoting job satisfaction. Interaction among workers is encouraged, workers are divided into teams, and rewards for speedy processing of customers' claims are distributed quarterly.

More Focus and Flexibility

Good planning improves focus and flexibility. An *organization with focus* knows what it does best, knows the needs of its customers, and knows how to serve them well. An *individual with focus* knows where he or she wants to go in a career or situation and is able to retain that objective even in difficult circumstances. An *organization with flexibility* is willing and able to change and adapt to shifting circumstances and operates with an orientation toward the future rather than the past or present. An *individual with flexibility* factors into career plans the problems and opportunities posed by new and developing circumstances—personal and organizational.

Action Orientation

Planning provides an action orientation. It makes people and organizations more: (1) *results oriented*—creating a performance-oriented sense of direction; (2) *priority oriented*—making sure the most important things get first attention; (3) *advantage oriented*—ensuring that all resources are used to best advantage; and (4) *change oriented*—anticipating problems and opportunities so they can be dealt with best. It helps them avoid the complacency trap of simply being carried along by the flow of events or being distracted by successes or failures of the moment. It keeps the future visible as a performance target and reminds everyone that the best decisions are often made before events force them upon us. Management consultant Stephen Covey, for example, points out that the most successful executives "zero in on what they do that 'adds value' to an organization." He suggests that instead of working on too many things, it is important to step back and identify the most important things to be doing.[5]

Improved Coordination

Planning improves coordination. As the many different individuals, groups, and subsystems in organizations each pursue different tasks and objectives, their accomplishments must collectively meet the needs of the organization as a whole. Good planning creates a *hierarchy of objectives* in which objectives at each level of an organization are linked together in means-ends fashion. Higher-level objectives as *ends* are directly tied to lower-level objectives as the *means* for their accomplishment. This is illustrated in *Figure 5.2* with a

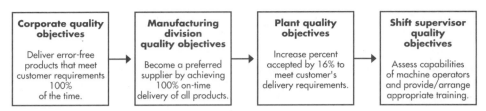

Figure 5.2   A sample hierarchy of objectives for total quality management.

hierarchy of quality objectives in a large manufacturing firm. The corporate-level quality objective is "deliver error-free products that meet customer requirements 100 percent of the time." This translates down the hierarchy in means-ends fashion to the level of the shift supervisor, where it becomes a formal commitment to "assess capabilities of machine operators and provide appropriate training."

Better Control

Planning facilitates control. It sets the stage for control by defining the objectives—desired performance results—and identifying the specific actions through which they are to be pursued. If results are less than expected, the original objectives, the actions being taken, or both, can be evaluated and then adjusted to improve future accomplishments. Without planning, the control process lacks a framework for measuring how well things are going and determining what can be done to make them go better.

Better Time Management

Planning helps with time management. Most of us have experienced the difficulties of balancing available time with the many commitments and opportunities we would like to fulfill.[6] Each day, we are bombarded by a multitude of tasks and demands in a setting of frequent interruptions, crises, and unexpected events—the manager's job is especially subject to such complications. In these circumstances it is easy to fall prey to "time wasters," allowing our time to be dominated by other people or by nonessential activities. Lewis Platt, former chairman of Hewlett-Packard, says for example: "basically, the whole day is a series of choices."[7] These choices have to be made in ways that allocate your time to the most important priorities. Platt says that he is "ruthless about priorities" and that you "have to continually work to optimize your time." Planning helps us to do this. One key to time management is to determine which items on our "to do" lists are the priorities, and then address them.

TYPES OF PLANS

Complex organizations operate with a wide variety of plans. The plans vary in terms of time spans, scope, and level of application. In all cases, plans must be both well made and well implemented for success.

SHORT-RANGE AND LONG-RANGE PLANS

When it comes to time horizons, a rule of thumb is that *short-range plans* cover one year or less, *intermediate-range plans* cover one to two years, and *long-range plans* look three or more years into the future. Top management is most likely to be involved in setting long-range plans and directions for the organization as a whole. Lower management levels focus more on short-run activities and plans that serve the long-term objectives.

STRATEGIC AND OPERATIONAL PLANS

Plans differ not only in time horizons but also in scope. **Strategic plans** address long-term needs and set comprehensive action directions for an organization. Top management planning of this scope involves determining objectives for the entire organization and then deciding on the actions and resource allocations to achieve them. **Operational plans** define what needs to be done in specific areas to implement the strategic plans. Typical operational plans in a business firm include *production plans*—dealing with the methods and technology needed to create valuable goods and services; *financial plans*—dealing with the money required to support various operations; *facilities plans*—dealing with the facilities and work layouts required to support task activities; *marketing plans*—dealing with the requirements of selling and distributing goods or services; and *human resource plans*—dealing with the recruitment, selection, and placement of people into various jobs.

Figure 5.3 uses the case of a firm undergoing a restructuring to show how a clear hierarchy of strategic and operational plans can integrate and direct actions toward a common purpose throughout an organization. In the example, the organization's strategic direction involves restructuring to focus growth in core product areas. This direction is supported operationally by very specific marketing, production, and financial plans. The operational plans serve the strategic plans by identifying the activities and committing the resources needed to accomplish them.

● A **strategic plan** is comprehensive and addresses longer term needs and directions of the organization.

● An **operational plan** is of limited scope and addresses activities to implement strategic plans.

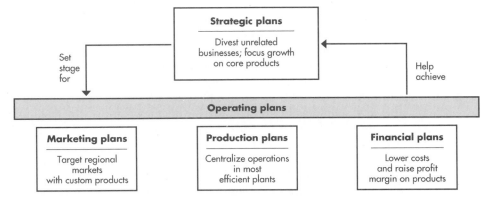

Figure 5.3 How strategic and operational plans should support each other.

POLICIES AND PROCEDURES

● A **policy** communicates broad guidelines for decisions and action.

Organizations typically operate with many policies and procedures. These *standing plans* are used over and over again to direct behavior in certain types of situations. A **policy** communicates broad guidelines for making decisions and taking action in specific circumstances. In human resource management, policies on matters such as AIDS/HIV, alcohol and substance abuse, and sexual harassment, for example, can help ensure that employees' daily actions and decisions are consistent with organizational values, strategies, and objectives.[8]

● A **procedure** describes exact rules to be followed in specific situations.

Procedures describe exact rules for dealing with specific situations. They are often found stated in employee handbooks or manuals as "SOPs"—standard operating procedures. Whereas a sexual harassment policy sets expectations for employee behavior, sexual harassment procedures define precise actions to be taken when someone believes he or she has been harassed on the job. The procedures help to ensure that everyone receives fair, equal, and nondiscriminatory treatment.

PROJECT SCHEDULES AND BUDGETS

● A **project schedule** is a single-use plan for accomplishing a specific set of tasks.

At another level of operations, plans are needed to manage the use of resources to accomplish defined tasks. The new workplace is increasingly organized around "projects" that are accomplished by teams working under tight deadlines. In such cases, **project schedules** identify the activities required to accomplish a specific major project. For example, project schedules would guide the completion of a new student activities building on a campus, the development of a new computer software program, or the implementation of a new advertising campaign for a sports team. In each case, the project schedule would define specific task objectives, activities to be accomplished, due dates and timetables for the activities, and resource requirements. Importantly, a good project schedule sets priorities so that everyone involved knows not only what needs to be done but also in what order so that the entire project gets finished on time.

● A **budget** is a plan that commits resources to projects or activities.

Budgets are plans that commit resources to activities, projects, or programs. They are powerful tools that allocate scarce resources among multiple and often competing uses. Good managers are able to bargain for and obtain adequate budgets to support the needs of their work units or teams. They are also able to achieve performance objectives while keeping resource expenditures within the allocated budget.

● A **zero-based budget** allocates resources to a project or activity as if it were brand new.

Projects and work units sometimes have *fixed budgets* that allocate a fixed pool of resources that can be used, but not exceeded, for the specified purpose. For example, a manager may have a $25,000 budget for equipment purchases in a given year. A *flexible budget*, by contrast, allows the allocation of resources to vary in proportion with various levels of activity. For example, a project leader's budget may increase to allow for hiring temporary workers when the timetable for completion is shortened due to competitive pressures. In a **zero-based budget,** a project or activity is budgeted as if it were brand new. There is no assumption that resources previously allocated will simply be continued in the future. All projects compete anew for available funds in each budget cycle. Zero-based budgeting is used by businesses, government agencies, and other organizations to make sure that only the most desirable and timely programs receive funding.

PLANNING AND DECISION MAKING

Planning is an exercise in decision making. It involves the use of information to make plans that address significant problems and opportunities.

THE DECISION MAKING PROCESS

Figure 5.4 describes a typical approach to decision making as applied in the planning process. The process begins with identification of a problem and ends with evaluation of implemented solutions.[9] The five steps in this approach are (1) identifying and defining the problem, (2) generating and evaluating possible solutions, (3) choosing a preferred solution *and* conducting the "ethics double-check," (4) implementing the solution, and (5) evaluating results.

Step 1: Identify and Define the Problem

The first step of decision making—finding and defining the problem, is a stage of information gathering, information processing, and deliberation. It often begins with the appearance of *problem symptoms* that signal the presence of a performance deficiency or opportunity. The planning goal at this stage is to assess a situation properly by looking beyond symptoms to find out what is really happening. Special care must be taken to not just address a symptom while ignoring the true problem.

The way a problem is originally defined can have a major impact on how it is eventually resolved. Three common mistakes can result in poor or ineffective plans. *Mistake number 1* was just introduced—focusing on symptoms instead of causes. Symptoms are indicators that problems may exist, but they shouldn't be mistaken for the problems themselves. Managers should be able to spot problem symptoms (e.g., a drop in performance). But instead of treating symptoms (such as simply encouraging higher performance), managers should address their root causes (such as discovering the worker's need for training in the use of a complex new computer system). *Mistake number 2* is defining the problem too broadly or too narrowly. To take a classic example, the problem stated as "Build a better mousetrap" might be better defined as "Get rid of the mice." That is, managers should define problems so as to give themselves the best possible range of planning options. *Mistake number 3* is choosing the wrong problem to deal with. Managers should set priorities and make plans that deal with the most

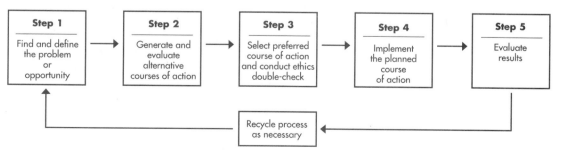

Figure 5.4 How decision making is utilized in the planning process.

important problems first. They should also give planning priority to problems that are truly solvable.

Step 2: Generate and Evaluate Possible Courses of Action

Once the problem is defined, it is possible to formulate one or several potential solutions. At this stage of decision making, more information is gathered, data are analyzed, and the pros and cons of possible alternative courses of action are identified. The involvement of others is important here in order to maximize information and build commitment. The plans can only be as good as the quality of the alternative solutions generated in this step. The better the pool of alternatives, the more likely a good solution will be achieved.

● **Cost-benefit analysis** involves comparing the costs and benefits of each potential course of action.

A very basic evaluation used in at this step involves **cost-benefit analysis,** the comparison of what an alternative will cost in relation to the expected benefits. At a minimum, the benefits of a preferred alternative should be greater than its costs. Although the analysis of costs and benefits is often quantitative, the insights should also be tempered with human judgment to ensure that a full and appropriate set of criteria are considered. More broadly, typical criteria for evaluating planning alternatives include the following:

Criteria for evaluating alternatives

- *Benefits:* What are the "benefits" of using the alternative to solve a performance deficiency or take advantage of an opportunity?
- *Costs:* What are the "costs" of implementing the alternative, including direct resource investments as well as any potential negative side effects?
- *Timeliness:* How fast will the benefits occur and a positive impact be achieved?
- *Acceptability:* To what extent will the alternative be accepted and supported by those who must work with it?
- *Ethical soundness:* How well does the alternative meet acceptable ethical criteria in the eyes of the various stakeholders?

Step 3: Choose a Preferred Course of Action

At this point, a "decision" is made to select a particular course of action. Just how this is done and by whom must be successfully resolved in each planning situation. In some cases, the best alternative may be selected using a cost-benefit criterion; in others, additional criteria may come into play. Once alternatives are generated and evaluated, however, a final choice must be made.

Historically, management theory has recognized two major models of how decisions get made in organizations—the classical model and the behavioral model.[10] The *classical decision model* views the manager as acting in a certain world. Here, the manager faces a clearly defined problem and knows all possible action alternatives as well as their consequences. As a result, he or she makes an *optimizing decision* that gives the absolute best solution to the problem. The classical approach is a very rational model that assumes perfect information is available for decision making.

Behavioral scientists question the assumptions underlying the classical model. Represented by the work of Herbert Simon, they recognize the existence of cognitive limitations, or limits to our human information-processing

Browser

Go to: http://www.wiley.com/college/schermerhorn

 THE WALL STREET JOURNAL.

WILEY

IN PRACTICE

Planning is one of the dominant activities that differentiate managers from non-managers. Information is a key ingredient that determines the usefulness of any planning activity. The Interactive Journal provides a valuable source of information to the serious student.

From the Front Section, select **Economy** under the **In this Section** of the left-hand menu. Forward-looking economic data often provides insight into future economic performance of various world economies.

At the bottom of the Front Section, you can locate major

ALSO IN TODAY'S EDITION

articles from various sections of the current wsj.com under **Also in Today's Edition.**

Customize Your Journal

It is possible to customize your Interactive Journal to filter only articles concerning particular firms or industries. Select **Personal Journal** from the left-hand menu list and you can select up to four Interactive Journal sections to scan for select articles. This can provide a semester-long search process for recurring news items.

The Career Plan

Career Planning is one major area on which students should concentrate. In the left-hand menu, under **Other wsj.com Sites,** click on the **Careers** link to access career information from the Interactive Journal.

The Careers Web site offers a wealth of information on the career search. Click on **Job Hunting Advice** for help on resumes, cover letters, and other helpful job hunting advice. The **Salaries and Profiles** link provides information on salary ranges that can prove useful during the interview process. **Working Globally** provides insights into working on the international stage. Links provided under **Job Seek** provide in-

teresting Question and Answers involving the career search.

Additional Career Web Sites:

Reports on over 1000 companies at **Vault Reports** http://www.VaultReports.com/.

Career Magazine at http://www.careermag.com/.

DELIVERABLES:

Develop a set of three to five performance objectives for yourself for the next year. These may be academic or career-related in nature. Attempt to identify relationships between your career aspirations and your course selections. Use information from the Interactive Journal to support your choices.

DISCUSSION QUESTIONS:

1. How can planning now pay off for you once you begin to do your career search?

2. How might identifying clear objectives improve your job-search activities in the future?

3. What might a 3–5 year career plan look like for you?

*Note: The underscored words/phrases in the Interactive Journal feature indicate Internet links provided in the online versions. See the *Introducing Management* Web site at www.wiley.com/college/schermerhorn.

capabilities. These limitations make it hard for managers to become fully informed and make perfectly rational decisions.

Accordingly, the *administrative decision model* assumes that people act only in terms of what they perceive about a given situation. Because perceptions are frequently imperfect, the decision maker has only partial knowledge about the available action alternatives and their consequences. Consequently, the first alternative that appears to give a satisfactory resolution of the problem is likely to be chosen. Simon, who won a Nobel Prize for his work, calls this tendency **satisficing**—choosing the first satisfactory alternative that comes to your attention. This model seems expecially accurate in describing how people make decisions about ambiguous problems in risky and uncertain conditions.

A potential decision-making error in this phase of the planning process is called **escalating commitment.** This is a decision to increase effort and perhaps apply more resources to pursue a course of action that is *not* working.[11] In such cases, managers let the momentum of the situation overwhelm them. They are unable to decide to "call it quits" and cancel an existing plan, even when experience indicates that this is the most appropriate thing to do. *Manager's Notepad 5.1* offers advice on avoiding this tendency.

Any decision to follow a particular plan of action should also be tested by performing an "ethics double-check" described in Chapter 4. This ensures that the ethical aspects of a situation are properly considered in the complex, fast-paced planning environments common in today's organizations.

- **Satisficing** involves choosing the first satisfactory alternative that appears.

- **Escalating commitment** is the tendency to continue to pursue a course of action, even though it is not working.

Step 4: Implement the Planned Course of Action

Given the preferred solution to a problem, appropriate action plans must be established and fully implemented. This is the stage at which directions are finally set and problem-solving actions are initiated. Nothing new can or will happen according to plan unless action is taken. Managers not only need

MANAGER'S NOTEPAD 5.1

HOW TO AVOID THE ESCALATION TRAP

- Set advance limits on your involvement and commitment to a particular course of action; stick with these limits.
- Make your own decisions; don't blindly follow the lead of others since they are also prone to escalation.
- Carefully determine just why you are continuing a course of action; if there are insufficient reasons to continue, don't.
- Remind yourself of what a course of action is costing; consider the cost savings of discontinuing it.
- Watch for escalation tendencies; be on guard against their influence on both you and others involved in the course of action.

Management Across Functions

PURCHASING

Plans Fuel Mexico's Home-Appliance Industry

It didn't take long for low cost labor, zero tariffs under NAFTA on exports to the United States, and a growing domestic market caught the eye of strategic planners for the home appliance industry. Sears, Whirlpool, and GE are all major corporate players in the manufacturing base evolving around the central Mexican city of San Luis Potosi. Workers at GE affiliate Mabe, SA, can make a stove for what it costs the firm to pay one of its appliance workers in Georgia for an hour of labor—about $15. But there's more to the strategy than just low-cost manufacturing. Purchasing efficiencies are also driving the expansion. As the appliance makers invest in Mexico, their suppliers are too—some 30 percent of them so far, and the number keeps growing. The automobile industry led the way in building strong and efficient purchasing relationships with suppliers. The appliance makers have benchmarked and learned those lessons well. U.S. Steel recently opened a major steel finishing operation next door to Mabe's sheet metal stamping shop. As the investment plans continue, Mexico is fast becoming a center point in home appliance manufacturing.[12]

the determination and creativity to make a plan, they also need the ability and willingness to implement it. Difficulties at this stage can often be traced to the *lack-of-participation error*, or the failure to adequately involve those persons whose support is necessary to ensure a plan's complete implementation. Managers who use participation wisely get the right people involved in decisions and problem solving from the beginning. When they do, plans are more likely to be implemented quickly, smoothly, and to everyone's satisfaction.

Step 5: Evaluate Results

Planning and decision making are not complete until results are evaluated. This is a stage of measurement, where accomplishments are compared with objectives. If the desired results are not achieved, the process must be renewed to allow for corrective actions. Both the positive and negative consequences of the chosen course of action should be examined. If the original solution appears inadequate, a return to earlier steps may be required to generate a modified or new plan. Evaluation is also made easier if the original plan includes objectives with measurable targets and timetables.

PLANNING AS PROBLEM SOLVING

Managers face many problems as they make and implement plans. Some are **structured problems** that are familiar, straightforward, and clear with respect to the information needed to resolve them. Such problems can often be ex-

● A **structured problem** is familiar, straightforward, and clear in its information requirements.

pected to arise in common situations that regularly occur. The manager can therefore plan ahead and develop specific ways to deal with them or even take action to prevent their occurrence. For example, "personnel" problems are common whenever decisions are made on pay raises and promotions, vacation requests, committee assignments, and the like. Knowing this, proactive managers plan ahead so they can handle complaints effectively when they arise.

When problems are structured and routine and tend to arise on a regular basis, they can be addressed through standard plans or prepared responses. Called *programmed decisions*, these are solutions already available from past experience that are appropriate for the problem at hand. A good example is the decision to reorder inventory automatically when on-hand stock falls below a predetermined level. Today, an increasing number of programmed decisions are being assisted or handled by computers using decision-support software.

● An **unstructured problem** involves ambiguities and information deficiencies.

Managers must also deal with **unstructured problems** that involve ambiguities and information deficiencies and that often occur unexpectedly. Unstructured problems require novel solutions. Proactive managers get a jump on them by realizing that a situation is susceptible to problems and then making plans that can be implemented when and if the situation occurs. For example, at the Vanguard Group executives are tireless in their preparation for a variety of events that could disrupt their mutual fund business. Their biggest fear is an investor panic that overloads their customer service system during a major plunge in the bond or stock markets. In anticipation of this eventuality, the firm has trained its accountants, lawyers, and money fund managers to staff the telephones if needed.

● A **crisis problem** is an unexpected problem that can lead to disaster if not resolved quickly and appropriately.

When new and unfamiliar problems arise, *nonprogrammed decisions* must be made to specifically tailor plans and soultions to the situation at hand. The information requirements for defining and resolving such problems are typically high. An extreme situation is the **crisis problem** that is unexpected and can lead to disaster if not resolved quickly and appropriately.[13] No one can avoid crises, and the public is well aware of the immensity of corporate crises in the modern world. The Chernobyl nuclear plant explosion in the former Soviet Union and the *Exxon Valdez* oil spill of years past are but two sensational examples. Managers in more progressive organizations now anticipate that crises, unfortunately, will occur. They are installing "early-warning" crisis information systems and developing crisis management plans to deal with them in the best possible ways.

PLANNING ENVIRONMENTS

Figure 5.5 illustrates three different planning environments in which plans must be made and problems must be solved in organizations: certainty, risk, and uncertainty. In a **certain environment,** there is sufficient information for the problem solver to know the possible alternatives and what the results of each would be. This is an ideal condition for planning. The challenge is simply to study the alternatives and choose the best solution. But realistically speaking, very little managerial planning occurs in certain environments.

● A **certain environment** offers complete information on possible action alternatives and their consequences.

● A **risk environment** lacks complete information, but offers "probabilities" of the likely outcomes for possible action alternatives.

In a **risk environment,** the problem solver lacks complete information on action alternatives and their consequences. However, there is some sense of the "probabilities" associated with their occurrence—that is, is the degree of likelihood (e.g., 4 chances out of 10). Risk is a common planning environment for managers.

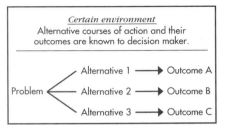 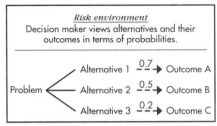 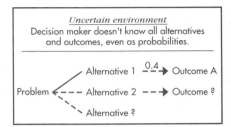

Figure 5.5   Three environments for managerial decision making and problem solving.

When information is so poor that planners are unable even to assign probabilities to the likely outcomes of alternatives that are known, an **uncertain environment** exists. This is the most difficult planning environment.[14] Uncertainty forces managers to rely heavily on creativity in solving problems; it requires unique, novel, and often totally innovative alternatives to existing patterns of behavior. Today's global economy, highly competitive industry environments, and dramatic technological changes have increased uncertainty for most organizational planners.

- An **uncertain environment** is so poor in information that it is difficult even to assign probabilities to the likely outcomes of alternatives.

PLANNING TOOLS AND TECHNIQUES

Planning is challenging in any circumstances, and the difficulties increase as the environment becomes more uncertain. To help master these challenges a number of useful planning tools and techniques have been developed. They include forecasting, contingency planning, scenario planning, benchmarking, participation and involvment, and the use of staff planners.

FORECASTING

Forecasting is the process of making assumptions about what will happen in the future.[15] A **forecast** is a specific vision of the future. All good plans involve forecasts. Some are based on *qualitative forecasting*, which uses expert opinions to predict the future. In this case, a single person of special expertise or reputation or a panel of experts may be consulted. Others are based on *quantitative forecasting*, which uses mathematical and statistical analysis of data banks to predict future events. Even the results of highly sophisticated quantitative approaches, however, still require interpretation. In the final analysis, forecasting always relies on human judgment, is subject to error, and should be treated cautiously. Forecasting is not planning; it is a planning tool.

- A **forecast** is an attempt to predict future outcomes.

CONTINGENCY PLANNING

Planning always involves thinking ahead. But the more unstructured the problems and more uncertain the planning environment, the more likely that one's original assumptions, predictions, and intentions may prove to be in error. Even the most carefully prepared plans may prove inadequate as experience develops. Unexpected problems and events frequently occur. When they do, plans have to be changed. It is better to anticipate this eventuality than be surprised by it.

● **Contingency planning** identifies alternative courses of action that can be taken if and when circumstances change with time.

Contingency planning is the process of identifying alternative courses of action that can be implemented if and when an original plan proves inadequate because of changing circumstances. The earlier that changes in the planning environment can be detected, the better. "Trigger points" that indicate that an existing plan is no longer desirable can and should be preselected and then monitored. Sometimes this is accomplished simply by good forward thinking on the part of managers and staff planners. At other times, it can be assisted by a "devil's advocate" method, in which planners are formally assigned to develop plans for "worst-case" forecasts of future events.

SCENARIO PLANNING

● **Scenario planning** identifies alternative future "scenarios" and makes plans to deal with each.

A popular and long-term version of contingency planning used extensively today is called **scenario planning.** This involves identifying several alternative future "scenarios" or states of affairs that may occur. Plans are then made to deal with each should it actually occur.[16] This helps organizations operate more flexibly in dynamic environments.

Royal Dutch/Shell has been doing scenario planning for many years. The process began years ago when top managers asked themselves a perplexing question: "What would Shell do after its oil supplies ran out?" The question was approached by creating alternative future scenarios while remaining sensitive to the nature of growing environmental changes. Although recognizing that planning scenarios can never be inclusive of all future possibilities, a Royal Dutch/Shell planning coordinator once said that scenarios help "condition the organization to think" and remain better prepared than its competitors for "future shocks."

BENCHMARKING

● **Benchmarking** uses external comparisons to gain insights for planning.

Another important influence on the success or failure of planning is the frame of reference used as a starting point. All too often, planners have only a limited awareness of what is happening outside the immediate work setting. Successful planning must challenge the status quo; it cannot simply accept things the way they are. One way to do this is through **benchmarking,** a technique that uses external comparisons to evaluate one's current performance and identify possible future actions. The purpose is to find out what other people and organizations are doing very well and plan how to incorporate these ideas into one's own operations. This is a way for progressive companies to learn from other "excellent" companies, not just direct competitors. It allows them to analyze and thoroughly compare all organizational systems and processes to locate possible areas to improve efficiencies and pursue opportunities for innovation. For example, a planning team from Xerox once visited L.L. Bean, Inc. and prepared a report that helped revamp the firm's warehouse and distribution systems.

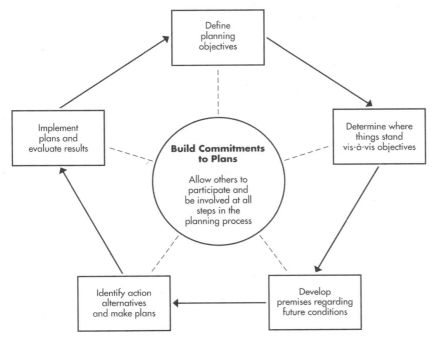

Figure 5.6 How participation and involvement build commitments to plans.

PARTICIPATION AND INVOLVEMENT

"Participation" is a key word in the planning process. The concept of **partici-pative planning** requires that the process include people who will be affected by the resulting plans and/or will be asked to help implement them. Participation can increase the creativity and information available for planning. It can also increase the understanding, acceptance, and commitment of people to final plans. Indeed, planning in organizations should rarely, if ever, be done by individuals. It should be organized and accomplished in a participatory manner that includes the contributions of many people representing diverse responsibilities and vantage points.

The centrality of participation and involvement in the planning process is highlighted in *Figure 5.6*. To create and implement the best plans, proper attention must always be given to genuinely involving others during all planning steps. Even though this process may mean that planning takes more time, it can improve results by improving implementation.

● **Participative planning** includes the people who will be affected by plans and/or asked to help implement them.

ROLE OF STAFF PLANNERS

As the planning needs of organizations grow, there is a corresponding need to increase the sophistication of the overall planning system itself. In some cases, staff planners are employed to take responsibility for leading and coordinating planning for the organization as a whole or for one of its major components. These planners should be skilled in all steps of the formal planning process as well as in the use of the participative, benchmarking, and scenario-planning approaches just discussed. They should also understand the staff, or advisory, nature of their roles. In general, this means a staff planner is expected to assist line managers in preparing plans, develop special plans upon request, gather and maintain planning information, assist in communicating plans to others, and monitor plans in progress and suggest changes.

Given clear responsibilities and their special planning expertise, staff planners can bring focus to efforts to accomplish important, often strategic, planning tasks. But one risk is a tendency for a communication "gap" to develop between staff planners and line managers. This can cause a great deal of difficulty. Resulting plans may lack relevance, and line personnel may lack commitment to implement them even if they are relevant. A trend in organizations today is to deemphasize the role of large staff planning groups and to place much greater emphasis on the participation and involvement of line managers in the planning process. At General Electric, CEO Jack Welch carefully limits the size of the firm's planning staff. He once dismantled a large planning group that emphasized voluminous written reports. Now, GE employs only a few planners whose responsibilities are limited to advising line managers.

SUMMARY

How Does Planning Work?

- Planning is the process of setting performance objectives and determining what should be done to accomplish them.
- A plan is a set of intended actions for accomplishing important objectives.
- Planning sets the stage for the other management functions—organizing, leading, and controlling.
- Good planning improves performance through better focus and flexibility, action orientation, coordination, control, and time management.

What Types of Plans Are Used By Managers?

- Short-range plans tend to cover a year or less, while long-range plans extend up to five years or more.
- Strategic plans set critical long-range directions; operational plans are designed to implement strategic plans.
- Standing plans, such as policies and procedures, are used over and over again.
- Single-use plans, such as project schedules and budgets, are established for a specific purpose and time frame.

How Does Planning Utilize Decision Making?

- The decision-making steps in the planning process are find and define the problem, generate and evaluate alternatives, choose the preferred solution, implement the plan, and evaluate the results.
- In the classical model, optimizing or best-chance decisions are made; in the behavioral model, satisficing or acceptable-choice decisions are made.

- As a problem-solving process, planning addresses structured and unstructured problems in organizations.
- The most threatening type of problem is the crisis, which occurs unexpectedly and can lead to disaster if it is not handled quickly and properly.
- Planning is more often done under environmental conditions of risk and uncertainty, than under certainty.

What Planning Tools and Techniques Are Available?

- Forecasting, a prediction of what will happen in the future, is a planning aid but not a planning substitute.
- Contingency planning identifies alternative courses of action that can be implemented if and when circumstances change in certain ways over time.
- Scenario planning through the use of alternative versions of the future is a useful long-term form of contingency planning.
- Planning through benchmarking utilizes external comparisons to identify desirable action directions.
- Participation and involvement open the planning process to valuable inputs from people whose efforts are essential to the effective implementation of plans.
- Specialized staff planners can help with the planning of details, although care must be taken to make sure they work well with line personnel.

KEY TERMS

Benchmarking (p. 84)

Budget (p. 76)

Contingency planning (p. 84)

Certain environment (p. 82)

Cost-benefit analysis (p. 78)

Crisis problem (p. 82)

Escalating commitment (p. 80)

Forecast (p. 83)

Objectives (p. 71)

Operational plan (p.75)

Participative planning (p. 85)

Planning (p. 71)

Policy (p. 76)

Procedure (p. 76)

Project schedule (p. 76)

Risk environment (p. 82)

Satisficing (p. 80)

Scenario planning (p. 84)

Strategic plan (p. 75)

Structured problem (p. 81)

Uncertain environment (p. 83)

Unstructured problem (p. 82)

Zero-based budget (p. 76)

  SELF-TEST Take the interactive Self-Test for this chapter on the Schermerhorn Web Site

Chapter Six

Strategic Management and Entrepreneurship

PLANNING AHEAD—
Chapter 6 Study Questions

- What is strategic management?
- How are strategies formulated?
- How are strategies implemented?
- What is entrepreneurship?

GET (AND STAY) AHEAD WITH STRATEGY

Wal-Mart's master plan is famous in the world of retail strategy—consistently low prices and high customer service. The firm was started by the late Sam Walton in Bentonville, Arkansas. "Mr. Sam" started in small southern towns. Now America's largest retailer and employer, Wal-Mart is located in all fifty states. With success came entry into broader national markets and international expansion. Industry analysts point to Wal-Mart's "productivity loop"—ability to offer lower prices and better service than its rivals—as a major competitive advantage. All this is backed up by the latest in technology. A sophisticated corporate satellite system and computer network keeps the home office in touch with operations at all stores. Inventories are monitored around the clock so that stores are rarely out of the items customers are seeking. Given Wal-Mart's impressive track record and strength, the question is, "Can other budget retailers keep up?" Of course, the visionaries at Wal-Mart are probably asking another question: "How can we stay ahead?" [1]

Even as Wal-Mart sets the pace, we will surely see many changes in competitive retailing in the years ahead. The industry is being challenged on many fronts, including catalog sales, home shopping by television, and the growth of electronic commerce. Success will come to those with a sense of future opportunities, clear vision about what needs to be done, and the strong management and organizational systems needed to get them accomplished.

STRATEGY AND COMPETITIVE ADVANTAGE

The opening example introduces the competitive domain of strategy and strategic management. A **strategy** is a comprehensive action plan that identifies long-term direction and guides resource utilization to accomplish an organization's mission and objectives with sustainable competitive advantage. It is a plan for using resources with consistent *strategic intent*, that is, with all organizational energies focused on a unifying and compelling target.[2] In the case of Coca-Cola that intent has been described as "To put a Coke within 'arm's reach' of every consumer in the world." To gain competitive advantage, an organization must deal with market and environmental forces better than its competitors.[3] The task of crafting strategies with this potential can be daunting. Consider the retailing industry again. Wal-Mart, Kmart, and Target each began operating in 1962. Of the 10 top discounters they faced in that year, none exists today. They were killed by competition.

● A **strategy** is a comprehensive plan that sets direction and guides the allocation of resources to achieve long-term objectives.

THE STRATEGIC MANAGEMENT PROCESS

The demands of intense competition in the global economy call for strategies that are often bold, aggressive, and fast-moving. **Strategic management** is the process of formulating and implementing strategies that create competitive advantage and advance an organization's mission and objectives. The essence of strategic management is to look ahead, understand the environment, and effectively position an organization for competitive success in changing times.

● **Strategic management** is the process of formulating and implementing strategies.

Figure 6.1 describes two major responsibilities in the strategic management process. The first is *strategy formulation*. This involves assessing existing stratgies,

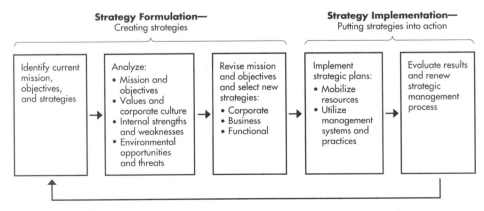

Figure 6.1   The strategic management process of strategy formulation and strategy implementation.

MANAGER'S NOTEPAD 6.1

FIVE STRATEGIC MANAGEMENT TASKS

1. Identify organizational mission and objectives.
   Ask: "What business are we in? Where do we want to be in the future?"
2. Assess current performance vis-à-vis mission and objectives.
   Ask: "How well are we currently doing?"
3. Create strategic plans to accomplish purpose and objectives.
   Ask: "How can we get where we really want to be?"
4. Implement the strategic plans.
   Ask: "Has everything been done that needs to be done?"
5. Evaluate results; change strategic plans and/or implementation processes as necessary.
   Ask: "Are things working out as planned, and what can be improved upon?"

Five strategic questions →

organization, and environment to develop new strategies and strategic plans capable of delivering future competitive advantage. Peter Drucker associates this process with a set of five strategic questions: (1) What is our business mission? (2) Who are our customers? (3) What do our customers consider value? (4) What have been our results? (5) What is our plan?[4]

The second strategic management responsibility is *strategy implementation.* Once strategies are created, they must be acted upon successfully to achieve the desired results. As Drucker says, "The future will not just happen if one wishes hard enough. It requires decision—now. It imposes risk—now. It requires action—now. It demands allocation of resources and above all, of human resources—now. It requires *work*—now."[5] This "work" is the responsibility for actually putting strategies and strategic plans into action—the process of implementation. All of this, in turn, requires a commitment to mastering the full range of strategic management tasks listed in *Manager's Notepad 6.1.*

MISSION, VALUES, AND OBJECTIVES

The strategic management process begins with a careful assessment and clarification of organizational mission, values, and objectives.[6] In today's quality-conscious and highly competitive environments, all must be directly centered on serving the needs of customers or clients. After all, their satisfaction and continued support are the ultimate keys to organizational survival.

● The **mission** of an organization is its reason for existence as a supplier of goods and services to society.

Mission

The **mission** or *purpose* of any organization may be described as its "reason" for existence as a supplier of goods and/or services to society. The best organizations have a clear and compelling mission. At Mary Kay Cosmetics, for example, it is "To give unlimited opportunity to women;" at 3M it is "To solve unsolved problems innovatively;" at Merck it is "To preserve and improve human life." A good mission statement is precise in identifying the *domain* in which the organization intends to operate—including the *customers* it intends to serve, the *products* and/or *services* it intends to provide, and the *location* in which it intends to operate. The mission statement should also communicate the underlying *philosophy* that will guide employees in these operations. America West's mission statement seems to meet each of these requirements. It reads "America West will support and grow its market position as a low-cost, full-service nationwide airline. It will be known for its focus on customer service and its high-performance culture. America West is committed to sustaining financial strength and profitability, thereby providing stability for its employees and shareholder value for its owners."

An important test of corporate mission is how well it serves the organization's *stakeholders*. These are employees and members of the external environment, customers, shareholders, suppliers, creditors, community groups, and others who are directly involved with the organization and/or affected by its operations. In a *strategic constituencies analysis* the specific interests of each stakeholder are assessed along with the organization's record in responding to them. *Figure 6.2* gives an example of how stakeholder interests can be addressed in a mission statement.

Core Values

Behavior in and by organizations will always be affected in part by *values*, which are broad beliefs about what is or is not appropriate. The predominant value system of the organization as a whole forms its **corporate culture.**[8] The presence of strong core values gives character to an organization, backs up the mission statement, and helps guide the behavior of members in meaningful and consistent ways. For example, core values at Merck include corporate social responsibility, science-based innovation, honesty and integrity, and profit from work that benefits humanity.

● **Corporate culture** is the predominant value system for the organization as a whole.

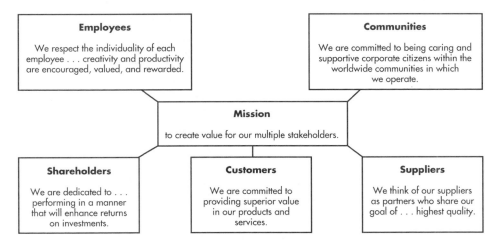

Figure 6.2 Stakeholder interests and the corporate mission statement.

Objectives

● **Operating objectives** are specific results that organizations try to accomplish.

Operative objectives

Whereas a mission statement sets forth an official purpose for the organization, **operating objectives** direct activities toward key and specific results. They are shorter term targets against which actual performance can be measured. Examples of business operating objectives include:[9]

● *Profitability:* Producing at a net profit in business.
● *Market share:* Gaining and holding a specific share of a product market.
● *Human talent:* Recruiting and maintaining a high-quality workforce.
● *Financial health:* Acquiring financial capital and earning positive returns.
● *Cost efficiency:* Using resources well to operate at low cost.
● *Product quality:* Producing high-quality goods or services.
● *Innovation:* Developing new products and/or processes.
● *Social responsibility:* Making a positive contribution to society.

SWOT ANALYSIS

● A **SWOT analysis** examines organizational strengths and weaknesses and environmental opportunities and threats.

● A **core competency** is a special strength that gives an organization a competitive advantage.

An important initial step in the strategic management process is analysis of the organization and its environment. This can be accomplished by a technique known as **SWOT analysis:** the analysis of organizational *S*trengths and *W*eaknesses as well as well as of environmental *O*pportunities and *T*hreats.

As shown in *Figure 6.3*, a SWOT analysis includes a systematic internal assessment of the organization's resources and capabilities. A major goal is to identify **core competencies,** special strengths that the organization has or does exceptionally well, that can become sources of competitive advantage.[10] Core competencies may be found in efficient manufacturing approaches, special

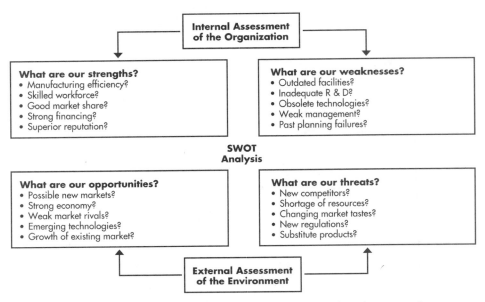

Figure 6.3 SWOT analysis of organizational strengths and weaknesses and environmental opportunities and threats.

knowledge or expertise, superior technologies, or unique product distribution systems, among many other possibilities.

The SWOT analysis is not complete until opportunities and threats in the external environment are also analyzed. It is necessary to assess how actual and future environmental conditions may affect mission accomplishment. This analysis should include *macro environment* developments in areas like technology, government, social structures and population demographics, the global economy, and the natural environment. It should also include the specific influences of the *industry environment* with respect to an organization's resource suppliers, competitors, and customers.

When Howard Schultz joined Starbucks in 1982, the firm was a small coffee retailer in Seattle. But Schultz envisioned more future potential. He had a vision that included Starbuck's becoming a national chain of stores offering the finest coffee drinks with a clear mission: "To educate consumers everywhere about fine coffee." The stores would be staffed by expert brewers who explained coffees as they were served. And, these employees would be given stock options to provide a sense of ownership in the company. Today Starbucks has grown to over 2,300 stores across North America and is expanding internationally. CEO Schultz says: "Moving forward, we will continue to pursue opportunities that increase long-term value for our shareholders and our partners, provide unique experiences for our customers, and bring us ever closer to our goal of becoming the most recognized and respected brand of coffee in the world." [11]

LEVELS AND TYPES OF STRATEGY

Organizations utilize different levels and types of strategies. The challenges of choosing and integrating these increase with the complexity of the setting.

Levels of Strategy

The level of **corporate strategy** directs the organization as a whole toward sustainable competitive advantage. As shown in *Figure 6.4*, it describes the scope of operations by answering this *strategic question:* "In what industries and markets should we compete?" In diversified conglomerate organizations like General Electric, corporate strategy identifies the different areas of business in which a company intends to compete. The firm pursues business interests in aircraft engines, appliances, capital services, lighting, medical systems, broadcasting, plastics, and power systems, for example. Typical strategic decisions at GE's corporate level relate to the allocation of resources for acquisitions, new business development, divestitures, and the like across this business portfolio. Increasingly, corporate strategies for many businesses include an important role for global operations such as international joint ventures and strategic alliances.

- A **corporate strategy** sets long-term direction for the total enterprise.

At the level of **business strategy,** strategy is set for a single business unit or product line. It describes strategic intent with respect to a given industry or market, such as GE's appliances division. In large conglomerates like General Electric, the term *strategic business unit* (SBU) is often used to describe such divisions when they operate with separate missions within a larger enterprise. The selection of business

- A **business strategy** identifies how a division or strategic business unit will compete in its product or service domain.

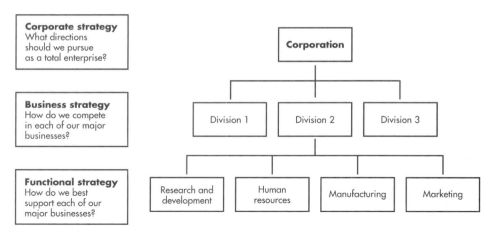

Figure 6.4 Levels of strategy in a large and complex business.

strategy involves answering this *strategic question:* "How are we going to compete for customers within this industry and market?" Typical business strategy decisions include choices about product/service mix, facilities locations, new technologies, and the like. In single-business enterprises, business strategy is the corporate strategy.

Functional strategy guides the use of resources to implement business strategy. This level of strategy focuses on activities within a specific functional area of operations such as marketing, manufacturing, finance, human resources and research and development. The *strategic question* to be answered in selecting functional strategies is: "How can we best utilize resources to implement our business strategy?" For example, Worthington Industries, a premier supplier of steel and plastic products, pursues a distinct human resource strategy based on trust. There are no time clocks, and all full-time employees are on salaries. Almost all absences are fully paid. The firm provides free coffee, in-plant barbershops, and medical-wellness centers. Not surprisingly, Worthington has made Fortune's list of "100 Best Companies to Work for in America."

Types of Strategies

Strategies used at any level can be breadly described for their relative emphasis on growth, retrenchment or stability. **Growth strategies** pursue larger size and expanded operations. They are popular in part because growth is necessary for long-run survival in some industries. Coca-Cola, for example, pursues a highly aggressive and global growth strategy. There is a tendency to equate growth with effectiveness, but that is not necessarily true. Any growth must be well managed to achieve the desired results. Some organizations grow through *concentration*— that is, by using existing strengths in new and productive ways and without taking the risks of great shifts in direction. Others grow through *diversification*, the acquisition of or investment in new businesses in unrelated areas.

Retrenchment strategies reduce the scale of operations in order to gain efficiency and improve performance. The decision to retrench can be difficult to make since it seems to be an admission of failure. But in today's era of challenging economic conditions and environmental uncertainty, retrenchment strategies have gained renewed respect. Retrenchment by *turnaround* is a strategy of "downsizing" to reduce costs and "restructuring" to improve operating

● A **functional strategy** guides activities within one specific area of operations.

● A **growth strategy** involves expansion of the organization's current operations.

● A **retrenchment strategy** involves reducing the scale of current operations.

efficiency. Retrenchment by *divestiture* involves selling parts of the organization to refocus on core competencies, cut costs, and improve operating efficiency. Retrenchment by *liquidation* involves closing operations through the complete sale of assets or the declaration of bankruptcy.

A **stability strategy** maintains the present course of action without major operating changes. Stability is sometimes pursued when an organization is doing well and the environment is not perceived to be changing. It is also used when time is needed to consolidate organizational strengths after a period of growth or retrenchment. Of course, stability can also be pursued by default when decision makers are unwilling to make strategic changes.

- A **stability strategy** maintains the present course of action.

STRATEGY FORMULATION

When strategies are being developed, it is important to remember the goal—to achieve sustainable competitive advantage. The major *opportunities for competitive advantage* have been traditionally found in the following areas:[12]

- *Cost and quality*—where strategy drives an emphasis on operating efficiency and/or product or service quality.
- *Knowledge and timing*—where strategy drives an emphasis on learning, innovation and speed of delivery to market for new ideas.
- *Barriers to entry*—where strategy drives an emphasis on creating a market stronghold that is protected from entry by others.
- *Financial resources*—where strategy drives an emphasis on investments and/or loss sustainment that competitors can't match.

◄── Opportunities for competitive advantage

In today's global economy of intense hypercompetition any advantage is likely to be temporary as changing environments and the moves of competitors take their toll over time.[13] The "burgerwars" of the fast-food industry, for example, are typically waged with a strategy of "if-you-can't-beat-them, copy-them." In competitive settings, strategy formulation must be considered a dynamic and continuing activity.

PORTFOLIO PLANNING

The **portfolio planning** approach to strategy formulation is designed to help allocate scarce organizational resources among competing opportunities, including the mix of product lines and business units.[14] *Figure 6.5* summarizes a portfolio planning approach developed by the Boston Consulting Group know as the **BCG matrix.** It ties strategy formulation to an analysis of business opportunities according to market growth rate and market share.[15] The matrix shows the following four possibilities, with each linked to a possible strategic direction.

Stars are high market share businesses in high-growth markets. They produce large profits through substantial penetration of expanding markets. The preferred strategy for stars is growth, and further resource investments in them are recommended. *Question marks* are low market share businesses in high-growth markets. They do not produce much profit but compete in rapidly growing markets. They are the source of difficult strategic decisions. The

- A **portfolio planning** approach seeks the best mix of investments among alternative business opportunities.

- The **BCG matrix** analyzes business opportunities according to market growth rate and market share.

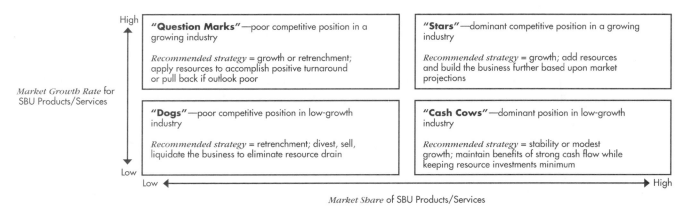

Figure 6.5   The BCG matrix: a portfolio model for corporate strategy formulation.

preferred strategy is growth, but the risk exists that further investments will not result in improved market share. The most promising question marks should be targeted for growth; others are retrenchment candidates.

Cash cows are high market share businesses in low-growth markets. They produce large profits and a strong cash flow. Because the markets offer little growth opportunity, the preferred strategy is stability or modest growth. The choice of terms is very descriptive "cows" should be "milked" to generate cash that can be used to support needed investments in stars and question marks. *Dogs* are low market share businesses in low-growth markets. They do not produce much profit, and they show little potential for future improvement. The preferred strategy for dogs is retrenchment by divestiture.

COMPETITIVE STRATEGIES

A strategic planning approach developed by Michael Porter of Harvard University gives special attention to the organization's current and potential competitive environment.[16] As described in *Figure 6.6*, his *five forces model* focuses attention on: the threats of new competitors entering the market, the bargaining power of suppliers, the bargaining power of customers, the threats of substitute products or services, and rivalry or jockeying for position among existing firms in the industry. From Porter's perspective, a good SWOT analysis includes careful examination of these five forces in the competitive environment. Strategies can then be chosen to give the organization a strategic advantage relative to its competitors. The three *generic strategies* in Porter's model are: differentiation, cost leadership, and focus.

Organizations pursuing a **differentiation strategy** seek competitive advantage through uniqueness. They try to develop goods and services that are clearly different from those of the competition. The objective is to attract loyal long-term customers. This strategy requires organizational strengths in marketing, research and development, technological leadership, and creativity. It is highly dependent for its success on continuing customer perceptions of product quality and uniqueness.

Organizations pursuing a **cost leadership strategy** try to continuously improve the efficiency of production, distribution, and other organizational systems. The objective is to have lower costs than competitors and therefore achieve higher

● A **differentiation strategy** offers goods and/or services that are clearly different from the competition.

● A **cost leadership strategy** seeks efficiency of organizational systems to have lower costs than competitors.

A family-owned company in New Philadelphia, Ohio, Endres Floral Company found its niche by selling "a better rose." And sell it does, shipping more than 5 million roses per year to wholesalers. The firm grows 170,000 rose bushes and harvests twice each day. To compete with lower cost producers from South America, the firm differentiates itself on quality. Endres red roses are supposed to last 10 days to 2 weeks without drooping. They are stored in computer-controlled coolers and shipped in special containers. No Endres rose is out of water more than 10 minutes after cutting and one can be in a customer's home within 24 hours.[17]

profits. This requires efficient systems and tight controls, as well as products that are easy to manufacture and distribute. Of course, quality must not be sacrificed in the process. Wal-Mart, for example, aims to keep its costs so low that it can always offer customers the lowest prices and still make a reasonable profit.

Organizations pursuing a **focus strategy** concentrate attention on a special market segment with the objective of serving its needs better than anyone else. The strategy focuses organizational resources and expertise on a particular customer group, geographical region, or product or service line. This requires a willingness to concentrate attention and the ability to use resources to special advantage in a single area. Cathay Pacific, long one of Asia's leading airlines, refocused on the tourist trade to bolster lagging revenues during the region's economic crisis. The firm offered dramatic discounts and special travel packages in attempting to lure customers from its rivals.

● A **focus strategy** concentrates a special market segment to serve its needs better than the competition.

PRODUCT LIFE CYCLES

A **product life cycle** is the series of stages a product or service goes through in the "life" of its marketability. Different business strategies are typically needed to support products in the life cycle stages of *introduction*, *growth*, *maturity*, and *decline*.[18] Products in the introduction and growth stages lend themselves to differentiation strategies. They require investments in advertising and market research to establish a market presence and build a customer base. In the maturity

● **Product life cycle** is the series of stages a product or service goes through in the "life" of its marketability.

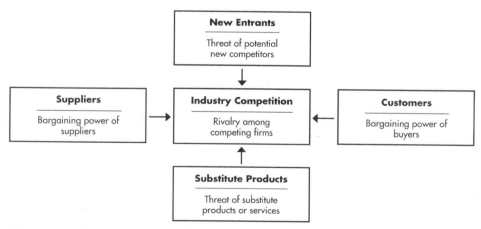

Figure 6.6 Five strategic forces affecting industry competition. *Source:* See Michael E. Porter, *Competitive Strategy* (New York: The Free Press, 1980).

Browser

Go to: http://www.wiley.com/college/schermerhorn

 THE WALL STREET JOURNAL.

WILEY

IN PRACTICE

Entrepreneurship is a major watch-word for the new economy. The Internet, global business climate, and other environmental and demographic forces are supporting huge opportunities for new and emerging businesses.

The Interactive Journal tracks these new businesses daily. Under the **Marketplace** heading, you can click on a **Small Business** link in the left-hand menu options. This supplies you with articles specifically targeted toward small and emerging growth companies.

Under the Small Business section, there are several helpful resource links, including:

The **resources** icon provides helpful links to assist entrepreneurs in their search for ideas, customers, and information.

The **text search** icon identifies and searches for articles on small businesses.

Another feature of **Marketplace** is the **Business Focus** link located in the left-hand menu.

This directs you to articles involving business strategies from a wide range of companies.

A collection of small business articles is contained in a section of **Special Reports,** which can be accessed from the left-hand menu near the bottom, under **Resources.** Locate the series "Small Business" from May 24, 1999. This link provides a wealth of information on trends in this area.

In the left-hand menu, locate **Starting a Business** under the heading: **Other wsj.com Sites.** This link sends you to a companion Interactive Journal Web site (http://startup.wsj.com/) that provides assistance to new businesses.

The link **Running a Business** provides a large number of articles involving starting and running small businesses.

Additional small business news sites include:

CNNfn.com at http://cnnfn.com/news/smbusiness/.
Fortune online at http://www.pathfinder.com/yourco/.

Smart Money Small-Biz at http://www.smartmoney.com/smallbiz/.

Return to the **Marketplace** heading and under the **In this Section** select **Media/Marketing**. This section includes articles on many new product ideas, in addition to new ways to reach customers.

DELIVERABLES:

Under the **Business Focus** link, choose three articles to read and compare. Which of the three business decisions discussed do you think will be most successful and why? Rank order the three from most- to least-likely to succeed. Provide rationale and supporting facts for your decision.

DISCUSSION QUESTIONS:

1. Why do you think strategy is an important topic to businesses today?
2. Can you identify a "personal" strategy you are using in your career plan?
3. Identify three new business ideas. Be prepared to support your choices.

 *Note: The underscored words/phrases in the Interactive Journal feature indicate Internet links provided in the online versions. See the *Introducing Management* Web site at www.wiley.com/college/schermerhorn.

stage, the strategic emphasis shifts toward keeping customers and gaining production efficiencies. They may involve focus and an attempt at cost leadership. These strategies may perform adequately even as the product first moves into decline. But at some point new ways must be found to extend product life or action must be taken to shift resources to other more promising products.

Understanding product life cycles and adjusting strategy is an important business skill that is especially relevant in dynamic times. Consider what happened at Motorola. When the cellular phone industry was starting to use new digital technologies, the firm continued to emphasize its successful, but older, analog products. Motorola's top managers failed to properly address industry trends and their company suffered losses of momentum to very aggressive competitors. They had to fight their way back in the face of difficult and global competition.

EMERGENT STRATEGIES

The real world of strategy formulation is complex and demanding. Not all strategies are developed at one point in time and then implemented step by step. Many take shape, change, and develop over time as modest adjustments to past patterns. James Brian Quinn calls this a process of *logical incrementalism*, whereby incremental changes in strategy occur as managers learn from experience.[19] This approach has much in common with Henry Mintzberg's and John Kotter's descriptions of managerial behavior described in Chapter 1.[20] They view managers as planning and acting in complex interpersonal networks and in hectic, fast-paced work settings. Effective managers must have the capacity to stay focused on long-term objectives while still remaining flexible enough to master short-run problems and opportunities as they occur.

Such reasoning has led Mintzberg to identify what he calls *emergent strategies*.[21] These are strategies that develop progressively over time as "streams" of decisions made by managers as they learn from and respond to work situations. There is an important element of "craftsmanship" here that Mintzberg worries may be overlooked by managers who choose and discard strategies in rapid succession while using the formal planning models. He also believes that emergent strategies allow managers and organizations to become really good at implementing strategies, not just formulating them.

STRATEGY IMPLEMENTATION

No strategy, no matter how well formulated, can achieve long-term success if it is not properly implemented. Current issues in strategy implementation call attention to the need for excellence in all management systems and practices, the importance of leadership and top management teams, and the responsibilities of corporate governance.

MANAGEMENT PRACTICES AND SYSTEMS

In order to successfully put strategies into action, the entire organization and all of its resources must be mobilized in support of them. This involves the complete management process from planning and controlling through organizing and leading. Every strategy requires supporting structures, well-designed tasks and workflows, and the right people. And, it must be enthusiastically supported by leaders who are capable of motivating everyone, building individual performance commitments, and utilizing teams and teamwork to best advantage. Only with such total systems support can strategies be implemented well enough to actually achieve competitive advantage.

Common strategic planning pitfalls that hinder implementation include both failures of substance and failures of process. *Failures of substance* reflect inadequate attention to the major strategic planning elements—analysis of mission, values and objectives, organizational strengths and weaknesses, and environmental opportunities and threats. *Manager's Notepad 6.2* offers useful guidelines on how to double-check a strategy from a substance perspective.[22] *Failures of process* reflect poor handling of the strategic planning process itself. A good example is lack of participation error. This is failure to include key persons in the strategic planning effort.[23] As a result, they lack sufficient commitment to action and follow-through. This often occurs as a result of too much centralization of planning in top management or too much delegation of planning activities to staff planners or separate planning departments.

STRATEGIC LEADERSHIP

Strategy implementation is a distributed leadership responsibility. Full commitment by all managers to support and lead strategic initiatives within their areas of supervisory responsibility is essential. To successfully put strategies into action the entire organization and all of its resources must be mobilized from top to bottom, and from side to side. The whole system must work together. And for this to happen, every manager must be a strategic leader who always understands and helps implement corporate strategy.

Of course top managers bear a particular responsibility for strategic leadership. Amidst the complexity of environment and operations today, strategic leadership at the top is increasingly viewed as a team situation. A *top manage-*

MANAGER'S NOTEPAD 6.2

HOW TO DOUBLE-CHECK A STRATEGY

Check 1: Is the strategy consistent with mission and values?
Check 2: Is the strategy feasible, given strengths/weaknesses?
Check 3: Is the strategy responsive to opportunities and threats?
Check 4: Is the strategy sustainable in competitive advantage?
Check 5: Is the risk in the strategy a "reasonable" risk?
Check 6: Is the strategy flexible enough?

ment team is one that is headed by a chief executive officer or president and entails, at a minimum, the senior managers reporting directly to this position. Some organizations have gone so far as to formally define a chief executive committee that is responsible for running day-to-day operations and that reports directly to the CEO. Members of these executive committees contribute their respective expertise and energies to strategy oversight.[24]

CORPORATE GOVERNANCE

Organizations today are experiencing new pressures at the level of **corporate governance.** This is the system of control and performance monitoring of top management that is maintained by boards of directors and other major stakeholder representatives. In businesses, for example, corporate governance is enacted by boards, institutional investors in a firm's assets, and other ownership interests. Each in its own way is a point of strategic performance accountability for top management.[25]

> ● **Corporate governance** is the system of control and performance monitoring of top management.

Boards of directors are formally charged with ensuring that an organization operates in the best interests of its owners and/or the representative public in the case of nonprofit organizations. Controversies often arise over the role of *inside directors* who are chosen from the senior management of the organization and *outside directors* who are chosen from other organizations and positions external to the organization. In the past corporate boards may have been viewed as largely endorsing or confirming the strategic initiatives of top management. Today they are increasingly expected to take active roles in ensuring that strategies are well chosen and that the strategic leadership of an enterprise is successful.

If anything, the current trend is toward greater attention to issues of corporate governance. Top managers probably feel more accountability for performance than ever before to boards of directors and other stakeholder interest groups. Furthermore, this strategic accountability relates not only to financial performance but also to broader social responsibility concerns. For example, there are institutional investors who purposely buy stock in a company to gain a voice in shareholder meetings. They do this to bring pressure on organizations to behave in socially responsible ways. Such pressure was felt by PepsiCo and Texaco for their controversial involvements in Burma, a country whose totalitarian rulers were accused of human rights abuses. Under pressure from consumers and activist groups, both PepsiCo and Texaco terminated their business interests in that country.

STRATEGY AND ENTREPRENEURSHIP

In dynamic times organizations must adapt and renew themselves continually to become and remain successful. People and organizations not only must change—they must change *frequently* and at a rapidly accelerating pace. Success in the highly competitive business environments, in particular, depends on **entrepreneurship.** This term is used to describe strategic thinking and risk-

> ● **Entrepreneurship** is dynamic, risk-taking, creative, and growth-oriented behavior.

taking behavior that results in the creation of new opportunities for individuals and/or organizations. These opportunities frequently appear in the form of new business ventures, such as the now familiar Domino's Pizza and Federal Express's overnight package delivery, or as new goods or services, such as the popular 3M Post-It Note.

WHO ARE THE ENTREPRENEURS?

● An **entrepreneur** pursues opportunities in risk situations.

An **entrepreneur** is a risk-taking individual who takes action to pursue opportunities in situations others may fail to recognize as such or may even view as problems or threats.[26] In the business context, an entrepreneur starts new ventures that bring to life new product or service ideas. Typical *characteristics of entrepreneurs* include the following:

Characteristics of entrepreneurs

- *Internal focus of control:* Entrepreneurs believe that they are in control of their own destiny; they are self-directing and like autonomy.
- *High energy level:* Entrepreneurs are persistent, hard working, and willing to exert extraordinary efforts to succeed.
- *High need for achievement:* Entrepreneurs are motivated to act individually to accomplish challenging goals.
- *Tolerance for ambiguity:* Entrepreneurs are risk takers; they tolerate situations with high degrees of uncertainty.
- *Self-confidence:* Entrepreneurs feel competent, believe in themselves, and are willing to make decisions.
- *Action oriented:* Entrepreneurs try to act ahead of problems; they want to get things done quickly and do not want to waste valuable time.

A common image of an entrepreneur is as the founder of a new business enterprise that achieves large-scale success. Anita Roddick's Body Shop, Bill Gates's Microsoft, and Sam Walton's Wal-Mart are but a few dramatic examples of this type of entrepreneurship. But entrepreneurs also operate on a smaller scale. Those who take the risk of buying a local McDonald's or Subway Sandwich franchise, opening a small retail shop, or going into a self-employed service business are also entrepreneurs. Similarly, anyone who assumes responsibility for introducing a new product or change in operations within an organization is also demonstrating the qualities of entrepreneurship.

ENTREPRENEURSHIP AND SMALL BUSINESS DEVELOPMENT

● A **small business** has fewer than 500 employees, is independently owned and operated, and does not dominate its industry.

Entrepreneurship plays an important role in the formation of smaller enterprises. A **small business** is commonly defined as one with 500 or fewer employees. The U.S. Small Business Administration, or SBA, also states that a small business is one that is independently owned and operated and that does not dominate its industry.[27] Almost 99 percent of American businesses meet this definition, and the small business sector is very important in most nations of the world. Among other things, small businesses offer major economic advantages by creating job opportunities and providing new goods and services. The most common ways to get involved in a small business are to (1) start one, (2) buy an existing one, or (3) buy and run a franchise.

Unfortunately, small businesses have a high failure rate. As many as 60 to 80 percent fail in their first five years of operation. Although many factors affect such outcomes, an important foundation for such success is a *business plan*. This is a written document that describes the nature of the business and its strategy, as well as exactly how an entrepreneur intends to start and operate it. Writing such a business plan helps the entrepreneur craft strategy and "think" through the various details of setting up a business.[28] Typically, this plan will be shared with banks, venture capitalists, and other potential investors in order to attract any additional funds that may be needed to make the startup possible.

A variety of resources are available to promote the development of small and medium scale enterprises. The United States Small Business Administration, for example, works with state and local agencies to support over 1,000 Small Business Development Centers (SBDCs) nationwide. They advise entrepreneurs and small business owners on how to set up and successfully run a business. Often these centers are associated with universities or colleges and

Management Across Functions

ACCOUNTING

Small Businesses Need Better Budgeting

"My annual plan—in my head—is to sell as much product for as much profit as possible," says Larry Southard, president of his own farm equipment sales firm in Iowa. He adds: "I hate paperwork." That's fine, but you have to worry whether or not he is adequately prepared for changes in the economy, adverse farming cycles, and even the hand-over of his business to someone else upon retirement. Consultants claim many small business owners aren't ready, especially when it comes to budgets and finances. One says: "I think you've got a whole group of people who are basically doing it on the fly." Many rely on accountants to supply monthly results and compare them on a year-to-year basis. Others struggle by with little attention to the numbers. Only 13 percent of small businesses included in a recent survey by the Willard & Shullman Group reported having an annual budget in writing. Only 14 percent had a written annual business plan; and 60 percent had no written plans at all. The result can be missed opportunities, or worse. Toby Fancher and a partner started a Web and graphic design business in southwestern Pennsylvania. Their budget was easy at first—just making payroll and paying office expenses. It's getting harder now that they have over 120 clients and eight staff. Fancher worries that it is hard for him to know which projects are profitable. "We need a budget," he says. "I know that." In the meantime the pressures of 14-hour days and a growth business leave him little time for planning.[29]

offer opportunities for students to learn first-hand the nature of small business and entrepreneurship. At the Silicon Valley Small Business Development Center, for example, Jean Jaffess and her partners in Mambo Design & Consulting were able to find assistance on writing a business plan, understanding financial reports, and tax requirements.[30]

There is also considerable attention devoted to *business incubation*, where special facilities provide a variety of shared administrative services and facilities to help small businesses get started. The idea is that by nurturing the new businesses in the incubators they will be able to grow more quickly and become healthy enough to survive on their own. And, of course, with survival the economic benefits of job creation and new community businesses are expected. The National Business Incubation Association, headquartered at Ohio University, serves as the network hub of business incubation professionals around the United States.

ENTREPRENEURSHIP AND LARGE ENTERPRISES

Larger organizations also depend on entrepreneurial workers who are willing to assume risk and display creativity. Such entrepreneurship helps drive the innovation so important to continued success in dynamic and competitive environments. Yet this task is especially challenging in very large and complex systems whose natural tendencies may be toward stability, rigidity, and avoidance of risk. The concept of **intrapreneurship** specifically describes entrepreneurial behavior on the part of people and subunits operating within large organizations.[31]

● **Intrapreneurship** is entrepreneurial behavior displayed by people or subunits within large organizations.

To enhance their competitive edge through intrapreneurship, large organizations must find ways to act like small ones. This is often accomplished with an emphasis on teams and teamwork. Some large organizations create small subunits allowed to work in a setting that is highly creative and free of bureaucratic restrictions. A classic example is the small group of enthusiastic employees once sent off to create Apple Computer's original Macintosh. The group operated free of the firm's normal product development bureaucracy, set its own norms, and even operated in a special location. It worked. And, the legendary success of the Macintosh is a fitting reminder of the importance of strategic management and entrepreneurship in organizations.

SUMMARY

What Is Strategic Management?

● A strategy is a comprehensive plan that sets long-term direction and guides resource allocation to accomplish an organization's mission.

● The strategic management process begins with analysis of mission, clarification of core values, and identification of objectives.

● The strategic management process involves a SWOT analysis of organizational resources and capabilities and industry/environment opportunities and threats.

- Corporate strategy sets direction for an entire organization; business strategy sets direction for a business division or product/service line; functional strategy sets direction for the operational support of business and corporate strategies.

- The grand or master strategies used by organizations include growth, retrenchment, and stability, which can be used singly or in combinations.

How Are Strategies Formulated?

- The BCG matrix is a portfolio planning approach that classifies businesses or product lines as "stars," "cash cows," "question marks," or "dogs."

- Porter's model of competitive strategy identifies three major generic strategic options: differentiation—distinguishing one's products from the competition; cost leadership—minimizing costs relative to the competition; and focus—concentrating on a special market segment.

- The product life-cycle model focuses on different strategic needs at the introduction, growth, maturity, and decline stages of a product's life.

- The incremental or emergent model recognizes that many strategies are formulated and implemented incrementally over time.

How Are Strategies Implemented?

- Management practices and systems—including the functions of planning, organizing, leading, and controlling—must be mobilized to support strategy implementation.

- Among the pitfalls that inhibit strategy implementation are failures of substance, such as poor analysis of the environment, and failures of process, such as lack of participation in the planning process.

- Strategic leadership responsibilities are distributed among all managers throughout an organization.

- Increasingly, organizations utilize top management teams to energize and direct the strategic management process.

- Corporate governance, involving the role of boards of directors in the performance monitoring of organizations, is an important element in strategic performance accountability.

What Is Entrepreneurship?

- Entrepreneurship is risk-taking behavior that results in the creation of new opportunities for individuals and/or organizations.

- An entrepreneur is someone who takes strategic risks to pursue opportunities in situations others may view as problems or threats.

- Entrepreneurship results in the founding of many small business enterprises that offer job creation and other economic benefits.

- In the United States, small businesses have access to a variety of forms of support and assistance, including Small Business Development Centers and business incubators.

- Intrapreneurship, or entrepreneurial behavior within larger organizations, is an important impetus to creativity and innovation in organizations.

KEY TERMS

Business strategy (p. 93)

BCG matrix (p. 95)

Core competency (p. 92)

Corporate culture (p. 91)

Corporate governance (p. 101)

Corporate strategy (p. 93)

Cost leadership strategy (p. 96)

Differentiation strategy (p. 96)

Entrepreneur (p. 102)

Entrepreneurship (p. 101)

Focus strategy (p. 97)

Functional strategy (p. 94)

Growth strategy (p. 94)

Intrapreneurship (p. 104)

Mission (p. 90)

Operating objectives (p. 92)

Portfolio planning (p. 95)

Product life cycle (p. 97)

Retrenchment strategy (p. 94)

Small business (p.102)

Stability strategy (p. 95)

Strategic management (p. 89)

Strategy (p. 89)

SWOT analysis (p. 92)

SELF-TEST   Take the interactive Self-Test for this chapter on the Schermerhorn Web Site

Chapter Seven

Controlling—To Ensure Results

PLANNING AHEAD—
Chapter 7 Study Questions

- How do controls work in organizations?
- How do organizational systems assist in control?
- How can operations management improve control?
- How can planning and controlling be integrated?

FACTS CAN BE YOUR BEST FRIENDS

Volant Inc., a Colorado-based ski maker, was in trouble when consultant Mark Soderberg was hired. A plant tour revealed thousands of half-finished skis stacked here and there, up to 40 percent of a day's production being scrapped, and many unfilled customer orders. His approach? Admit the facts, stop production, analyze systems, and address quality problems. Doing what he calls "just the basics of manufacturing," Soderberg cut work-in-process inventories, set up control systems to track defects during production, and organized workers into "process analysis" teams to tap their ideas. Within two years the orders were flowing again and production was smooth and efficient. As quality went up, costs went down. And with the ski business under control, Volant's management was free to consider a shift in strategy to offset the seasonality of skis, such as entering the golf or biking markets.[1]

"Keeping in touch . . . Staying informed . . . Being in control." These are important responsibilities for every manager. But *control* is a word like power; if you aren't careful when it is used, it leaves a negative connotation. Yet, as the example from Volant Inc. shows, control plays a positive and necessary role in the management process. To have things "under control" is good; for things to be "out of control" generally is bad. This chapter introduces the fundamentals of controlling as a basic managerial responsibility and as an important key to sustained organizational productivity.

HOW CONTROLS WORK

● **Controlling** is the process of measuring performance and taking action to ensure desired results.

When the management functions were first introduced in Chapter 1, **controlling** was defined as a process of measuring performance and taking action to ensure desired results. The purpose of controlling is straightforward—to make sure that plans are fulfilled and that actual performance meets or surpasses objectives.

Figure 7.1 shows how controlling fits in with the rest of the management process. *Planning* sets the directions and allocates resources. *Organizing* brings people and material resources together in working combinations. *Leading* inspires people to best utilize these resources. *Controlling* sees to it that the right things happen, in the right way, and at the right time. It helps ensure that the performance contributions of individuals and groups are consistent with strategic and operational plans. It helps ensure that performance accomplishments throughout an organization are well integrated in means–ends fashion. And it helps ensure that people comply with organizational policies and procedures.

STEPS IN THE CONTROL PROCESS

The control process, as shown in *Figure 7.2*, involves four steps: (1) establish objectives and standards; (2) measure actual performance; (3) compare results with objectives and standards; and (4) take corrective action as needed.

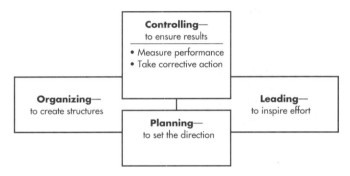

Figure 7.1 The role of controlling in the management process.

Figure 7.2 Four steps in management control.

Step 1: Establishing Objectives and Standards

The control process begins when performance objectives and standards are set through planning. The objectives provide the performance targets and the standards provide the yardstick for assessing actual accomplishments. Two types of standards can be used for this purpose. **Output standards** measure results in terms of performance quantity, quality, cost, or time. Examples include percentage error rate, dollar deviation from budgeted expenditures, and the number of units produced or customers serviced in a time period. **Input standards,** by contrast, measure effort in terms of the amount of work expended in task performance. They are used in situations where outputs are difficult or expensive to measure. Examples include conformance to rules and procedures, efficiency in the use of resources, and work attendance or punctuality.

● An **output standard** measures performance results in terms of quantity, quality, cost, or time.

● An **input standard** measures work efforts that go into a performance task.

Step 2: Measuring Actual Performance

The second step of the control process is to measure actual performance. The measurement must be accurate enough to spot significant differences between what is really taking place and what was originally planned. A common failure in organizations is an unwillingness or inability to rigorously measure performance. Often, this involves a reluctance by managers to specifically assess the accomplishments of other people at work. Yet without measurement, effective control is not possible. Managers need to get comfortable with the act of measurement and they need to be consistent in doing it. When Linda Sanford was appointed head of IBM's sales force, for example, she came with an admirable performance record during a 22-year career with the company. And she was known for walking around the factory just to see "at the end of the day how many machines were going out of the back dock." [2]

Step 3: Comparing Results with Objectives and Standards

Step three in the control process is to compare measured performance with objectives and standards. This establishes whether or not there is a need for corrective action. This step can be expressed as the following *control equation:*

$$\text{Need for Action} = \text{Desired Performance} - \text{Actual Performance}$$

The control equation can be applied in an *historical comparison* that uses past performance as a standard for evaluating current performance.[3] It can be based on *relative comparison* that uses the performance achievements of other persons, work units, or organizations as evaluation benchmarks. Or, it can be an *engineering comparison* that uses standards set scientifically through such methods as time and motion studies.

Step 4: Taking Corrective Action

● **Management by exception** focuses managerial attention on substantial differences between actual and desired performance.

The last step in the control process is to take any action necessary to correct or improve future performance. This allows for a judicious use of **management by exception**—the practice of giving priority attention to situations that show the greatest need for action. This approach can save valuable time, energy, and other resources, while allowing all efforts to be concentrated on the areas of greatest need.

Two types of exceptions may be encountered. In a *problem situation* actual performance is below the standard. The reasons for this performance deficiency must be understood. This allows for corrective action to restore performance to the desired level. In an *opportunity situation* actual performance is above the standard. The reasons for this extraordinary performance must also be understood. This allows for action to continue the higher level of accomplishment in the future.

EFFECTIVE CONTROLS

One of the problems with the control process is that many managers are too busy and/or unwilling to follow it. They make a decision, take action and then forget about it as they go on to other tasks. The best managers, by contrast, are proactive and positive in applying the control process to full advantage. Rather than simply assuming that everything is working out as intended, they make sure that things are going right.

Effective controls in organizations share the following characteristics:

Characteristics of effective control systems

- *Controls should be strategic and results oriented.* They should support strategic plans and focus on significant activities that make a real difference to the organization.
- *Controls should be understandable.* They should support decision making by presenting data in understandable terms; they should not involve complex reports and hard-to-understand statistics.
- *Controls should encourage self-control.* They should allow for mutual trust, good communication, and participation among everyone involved.

- *Controls should be timely and exception oriented.* They should report deviations quickly, lending insight into why a performance gap exists and what might be done to correct it.
- *Controls should be positive in nature.* They should emphasize their contribution to development, change, and improvement; they should deemphasize their role in penalties and reprimands.
- *Controls should be fair and objective.* They should be considered impartial and accurate by everyone; they should be respected for one fundamental purpose—performance enhancement
- *Controls should be flexible.* They should leave room for individual judgment and they should be modified to fit new circumstances as they arise.[4]

At Bell Atlantic, senior-level executives specifically monitor corporate performance on the top 20 to 30 priorities. In this way, objectives are revisited, results analyzed, new conditions taken into account, and plans and activities adjusted to maximize performance. Such an independent review helps to ensure that the control process operates even at the highest levels of the organization.[5]

TYPES OF CONTROLS

Three major types of managerial controls are found in organizations—feedforward, concurrent, and feedback control.[6] Shown in *Figure 7.3*, each is relevant to a different phase of the organization's input–throughput–output cycle of activities. And importantly, each has an important role to play in the quest for long-term productivity and high performance.

Feedforward Controls

The controls that are accomplished before a work activity begins are called **feedforward controls,** or *preliminary controls.* They ensure that objectives are clear, that proper directions are established, and that the right resources are available to accomplish them. By making sure that the stage is properly set for high performance, feedforward controls are preventive in nature. They help eliminate later problems by asking an important but often neglected question: "What needs to be done before we begin?" A good example is the inportance of quality resources in feedback control. At McDonald's preliminary control of food ingredients plays a major role in the firm's quality program. The company requires that suppliers

- A **feedforward control** ensures that the right directions and resources are available before work begins.

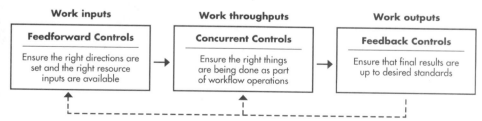

Work inputs	Work throughputs	Work outputs
Feedforward Controls	**Concurrent Controls**	**Feedback Controls**
Ensure the right directions are set and the right resource inputs are available	Ensure the right things are being done as part of workflow operations	Ensure that final results are up to desired standards

Figure 7.3   Three types of controls: feedforward, concurrent, and feedback controls.

Browser

Go to: http://www.wiley.com/college/schermerhorn

 THE WALL STREET JOURNAL. **WILEY**

IN PRACTICE

Controlling is defined as "measuring performance and taking action to ensure desired results." Grades are one means of controlling performance in higher education. Similarly, business establishments use a variety of performance outcomes to measure results.

The Interactive Journal provides you excellent "benchmarking" data by which to compare results from a wide range of industries and firms.

Select **Money and Investing** from the menu in the left-hand of the Front Section. This section focuses on performance results for the complete list of stocks and bonds. Articles identify which firms are doing well and which need to improve.

The text notes the importance of compensation and benefits systems for employee control. Check out the Web site at the Society for Human Resource Management (http://www.shrm.org/hrlinks/comp.htm) for a list of benefit sites.

Use the **Search** mechanism under **Journal Atlas** in the left-hand menu wsj.com to search "pay for performance" and "executive pay" to determine what articles have been written regarding those subjects.

Dowjones.com

Your subscription to the Interactive Journal also entitles you access to additional Dow Jones publications. Under **More Dow Jones Sites** in the left-hand menu, click on **dowjones.com.** This site searches over 2000 business Web sites for the most up-to-date news items available.

Click on the **Go to Industries Pages** drop-down box to search for information on a wide variety of industries. Under the **Business Search** box, type in "pay for performance" (with the quotation marks) to see stories and press releases on this subject.

Dowjones.com limits its search to business-related Web sites, thereby increasing your chances to find relevant business infor-

mation. It serves as a valuable complement to the Interactive Journal as a source of business news.

DELIVERABLES:

Using the objectives you identified in Chapter 4 (if you did not do that assignment, begin by identifying 3–5 objectives for yourself), develop a list of specific measurements that you can use to evaluate the results.

Be as specific as possible, including dates, amounts, numbers, and percentages. The measures should provide a useful target upon which to measure your results.

DISCUSSION QUESTIONS:

1. What examples of "controls" are evident in your family life? Your work?

2. Does it appear that "pay-for-performance" schemes work as intended?

3. What performance measures do firms use to determine their performance?

 *Note: The underscored words/phrases in the Interactive Journal feature indicate Internet links provided in the online versions. See the *Introducing Management* Web site at www.wiley.com/college/schermerhorn.

of its hamburger buns produce them to exact specifications, covering everything from texture to uniformity of color. Even in overseas markets, the firm works hard to develop local suppliers that can offer dependable quality.[7]

Concurrent Controls

The controls that focus on what actually happens during the work process are called **concurrent controls,** or *steering controls*. They monitor ongoing operations and activities as they take place to make sure things are being done according to plan. The key question is, "Now that we've started, what can we do to improve things before we finish?" Taking McDonald's again as an example, ever-present shift leaders provide concurrent control through direct supervision. They constantly observe what is taking place even while helping out with the work. They are trained to intervene immediately when something is not done right and to correct things on the spot.

● A **concurrent control** focuses on what happens during the work process.

Feedback Controls

The controls that take place after work is completed are called **feedback controls** or *postaction controls*. They focus on the results achieved rather than on work inputs and activities. They ask the question "Now that we are finished, how well did we do?" Restaurants, for example, ask how you like a meal . . . after it is eaten; a final exam grade tells you how well you performed . . . after the course is over; a budget summary informs managers of any cost overruns . . . after a project is completed. In these and other similar cases the feedback gained is most useful for improving things in the future. Employees at a McDonald's restaurant never know when a corporate evaluator may stop in to sample the food and the service. When this happens, however, the evaluator provides feedback with the goal of improving future operations.

● A **feedback control** takes place after an action is completed.

CONTROL STRATEGIES

Managers have two broad options with respect to control. First, they can rely on people to exercise self-control. This strategy of **internal control** allows motivated individuals and groups to exercise self-discipline in fulfilling job expectations.[8] Second, managers can take direct action to control the behavior of others. This is a strategy of **external control** that occurs through personal supervision and the use of formal administrative systems. Organizations with effective controls typically use both strategies to good advantage. Importantly, the new workplace is rich with a renewed emphasis on internal or self-control. This is consistent with trends toward more participation, empowerment, and employee involvement.

● **Internal control** occurs through self-discipline and self-control.

● **External control** occurs through direct supervision or administrative systems.

ORGANIZATIONAL CONTROL SYSTEMS

Each component in an organization's control systems should contribute to maintaining predictably high levels of performance. At the same time that internal control is encouraged and supported, external control should be appropriate and rigorous.

Sun Microsystems posts plastic laminated instructions by each workstation used by temporary workers who fill in for fulltimers. The instructions help ensure that the work gets done the same way. This type of quality safeguard is typical in organizations that have ISO 9000 certification. Sun's worldwide operations vice president believes in the standard as a requirement in the global marketplace. According to him, "Among ISO's strengths are that it requires you to do what you say you're going to do." One of the things ISO requires is the monitoring of customer complaints. Sun established an on-line system to track product defects found anywhere by an employee or customer. Sun wants its own suppliers to have ISO certification—just another form of quality assurance for this maker of network computer systems.[9]

MANAGEMENT PROCESS CONTROLS

The discipline of the management process itself facilitates control. In planning, *control via strategy and objectives* occurs when work behaviors are initially directed toward the right end results. When performance goals are clearly set and understood, lack of performance because of poor direction in one's work is less likely to occur. *Control via policies and procedures* operates in similar ways. To the extent that good policies and procedures exist to guide behavior, an organization's members are more likely to act uniformly on important matters. *Control via learning* occurs when past experience is systematically considered and incorporated into future strategies, objectives, policies, and procedures.

Management control is also facilitated by good organizing. *Control by selection and training* occurs when capable people are hired and given the ongoing training needed to perform their jobs at high levels of accomplishment. The closer the match between individual skills and job requirements, the less need there is for external control and the greater the opportunity for internal control. *Control via performance appraisal* occurs when individual performance is assessed and evaluated to ensure high performance results. This also helps to identify areas where training and development is needed. *Control via job design and work structures* operates in similar fashion. It puts people in jobs designed to best fit their talents. When all jobs are well coordinated in workflows and operations, this structures activities and adds substantially to control.

Leadership contributes to *control through performance modeling*. This occurs as leaders set the examples so that workers have good models to follow in their job activities. *Control by performance norms* occurs when team or group members share commitments to high performance standards and reinforce one another's efforts to meet them. *Control via organization culture* occurs in similar fashion when core values add a shared sense of meaning and adds purpose throughout the organization.

EMPLOYEE DISCIPLINE SYSTEMS

Absenteeism . . . tardiness . . . sloppy work . . . , the list of possible misbehaviors in the workplace can go on to even more extreme actions—falsifying records . . . sexual harassment . . . embezzlement, and more. All are examples of behaviors that can and should be formally addressed in employee discipline systems. **Discipline** is the act of influencing behavior through reprimand. Ideally, the use of discipline in managerial control is handled in a fair, consistent, and systematic way.

Progressive discipline ties reprimands to the severity and frequency of misbehavior. Under such a system, penalties for employees vary according to how significant the inappropriate behavior is and how often it occurs. The goal is to achieve compliance with organizational expectations through the least extreme reprimand possible. However, the system should still be strict and rigorous. For example, the progressive discipline guidelines of one university state: "The level of disciplinary action shall increase with the level of severity of behavior engaged in and based on whether the conduct is of a repetitive nature." In this particular case, the ultimate penalty of "discharge" is reserved for the most severe behaviors (e.g., any felony crime) or for continual infractions of a less severe nature (e.g., being continually late for work and failing to respond to a series of written reprimands and/or suspensions).

Managers must also be comfortable and fair in exercising discipline as needed on a case-by-case basis. One way to develop a consistent personal approach to disciplinary situations is to remember the "hot stove rules" of discipline. They begin with a simple rule: "When a stove is hot, don't touch it." We also know that when this rule is violated, you get burned—immediately, consistently, but usually not beyond the possibility of repair. Six "hot stove rules" for using reprimands in disciplinary action are described in the accompanying *Manager's Notepad 7.1.*[10]

Discipline is the act of influencing behavior through reprimand.

Progressive discipline ties reprimands to the severity and frequency of misbehavior.

MANAGER'S NOTEPAD 7.1

"HOT STOVE RULES" OF EMPLOYEE DISCIPLINE

- *A reprimand should be immediate:* A hot stove burns the first time you touch it.
- *A reprimand should be directed toward someone's actions, not their personality:* A hot stove doesn't hold grudges, doesn't try to humiliate people, and doesn't accept excuses.
- *A reprimand should be consistently applied:* A hot stove burns anyone who touches it, and it does so every time.
- *A reprimand should be informative:* A hot stove lets a person know what to do to avoid getting burned in the future—"Don't touch."
- *A reprimand should occur in a supportive setting:* A hot stove conveys warmth but also operates with an inflexible rule—"Don't touch."
- *A reprimand should support realistic rules:* The don't-touch-a-hot-stove rule isn't a power play, a whim, or an emotion of the moment; it is a necessary rule of reason.

INFORMATION AND FINANCIAL CONTROLS

When resource utilization is considered from the standpoint of managerial control, the use of information in the financial analysis of firm or organizational performance is critical. The pressure is ever present today for all organizations to use their resources well and to perform with maximum efficiency.

For control purposes managers should be able to understand the following important financial aspects of organizational performance: (1) *Liquidity*—ability to generate cash to pay bills; (2) *Leverage*—ability to earn more in returns than the cost of debt; (3) *Asset management*—ability to use resources efficiently and operate at minimum cost; and (4) *Profitability*—ability to earn revenues greater than costs. These financial aspects of organizational performance are typically assessed using a variety of financial ratios. Importantly, the ratios can be used to initially set goals and then track actual performance. They can also provide for historical comparisons within the firm or in external benchmarking relative to industry performance. A number of popular financial ratios are listed here along with up [⇧] and down [⇩] arrows showing their preferred directions.

Popular financial ratios

- *Liquidity Ratios:*
  [⇧] Current ratio = Current assets/Current liabilities
  [⇧] Acid test = (Current assets − inventory)/Current liabilities
- *Leverage Ratios:*
  [⇩] Debt ratio = Total debts/Total assets
  [⇧] Times interest earned = Profits before interest and taxes/Total interest
- *Asset Management Ratios:*
  [⇧] Inventory turnover = Sales/Average inventory
  [⇧] Total asset turnover = Sales/Total assets
- *Profitability Ratios:*
  [⇧] Net margin = Net profit after taxes/Sales
  [⇧] Return on investment (ROI) = Net profit after taxes/Total assets

OPERATIONS MANAGEMENT AND CONTROL

Control is an essential part of operations management, where the emphasis is always on utilizing people, resources, and technology to the best advantage. Among the important aspects of operations management today, purchasing control, inventory control, and—of course, quality control, deserve special attention.

PURCHASING CONTROL

In today's economy the rising costs of materials seem to be a fact of life. Controlling these costs through efficient purchasing management is an important productivity tool. Like an individual, a thrifty organization must be concerned about how much it pays for what it buys. In respect to the purchasing function, an AT&T vice president says, "Nothing we do is more important." [11]

Management Across Functions

MANUFACTURING

Lack of Control Costly for Coke

The crisis was devasting for Coke. Hundreds of European consumers of the firm's products became ill and governments forced retailers to stop selling Coke. At the bottom of it all was contaminated carbon dioxide, the gas that gives Coke its "fizz." The bad CO_2 was inadvertently used at a Coke bottler in Antwerp, Belgium. But the real problem was poor control. Standard quality control procedures weren't followed—the plant was supposed to receive certificates of analysis from its supplier of the gas. It didn't. Also the plant was supposed to conduct its own analysis. It didn't. The result was a public relations disaster. Some 14 million cases of Coke were recalled in five countries. And if that wasn't all, quality control failures elsewhere also turned up. Fungicide used on wooden pallets rubbed off on cans at a French plant and caused a bad smell. Consumers complained it made them ill. When the facts were finally clear, Coke's top scientist Anton Amon issued strict instructions regarding enforcement of the required certificate of analysis from gas suppliers and the self-testing by each plant. He also declared that no treated wooden pallets were to be used and that all contaminated pallets were to be destroyed. The quality-conscious company was reasserting its commitment to quality control in all manufacturing stages—from point of supply through the production process to the point of delivery.[12]

The following trends are evident in purchasing control. To *leverage buying power* more organizations are centralizing purchasing to allow buying in volume. They are committing to a *small number of suppliers* with whom they can negotiate special contracts, gain quality assurances, and get preferred service. They are also finding ways to work together in *supplier-purchaser partnerships* so they can operate in ways that allow each partner to contain its costs. An example would be a parts supplier that keeps a warehouse in a customer's factory, and then stocks it according to bimonthly order forecasts. The customer provides the space, while the supplier does the rest. The customer lowers its purchasing costs and gains preferred service; the supplier gains an exclusive contract and more sales volume.

INVENTORY CONTROL

Organizations maintain inventories of raw materials, work in process, and/or finished goods. They keep them to smooth out periods of excess or undercapacity, meet periods of unusual demand, and/or achieve economies from large-scale purchases. But because inventories represent costs, they must be well managed. The basic principle of inventory control is to make sure that it is just the right size for the tasks at hand.

● The **economic order quantity (EOQ)** method orders a fixed number of items every time an inventory level falls to a predetermined point.

● **Just-in-time scheduling (JIT)** schedules materials to arrive at a work station or facility "just in time" to be used.

Some inventory controls are quantitative and even computerized. For example, the **economic order quantity (EOQ)** is a method of inventory control that involves ordering a fixed number of items every time an inventory level falls to a predetermined point. When this point is reached, a decision is automatically made (more and more often now by computer) to place a standard order. The objective is always to have new inventory arrive just as old inventory runs out. This minimizes the total cost of the inventory.

Another approach to inventory control is **just-in-time scheduling** or "**JIT**." Made popular by the productivity of Japanese industry, JIT systems try to reduce costs and improve workflow by scheduling materials to arrive at a work station or facility "just in time" to be used. This minimizes carrying costs since almost no inventories are maintained—materials are ordered or components produced only as needed. *Kanban*, for example, is a Japanese word for the piece of paper that accompanies a bin of parts. When a worker first takes parts from a new bin, the *kanban* is routed back to the supplier and serves as an order for new parts. JIT systems not only reduce costs in many instances, but they can also help to maximize the use of space and improve the quality of results.

QUALITY CONTROL

● **Quality control** involves checking processes, material, products, or services to ensure that they meet high standards.

The theme of total quality management has been with us since Chapter 1. In the context of managerial control systems, **quality control** involves checking processes, materials, products, and services to ensure that they meet high standards. This responsibility applies to all aspects of production and operations, from the selection of raw materials and supplies right down to the last task performed on the finished good or service.

Consider the case of an engine crankshaft for an automobile. These crankshafts are first molded and then machined to the correct dimensions. Because of variation in the parts, wear on the equipment, and/or differences in the skills of machine operators, not all crankshafts will have exactly the same dimensions after machining. That's not completely bad in itself because the crankshaft will still perform properly as long as its dimensions are within certain limits. The quality of crankshafts might be checked by measuring each one as it is completed. If the diameter of a crankshaft is within the control limits, it passes; otherwise, it fails. An occasional crankshaft falling outside the limits would not be cause for managerial concern; it would simply be rejected. However, several rejects might mean that the machining process is out of control and requires correction.

This same quality control can be accomplished through *statistical quality control*, the use of statistical techniques to improve operations quality. In such cases, instead of checking every crankshaft, whole batches are checked by taking random samples. Because of the inherent difficulty of carefully inspecting quality on a item-by-item basis, large complex operations accomplish most quality control in this way.

When statistics and quality come together in a systematic quality control program, great things can happen. At General Electric, for example, the firm's quest for competitive advantage in global markets is driven by a quality program known as "Six Sigma."[14] This program commits GE to always delivering quality goods within six standard deviations of a desired result. This means that statistically the firm's quality performance will tolerate no more than 3.4 defects per million—a perfection rate of 99.9997 percent! As tough as it sounds, six sigma is a recognized standard for quality and control in the new workplace.

INTEGRATED PLANNING AND CONTROLLING

When planning is done well, control gets better—and vice-versa. Without good planning, control lacks a framework for performance measurement. Without good control, planning lacks the follow-through needed to ensure results. A useful technique that helps to integrate planning and controlling is **management by objectives,** or **MBO** for short.

● **Management by objectives (MBO)** is a process of joint objective setting between a superior and subordinate.

WHAT IS MANAGEMENT BY OBJECTIVES?

Formally defined, MBO is a structured process of regular communication in which a supervisor and subordinate jointly set performance objectives for the subordinate and review results accomplished.[15] MBO requires a formal agreement between the supervisor and subordinate concerning: (1) the subordinate's performance objectives for a given time period, (2) the plans through which they will be accomplished, (3) standards for measuring whether or not they have been accomplished and (4) procedures for reviewing performance results.

The way MOB might be used in a work team is illustrated in *Figure 7.4.* Note that the team leader and team member *jointly* establish plans and *jointly* control results in any good MBO action framework. They agree on the high-priority performance objectives for the member along with a timetable for their accomplishment and the criteria to be used in evaluating results.

A major advantage of management by objectives is that the process clearly focuses a person's work efforts on the most important tasks and objectives. Another is that it focuses a supervisor's work efforts on areas of support that can truly help the individual meet the agreed-upon objectives. Good advice is available on what to do and what not to do if MBO is to be used to maximum advantage.[16] Things to avoid doing in MBO include tying it to pay, focusing too much attention on only those objectives that are easily quantified, requiring excessive paperwork, and having supervisors simply *tell* subordinates their objectives. On the other hand, *Manager's Notepad 7.2* offers six steps for making sure MBO succeeds in practice.

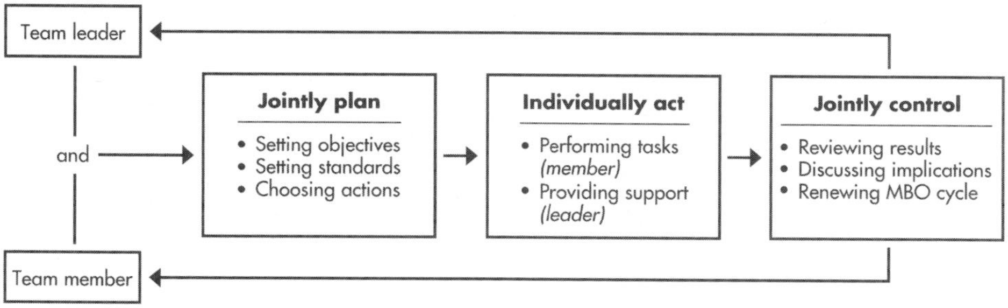

Figure 7.4   The management by objectives framework for integrated planning and controlling in a work team.

MANAGER'S NOTEPAD 7.2

STEPS TO SUCCESSFUL MBO

Step 1. An individual lists key performance objectives for a time period with target dates for accomplishing them.

Step 2. Objectives are reviewed and discussed with the supervisor, and an agreed-upon set of objectives is documented.

Step 3. The supervisor and subordinate meet regularly to review progress and make revisions or update objectives as needed.

Step 4. At a specified time, such as after six months, the individual prepares a "performance report" that lists major accomplishments and comments on discrepancies between expected and actual results.

Step 5. This self-appraisal is discussed with the supervisor with an emphasis on its implications for future performance.

Step 6. A new set of objectives is established for the next time period, as in Step 1, and the MBO cycle begins anew.

PERFORMANCE OBJECTIVES

Performance objectives are clearly essential to the MBO process. But the ways objectives are specified and established will influence how well MBO works. Three types of objectives may be specified in an MBO contract. *Improvement objectives* document intentions for improving performance in a specific way and with respect to a specific factor. An example is "to reduce quality rejects by 10 percent." *Personal development objectives* pertain to personal growth activities, often those resulting in expanded job knowledge or skills. An example is "to learn the latest version of a computer spreadsheet package." Some MBO contracts also include *maintenance objectives*, which formally express intentions to maintain performance at an existing level. In many organizations, the MBO process emphasizes improvement and personal growth objectives. In all cases, performance objectives are written and formally agreed to by both the superior and subordinate. They also meet the following *criteria of a good performance objective:*

Criteria of a good performance objective →

1. *Specific*—targets a key result to be accomplished.
2. *Time defined*—identifies a date for achieving results.
3. *Challenging*—offers a realistic and attainable challenge.
4. *Measureable*—is as specific and quantitative as possible.

One of the more difficult aspects of MBO relates to the last criterion—the need to state performance objectives as specifically and quantitatively as possible. Ideally, this occurs as agreement on a *measurable end product*, for example, "to reduce housekeeping supply costs by 5 percent by the end of the fiscal year." But some jobs, particularly managerial ones, involve performance areas that are hard to quantify. Rather than abandon MBO in such cases, it is often possible to agree on performance objectives that are stated as *verifiable work activities*. The accomplishment of the activities can then serve as an indicator of progress under the performance objective. An example is "to improve communications with my subordinates in the next 3 months by holding weekly group meetings." Whereas it can be difficult to measure "improved communications," it is easy to document whether or not the "weekly group meetings" have been held.

INTERNAL CONTROL AND SELF MANAGEMENT

Internal control, as described earlier is self-control. It is exercised by people who are motivated to take charge of their own behavior on the job. Of course, people are most likely to do this when they participate in setting performance objectives and their standards of measurement. This, of course, is what the notion of management by objectives is all about. Given clear objectives to which they are commited, people are likely to manage themselves in pursuit of performance excellence. MBO provides just this opportunity. Because the MBO involves direct face-to-face communication between supervisor and subordinate, it contributes to relationship building. Because MBO provides structured opportunities for people to participate in decisions that affect their work, it is empowering and motivating. Because it creates enthusiasm to fulfill one's performance obligations, MBO encourages self-management rather than external control.[17]

None of this advice is lost on today's best managers. Although they may describe what they are doing by different names, it has a common thread that is consistent with the MBO concept. If you want high performance from individual contributors, you must hire the best people, work with them to set challenging performance objectives, give them the best possible support, and hold them accountable for results.

SUMMARY

How Do Controls Work?

- Controlling—the fourth management function, is the process of monitoring performance and taking corrective action as needed.

- The four steps in the control process are (1) establish performance objectives, (2) measure actual performance, (3) compare results with objectives, and (4) take necessary action to resolve problems or explore opportunities.

- Feedforward controls are accomplished before a work activity begins; concurrent controls monitor ongoing operations and activities, feedback controls take place after an action is completed.

- External control is accomplished through direct supervision and formal administrative systems; internal control occurs as individuals exercise self-discipline in their work.

How Do Organizational Systems Assist In Control?

- Control through the management process occurs when the management functions of planning, organizing, and leading are well implemented.

- Discipline, the act of influencing behavior through reprimand, is an essential part of control in organizations.
- Progressive discipline systems link reprimands to the severity and frequency of any misbehaviors.
- Information and financial controls are assisted by useful financial ratios addressing issues of liquidity, leverage, asset management, and profitability.

How Can Operations Management Improve Control?

- The economic order quanity (EOQ) method controls inventories by ordering a fixed number of items every time the inventory level falls to a given point.
- Just-in-time scheduling (JIT) attempts to reduce costs and improve workflows by scheduling materials to arrive at a work station "just in time" to be used.

How Can Planning and Controlling Be Integrated?

- In Management by Objectives supervisors work together with their subordinates to "jointly" set performance objectives and review performance results.
- The MBO process is a highly participative form of integrated planning and controlling.
- MBO should clarify performance objectives for the subordinate and also identify support needed from the supervisor.
- The full benefits of MBO for individuals and organizations will be realized only when the process is truly mutual and participative.

KEY TERMS

Concurrent control (p. 113)

Controlling (p. 108)

Discipline (p. 115)

Economic order quantity (EOQ) (p. 118)

External control (p. 113)

Feedback control (p. 113)

Feedforward control (p. 111)

Input standard (p. 109)

Internal control (p. 113)

Just-in-time scheduling (JIT) (p. 118)

Management by exception (p. 110)

Management by objectives (p. 119)

Output standard (p. 109)

Progressive discipline (p. 115)

Quality control (p. 118)

SELF-TEST

Take the interactive Self-Test for this chapter on the Schermerhorn Web Site

Chapter Eight

Organizing—To Create Structures

PLANNING AHEAD—
Chapter 8 Study Questions

- What is organizing as a management function?
- What are the traditional organization structures?
- What are the new developments in organization structures?
- What organizing trends are changing the workplace?

STRUCTURES MUST SUPPORT STRATEGIES

Management scholar and consultant Peter Drucker describes the brokerage firm Edward Jones "the Wal-Mart of Wall Street." He describes the firm as having an innovative structure that directly supports its strategy. The firm, like Wal-Mart, established itself in rural America. With a strong core surrounded by largely independent satellite units, Drucker likens it to a "confederation of highly autonomous entrepreneurial units bound together by a highly central-ized core of values and services." A values-driven commitment to the customers is a common bond among the firm's brokers. They have the freedom to deal with customers in their own way and in their small-town settings. The firm is now testing its face-to-face and customer-oriented brokerage strategy with ex-pansion into the suburbs of large cities. Of course, it's a competitive business. Brokerage giant Merrill Lynch is starting a new push of its own—to open small brokerage offices in small rural towns.[1]

By building a well-focused yet market-responsive structure, Edward Jones has established and sustained a niche in the highly competitive financial services industry. But the approach is only one among many possibilities. Organizations in all industries are trying a variety of new forms or structures in the quest for productivity and competitive advantage. Some follow traditional patterns, while others experiment with nontraditional directions, emphasizing teams, networks, and even "boundaryless" organizations. Athough their forms vary according to the situation, the vanguard organizations—those that outperform the rest, always share a common emphasis. They are superb at supporting employees, responding to client or customer needs, staying flexible in dealing with a dynamic environment, and giving continual attention to quality improvements.

ORGANIZING AS A MANAGEMENT FUNCTION

● **Organizing** is the process of arranging people and resources to work toward a common purpose.

Formally defined, **organizing** is the process of arranging people and other resources to work together to accomplish a goal. It involves both dividing up the tasks to be performed and coordinating results to achieve a common purpose. *Figure 8.1* shows the central role organizing plays in the management process. Once plans are created, the manager's task is to see to it that they are carried out. Given a clear mission, core values, objectives, and strategy, organizing begins the process of implementation. It identifies who is to do what, who is in charge of whom, and how different people and parts of the organization relate to one another. The challenge is to choose the best form to fit the demands of a given situation.[2]

WHAT IS ORGANIZATION STRUCTURE?

● **Organization structure** is a system of tasks, reporting relationships, and communication linkages.

The **organization structure** is the system of tasks, workflows, reporting relationships, and communication channels that link together the diverse parts of an organization. Any structure should both allocate tasks and provide for the coordination of performance results. Unfortunately, it is easier to talk about good structures than it is to actually create them. This is why you often read and hear about *restructuring*, the process of changing an organization's structure in an attempt to improve performance.

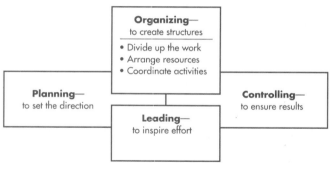

Figure 8.1 Organizing viewed in relationship with the other management functions.

FORMAL AND INFORMAL STRUCTURES

You may know the concept of structure best in the form of an *organization chart*. A typical organization chart identifies by diagram key positions and job titles within an organization. It also shows the lines of authority and communication between them.[3] This is the **formal structure,** the intended or official structure, and it represents the way the organization is intended to function.

Behind every formal structure typically lies an **informal structure.** This is a "shadow" organization made up of the unofficial, but often critical, working relationships between organizational members. If the informal structure could be drawn, it would show who talks to and interacts regularly with whom, regardless of their formal titles and relationships. The lines of the informal structure would cut across levels and move from side to side. They would show people meeting for coffee, exercise groups, and in friendship cliques, among other possibilities.

- **Formal structure** is the official structure of the organization.

- **Informal structure** is the set of unofficial relationships among an organization's members.

When the Center for Workforce Development conducted a study at a Siemens factory in North Carolina, the focus was on informal learning. What they found was that the cafeteria was a "hotbed" of learning as workers shared ideas, problems, and solutions with one another over snacks and meals. Says the Director of Training for Siemens, Barry Blystone: "The assumption was made that this was chitchat, talking about the golf game. But there was a whole lot of work activity." For Blystone and others the lesson is to mobilize informal learning opportunities as a resource for organizational improvement.[5]

HOW STRUCTURES WORK

No organization can be fully understood without gaining insight into the formal structures as well as the informal ones.[4] *Manager's Notepad 8.1* identifies some of the things that you can learn from an organization chart. But, the informal or shadow organization counts too. Because of the complex nature of organizations and constantly shifting performance demands, informal structures can be very helpful in getting needed work accomplished. Through the emergent and spontaneous relationships of informal structures, people gain access to interpersonal networks of emotional support and friendship that satisfy important social needs. They also benefit from contacts with others who can help them better perform their jobs and tasks. Importantly, valuable learning and knowledge sharing takes place as people interact informally throughout the work day and in a wide variety of unstructured situations.

Of course, informal structures also have potential disadvantages. They can be susceptible to rumor, carry inaccurate information, breed resistance to change, and even divert work efforts from important objectives. People who feel left out of informal groupings may become dissatisfied. Some American managers of Japanese firms, for example, have complained about being excluded from the "shadow cabinet"—an informal group of Japanese executives who hold the real power to get things done.[6]

> ### MANAGER'S NOTEPAD 8.1
>
> #### WHAT YOU CAN LEARN FROM AN ORGANIZATION CHART
>
> - *The division of work:* Positions and titles show how work responsibilities are assigned.
> - *Supervisory relationships:* Lines among positions show who reports to whom.
> - *Communication channels:* Lines among positions show formal communication channels.
> - *Major subunits:* Positions reporting to a common manager are identified as a group.
> - *Levels of management:* Layers of management from top to bottom are shown.

TRADITIONAL ORGANIZATION STRUCTURES

Organizations operate with a division of labor that allows people to specialize and become expert in certain jobs or tasks. Given this, however, decisions must be made on how to group people into teams or departments and then link them in a coordinated fashion within the larger organization.[7] Traditional approaches for accomplishing this include the functional, divisional, and matrix structures.

FUNCTIONAL STRUCTURES

● A **functional structure** groups together people with similar skills who perform similar tasks.

In **functional structures,** people with similar skills and performing similar tasks are grouped together. The example in *Figure 8.2* shows a business organized by the functions of marketing, finance, production, and human resources. In this functional structure, manufacturing problems are the responsibility of the manufacturing vice president, marketing problems are the province of the marketing vice president, and so on. Members of each function work within their areas of expertise. If each function does its jobs well, the expectation is that the business will operate successfully. The major advantages of a functional structure include:

Advantages of functional structures

- Economies of scale with efficient use of resources.
- Task assignments consistent with expertise and training.
- High-quality technical problem solving.
- In-depth training and skill development within functions.
- Clear career paths within functions.

● The **functional chimneys problem** is a lack of communication and coordination across functions.

The very strong focus on functions, functional expertise, and functional careers sometimes creates problems for organizations using this type of structure. The **functional chimneys problem** appears as a lack of communication, coor-

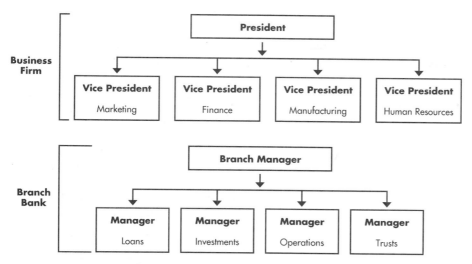

Figure 8.2 Functional structures in a business, and branch bank.

dination, and problem solving among functions. Here members of functional groups develop self-centered and narrow viewpoints, become uncooperative with other groups, and otherwise lose the total systems perspective. When problems occur with another function, they are too often referred up to higher levels for resolution rather than being addressed directly at the level of action. This slows decision making and problem solving, and can result in a loss of competitive advantage. Other problems with functional structures involve the blurring of responsibility for cost containment, product or service quality and timeliness, and innovation in response to environmental changes.

DIVISIONAL STRUCTURES

A second traditional alternative is the **divisional structure.** It groups together people who work on the same product or process, serve similar customers, and/or are located in the same area or geographical region. As illustrated in *Figure 8.3*, divisional structures are common in complex organizations that have multiple and differentiated products and services, pursue diversified strategies, and/or operate in several competitive environments.[8] The potential advantages of divisional structures include the following:

- More flexibility in responding to environmental changes.
- Improved coordination across functional departments.
- Clear points of responsibility for product or service delivery.
- Expertise focused on specific customers, products, and regions.
- Greater ease in changing size by adding or deleting divisions.

Divisional structures also have potential disadvantages. They can reduce economies of scale and increase costs through the duplication of resources and efforts across divisions. Unhealthy rivalries can emerge as divisions compete for resources and attention. Divisions may also emphasize their needs and goals rather than the best interests of the organization as a whole.

> A **divisional structure** groups together people who work on the same product, work with similar customers, or work in the same area or processes.

← Advantages of divisional structures

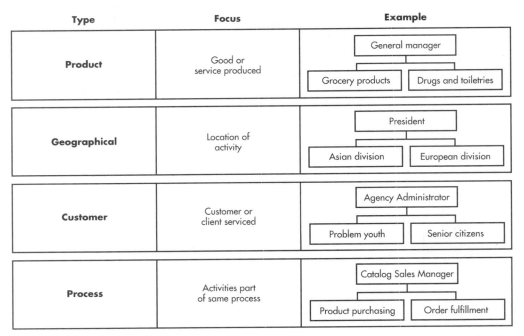

Figure 8.3 Divisional structures based on product, geography, customer, and process.

MATRIX STRUCTURES

● A **matrix structure** combines functional and divisional approaches to emphasize project or program teams.

The **matrix structure** combines elements of both the functional and divisional structures. The goal is to combine the advantages of each, while minimizing disadvantages. As shown in *Figure 8.4*, a matrix uses permanent cross-functional teams to integrate functional expertise with a divisional focus.[9] Workers in a matrix structure belong to at least two formal groups at the same time—a functional group and a product, program, or project team. They also report to two bosses—one within the function and the other within the team. The cross-functional team members work closely together to share functional expertise and information to solve problems in a timely manner. The potential advantages of matrix structures include the following:

Advantages of a matrix structure

● More interfunctional cooperation in operations.
● Increased flexibility in meeting changing demands.
● Better customer service championed by project managers.
● Better performance accountability through the project managers.
● Improved problem solving at the team level, where the best information is available.
● Improved strategic management as top managers are freed to focus on strategic issues.

Predictably, the matrix structure also has potential disadvantages. The two-boss system is susceptible to power struggles, as functional supervisors and team leaders vie with one another to exercise authority. Members of the matrix

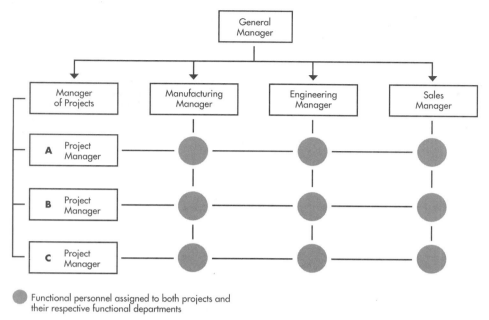

Functional personnel assigned to both projects and their respective functional departments

Figure 8.4 Matrix structure in a small multiproject business firm.

may suffer task confusion when taking orders from more than one boss. Teams may develop "groupitis" or strong loyalties that focus attention more on the team than on larger organizational goals. The use of formal team leaders in a matrix structure can also result in increased personnel costs.

DEVELOPMENTS IN ORGANIZATION STRUCTURES

The global economy and the demands of hyper-competition have managers everywhere searching for structures that can best meet ever-changing environmental challenges. Current developments emphasize integration and cross-functional teamwork, and the advantages of networking through information technology. Organizations like American Express, General Electric, and Ford are dismantling more traditional vertical structures in favor of more horizontal ones.

TEAM STRUCTURES

Teams are the building blocks of the new and more horizontal organizational forms. **Team structures** formally designate and use permanent and temporary teams extensively to accomplish tasks.[10] As illustrated in *Figure 8.5*, teams of various types work together as needed to solve problems and explore opportunities, either on a full-time or part-time basis. These are often *cross-functional teams* composed of members from different functional areas of work responsibility.[11] The intention is to break down functional chimneys, increase information sharing, and create more effective lateral relations that improve problem solving and

● A **team structure** uses permanent and temporary cross-functional teams to improve lateral relations.

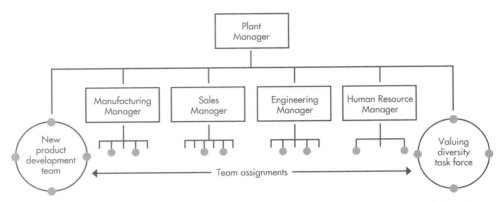

Figure 8.5 How a team structure uses cross-functional teams for improved lateral relations.

performance. At Intel, for example, most workers are assigned to one or more projects under the direction of team leaders. The traditional hierachy takes a back seat to the focus on team activities and project accomplishments. Team members feel responsible for meeting performance targets and act accordingly. Says one team member, "We report to each other."

The potential advantages of team structures begin with better communication across functions. Team assignments help to break down barriers between operating departments and can also boost morale as people from different parts of an organization get to better know one another. Because the teams focus shared knowledge and expertise on specific problems they can also improve the speed and quality of decisions in many situations. Of course, the complexities of teams and teamwork, as discussed in Chapter 14, can create *potential disadvantages* as well. These include conflicting loyalties among members to both team and functional assignments, issues of time management, and difficulties with interpersonal relations and group process.

NETWORK STRUCTURES

• A **network structure** consists of a central business core that works with networks of outside suppliers and service contractors.

Terms like "boundaryless organizations" and "virtual corporations" [12] are increasingly used to describe new organizations. They typically indicate the utilization of advanced information technology that improves linkages within an organization and with environmental elements. A good example is the **network structure** where a central organizational core is linked through "networks" of relationships with outside contractors and suppliers of essential services. Such network organizations use the latest computer and information technologies to support a shifting mix of strategic alliances and business contracts that sustain operations without the costs of having to own all components.

Figure 8.6 illustrates a network structure as it might work for an e-commerce and mail-order company selling lawn and deck furniture through the Internet and a catalog. The firm itself is very small, with a core consisting of a few full-time employees working from a central headquarters. Beyond that, it is

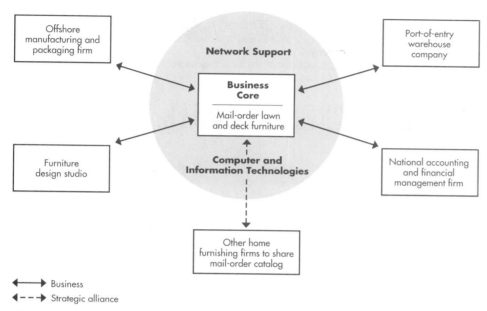

Figure 8.6 A network structure for an e-commerce and catalog-based retail business.

structured as a series of contracts and alliances. Merchandise is designed on contract with a furniture design firm; its manufacture and packaging are contracted to "offshore" companies; stock is maintained and shipped from a contract warehouse; and all of the accounting and financial details are managed on contract with an outside firm. The quarterly catalog is designed, printed, and mailed as a strategic alliance with two other firms that sell different home furnishings with a related price appeal.

The potential advantages of network structures in part derive from the creative use of technology. With the technological edge companies can operate with fewer full-time employees and less complex internal systems. They can easily develop and maintain partner linkages across great distances. The benefits of global commerce are unlocked as the Internet, and E-mail, bring international business opportunities into easy reach, and at minimum cost. Networks can also help organizations stay cost competitive through reduced overhead and increased operating efficiency. The potential disadvantages of network structures trace largely to the demands of coordinating the complex system of business relationships. If one part of the network breaks down or fails to deliver, the entire system suffers the consequences.

As information technology continues to develop network structures are growing in number and range of applications.[13] They are useful for smaller businesses and organizations, including entrepreneurial ones. They are also appropriate components in larger organizational structures. Many corporations, for example, are using network concepts internally as they outsource specialized business functions rather than maintain full-time staff to do them. A bank may contract with local firms to provide mailroom, cafeteria, and legal services; an airline might contract out customer service jobs at various airports.

Browser

Go to: http://www.wiley.com/college/schermerhorn

 THE WALL STREET JOURNAL.
WILEY

The organization that a business firm chooses has a direct impact on its ultimate performance. With the advent of the Internet, new and exciting "virtual" business forms are evolving. The Interactive Journal tracks these new organizational structures on a daily basis.

Formerly unrelated businesses are merging to form entirely new industries. Telephone/cable television, banks/brokerage houses, and Internet/Everything are a few examples.

The Internet has spawned the development of "Virtual" businesses where location is irrelevant. As such, these new businesses operate in a way entirely foreign to regular "brick-and-mortar" establishments.

Under **Tech Center, Company Profiles** provides in-depth looks at high-tech firms. Their attempts to create competitive advantages through the use of technology provide insight into leading-edge business practices.

Look under **Special Reports** in the **Resources** section of the left-hand menu to see if there

are any article series about new business forms. Also, using the **Search** link, enter "virtual" or "virtual business" to see what articles are identified.

Go to **dowjones.com** from the link in the left-hand menu under **More Dow Jones Sites.** Type "organizational structure" (with the quotation marks) in the **Business Search** window. Investigate some of the news articles and company Web sites listed to determine different organizational structures. Why do firms choose different means to structure their operations?

Chapter 8—Organizing—To Create Structures defines structuring as a "process of arranging people and other resources to work together to accomplish a goal." Perhaps the most important factor to encourage new ways of structuring companies has been technology. The Internet and new communication devices (pagers, cell phones, computers) have significantly changed the way people interact.

Firms react to these new opportunities by changing the ways

they structure their operations to take advantage of new efficiencies. They can offer better service at lower costs, and pass some of the savings on to their customers.

DELIVERABLES:

Based on the discussion in the textbook, describe the organizational structure of your academic institution. Provide suggestions as to how it might change to become more effective.

DISCUSSION QUESTIONS:

1. What examples of "informal" structures can you identify from student associations with which you are a member?

2. How has technology affected the way YOU work at college? The ways you interact with fellow students (email, video conferencing, chat rooms)?

3. How has the Internet changed the way companies interact with their suppliers; customers; employees? Give some examples from your own experience.

 *Note: The underscored words/phrases in the Interactive Journal feature indicate Internet links provided in the online versions. See the *Introducing Management* Web site at www.wiley.com/college/schermerhorn.

June Holley, president of the Appalachian Center for Economic Networks (ACEnet), uses network organization concepts to support economic development in rural America. The Athens, Ohio, center serves as a networking hub for small businesses, or microenterprises, that share expertise and connections. ACEnet offers information and business incubator support, including a large community kitchen. Some 100 area farmers and entrepreneurs have so far rented kitchen space to test new products. As they cook, they rub elbows with one another. When Chris Chmiel started experimenting with a wild local fruit, pawpaws, he ended up talking with someone from the local Casa Nueva restaurant. Now the restaurant serves "pawpaw coladas." Networking works for ACEnet. Holley says: "Poverty is due to isolation. So we set up a networking hub." [14]

ORGANIZING TRENDS IN THE MODERN WORKPLACE

In Chapter 1 the concept of the "upside-down pyramid" was introduced as an example of the new mindset in management. By putting customers on top, served by workers in the middle, who are in turn supported by managers at the bottom, this notion tries to refocus attention on the marketplace and customer needs. Although more of a concept than a depiction of a formal organization structure, such thinking is representative of forces behind new trends in how the modern workplace is organized. Among these trends is a common theme — making the adjustments needed to streamline for cost efficiency and to allow increased worker involvement in all aspects of operations.

SHORTER CHAINS OF COMMAND

A typical organization chart shows a **chain of command,** or line of authority that vertically links all positions with successively higher levels of management. When organizations grow in size, they tend to get taller as more levels of management are added to the chain of command. This increases overhead costs, adds distance in communication and limits access between top and bottom levels, and can slow decision making. These are all reasons why "tall" organizations with many levels of management are often criticized for inefficiencies and poor productivity. The *current trend* is to streamline organizations by cutting unnecessary levels of management. Flatter structures are viewed as a potential source of competitive advantage.

● The **chain of command** links all persons with successively higher levels of authority.

WIDER SPANS OF CONTROL

The **span of control** is the number of persons reporting directly to a manager. When span of control is "narrow," only a few people are directly supervised; a "wide" span of control indicates that a manager supervises many people. *Figure 8.7* shows the relationship between span of control and the number of management levels. Organizations with wider spans of control tend to be flat and have few levels of management. Those with narrow spans of control tend to be tall and have many levels of management.[15] As just discussed, tall organizations are more costly, and may be less efficient, less flexible, and less customer sensitive than flatter ones. The *current trend* is toward wider spans of control that shorten chains of command and increase worker empowerment.

● **Span of control** is the number of subordinates reporting directly to a manager.

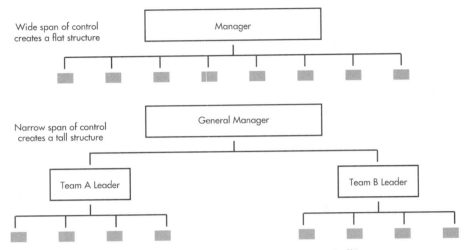

Figure 8.7   How span of control creates "flat" versus "tall" structures.

LESS UNITY OF COMMAND

Traditional management theory emphasized the *unity-of-command principle*—each person in an organization should report to one and only one supervisor. This one person/one boss notion is intended to avoid the confusion created when a person gets work directions from more than one source. The "two-boss" system of matrix structure violates unity of command. It does so on purpose and in an attempt to improve lateral relations and project teamwork. Unity of command is also less predominant in structures that use cross-functional teams or task forces. The *current trend* is for less, not more, unity of command in organizations.

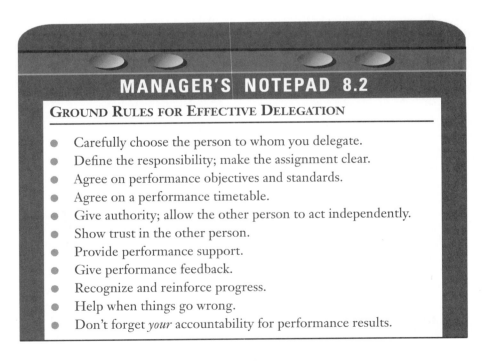

MANAGER'S NOTEPAD 8.2

GROUND RULES FOR EFFECTIVE DELEGATION

- Carefully choose the person to whom you delegate.
- Define the responsibility; make the assignment clear.
- Agree on performance objectives and standards.
- Agree on a performance timetable.
- Give authority; allow the other person to act independently.
- Show trust in the other person.
- Provide performance support.
- Give performance feedback.
- Recognize and reinforce progress.
- Help when things go wrong.
- Don't forget *your* accountability for performance results.

MORE DELEGATION AND EMPOWERMENT

All managers and team leaders must decide what work they should do themselves and what should be left for others. At issue here is **delegation**—the process of distributing and entrusting work to other persons. Useful guidelines for delegating are offered in *Manager's Notepad 8.2.*[16] Unfortunately, a common management mistake is failure to delegate. In so doing, a manager easily becomes overloaded with work that could and should be done by others. And, failure to delegate denies others the opportunity to fully utilize their talents on the job. When done well, by contrast, delegation leads to empowerment. It gives people the freedom to contribute ideas and do their jobs in the best possible ways. When Leo F. Mullin became CEO of Delta airlines, for example, he began at once to focus on employees. Mullin met with workers all over the system to gather ideas and rebuild morale. He gave managers more day-to-day decision-making power to speed problem solving and improve service. The *current trend* is to delegate more so that people at all levels are empowered to make decisions about their work.

 Delegation is the process of distributing and entrusting work to other persons.

DECENTRALIZATION WITH CENTRALIZATION

A question frequently asked by managers is, "Should most decisions be made at the top levels of an organization, or should they be dispersed by extensive delegation throughout all levels of management?" The former approach is referred to as **centralization;** the latter is called **decentralization.** This really isn't an "either/or" choice. Today's organizations can operate with greater decentralization without losing centralized control. They do so by using computer

 Centralization is the concentration of authority for most decisions at the top level of an organization.

Decentralization is the dispersion of authority to make decisions throughout an organization.

Management Across Functions

HUMAN RESOURCES

Intranet + Human Resources Department = Efficiency

Human resource departments are being transformed by the use of Intranets and advancing information technologies. Says one professional: "The old school rule was one HR person for every 100 employees. Now we have one for every 500 to 600." That's quite a gain in efficiency and its quite a streamlining of traditional structures in Human Resource Departments. Online communication with employees is changing more than structures, it's also changing the relationship between HR staff and their internal customers. Members of the HR groups stay in closer touch with employee needs. Employees stay in closer touch with health-care benefits, employment policies and opportunities, retirement plans, and more. All this cuts down on staff time and resources at the same time that service improves. At Sharkey Financial Group Inc. in New Jersey, HR executives were able to free 25–30 percent more time to work on strategic needs of the company, such as corporate recruiting. The HR group also benefits from improved communication with employees. The questions asked help shape the services and policies of the function for future improvements.[18]

networks and advanced information systems that allow higher levels to more easily stay informed about a wide range of day-to-day performance matters. Because the top has information on results readily available, it can allow more decentralization.[17] If something goes wrong, presumably the information systems will sound an alarm in time for corrective action to be taken quickly. The *current trend* is toward more decentralization in organizations, while utilizing advances in information systems to retain centralized control.

REDUCED USE OF STAFF

The role of staff assignments in organizations is largely one of providing expert advice and guidance to line personnel. This can help ensure that performance standards are maintained in areas of staff expertise. The problem is that the size of staff can grow to the point where it costs more in administrative overhead than it is worth. This is why staff cutbacks are a common first-choice in downsizing and other cost-saving efforts. What is best for any organization will be a cost-effective staff component that satisfies, but doesn't overreact to, needs for specialized technical assistance to line operations. The *current trend* is for organizations to minimize the use of staff components in the quest for increased operating efficiency.

SUMMARY

What Is Organizing as a Management Function?

- Organizing is the process of creating work arrangements of people and resources, be it for a small unit, a large division, or an entire enterprise.

- To organize a work setting, decisions must be made about how to divide up the work that needs to be done, allocate people and resources to do it, and coordinate results to achieve productivity.

- Structure is the system of tasks, reporting relationships, and communication that links together the people and positions within an organization.

- Formal structure, such as shown on an organization chart, describes how an organization is supposed to work.

- The informal structure of an organization consists of the unofficial working relationships among members.

What Are the Traditional Organization Structures?

- The division of labor in organizations is coordinated in part by grouping people together into formal work units, departments or teams.

- In functional structures, people with similar skills and performing similar tasks work together under a common manager.

- In divisional structures, people who work on a similar product, work in the same geographical region, serve the same customers, or participate in the same work process are grouped together under common managers.

- A matrix structure combines the functional and divisional approaches to create permanent cross-functional project teams.

What Are the New Developments In Organization Structures?

- Increasing complexity and greater rates of change in the environment are challenging the performance capabilities of traditional organization structures.

- New structures are more horizontal and less veritcal in nature.

- There is growing use of team structures that create horizontal organizations using cross-functional teams and task forces to improve lateral relations and problem solving at all levels.

- More organizations are adopting network structures that use information technology to cluster systems of contracted services and strategic alliances around a "core" business or organizational center.

What Organizing Trends Are Changing the Workplace?

- Traditional vertical command-and-control structures are giving way to more horizontal structures strong on employee involvement and flexibility.

- Organizations today often operate with shorter chains of command and less unity of command.

- Organizations today often operate with wider spans of control and fewer levels of management.

- The emphasis in many organizations today is on effective delegation and empowerment.

- Advances in information technology are making it possible to operate with decentralization while still maintaining centralized control.

- Reduction in the size of staff is common in organizations seeking greater efficiency and productivity.

KEY TERMS

Centralization (p. 135)

Chain of command (p. 133)

Decentralization (p. 135)

Delegation (p. 134)

Divisional structure (p. 127)

Formal structure (p. 125)

Functional chimneys problem (p. 126)

Functional structure (p. 126)

Informal structure (p. 125)

Matrix structure (p. 128)

Network structure (p. 130)

Organization structure (p. 124)

Organizing (p. 124)

Span of control (p. 133)

Team structure (p. 129)

  Take the interactive Self-Test for this chapter on the Schermerhorn Web Site

Chapter Nine

Organizational Culture and Design

PLANNING AHEAD—
Chapter 9 Study Questions

- What is organizational culture?
- What are current directions in organizational cultures?
- What is organizational design?
- What are current directions in subsystems and work process design?

DESIGN FOR INTEGRATION AND EMPOWERMENT

Fortune magazine once called Nestle a "Swiss powerhouse . . . racing across the developing world, building roads, farms, factories, and whatever else it needs to capture new markets." It is both the largest branded food company in the world and a truly global company that is always looking for opportunities. Nestle grows by adapting its strategies to fit regional conditions and by allowing managers autonomy to pursue opportunities specific to their countries and regions. The company builds a strong cadre of local managers who transfer around regions and continuously share new ideas for improved operations. Local units operate with self-management ideas gained at the firm's Switzerland training center.[1]

Competitive demands and changing times require flexible and well-integrated organizations that can deliver high-quality products and services while still achieving the innovation needed for sustained future performance.[2] Yet organizations face widely varying problems and opportunities. There is no one best way to deal with them. The key to success is finding the best design to master the unique situational needs and challenges for each organization.[3]

ORGANIZATIONAL CULTURE

Culture is a popular word in management. Important differences in national cultures were discussed in Chapter 3 on globalization and international management. Now it is time to talk about **organizational culture,** defined by noted scholar and consultant Edgar Schein as the system of shared beliefs and values that develops within an organization and guides the behavior of its members.[4] Whenever someone speaks of "the way we do things here," for example, they are talking about the organizational culture.

● **Organizational culture** is the system of shared beliefs and values that develops within an organization and guides the behavior of its members.

WHAT STRONG CULTURES DO

Although culture is not the sole determinant of what happens in organizations, it is an important influence on what the members accomplish . . . and how. The internal culture has the potential to shape attitudes, reinforce common beliefs, direct behavior, establish performance expectations and create the motivation to fulfill them.

A recent study of successful businesses concluded that organizational culture made a major contribution to long-term performance.[5] The best organizations have *strong cultures* that are clear, well defined and widely shared as they discourage dysfunctional work behaviors and encourage positive ones.[6] These cultures commit members to do things for and with one another that are in the best interests of the organization. They show respect for members and expect adaptability and continuous improvement in all areas of operations. Strong and positive cultures are performance oriented, emphasize teamwork, allow for risk taking, encourage innovation, and make the well-being of people a top management priority.[7]

ELEMENTS OF ORGANIZATIONAL CULTURE

Figure 9.1 shows two levels of culture in organizations—the "observable" culture and the "core" culture.[8] The *observable culture* is what one sees and hears when walking around an organization as a visitor, a customer, or an employee. It is apparent in the way people dress at work, how they arrange their offices, how they speak to and behave toward one another, the nature of their conversations, and how they talk about and treat their customers. The observable culture also includes the following elements that help members share and reinforce an organization's special qualities or personality.

● *Stories*—Oral histories and tales, told and retold among members, about dramatic sagas and incidents in the life of the organization.

● *Heroes*—The people singled out for special attention and whose accomplishments are recognized with praise and admiration among members; they include founders and role models.

Observable elements of organizational cultures

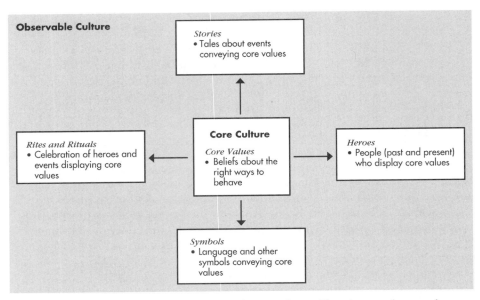

Figure 9.1   Levels of organizational culture—observable culture and core culture.

- *Rites and rituals*—The ceremonies and meetings, planned and spontaneous, that celebrate important occasions and performance accomplishments.
- *Symbols*—The special use of language and other nonverbal expressions to communicate important themes of organizational life.[9]

The foundation for what one observes in the daily life of an organization rests with a second and deeper level of culture—the *core culture*. It consists of **core values** or underlying beliefs that influence the behavior of organization members. Values are essential to strong culture organizations and are often widely publicized in formal statements of corporate mission and purpose. Successful companies, for example, typically emphasize the values of performance excellence, innovation, social responsibility, integrity, worker involvement, customer service, and teamwork.[10]

- **Core values** are underlying beliefs shared by members of the organization and that influence their behavior.

DIRECTIONS IN ORGANIZATIONAL CULTURES

Progressive leadership and worker empowerment are important themes as organizations seek to gain competitive advantages and build cultures to meet the challenges of the new workplace. The best cultures also value diversity in the workforce and ensure that high ethical standards are maintained. Stride Rite, Inc., for example, has achieved a reputation as a family-friendly company. Concerns for children are center stage in Stride Rite's organizational culture. The firm believes in helping its employees meet the needs of dependent relatives. It was the first American company to have an on-site child care facility. It also started the Stride Rite Intergenerational Day Care Center to accommodate the elderly as well as the very young.

LEADERSHIP AND ORGANIZATIONAL CULTURE

Leadership in organizations involves a responsibility for building and maintaining a strong and positive culture. Whereas this is often considered a top management task, the responsibility holds for all levels of management, including team leaders. Just like the organization as a whole, any work team or group will have a culture. How well this culture operates to support performance will depend in part on the strength of the team's core values. At any level, leaders should advance values that meet the test of: (1) *relevance*—core values should support key performance objectives; (2) *pervasiveness*—core values should be known by all members of the organization or group; and (3) *strength*—core values should be accepted by everyone involved.[11] At this highly regarded Nordstrom department store chain, for example, core values emphasized at all levels include: service to the customer, hard work and individual productivity, never being satisfied, and reputational excellence.

Attention is now being increasingly given to the concept of a **symbolic leader,** someone who uses symbols well to establish and maintain a desired organizational culture. Symbolic leaders and managers talk the "language" of the organization or team. They are careful always to use spoken and written words to describe people, events, and even the competition in ways that reinforce and communicate core values. *Language metaphors* that convey positive examples from other contexts are very powerful in this regard. For example, newly hired workers at Disney World and Disneyland are counseled to always think of themselves as key "members of the cast," who work "on stage." After all, they are told, Disney isn't just any business—it is an "entertainment" business.

 A **symbolic leader** uses symbols to establish and maintain a desired organizational culture.

 Management Across Functions

OPERATIONS MANAGEMENT

The Best Cultures Treat People Well

The organizational culture at Southwest Airlines is known for its tight knit and family character. The person behind the culture is president and CEO Herb Kelleher who co-founded the airline in 1978. When asked to explain how his operations beat by half the average industry time for getting planes in and out of the gate, Kelleher points to people. "It's just a lot of people taking pride in what they are doing," he says. And the people are part of the culture, not by chance but by design. Positive attitudes are an important hiring criterion at Southwest; training is conducted with an emphasis on people working together and sharing diverse talents; feedback from customers is shared with employees so that they see the results of their efforts. Kelleher recognizes that continued growth and larger size for the airline put pressure on the culture and systems. But, he says that Southwest always fights bureaucracy and hierarchy. He sends people around the firm to do other people's jobs so that they understand the problems of each operations aspect. About culture and competitive advantage at Southwest, Kelleher says: "I've tried to create a culture of caring for people . . . Someone can go out and buy a bunch of planes from Boeing, but they can't buy our culture, our esprit de corps."[12]

Good symbolic leaders highlight the observable culture. They tell key stories over and over again, and they encourage others to tell them. They often refer to the "founding story" about the entrepreneur whose personal values set a key tone for the enterprise. They often tell about organizational heroes, past and present, whose performances exemplify core values. They engage in symbolic rites and rituals that glorify the performance of the organization and its members. Such ceremonies may be as simple as a spontaneous public congratulation of a work group that exceeded its quality goals or as formal as a mass meeting called to announce major organizational accomplishments. Rites, rituals, and ceremonies are almost a corporate symbol at Mary Kay Cosmetics. Gala events at which top sales performers share their tales of success are legendary. The lavish incentive awards presented at these ceremonies, especially the pink luxury cars given to the most successful salespeople, are highly valued.

ORGANIZATIONAL CULTURE AND DIVERSITY

Managers at all levels of responsibility are finding that the best way to benefit from a strong culture is through an underlying commitment to employee participation, and involvement. The old-fashioned top-down or "paternalistic" approach just doesn't work well anymore. Progressive managers know this and are trying to create and rebuild organizational cultures on the foundations of empowerment.

The culture at Patagonia, Inc. supports and respects workforce diversity. The firm sets an interesting standard for employers that want best to meet the needs of workers with diverse backgrounds and interests. Casual is in at Patagonia; formal is out. If you look at the Patagonia's website you might find depicted there a casually dressed employee with feet on the desk. Today, especially for the Gen-xers, jobs should be fun, self-fulfilling, and rewarding.

Patagonia sets an interesting standard for empowerment and corporate culture.[13] But, there is no reason why organizational cultures everywhere cannot reflect core values and encourage common work directions that respect workforce diversity. The "best" organizational cultures in this sense are those that value the talents, ideas, and creative potential of all members.[14] They allow all the human resources of an organization to be utilized to their fullest potential, and they allow the people involved to feel good about it.

The term *multiculturalism* refers to pluralism and respect for diversity in the workplace. A truly **multicultural organization,** operates with an organizational culture and characteristics such as these:

* *Pluralism*—Members of both minority cultures and majority cultures are influential in setting key values and policies.
* *Structural integration*—Minority-culture members are well represented in jobs at all levels and in all functional responsibilities.
* *Informal network integration*—Various forms of mentoring and support groups assist in the career development of minority-culture members.
* *Absence of prejudice and discrimination*—A variety of training and task force activities continually address the need to eliminate culture-group biases.

● A **multicultural organization** is based on pluralism and operates with respect for diversity in the workplace.

Characteristics of multicultural organizations

● *Minimum intergroup conflict*—Diversity does not lead to destructive conflicts between members of majority and minority cultures.[15]

ETHICAL ORGANIZATIONAL CULTURES

Along with valuing diversity, there is an important ethical aspect to any strong organizational culture. Part of the leadership role is to set the ethical tone. Organizational culture should communicate a desired *ethical climate*—a shared set of understandings about what is considered ethically correct behavior in the organization.[16]

Organizations with positive ethical climates establish clear expectations for their members. They leave little doubt as to what should be done when the inevitable ethical dilemmas occur. They also remind everyone that managers and organizational policies stand behind these expectations. Consider the example of Service Performance Corporation—rated as "outstanding" in the Enterprise Awards for Best Business Practices conducted by Arthur Andersen. The privately held San Francisco company makes the ultimate commitment to customer service in a policy called "The Difficult Yes." CEO David Pasek says, "Our company policy is to find a way to say 'yes' to customer requests . . . Employees don't need approval to satisfy the customer's request, although we do expect them to use good judgment." [17]

ORGANIZATIONAL DESIGN

Organizational design is the process of aligning organizational structures and cultures to best serve the organization's mission, strategy, and objectives.[18] Key directions today involve a basic shift in attention away from a traditional emphasis on more vertical or authority-driven organizations toward those that are more horizontal and task-driven.

● **Organizational design** is the process of aligning structures and cultures to best serve mission, strategy, and objectives.

BUREAUCRATIC DESIGNS

A **bureaucracy** is a form of organization based on logic, order, and the legitimate use of formal authority. Originally described by Max Weber as "ideal" organizational forms, bureaucracies are supposed to be fair and highly efficient.[19] They operate with a clear-cut division of labor, strict hierarchy of authority, formal rules and procedures, and career advancement based on competency.

Today we recognize that there are limits to bureaucracy.[20] Organizations that rely too much on rules and procedures can become unwieldy, rigid, and slow in responding to changing environments. Thus, management theory asks critical contingency questions: When is a bureaucratic form a good choice for an organization? What alternatives exist when it is not a good choice?

A basis for answering the prior questions lies in a classic research study conducted in England during the early 1960s by Tom Burns and George Stalker.[21] They concluded that different organizational forms could be successful, depending on the nature of a firm's external environment. A more bureaucratic or "mechanistic" form thrived when the environment was stable, but struggled when the environment was changing and uncertain. In the latter and more dynamic situations, a much less bureaucratic and more "organic" form performed best.

● **Bureaucracy** is an organizational form based on logic, order, and formal authority.

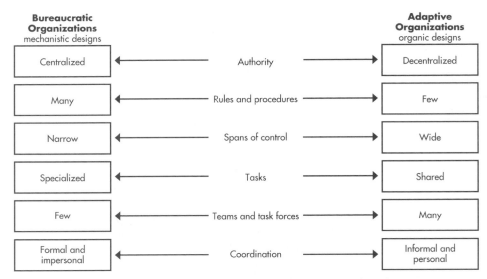

Figure 9.2   A continuum of organizational design alternatives: from bureaucratic to adaptive organizations.

● A **mechanistic design** has centralized authority, many rules and procedures, a clear-cut division of labor, narrow spans of control, and formal coordination.

On the continuum of organizational design alternatives in *Figure 9.2*, bureaucratic organizations use **mechanistic designs** with centralized authority, many rules and procedures, a precise division of labor, narrow spans of control, and formal means of coordination. These are "tight" structures of the traditional "pyramid" form.[22] An example is your local McDonald's restaurant. A relatively small operation, each store operates much like every other and under the close watch of corporate management. Restaurant staff work in disciplined ways guided by many rules and procedures. Crew leaders in special uniforms work alongside counter personnel and cooks to further ensure quality and consistency.

ADAPTIVE DESIGNS

The ability to respond quickly to shifting challenges in rapidly changing environments often distinguishes successful organizations from less successful ones.[23] High performance in these circumstances is achieved by *adaptive organizations* with a minimum of bureaucratic features and with cultures that encourage worker empowerment and participation.[24] The **organic designs** shown in *Figure 9.2* operate with more decentralized authority, fewer rules and procedures, less precise division of labor, wider spans of control, and more personal means of coordination.

● An **organic design** is decentralized with fewer rules and procedures, more open divisions of labor, wide spans of control, and more personal coordination.

Adaptive organizations are flatter systems in which a lot of work gets done through informal structures and networks of interpersonal contacts. The horizontal design features value teamwork and legitimate cross-functional linkages. They try to give otherwise capable employees the freedom to do what they can do best—get the job done. Above all, adaptive organizations are built upon eliminating restrictive centralized controls and trusting that people will do the right things on their own initiative.

Especially in our age of information technology and knowledge workers, organic designs with their emphasis on empowerment are important. When IBM purchased the software firm Lotus, for example, the intention was to turn it into a building block for the firm's networking business. But Lotus was small and IBM was huge. The whole thing had to be carefully handled or IBM might lose many of the talented people who created the popular LotusNotes software and related products. The solution was to adapt the design to fit the people. IBM gave Lotus the space it needed to retain the characteristics of a creative software house. Says the firm's head of software at the time: "You have to keep the people, so you have to ask yourself why it is they like working there." [25]

CONTINGENCIES IN ORGANIZATIONAL DESIGN

Good organizational design decisions should satisfy situational demands and allow all resources to be used to best advantage. This is true contingency thinking and it involves the discipline shown in *Manager's Notepad 9.1*.

The notion that "structure follows strategy" is an important premise of organizational design. [26] When strategy is stability oriented, the premise is that little significant change will be occurring in the external environment. The supporting organization's structure should be well defined and predictable, as found in bureaucratic organizations using more mechanistic design alternatives. But when strategy is growth oriented, operating objectives are likely to include the need for innovation and flexible responses to changing competition in the environment. The most supportive structure is likely to be one that is more decentralized and empowered, as found in adaptive organizations using more organic design alternatives. [27]

Size is another factor that plays a role in organizational design. [28] Although research indicates that larger organizations tend to have more mechanistic structures than smaller ones, it is clear that this is not always best for them. In fact, a perplexing managerial concern is that organizations tend to become more bureaucratic as they grow in size and consequently have difficulty adapting to changing environments. Good managers constantly search for unique ways to overcome the disadvantages of large size. They are creative in forming teams and smaller units,

---

MANAGER'S NOTEPAD 9.1

ORGANIZATIONAL DESIGN CHECKLIST

Check 1: Does the design fit well with the major problems and opportunities of the external environment?

Check 2: Does the design support the implementation of strategies and the accomplishment of key operating objectives?

Check 3: Does the design support core technologies and allow them to be used to best advantage?

Check 4: Can the design handle changes in organizational size and different stages in the organizational life cycle?

Check 5: Does the design support and empower workers and allow their talents to be used to best advantage?

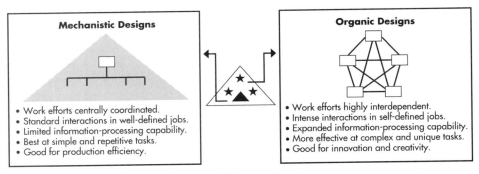

Figure 9.3 Simultaneous "loose-tight" properties of team structures support efficiency and innovation.

and allowing them to operate with considerable autonomy within the larger organizational framework. Such *simultaneous structures*, combine mechanistic and organic designs to meet the need for both production efficiency and continued innovation. This loose–tight concept in organizational design is depicted in *Figure 9.3*.

SUBSYSTEMS AND WORK PROCESS DESIGN

● A **subsystem** is a work unit or smaller component within a larger organization.

Small departments, work units, or teams headed by managers are **subsystems** that perform specialized tasks within organizations. Ideally, their work is efficient and well integrated to meet the needs of the larger organization.

SUBSYSTEMS DESIGN

Important research in subsystems design was reported in 1967 by Paul Lawrence and Jay Lorsch of Harvard University.[29] They found that not only did the overall organizational designs of successful firms match their respective environmental challenges, but also that their subsystem designs matched the challenges of their respective subenvironments. Differences among the subsystem structures accommodated the special problems and opportunities of their unique operating situations. This illustrates **differentiation,** or the degree of difference that exists between the internal components of the organization. Furthermore, subsystems in the successful firms worked well with one another even though they had very different structures. This illustrates **integration,** the level of coordination achieved among an organization's internal components.

● **Differentiation** is the degree of difference between subsystems in an organization.

● **Integration** is the level of coordination achieved between subsystems in an organization.

Figure 9.4 shows how research and development, manufacturing, and sales units in one of the firms studied by Lawrence and Lorsch operated differently in response to unique needs. There are four common sources of differentiation among these and other subsystems. First, *differences in time orientation* become characteristic of work units themselves. This occurs as the planning and action horizons of managers vary from short term to long term. In a business firm, for example, the manufacturing subsystem may have a shorter term outlook than does the research and development group. These differences can make it difficult for personnel from the two units to work well together. Second, different tasks assigned to work units may result in *differences in objectives*. For example, cost-con-

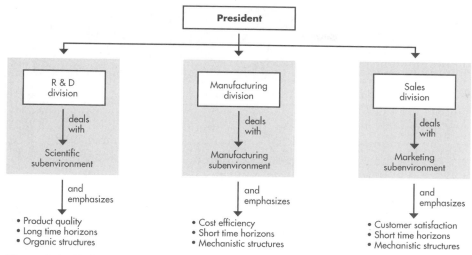

Figure 9.4   Differentiation among research and development (R&D), manufacturing, and sales divisions.

scious production managers and volume-conscious marketing managers may have difficulty agreeing on solutions to common problems. Third, *differences in interpersonal orientation* can affect subsystem relations. To the extent that patterns of communication, decision making, and social interaction vary, it may be harder for personnel from different subsystems to work together. Fourth, *differences in formal structure* can also affect subsystem behaviors. Someone who is used to flexible problem solving in an organic setting may find it very frustrating to work with reprersentatives from a mechanistic setting that operates with very strict rules.

As described by the Lawrence and Lorsch study, successful organizations operate with both differentiated structures and appropriate integrating mechanisms. A basic paradox, however, makes this a particularly challenging task in organizational design: Increased differentiation among organizational subsystems creates the need for greater integration, but integration becomes harder to achieve as differentiation increases.

Manager's Notepad 9.2 identifies several mechanisms for achieving subsystem integration in organizational design.[30] Integrating mechanisms that rely more on vertical coordination and the use of authority relationships—rules and procedures, hierarchical referral, and planning—work best when differentiation is low. Integrating mechanisms that emphasize horizontal coordination and improved lateral relations work better when differentiation is high. They include the use of direct contact between managers, liaison roles, task forces, teams, and matrix structures.

WORK PROCESSES

In his book *Beyond Reengineering*, Michael Hammer defines a **work process** as "a related group of tasks that together create a result of value for the customer."[31] He highlights the following key words and their implications: (1) *group*—tasks are viewed as part of a group rather than in isolation; (2) *together*—everyone must share a common goal: (3) *result*—the focus is on what

● A **work process** is a related group of tasks that together create a value for the customer.

MANAGER'S NOTEPAD 9.2

HOW TO IMPROVE SUBSYSTEMS INTEGRATION

- *Rules and procedures:* Clearly specify required activities.
- *Hierarchical referral:* Refer problems upward to a common boss.
- *Planning:* Set targets to head everyone in same direction.
- *Direct contact:* Have subunit managers coordinate directly.
- *Liaison roles:* Assign formal coordinators to link subunits.
- *Task forces:* Form temporary task forces to coordinate activities and solve specific problems.
- *Teams:* Form permanent teams with the authority to coordinate and solve problems as they occur over time.
- *Matrix organizations:* Create a matrix structure to improve coordination among multiple and diverse projects.

is accomplished not on activities; (4) *customer*—processes serve customers, and their perspectives are the ones that really count.

● **Process reengineering** systematically analyzes work processes to design new and better ones.

Along with the emphasis on horizontal structures and systems integration in organizational design has come a development known as **process reengineering.**[32] This is defined as the systematic and complete analysis of work processes and the design of new and better ones. The goal of a reengineering effort is to focus attention on the future, on customers, and on improved ways of doing things. It tries to break people and mindsets away from habits, preoccupation with past accomplishments, and tendencies to continue implementing old and outmoded ways of doing things. Simply put, reengineering is a radical and disciplined approach to changing the way work is carried out in organizations.

The Patricia Seybold Group of Boston is a worldwide consulting firm specializing in information technology and e-business. One of the firm's areas of expertise is in work group products. To improve a process, Seybold consultants determine how it works, the sequence of activities or tasks involved, the responsibilities of the people involved, and the rules of the process or conditions under which it might change. This is often done with the assistance of special software tools and a focus on improved customer service.[33]

HOW TO REENGINEER CORE PROCESSES

● **Process value analysis** identifies and evaluates core processes for their performance contributions.

In the reengineering approach to work process design, a process is viewed as a "black box" with inputs and outputs. The process is what turns the inputs into outputs, and the outputs should have greater value coming out than did the inputs as they went in. Through a technique called **process value analysis,** core

Browser

Go to: http://www.wiley.com/college/schermerhorn

 THE WALL STREET JOURNAL.

WILEY

IN PRACTICE

The text defines corporate culture as the "predominant value system for the organization as a whole." It encompasses factors that the organization deems as important, such as hard work, high performance results, or even negative factors such as not rocking the boat, or doing as little as possible.

High performance cultures represent values that encourage positive results. *Fast Company*, a business magazine, attempts to support values that lead to success. View their mission statement at http://www.fastcompany.com/partners/mission.html.

Under the Interactive Journal Search feature, type in "corporate culture" and view articles reporting on various culture changes within businesses. Culture is increasingly recognized as a valuable competitive advantage between firms. As such, it becomes important for managers to recognize and influence their respective cultures.

Careers.com

Click on the Careers link under the **Other wsj.com sites** heading in the left-hand menu.

Select College Connection from the left-hand menu, and look for Career and Industry Profiles from Vault Reports.

Vault Reports provides inside looks at working conditions and culture factors across over 30 careers. Click on some you are interested in to see what you can find.

You can also get company information at Vault Reports homepage. Try some of the following links at http://www.VaultReports.com/.

These reports provide a rare glimpse at candid looks inside organizations. Present employees include comments regarding culture and work attitudes from within the firm.

Chapter 9 suggests major changes in how we perceive work in the future. Technology, communication options, and work itself are all changing the ways in which we conduct business. We are moving away from manufacturing products to a service-oriented economy, where information and knowledge provide the value-added inputs to work.

One interesting phenomenon has been the increase in home office businesses. An entire industry has

evolved that caters exclusively to these firms. Check out one example at http://www.theoffice.com/.

As employees become increasingly detached from a centralized office, questions arise about loyalty and commitment to the organization. Will these new work processes improve or detract from employees' sense of belonging?

DELIVERABLES:

Examine the culture at one of your student associations. Does it encourage and support high performance, or does it serve to stifle innovation and change? What procedures would you suggest to improve the culture of your group? Support your assessment.

DISCUSSION QUESTIONS:

1. Analyze the undergraduate culture of your academic institution. Would you describe it as positive or negative?

2. View some of the career descriptions from Vault Reports. Which did you find interesting?

3. Do you want to work for a high performance culture when you graduate? Describe what you think that includes.

 *Note: The underscored words/phrases in the Interactive Journal feature indicate Internet links provided in the online versions. See the *Introducing Management* Web site at www.wiley.com/college/schermerhorn.

processes can be identified and carefully evaluated for their performance contributions. Each step in a workflow is examined. Unless a step is found to be important, useful, and contributing to the value-added, it is eliminated. Process value analysis typically involves the following design activities.[34]

Steps in process value analysis →

1. Identify the core processes.
2. Map the core processes in respect to workflows.
3. Evaluate all tasks for the core processes.
4. Search for ways to eliminate unnecessary tasks or work.
5. Search for ways to eliminate delays, errors, and misunderstandings.
6. Search for efficiencies in how work is shared and transferred among people and departments.

Customers, teamwork, and efficiency are central to Hammer's notion of process reengineering. The goal is to redesign core processes to center control for them with an identifiable group of people, and to focus the entire system on best meeting customer needs and expectations. Process reengineering tries to eliminate duplications of work and systems bottlenecks. In so doing it tries to reduce costs and streamline operations efficiency. Hammer describes the case of Aetna Life & Casualty Company where a complex system of tasks and processes once took as much as 28 days to accomplish.[35] Customer service requests were handled in step-by-step fashion by many different persons. After an analysis of workflows, the process was redesigned into a "one and done" format—a single customer service provider handled each request from start to finish. One of Aetna's customer account managers said after the change was made: "Now we can see the customers as individual people. It's no longer 'us' and 'them.'"

SUMMARY

What Is Organizational Culture?

- The organizational culture establishes a personality for the organization as a whole and has a strong influence on the behavior of its members.
- The observable culture is found in the rites, rituals, stories, heroes, and symbols of the organization.
- The core culture consists of the core values and fundamental beliefs on which the organization is based.
- In organizations with strong and positive cultures members behave with shared understandings that support the accomplishment of key organizational objectives.

What Are Current Directions In Organizational Cultures?

- Symbolic leaders are good at building shared values and using stories, ceremonies, heroes, and language to reinforce core values in daily affairs.
- Multicultural organizations operate through a culture that values pluralism and respects workforce diversity.

- The organizational culture should display a positive ethical climate or shared set of understandings about what is considered ethically correct behavior.

What Is Organizational Design?

- Organizational design is the process of choosing and implementing structures and cultures that best arrange resources to serve organizational mission, strategy, and objectives.
- Bureaucratic or mechanistic organizational designs are vertical in nature and perform best for routine and predictable tasks.
- Adaptive or organic organizational designs are horizontal in nature and perform best in conditions requiring change and flexibility.
- Although organizations tend to become more mechanistic as they grow in size, designs must be used to allow for innovation and creativity in changing environments.

What Are Current Directions In Subsystems And Work Process Design?

- Differentiation is the degree of difference that exists between various subsystems; integration is the level of coordination achieved among them.
- As organizations become more highly differentiated they have a greater need for integration, but as differentiation increases integration is harder to accomplish.
- Greater differentiation requires more intense coordination through horizontal organizational designs, with an emphasis on cross-functional teams and lateral relations.
- A work process is a related group of tasks that together create value for a customer.
- Business process engineering is the systematic and complete analysis of work processes and the design of new and better ones.

KEY TERMS

Bureaucracy (p. 143)

Core values (p. 140)

Differentiation (p. 146)

Integration (p. 146)

Mechanistic design (p. 143)

Multicultural organization (p. 142)

Organic design (p. 144)

Organizational culture (p. 139)

Organizational design (p. 143)

Process reengineering (p. 148)

Process value analysis (p. 148)

Subsystem (p. 146)

Symbolic leader (p. 141)

Work process (p. 147)

SELF-TEST  Take the interactive Self-Test for this chapter on the Schermerhorn Web Site

Chapter Ten

Human Resource Systems

> **PLANNING AHEAD—**
> **Chapter 10 Study Questions**
>
> - What is human resource management?
> - How do organizations attract quality workers?
> - How do organizations develop quality workers?
> - How do organizations maintain quality workers?

MAKE PEOPLE YOUR TOP PRIORITY

At Coopers & Lybrand (C&L), human resource development is a top priority. The firm is committed to hiring and retaining talented people who have the abilities, knowledge, and ideas to match the demands of the challenging twenty-first-century environment. Chairman and CEO Nicholas C. Moore says, "Attracting and retaining the highest intellectual capital are critical objectives of Coopers & Lybrand." The firm's commitment to talent is backed by a strong diversity program that includes a C&L mentoring initiative. In this program the top 100 partners in the company serve as mentors to at least one female or minority manager. The program seeks to increase their success rate in achieving partner status. Moore chairs a Diversity Advisory Group with the goal of fully understanding diversity as it relates to the business.[1]

People are precious in organizations. No one's talents can be wasted in the quest for high performance. In principle, at least, the following organizational slogans say it all: "*People* are our most important asset"; "It's *people* who make the difference"; "It's the *people* who work for us who . . . determine whether our company thrives or languishes."[2] Today, perhaps more than ever before, the pressures of global competition and social change have led to what *Fortune* magazine once refered to as "a human resources revolution" that affects organizations of all types and sizes.[3] "Build a portfolio of skills," "Protect your mobility," "Take charge of your destiny," "Add value to your organization" advise the modern career gurus. Test yourself by asking and answering the tough question: "Am I ready?"

HUMAN RESOURCE MANAGEMENT

The basic building blocks of any high performance organization are talented workers with relevant skills and great enthusiasm for their work. A manager at a California industrial design firm says, for example: "If you hire the right people . . . if you've got the right fit . . . then everything will take care of itself."[4]

The process of **human resource management** involves attracting, developing, and maintaining a talented and energetic workforce. Attracting a quality workforce involves human resource planning, recruitment, and selection. Developing a quality workforce involves employee orientation, training and development, and career planning and development. Maintaining a quality workforce involves management of employee retention and turnover, performance appraisal, and compensation and benefits.

● **Human resource management** is the process of attracting, developing, and maintaining a talented and energetic workforce.

HUMAN RESOURCE PLANNING

Any organization should at all times have the right people available to do the required work. This requires a commitment to **strategic human resource planning,** a process of analyzing staffing needs and planning how to satisfy these needs in a way that best serves organizational mission, objectives, and strategies.[5]

The elements in strategic human resource planning are shown in *Figure 10.1.* The process begins with a review of organizational mission, objectives, and strategies. This establishes a frame of reference for forecasting human resource needs and labor supplies, both within and outside the organization. Ultimately, the planning process should help managers identify staffing requirements, assess the existing workforce, and determine what additions and/or replacements are required to meet future needs.

The foundations for human resource planning are set by *job analysis.* This involves the orderly study of just what is done, when, where, how, why, and by whom in existing or potential new jobs. The job analysis provides useful information that can then be used to write and/or update *job descriptions.* These are written statements of job duties and responsibilities. The information in a job analysis can also be used to create *job specifications.* These are lists of the qualifications—such as formal education, prior work experience, and skill requirements, that should be met by any person hired for or placed in a given job.

● **Strategic human resource planning** analyzes staffing needs and identifies actions to fill those needs.

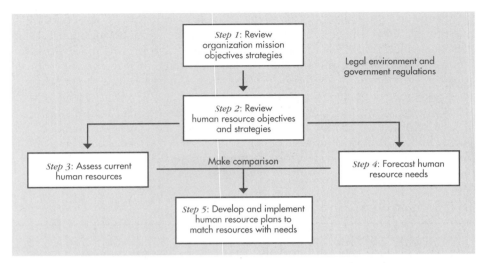

Figure 10.1   Steps in the strategic human resource planning process.

COMPLEX LEGAL ENVIRONMENT

All aspects of human resource management must be accomplished within a legal environment that grows increasingly complex as old laws are modified and new ones are added. A sample of major U.S. laws relating to human resource management is provided in *Figure 10.2.*

● **Equal employment opportunity (EEO)** is the right to employment and advancement without regard to race, sex, religion, color, or national origin.

An important cornerstone of protection for employees' rights to fair treatment was established by *Title VII of the Civil Rights Act of 1964*, as amended by the *Equal Employment Opportunity Act of 1972* and the *Civil Rights Act of 1991.* They provide for **equal employment opportunity (EEO)**—the right to employment without regard to race, color, national origin, religion, gender, age, or physical and mental ability. EEO is federally enforced by the Equal Employment Opportunity Commission (EEOC) and generally applies to all public and private organizations employing 15 or more people. These and related laws are designed to protect people from the *employment discrimination* that occurs when irrelevant criteria are used in hiring or job assignments. For example, the Americans With Disabilities Act, passed in 1990, prevents discrimination against people with disabilities. The law requires employers to focus attention on abilities and what a person can do in the workplace.

● An **affirmative-action program** tries to increase employment opportunities for women and minorities.

When discrimination in any human resource practice is encountered, legal charges can be filed and court action taken to resolve complaints. Under title VII, organizations doing business with the federal government are expected to have **affirmative-action programs** promoting the employment opportunities of women and other minorities, including veterans, the aged, and the disabled. The intent of such programs is to ensure that women and other minorities are represented in the workforce in proportion to their actual availability in the area labor market. Controversy over affirmative action is in the news, with the pros and cons being debated at both the federal and state levels. The debates involve such issues as hiring quotas and potential interference with the individual rights of members of majority populations.

Equal Pay Act of 1963	Prohibits pay differences for men and women doing equal work.
Title VII of the Civil Rights Act of 1964 (as amended 1972)	Prohibits discrimination in employment based on race, color, religion, sex, or national origin.
Age Discrimination Employment Act of 1967 (as amended 1978,1986)	Prohibits discrimination in employment against persons over 40; restricts mandatory retirement.
Occupational Safety and Health Act of 1970 (OSHA)	Establishes mandatory safety and health standards in workplaces.
Vocational Rehabilitation Act of 1973	Prohibits discrimination in employment based on physical or mental handicaps.
Pregnancy Discrimination Act of 1978	Prohibits employment discrimination against pregnant workers.
Immigration Reform and Control Act of 1986	Prohibits knowing employment of illegal aliens.
Americans with Disabilities Act of 1990	Prohibits discrimination against a qualified individual on the basis of disability.
Civil Rights Act of 1991	Reaffirms Title VII of the 1964 Civil Rights Act, reinstates burden of proof by employer, and allows for punitive and compensatory damages.
Family and Medical Leave Act of 1993	Allows employees up to 12 weeks of unpaid leave with job guarantees for childbirth, adoption, or family illness.

Figure 10.2 A sample of U.S. laws influencing human resource management practices.

ATTRACTING A QUALITY WORKFORCE

Once a human resource plan is prepared, the process of attracting a quality workforce can systematically begin. In order to attract the right people, an organization must first know exactly what it is looking for—it must have a clear understanding of the jobs to be done and the talents required to do them well. Then it must have the systems in place to excel at employee recruitment and selection.

THE RECRUITING PROCESS

Recruitment is a set of activities designed to attract a qualified pool of job applicants to an organization. Emphasis on the word "qualified" is important. Effective recruiting should bring employment opportunities to the attention of people whose abilities and skills meet job specifications. The three steps in a typical recruitment process are (1) advertisement of a job vacancy, (2) preliminary contact with potential job candidates, and (3) initial screening to identify all qualified applicants. In collegiate recruiting, for example, advertising is done by the firm posting short job descriptions in print or on Web sites through the campus placement center. Preliminary contact is made after candidates register for interviews with company recruiters on campus. This typically involves a short 20- to 30-minute interview, during which the candidate presents a written resume and briefly explains his or her job qualifications. The recruiter shares interview results and resumes from the campus visits with key decision makers at the place of employment. They choose a final pool of candidates to be invited for further interviews during a formal visit to the organization.

External versus Internal Recruitment

The collegiate recruiting example is one of *external recruitment* in which job candidates are sought from outside the hiring organization. Newspapers, employment agencies, colleges, technical training centers, personal contacts, walk-ins, employee referrals, and even competing organizations are all sources of external recruits. By contrast, *internal recruitment* seeks applicants from inside the organization. This involves notifying existing employees of job vacancies. Most organizations have a procedure for announcing vacancies through newsletters, electronic bulletin boards, and the like. They also rely on managers to recommend high-performing workers as candidates for advancement.

Both recruitment strategies offer potential advantages. External recruiting brings in outsiders with fresh perspectives. It also provides access to specialized expertise or work experience not otherwise available from insiders. Internal recruitment is usually less expensive. It also involves persons whose performance records are well established. A history of serious internal recruitment can also be encouraging to employees; it shows that one can advance in the organization by working hard and achieving high performance at each point of responsibility. One of the most famous "salarymen" in recent American corporate history was the late Robert Goizueta. CEO of Coca-Cola when he died, Goizueta owned over $1 billion of the company's stock. He worked his way up to the top position over a 43-year career in the firm. Hard work and a company commitment to internal advancement paid off for this respected business leader.

Realistic Job Previews

In what may be called *traditional recruitment*, the emphasis is on selling the organization to job applicants. Only the most positive features of the job and organization are communicated to potential candidates. The problem is that this may create unrealistic expectations that are difficult to fulfill. As a result, dissatisfied new hires may leave. The cost of job turnover, including lost productivity, search fees, and recruiting costs, can be very high.

● **Realistic job previews** provide all pertinent information about a job and the organization.

Realistic job previews, by contrast, try to provide the candidate with all pertinent information about the job and organization without distortion and before the job is accepted.[6] Instead of "selling" only positive features of a job, this approach tries to be realistic and balanced in the information provided. With more realistic job expectations, new employees should be less prone to premature turnover. They should also experience higher levels of initial job satisfaction.

THE SELECTION PROCESS

Selection is the process of choosing from a pool of applicants the person or persons who offer the greatest performance potential. Steps in a typical selection process are shown in *Figure 10.3*. They are (1) completion of a formal application form, (2) interviewing, (3) testing, (4) reference checks, (5) physical examination, and (6) final analysis and decision to hire or reject. Again, the best employers exercise extreme care in the selection process. For example, over 150,000 resumes are received each year by Southwest Airlines. Only 5,000 of the applicants are hired, and they go through a rigorous process of selection. Even humor counts; it goes with the corporate culture. An interviewee who appears a bit too tight may be asked to "tell a joke." It's a serious requirement—you can't work for Southwest if you can't pass the levity test.

Applications and Resumes

The application form declares the individual to be a formal candidate for a job. It documents the applicant's personal history and qualifications. The personal resume is often included with the job application. This important document should accurately summarize an applicant's special qualifications. As a job applicant, you should exercise great care in preparing your resume for job searches. As a recruiter, you should also learn how to screen applications and resumes for insights that can help you make good selection decisions. Importantly, the application should only request information that is directly relevant to the job and the applicant's potential job success.

Interviews

Interviews are extremely important in the selection process because of the information exchange they allow. It is a time when both the job applicant and potential employer can learn a lot about one another. However, interviews are also recognized as potential stumbling blocks in the selection process.

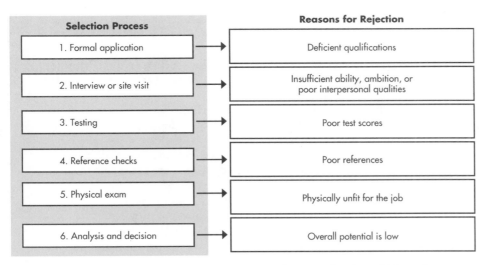

Figure 10.3 Steps in the typical selection process: the case of a rejected job applicant.

Sometimes interviewers ask the wrong things, sometimes they talk too much, sometimes the wrong people do the interviewing, and other times the interviewer falls prey to biases and fails to fully consider the applicant's capabilities. Among the recommendations for how to interview a job applicant are those shown in the *Manager's Notepad 10.1*.

Employment Tests

Whenever tests are used and in whatever forms, the goal should be to gather information that will help predict the applicant's eventual performance success. Like any selection device, an employment test should meet the criterion of *validity*. This means it measures exactly what it intends to relative to the job specification—for example, written communication skills or computer literacy. It should also meet the criterion of *reliability* by yielding approximately the same results over time if taken by the same person. Furthermore, any employment test used in the selection process should be legally defensible on the grounds that it actually measures an ability required to perform the job.

● An **assessment center** examines candidates' handling of simulated job situations.

New developments in testing allow for actual demonstrations of job-relevant skills and personal characteristics. An **assessment center** evaluates a person's potential by observing his or her performance in experiential activities designed to simulate daily work. Another form of this testing approach is *work sampling*, which directly assesses a person's performance in the job. Here, applicants are asked to work on actual job tasks while being graded by observers on their performance.

MANAGER'S NOTEPAD 10.1

How to Conduct Job Interviews

- *Plan ahead.* Review the job specifications and job description as well as the candidate's application; allow sufficient time for a complete interview.
- *Create a good interview climate.* Allow sufficient time; choose a quiet place; be friendly and show interest; give the candidate your full attention.
- *Conduct a goal-oriented interview.* Know what information you need and get it; look for creativity, independence, and a high energy level.
- *Avoid questions that may imply discrimination.* Focus all questioning on the job applied for and the candidate's true qualifications for it.
- *Answer the questions asked of you . . . answer others that may not be asked.* Do your part to create a realist job preview.
- *Write notes on the interview immediately upon completion.* Document details and impressions for later deliberation and decision making.

When Mercedes opened a new plant in Alabama, it had over 45,000 applicants for 1,500 jobs. To help make its selection decisions the firm set up job-specific exercises to determine who had the best of the required skills and attitudes. One was a tire-changing test, with color-coded bolts and a set of instructions. As Charlene Paige took the test, she went slow and followed directions carefully. Two men that went with her changed the tires really fast. She got the job because the firm wanted people who would follow directions and work for quality. Charlene soon worked into the position of team leader in an assembly shop.[7]

Reference Checks

Reference checks are inquiries to previous employers, academic advisors, co-workers, and/or acquaintances regarding the qualifications, experience, and past work records of a job applicant. Although they may be biased if friends are prearranged "to say the right things if called," reference checks can be helpful. The Society for Human Resources Management (SHRM), for example, estimates that 25 percent of job applications and resumes contain errors.[8]

Physical Examinations

Many organizations ask job applicants to take a physical examination. This health check helps ensure that the person is physically capable of fulfilling job requirements. It may also be used as a basis for enrolling the applicant in health-related fringe benefits such as life and health insurance programs. A recent and controversial development in this area is the emerging use of substance-abuse testing. This has become part of preemployment health screening and a basis for continued employment at some organizations. At a minimum, care must be exercised that any required test is job relevant and does not discriminate in any way against the applicant.

Final Decision to Hire or Reject

The best selection decisions are most likely to be those involving extensive consultation among the manager or team leader, potential co-workers, and human resource staff. Importantly, the emphasis in selection must always be comprehensive and focus on all aspects of the person's capacity to perform in a given job. Just as a "good fit" can produce long-term advantage, a "bad fit" can be the source of many and perhaps long-term problems. Sometimes the people who know this lesson best are those who run small businesses. Says one dairy store owner who knew the importance of customer service in retail sales, "If applicants have a good attitude, we can do the rest . . . but if they have a bad attitude to start with, everything we do seems to fail."[9]

DEVELOPING A QUALITY WORKFORCE

When people join an organization, they must "learn the ropes" and become familiar with "the way things are done." **Socialization** is the process of influencing the expectations, behavior, and attitudes of a new employee in a way

● **Socialization** is the process of systematically changing the expectations, behavior, and attitudes of a new employee.

Browser

Go to: http://www.wiley.com/college/schermerhorn

 THE WALL STREET JOURNAL.   **WILEY**

At a time when knowledge management is so important to companies, Human Resource Management takes on additional importance. Attracting and retaining a talented work force is increasingly difficult in the modern business environment.

Work Week is a regular Tuesday column in the Interactive Journal and can be accessed from the **Table of Contents** under **Journal Atlas. Page One Columns** is located in the left-hand listing.

In the same area, under **Marketplace Columns** in the second column, **Managing Your Career** is a regular Tuesday column. Click on it to see the latest in career suggestions from WSJ writers.

Human Resource activities increasingly take on an aspect of law, particularly in the areas of benefits and compensation. Also in the **Marketplace** section, there is a **Law** link in the left-hand menu that often contains information concerning labor issues.

Also, use the **Search** feature to investigate articles concerning

"labor relations." Union activity is a major news item in the WSJ.

ADDITIONAL SITES

The Society for Human Resource Management provides an excellent online links page for a variety of HR issues at http://www.shrm.org/docs/otherink.html.

The Kansas Net Library has excellent Internet links to a large variety of Human Resource topics, located at http://www.bschool.ukans.edu/IntBusLib/.

Cornell University provides a valuable source of links to Industrial and Labor relations information at http://www.ilr.cornell.edu/workindex.html.

CAREERS

The **Careers** link under **Other wsj.com sites** in the left-hand menu provides a primary link to Human Resource topics.

In the left-hand menu in the careers.wsj.com site, **HR Issues** provides access to a collection of articles.

Browse this site in order to view the full range of support services wsj.com the Interactive Journal offers to job seekers. The **Job Hunting** link provides assistance with resumes and interviewing tips.

Under the Job Hunting link, click on the hyperlink that provides contact data on over 5000 Human Resource departments nationwide. You can search this database by region and industry.

DELIVERABLES:

Using the resume suggestions from the **Careers** site, update and improve your resume. If you do not already have an online version of your resume, develop one. Ask for constructive critique from three fellow students.

DISCUSSION QUESTIONS:

1. What are the primary value-added inputs that Human Resource managers provide organizations?

2. How can a HR department add to a firm's competitive advantage?

3. What careers are available in HR departments?

 *Note: The underscored words/phrases in the Interactive Journal feature indicate Internet links provided in the online versions. See the *Introducing Management* Web site at www.wiley.com/college/schermerhorn.

considered desirable by the organization.[10] The intent of socialization in the human resource management process is to help achieve the best possible fit between the individual, the job, and the organization.

EMPLOYEE ORIENTATION

Socialization of newcomers begins with **orientation**—a set of activities designed to familiarize new employees with their jobs, co-workers, and key aspects of the organization as a whole. This includes clarifying the organizational mission and culture, explaining operating objectives and job expectations, communicating policies and procedures, and identifying key personnel.

- **Orientation** makes new employees familiar with their jobs, co-workers, and organizational context.

The first six months of employment are often crucial in determining how well someone is going to perform over the long run. It is a time when the original expectations are tested, and patterns are set for future relationships between an individual and employer. If orientation is neglected, newcomers are left to fend for themselves during this critical period. On their own or through casual interactions with co-workers, otherwise well-intentioned and capable persons may learn inappropriate attitudes and/or behaviors.[11] Good orientation, by contrast, enhances a person's understanding of the organization and adds a sense of common purpose as a member.

At Walt Disney World Resort in Buena Vista, Florida, workers are carefully selected and trained to provide high-quality customer service as "cast members." During orientation, newly hired employees are taught the corporate culture. They learn that everyone employed by the company, regardless of her or his specific job—be it entertainer, ticket seller, or groundskeeper—is there "to make the customer happy." The company's interviewers place a premium on personality, seeking people who are enthusiastic, take pride in their work, and can work without supervision.

TRAINING AND DEVELOPMENT

Training is a set of activities that provides the opportunity to acquire and improve job-related skills. This applies to both initial training of employees and to upgrading or improving their skills to meet changing job requirements.

- **Training** provides opportunities to acquire and improve job skills.

On-the-job training takes place in the work setting while someone is doing a job. *Job rotation* allows people to spend time working in different jobs and thus expand the range of their job capabilities. *Coaching* occurs when an experienced person gives technical advice to someone else. This can be done on a formal basis by supervisors or co-workers. It can also occur more informally in the form of help spontaneously offered in teams. *Apprenticeship* is a work assignment as understudy or assistant to someone who already has the desired job skills. Through this relationship, an apprentice learns a job over time and eventually becomes fully qualified to perform it.

Training also occurs through *modeling*, where someone demonstrates through personal behavior what is expected of others. One way to learn managerial skills, for example, is to observe and practice the techniques of good

● **Mentoring** occurs when senior employees coach and advise newer ones.

managers. **Mentoring** occurs when new or early-career employees are formally assigned as protégés to senior persons who then coach, model, and otherwise assist them to develop job skills and get a good start in their careers.

Management development is a special form of off-the-job training designed to improve a person's knowledge and skill in management and leadership. Progressive organizations are generous in providing management development opportunities. The Center for Creative Leadership, for example, hosts managers sent by their firms for special training. They learn by participating in the "Looking Glass" simulation that models the pressures of daily work. The simulation is followed by extensive debriefings and discussion in which participants give feedback to one another.

PERFORMANCE APPRAISAL

● **Performance appraisal** is the process of formally evaluating performance and providing feedback.

The process of formally assessing someone's work accomplishments and providing feedback is **performance appraisal.** It serves two basic purposes in the maintenance of a quality workforce. The *evaluation purpose* is intended to let people know where they stand relative to performance objectives and standards. The *development purpose* is intended to assist in their training and continued personal development.[12]

Like employment tests, performance appraisals should meet the criteria of reliability and validity. To be reliable, the method should consistently yield the same result over time and/or for different raters. To be valid, it should be unbiased and measure only factors directly relevant to job performance. These criteria are especially important in today's complex legal environment. A manager who hires, fires, or promotes someone is increasingly called upon to defend such actions—sometimes in specific response to lawsuits alleging that the actions were discriminatory. At a minimum, written documentation of performance appraisals and a record of consistent past actions will be required to back up any contested evaluations. Performance appraisal methods commonly used in organizations include graphic rating scales, narratives, behaviorally anchored rating scales, the critical-incident technique, and multi-person comparisons.

Graphic Rating Scales

● A **graphic rating scale** uses a checklist of traits or characteristics to evaluate performance.

Graphic rating scales offer checklists of traits or characteristics thought to be related to high performance outcomes in a given job. A manager rates the individual on each trait using a numerical score. The primary appeal of graphic rating scales is that they are relatively quick and easy to complete. Their reliability and validity are questionable, however, because the categories and scores are subject to varying interpretations.

Narratives

● The **narrative technique** uses a written essay approach to describe a person's performance.

The **narrative technique** is a written essay description of a person's job performance. The commentary typically includes actual descriptions of performance, discusses an individual's strengths and weaknesses, and provides an overall evaluation. Free-form narratives are sometimes used in combination with other performance appraisal methods, such as the graphic rating scale.

Behaviorally Anchored Rating Scales

A **behaviorally anchored rating scale (BARS)** offers rating scales for actual behaviors that exemplify various levels of performance achievement. Look at the case of a customer service representative illustrated in *Figure 10.4.* "Extremely poor" performance is clearly defined as rude or disrespectful treatment of a customer. Because performance assessments are anchored to specific descriptions of work behavior, a BARS is more reliable and valid than the graphic rating scale. The behavioral anchors can also be helpful in training people to master job skills of demonstrated performance importance.

● A **behaviorally anchored rating scale (BARS)** uses specific descriptions of actual behaviors to rate various levels of performance.

Critical-Incident Technique

The **critical-incident technique** involves keeping a running log or inventory of effective and ineffective job behaviors. By creating a written record of positive and negative performance examples, this method documents success or failure patterns that can be specifically discussed with the individual. Using the case of the customer service representative again, a critical-incidents log might contain the following types of entries: *Positive example*—"Took extraordinary care of a customer who had purchased a defective item from a company store in another city"; *negative example*—"Acted rudely in dismissing the complaint of a customer who felt that a sale item was erroneously advertised."

● The **critical-incident technique** involves keeping a running log of effective and ineffective job behaviors.

Multiperson Comparisons

Multiperson comparisons formally compare one person's performance with that of one or more others. They can be used on their own or in combination with some other method. They can also be done in different ways. In *rank ordering*, all persons being rated are arranged in order of performance achievement, with the best performer at the top of the list and the worst performer at

● A **multiperson comparison** compares one person's performance with that of others.

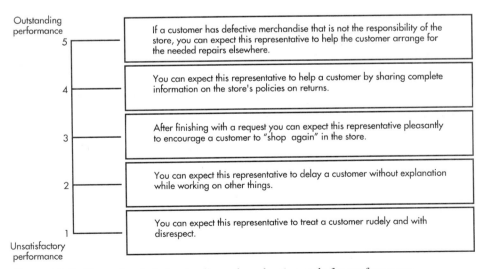

Figure 10.4 Example of a behaviorally anchored rating scale for performance appraisal: the case of a customer-service representative.

the bottom; no ties are allowed. In *paired comparisons*, each person is formally compared to every other person and rated as either the superior or the weaker member of the pair. After all paired comparisons are made, each person is assigned a summary ranking based on the number of superior scores achieved. In *forced distribution*, each person is placed into a frequency distribution that requires that a certain percentage fall into specific performance classifications, such as top 10 percent, next 40 percent, next 40 percent, and bottom 10 percent.

MAINTAINING A QUALITY WORKFORCE

It is not enough to attract and develop a qualified workforce; the workforce must be successfully nurtured and managed for long-term effectiveness. This requires proper attention to such maintenance issues as career planning and development, work-life balance, retention and turnover, and compensation and benefits.

CAREER PLANNING AND DEVELOPMENT

● **Career planning** is the process of systematically matching goals and capabilities with opportunities.

In his book *The Age of Unreason*, British scholar and consultant Charles Handy says, "The times are changing and we must change with them." [13] Everyone should take Handy's advice and take charge of their careers. **Career planning** is the process of systematically matching career goals and individual capabilities with opportunities for their fulfillment. It involves answering such questions as "Who am I?," "Where do I want to go?," "How do I get there?" While some suggest that a career should be allowed to progress in a somewhat random but always opportunistic way, others view a career as something to be rationally planned and pursued in a logical step-by-step fashion. In fact, a well-managed career will probably include elements of each. The carefully thought-out plan can point you in a general career direction; an eye for opportunity can fill in the details along the way.

WORK–LIFE BALANCE

● **Work–life balance** involves balancing career demands with personal and family needs.

Today's fast-paced and complicated life styles bring with them inevitable pressures on the balance between careers and personal time. This issue of **work–life balance** deals with how people balance the demands of work with their personal and family needs. Human resource policies and practices that support a healthy work–life balance are increasingly valued. Included among work-life balance concerns are the unique needs of *single parents*—who must balance complete parenting responsibilities with a job, and *dual-career couples*—who must balance the career needs and opportunities of each partner. [14] Not surprisingly, the "family-friendliness" of an employer is now frequently and justifiably used as a screening criterion by many job candidates. At First Union Bank in Charlotte, North Carolina, for example, employees have access to on-site day care as well as such additional services as medical and dental offices, dry cleaning, and even video rentals. All of this is aimed at improving employee welfare and productivity through an organizational commitment to work-life balance. [15]

Management Across Functions

INTERNATIONAL OPERATIONS

Moves Abroad Require Special Attention

Special human resource policies had to be drafted to support international assignments in DaimlerChrysler. Before the merger, Chrysler was much less international and had less experience with the demands of expatriate assignments than its German partner Daimler. Now a new program is in place to encourage employees from both to seek jobs abroad with the new firm. The goal is to make the assignments both attractive and possible, including support for families. Expatriates are kept on their home-country payrolls and receive their pay in home-country currency. Housing costs abroad are fully paid and costs of maintaining a domestic home are covered. Vacation is generous and includes airfares for a trip home for employee and family. Spouses also get assistance in entering the foreign job market and children are paid tuition and school expenses. Prior to the new policy it had proved difficult to get Americans to relocate to Germany. They were concerned about costs and housing, as well as their careers. It took time, teamwork and a good deal of cross-cultural understanding to develop the new policies. A special task force met regularly for several months in both Germany and America, and used extensive video conferencing and electronic communications. Although it was difficult to reconcile the different expatriate policies used by the former two companies, the process resulted in a new program that is expected to better encourage and support the expatriate assignments so critical to a truly global company.[16]

RETENTION AND TURNOVER

The several steps in the human resource management process both conclude and recycle with the management of promotions, transfers, terminations, layoffs, and retirements. Any replacement situation should be approached as an opportunity to review human resource plans and ensure that the best people are selected to perform the required tasks.

Some replacement decisions shift people between positions within the organization. *Promotion* is movement to a higher level position; *transfer* is movement to a different job at a similar level of responsibility. Another set of replacement decisions relates to *retirement*, something most people look forward to . . . until it is close at hand. Then the prospect of being retired often raises fears and apprehensions. Many organizations offer special counseling and other forms of support for preretirement employees, including advice on company benefits, money management, estate planning, and use of leisure time. Downsizing is sometimes accompanied by special offers of early retirement, that is, retirement before formal retirement age but with special financial incentives.

The most extreme replacement decisions involve *termination*, the involuntary and permanent dismissal of an employee. For the person being dismissed, accepting the fact of termination is difficult. The termination notice may come by surprise and without the benefit of advance preparation for either the personal or the financial shock. The experts' advice, though, is to ask at least three tough questions of the ex-boss: "Why am I being fired?" "What are my termination benefits?" "Can I have a good reference?" Advice for the manager who must do the firing is offered in *Manager's Notepad 10.2*.

COMPENSATION AND BENEFITS

● **Base compensation** is a salary or hourly wage paid to an individual.

When properly designed and implemented, compensation and benefit systems help attract qualified people to the organization and retain them. **Base compensation** in the form of salary or hourly wages can make the organization a desirable place of employment. It can help get the right people into jobs to begin with. By making outside opportunities less attractive, it can also help keep them there. Unless an organization's prevailing wage and salary structure is competitive, it will be difficult to attract and retain a staff of highly competent workers. A basic rule of thumb is to study the labor market carefully and pay at least as much as, and perhaps a bit more than, what competitors are offering.

● **Fringe benefits** are nonmonetary forms of compensation (e.g., health plans, retirement plans, etc.).

The organization's employee-benefit program also plays a role in attracting and retaining capable workers. **Fringe benefits,** the additional nonwage or nonsalary forms of compensation, now constitute some 30 percent or more of a typical worker's earnings. Benefit packages usually include various options on disability protection, health and life insurance, and retirement plans.

● A **flexible benefits** program allows employees to choose a range of benefit options.

The ever-rising cost of fringe benefits, particularly employee medical benefits, is a major worry for employers. Some are attempting to gain control over health-care costs by becoming more active in their employees' choices of health-care providers and by encouraging healthy lifestyles. An increasingly common approach overall is **flexible benefits,** sometimes known as *cafeteria benefits*, which let the employee choose a set of benefits within a certain dollar amount. The employee gains when such plans are better able to meet individ-

MANAGER'S NOTEPAD 10.2

THINGS TO REMEMBER WHEN HANDLING A DISMISSAL

● Dismissal can be as personally devastating as a divorce or the death of a loved one.
● Dismissal should always be legally defensible and done in complete compliance with organizational policies.
● Dismissal should not be delayed unnecessarily; it is best done as soon as the inevitability of the dismissal is known.
● Dismissal should include offers of assistance to help the former employee reenter the labor market.

ual needs; the employer gains from being more responsive to a wider range of needs in a diverse workforce.

LABOR-MANAGEMENT RELATIONS

A final aspect of human resource management relates to the influence of organized labor. **Labor unions** are organizations to which workers belong that deal with employers on the workers' behalf.[17] They are important forces in the modern workplace both in the United States and around the world. Today, slightly over 16 percent of American nonfarm workers belong to a union; the figures are over 30 percent for Canada and some 25 percent for Great Britain.[18]

Labor unions act as bargaining agents who negotiate legal contracts that affect many aspects of human resource management. Labor contracts typically include the rights and obligations of employees and management with respect to wages, work hours, work rules, seniority, hiring, grievances, and other aspects or conditions of employment. The foundation of any labor and management relationship is **collective bargaining,** which is the process of negotiating, administering, and interpreting labor contracts. Labor contracts and the collective bargaining process are governed closely in the United States by a strict legal framework. For example, the *Wagner Act of 1935* protects employees by recognizing their rights to join unions and engage in union activities; the *Taft-Hartley Act of 1947* protects employers from unfair labor practices by unions and allows workers to decertify unions; and the *Civil Service Reform Act Title VII of 1978* clarifies the rights of government employees to join and be represented by labor unions.

In *Figure 10.5* labor and management are viewed as "win-lose" adversaries, destined to be in opposition and possessed of certain weapons with which to fight one another. If labor-management relations take this form, a lot of energy on both sides can be expended in prolonged conflict. This model is, to some extent, giving way to a new and more progressive era of greater cooperation.[19] Today's union leaders and corporate leaders appear to recognize that labor-management relations must adapt to changing conditions if they are to survive

● A **labor union** is an organization to which workers belong and that deals with employers on their collective behalf.

● **Collective bargaining** is the process of negotiating, administering, and interpreting a labor contract.

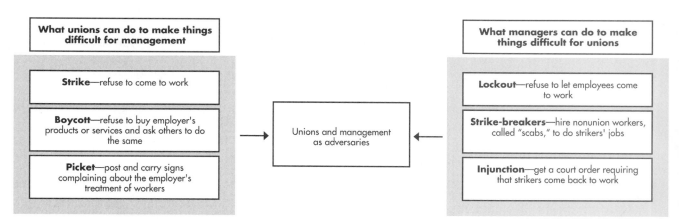

Figure 10.5   The traditional adversarial view of labor-management relations.

and prosper in the years ahead. For example, labor–management cooperation helped Xerox Corporation bring home to America jobs it had previously performed abroad. New team manufacturing concepts were developed with the assistance of the union representing its copier assemblers, the Amalgamated Clothing & Textiles Workers Union. CEO Paul A. Allaire said: " . . . if we have a cooperative model, the union movement will be sustained and the industries it's in will be more competitive."

SUMMARY

What Is Human Resource Management?

- The human resource management process is the process of attracting, developing, and maintaining a quality workforce.
- Human resource planning is the process of analyzing staffing needs and identifying actions to satisfy these needs over time.
- The purpose of human resource planning is to make sure the organization always has people with the right abilities available to do the required work.
- A complex legal environment influences human resource management, giving special attention to equal employment opportunity.

How Do Organizations Attract Quality Workers?

- Recruitment is the process of attracting qualified job candidates to fill vacant positions.
- Recruitment should involve realistic job previews that provide job candidates with accurate information on the job and organization.
- Managers typically use interviews, employment tests, and references to help make selection decisions; the use of assessment centers and work sampling is becoming more common.

How Do Organizations Develop Quality Workers?

- Orientation is the process of formally introducing new hires to their jobs, performance requirements, and the organization.
- On-the-job training may include job rotation, coaching, apprenticeship, modeling, and mentoring.
- Performance management systems focus on the establishment of work standards and the assessment of results through performance appraisal.
- Common performance appraisal methods are graphic rating scales, narratives, behaviorally anchored rating scales, and multiperson comparisons.

How Do Organizations Maintain Quality Workers?

- Career planning systematically matches individual career goals and capabilities with opportunities for their fulfillment.
- Programs that address work-life balance and the complex demands of job and family responsibilities are increasingly important in human resource management.

- Whenever workers must be replaced over time because of promotions, transfers, retirements, and terminations, the goal should be to treat everyone fairly while ensuring that jobs are filled with the best personnel available.

- Compensation and benefits packages must be continually updated so that the organization maintains a competitive position in external labor markets.

- Where labor unions exist, labor-management relations should be positively approached and handled with all due consideration of applicable laws.

KEY TERMS

Affirmative-action program (p. 154)

Assessment center (p. 158)

Base compensation (p. 166)

Behaviorally anchored rating scale (BARS) (p. 163)

Career planning (p. 164)

Collective bargaining (p. 167)

Critical-incident technique (p. 163)

Equal employment opportunity (EEO) (p. 154)

Flexible benefits (p. 166)

Fringe benefits (p. 166)

Graphic rating scale (p. 162)

Human resource management (p. 153)

Labor union (p. 167)

Mentoring (p. 162)

Multiperson comparison (p. 163)

Narrative technique (p. 162)

Orientation (p. 161)

Performance appraisal (p. 162)

Realistic job previews (p. 156)

Socialization (p. 159)

Strategic human resource planning (p. 153)

Training (p. 161)

Work–life balance (p. 164)

SELF-TEST Take the interactive Self-Test for this chapter on the Schermerhorn Web Site

Chapter Eleven

Leading—To Inspire Effort

PLANNING AHEAD—
Chapter 11 Study Questions

- What is leadership?
- What are the important leadership models and theories?
- What are current directions in leadership development?
- What are the leadership "anchors" for dynamic times?

YOU HAVE TO BELIEVE IN PEOPLE

WHAT IS GREAT LEADERSHIP? At Herman Miller, Inc., the innovative Michigan-based maker of office furniture, the answer lies in a belief in people. Max DePree, the firm's chairperson and the son of its founder, tells the story of a millwright who worked for his father. The millwright held an important job in the plant. He was responsible for keeping all of the machines supplied with power from a central boiler. When the man died, DePree's father, wishing to express his sympathy to the family, went to their home. There he listened as the widow read some beautiful poems, which, he was surprised to learn, had been written by the millwright. To this day, DePree says, he and his father still wonder, "Was he a poet who did millwright's work, or was he a millwright who wrote poetry?" [1]

Great leaders understand people and respect their great diversity of talents. According to Max DePree, when we recognize the unique qualities of others, we become less inclined to believe that we alone know what is best.[2] By valuing diversity, not only do we learn what may be needed to provide others with meaningful work and opportunities, we also benefit by allowing everyone's contribution to have an influence on the organization.

WHAT IS LEADERSHIP?

Leadership—the process of inspiring others to work hard to accomplish important tasks, is one of the most popular management topics.[3] As shown in *Figure 11.1*, it is also critical to the management process. Planning sets the direction and objectives; organizing brings the resources together to turn plans into action; *leading* builds the commitments and enthusiasm needed for people to apply their talents fully to help accomplish plans; and controlling makes sure things turn out right.

- **Leadership** is the process of inspiring others to work hard to accomplish important tasks.

LEADERSHIP AND VISION

"Great leaders," it is said, "get extraordinary things done in organizations by inspiring and motivating others toward a common purpose."[4] More and more frequently, great leadership is associated with **vision**. The term is generally used to describe someone who has a clear sense of the future and an understanding of the actions needed to get there successfully. But there is more. Leading requires turning vision into results. At GE, for example, the top management team says: "At the leadership level, an 'A' is a man or woman with vision and the ability to articulate that vision to the team, so vividly and powerfully that it also becomes their vision."[5] Five core principles for meeting the challenges of visionary leadership are:[6]

- **Vision** is a term used to describe a clear sense of the future.

1. *Challenge the process:* Be a pioneer—encourage innovation and support people who have ideas.
2. *Be enthusiastic:* Inspire others through personal enthusiasm to share in a common vision.
3. *Help others to act:* Be a team player and support the efforts and talents of others.

Principles for visionary leadership

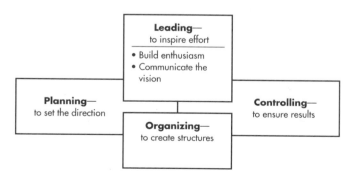

Figure 11.1   Leading viewed in relationship to the other management functions.

4. *Set the example:* Provide a consistent role model of how others can and should act.

5. *Celebrate achievements:* Bring emotion into the workplace and rally "hearts" as well as "minds."

LEADERSHIP AND POWER

● **Power** is the ability to get someone else to do something you want done or to make things happen the way you want.

Leadership involves influencing the behavior of other people. **Power** in this sense is the ability to get someone else to do something you want done. It is the ability to make things happen for the good of the group or organization as a whole.[7] This "positive" face of power is the foundation of effective leadership.[8] *Figure 11.2* divides the possible sources or bases of power into those that trace to one's position in an organization, and those that come from personal qualities.[9]

Position Power

A manager's official status, or position, in the organization's hierarchy of authority provides access to position power. This includes the power of rewards, punishments, and legitimacy.

● **Reward power** offers something of value as a means of influencing other people.

Reward power is the ability to influence through rewards. It is the capability to offer something of value—a positive outcome—as a means of influencing the behavior of other people. This involves the control of rewards or resources such as pay raises, bonuses, promotions, special assignments, and verbal or written compliments. To mobilize reward power, a manager says, in effect, "If you do what I ask, I'll give you a reward."

● **Coercive power** uses punishment as a means of influencing other people.

Coercive power is the ability to influence through punishment. It is the capacity to punish or withhold positive outcomes as a way to influence the behavior of other people. A manager may attempt to coerce someone by threatening him or her with verbal reprimands, pay penalties, and even termination. To mobilize coercive power, a manager says, in effect, "If you don't do what I want, I'll punish you."

● **Legitimate power** influences other people by formal authority, or the rights of office.

Legitimate power is the ability to influence through *formal authority*—the right by virtue of one's organizational position or status to exercise control over persons in subordinate positions. It is the capacity to influence the behavior of other people by virtue of the rights of office. To mobilize legitimate power, a manager says, in effect, "I am the boss and therefore you are supposed to do as I ask."

Sources of power...

Power of the POSITION:	Power of the PERSON:
Based on things managers can offer to others.	*Based on the ways managers are viewed by others.*

Rewards: "If you do what I ask, I'll give you a reward."

Coercion: "If you *don't* do what I ask, I'll punish you."

Legitimacy: "Because I am the boss; you *must* do as I ask."

Expertise—as a source of special knowledge and information.

Reference—as a person with whom others like to identify.

Figure 11.2   Sources of position power and personal power used by leaders.

Personal Power

Power can also derive from a manager's or leader's unique personal qualities. Two bases of personal power are expert power and referent power.

Expert power is the ability to influence through special expertise. It is the capacity to influence the behavior of other people because of one's knowledge, understanding, and skills. Expertise derives from the possession of technical know-how or information pertinent to the issue at hand.[10] This is developed by acquiring relevant skills or competencies or by gaining a central position in relevant information networks. It is maintained by protecting one's credibility and not overstepping the boundaries of true understanding. When a manager uses expert power, the implied message is, "You should do what I want because of my special expertise or information."

Referent power is the ability to influence through identification. It is the capacity to influence the behavior of other people because they admire you and want to identify positively with you. Reference is a power derived from charisma or interpersonal attractiveness. It is developed and maintained through good interpersonal relations that encourage the admiration and respect of others. When a manager uses referent power, the implied message is, "You should do what I want in order to maintain a positive self-defined relationship with me."

- **Expert power** influences other people by specialized knowledge.

- **Referent power** influences other people because of their desire to identify personally with you.

LEADERSHIP AND EMPOWERMENT

Management today is rich with the processes of *empowerment*, the process through which managers enable and help others to gain power and achieve influence within the organization. Effective leaders know that when people feel powerful, they are more willing to make the decisions and take the actions needed to get their jobs done.[11] They also realize that power in organizations is not a "zero-sum" quantity. That is, in order for someone to gain power, it isn't necessary for someone else to give it up. Indeed, to master the complexity and pace of challenges faced in today's environments, an organizations' success may well depend on how much power can be mobilized throughout an organizations' workforce.

When *Working Woman* was looking for a role model of business leadership in the 21st century it turned to Patricia Gallup, CEO of PC Connection. Gallup co-founded the computer mail-order firm in 1982 and has since gained a reputation for first-class leadership. She is considered the new breed of leader who emphasizes integration, teamwork, collaboration, and consensus rather than command and control. Of course it's hard work and the hours are long—some 60 or more in Gallup's typical week. She communicates via e-mail and directly with the firm's 284 employees, greets employees by name in the hallways, and prefers working with others out on the floor rather than spending time alone in her office.[12]

Manager's Notepad 11.1 offers tips on how to empower others.[13] They are well worth remembering. Max DePree, for example, praises leaders who are willing to focus on what is best for the organization and "permit others to share ownership of problems—to take possession of the situation."[14] This is leader-

MANAGER'S NOTEPAD 11.1

HOW TO EMPOWER OTHERS

- Get others involved in selecting their work assignments and the methods for accomplishing tasks.
- Create an environment of cooperation, information sharing, discussion, and shared ownership of goals.
- Encourage others to take initiative, make decisions, and use their knowledge.
- When problems arise, find out what others think and let them help design the solutions.
- Stay out of the way; give others the freedom to put their ideas and solutions into practice.
- Maintain high morale and confidence by recognizing successes and encouraging high performance.

ship through empowerment. It is helping others use their knowledge and judgment to make a real difference in daily workplace affairs. This occurs as people work in responsible jobs, as they participate in cross-functional task forces and teams, and as they function in work environments that respect them as capable and creative human beings.

LEADERSHIP MODELS AND THEORIES

For centuries, people have recognized that some persons perform very well as leaders, whereas others do not. The questions still debated are "Why?" "What determines leadership success?"

LEADERSHIP TRAITS

An early tradition in leadership research involved a search for universal traits that separate effective and ineffective leaders. The results of many years of research on leadership traits can be summarized as follows.[15] Physical traits such as a person's height, weight, and physique make no difference in determining leadership success. On the other hand, followers do appear to admire certain things about leaders. In one study of over 3,400 managers, for example, the most respected leaders were described as honest, competent, forward-looking, inspiring, and credible. Such positive feelings may enhance a leader's effectiveness, particularly with respect to creating vision and a sense of empowerment. Among the personal traits now considered important as personal foundations for leadership success are drive, desire to lead, motivation, honesty and integrity, self-confidence, intelligence, knowledge, and flexibility.[16]

LEADERSHIP BEHAVIORS

The behavioral theories of leadership sought to determine which **leadership style**—the recurring pattern of behaviors exhibited by a leader—worked best.[17] Given a preferred style, the goal was to be able to train leaders to become skilled at using it to best advantage.

● **Leadership style** is the recurring pattern of behaviors exhibited by a leader.

Now president of the Child Care Action Campaign, Faith Wohl was one of DuPont's first senior female managers. When she took over as the director of workforce partnering for the firm, she was committed to making the firm "family friendly." She advocated policies that help employees balance work and family needs, such as job sharing and Flextime schedules, day-care programs, elder care, and related matters. Knowing she needed management support to make them work, Wohl made data-filled presentations, held well-publicized meetings with employees to discuss the programs, met frequently with managers to determine their needs, set up "work life" committees to solicit employee suggestions, and made sure the CEO regularly expressed his public support.[18]

Most research in the leader behavior tradition has focused on the degree to which a leader's style displays concern for the task to be accomplished and/or concern for the people doing the work. The behaviors characteristic of each dimension are quite clear. A leader high in concern for task plans and defines work to be done, assigns task responsibilities, sets clear work standards, urges task completion, and monitors performance results. By contrast, a leader high in concern for people acts warm and supportive toward followers, develops social rapport with them, respects their feelings, is sensitive to their needs, and shows trust in them.

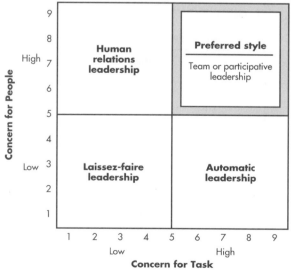

Figure 11.3 Implications of leader behavior research.

The results of leader behavior research at first suggested that followers of people-oriented leaders would be more productive and satisfied than those working for more task-oriented leaders. Later results, however, suggested that truly effective leaders were high in both concern for people and concern for task.[19] As shown in *Figure 11.3*, the preferred style of "team leader" shares decisions with subordinates, encourages participation, and supports the teamwork needed for high levels of task accomplishment.

FIEDLER'S CONTINGENCY THEORY

Instead of searching for the one best style, a contingency leadership theory developed by Fred Fiedler suggests that leadership success depends on a match between leadership style and situational demands.[20] He believes that leadership style is part of one's personality and is therefore relatively enduring and difficult to change. Rather then trying to train leaders to adopt new styles, he advises them to match their existing styles with situations for which they are the best "fit."

According to the theory, people's leadership styles tend to be either task motivated or relationship motivated. Extensive research by Fiedler suggests that neither style is effective all the time. Instead, each works best when used in the right situation.

To diagnose leadership situations three contingency variables must be understood. The *quality of leader-member relations* (good or poor) measures the degree to which the group supports the leader. The *degree of task structure* (high or low) measures the extent to which task goals, procedures, and guidelines are clearly spelled out. The *amount of position power* (strong or weak) measures the degree to which the position gives the leader power to reward and punish subordinates.

Figure 11.4 shows eight possible combinations that range from the most favorable situation for a leader (good leader–member relations, high task structure, strong position power), to the least favorable situation (poor leader–member relations, low task structure, weak position power). The implications of this figure and Fiedler's theory can be stated as two propositions. *Proposition 1* is

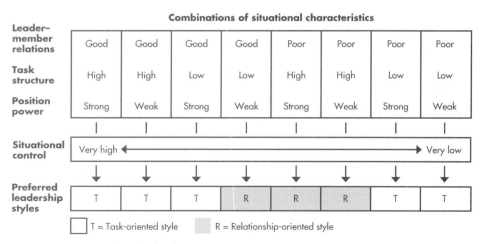

Figure 11.4 Matching leadership style and situation: predictions from Fiedler's contingency theory.

that a task-oriented leader will be most successful in either very favorable (high-control) or very unfavorable (low-control) situations. *Proposition 2* is that a relationship-oriented leader will be most successful in situations of moderate control.

HERSEY-BLANCHARD SITUATIONAL MODEL

The Hersey-Blanchard situational leadership model suggests that successful leaders adjust their styles depending on the readiness of followers to perform in a given situation.[21] "Readiness," in this sense, is based on how able, willing, and confident followers are to perform required tasks. As shown in *Figure 11.5*, the

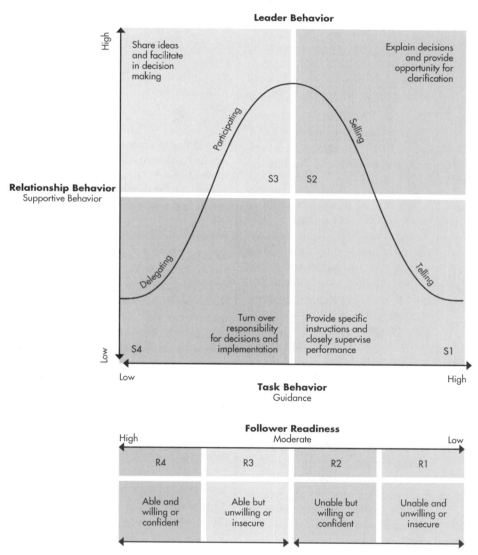

Figure 11.5   The Hersey-Blanchard model of situational leadership. *Source:* Paul Hersey and Kenneth H. Blanchard, *Management of Organizational Behavior* (Englewood Cliffs, NJ: Prentice-Hall, 1988), p. 171. Used by permission.

Browser

Go to: http://www.wiley.com/college/schermerhorn

 THE WALL STREET JOURNAL.
WILEY

IN PRACTICE

Leadership is described as the ability to "inspire" others to work towards a common goal. The Interactive Journal covers all the major players in the business community. Interviews, cover stories, and feature articles of successes and failures provide the reader a valuable insight into what constitutes leadership.

Much has been made recently about the difference between management and leadership. While managers are concerned with control, leaders seek to motivate change and innovation among their followers.

Check **Special Reports** under the **Resources** heading in the left-hand menu. Look for a set of articles involving leadership as a theme.

Utilizing the **Search** feature, look for news articles on business leaders, such as:

- Jack Welch—GE
- Michael Dell—Dell Computer
- Lou Gerstner—IBM
- Bill Gates—Microsoft

ADDITIONAL SITES

Take a leadership test to assess your ability at http://www.

leaderx.com/testyourlead.htm. Take some time to reflect on the findings.

Leader-Values at http://www.leadervalues.com/ is a meeting place for students and business leaders to discuss a variety of subjects relating to leadership.

The site New Leadership at http://www.newleadership.com/frame.htm pays particular attention to women and leadership.

General Electric makes a unique effort to train leaders as they move up the organization. The firm recognizes the importance of continued education as a source of new value and innovation in the company. The web site at http://www.ge.com/ibcroa18.htm introduces you to the program located at Crotonville, the world's first major corporate business school. Look over the site to better appreciate GE's commitment to excellence.

Chapter 11, Leading—To Inspire Effort, recognizes that leaders vary widely in attributes and behaviors. The question becomes, is there any common set of variables on which leaders can be evaluated? As leadership theories evolve, they move increasingly away from attributes

and more toward shared behaviors that make leaders unique.

The text's discussion of transactional leadership, aimed primarily at meeting organizational goals, versus transformational leadership that is concerned with change and innovation is topical given the dynamics of business markets today.

As you come across leaders in the Interactive Journal, assess which leadership approach they are projecting. What differences can you detect in the two perspectives?

DELIVERABLES:

Select a business leader that you are interested in and research him or her on the Interactive Journal. Remember that the **Search** feature allows you to search News, Company Info, and Web. Prepare a short summary as to why you think they are successful.

DISCUSSION QUESTIONS:

1. Pick a business leader you admire and analyze their leadership style based on one of the models described in the textbook.

2. Do you consider yourself a leader? Why or why not?

3. Identify 3–5 personal factors on which you intend to improve in order to be a better leader.

 *Note: The underscored words/phrases in the Interactive Journal feature indicate Internet links provided in the online versions. See the *Introducing Management* Web site at www.wiley.com/college/schermerhorn.

possible leadership styles that result from different combinations of task-oriented and relationship-oriented behaviors are as follows:

- *Delegating:* Allowing the group to make and take responsibility for task decisions; a low-task, low-relationship style.
- *Participating:* Emphasizing shared ideas and participative decisions on task directions; a low-task, high-relationship style.
- *Selling:* Explaining task directions in a supportive and persuasive way; a high-task, high-relationship style.
- *Telling:* Giving specific task directions and closely supervising work; a high-task, low-relationship style.

← Leadership styles in the situational model

Anyone using this model must be able to implement the alternative leadership styles as needed. The *delegating style* works best in high-readiness situations of able, willing, and confident followers; the *telling style* works best at the other extreme of low readiness. In between, the *participating style* is recommended for low to moderate readiness and the *selling style* for moderate to high readiness. Hersey and Blanchard further believe that leadership styles can and should be adjusted as followers in a given situation change over time. The model also implies that if the correct styles are used in lower readiness situations, followers will "mature" and grow in ability, willingness, and confidence. Not only is this a positive result in itself, it also allows the leader to become less directive.

HOUSE'S PATH-GOAL THEORY

A third contingency leadership approach is the path-goal theory advanced by Robert House.[22] This theory suggests that an effective leader is one who clarifies paths through which followers can achieve both task-related and personal goals. A good leader helps people progress along these paths, removes any barriers, and provides appropriate rewards for task accomplishment. House identifies four leadership styles that may be used in this "path-goal" sense:

- *Directive leadership:* Letting subordinates know what is expected; giving directions on what to do and how; scheduling work to be done; maintaining definite standards of performance; clarifying the leader's role in the group.
- *Supportive leadership:* Doing things to make work more pleasant; treating group members as equals; being friendly and approachable; showing concern for the well-being of subordinates.
- *Achievement-oriented leadership:* Setting challenging goals; expecting the highest levels of performance; emphasizing continuous improvement in performance; displaying confidence in meeting high standards.
- *Participative leadership:* Involving subordinates in decision making; consulting with subordinates; asking for suggestions from subordinates; using these suggestions when making a decision.

← Leadership styles in the path-goal theory

The path-goal leadership theory advises a manager always to use leadership styles that complement the needs of situations. This means that the leader "adds value" by contributing things that are missing from the situation or that need strengthening. She or he specifically avoids redundant behaviors. The important contingencies for making good path-goal leadership choices include the work environment (tasks, authority, and group) and subordinate personal characteristics (ability, experience, and locus of control). For example, when job assignments are unclear, the effective manager provides directive leadership to clarify task objectives and expected rewards. When worker self-confidence is low, the effective manager provides supportive leadership to clarify individual abilities and offers needed task assistance. When performance incentives are poor, the effective manager provides participative leadership to identify individual needs and appropriate rewards. When task challenge is insufficient, the effective manager provides achievement-oriented leadership to raise performance aspirations.

● **Substitutes for leadership** are factors in the work setting that influence behavior without the involvement of a leader.

Path-goal theory has led some theorists to identify what they call **substitutes for leadership.**[23] These are aspects of the work setting and the people involved that can reduce the need for a leader's personal involvement. In effect, they make leadership from the "outside" unnecessary because leadership is already built into the situation. Possible substitutes for leadership include *subordinate characteristics* such as ability, experience, and independence; *task characteristics* such as routineness and availability of feedback; and *organizational characteristics* such as clarity of plans and formalization of rules and procedures.

DIRECTIONS IN LEADERSHIP DEVELOPMENT

Current directions in leadership thinking seek to integrate and extend the many insights of the theories discussed so far.[24] The quest to understand leadership success is still there. Warren Bennis, a respected leadership scholar and consultant, claims that too many American corporations are "over-managed and under led." Grace Hooper, another management expert and the first female admiral in the U.S. Navy says, "You manage things; you lead people." [25] Given these challenges, where do we go from here?

● A **charismatic leader** is a leader who develops special leader–follower relationships and inspires followers in extraordinary ways.

TRANSFORMATIONAL LEADERSHIP

This is the era of "superleaders" who, through vision and strength of personality, have a truly inspirational impact on others.[26] Their leadership efforts result in followers not only meeting performance expectations but performing above and beyond them. These are **charismatic leaders** who develop special leader–follower relationships and inspire their followers in extraordinary ways. The presence of charismatic leadership is reflected in followers who are enthusiastic about the leader and his or her ideas, who work very hard to support them, who remain loyal and devoted, and who seek superior performance accomplishments.[27]

● **Transformational leadership** is inspirational leadership that gets people to do more in achieving high performance.

● **Transactional leadership** is leadership that directs the efforts of others through tasks, rewards, and structures.

The term **transformational leadership** is often used to describe someone who uses charisma and related qualities to raise aspirations and shift people and organizational systems into new high-performance patterns. This contrasts with **transactional leadership** in which a leader adjusts tasks, rewards, and structures to help followers meet their needs while working to accomplish organizational objectives.[28] Such transactional leadership meets only part of an organization's requirements in today's dynamic environment. A manager must also lead in an inspirational way and with a compelling personality. The transformational leader provides a strong aura of vision and contagious enthusiasm that substantially raises the confidence, aspirations, and commitments of followers. This leader arouses followers to be more highly dedicated, more satisfied with their work, and more willing to put forth extra effort to achieve success in challenging times.

The special qualities that are often characteristic of transformational leaders include the following:

- *Vision:* Having ideas and a clear sense of direction; communicating them to others; developing excitement about accomplishing shared "dreams."
- *Charisma:* Arousing others' enthusiasm, faith, loyalty, pride, and trust in themselves through the power of personal reference and appeals to emotion.
- *Symbolism:* Identifying "heroes," offering special rewards, and holding spontaneous and planned ceremonies to celebrate excellence and high achievement.
- *Empowerment:* Helping others develop, removing performance obstacles, sharing responsibilities, and delegating truly challenging work.
- *Intellectual stimulation:* Gaining the involvement of others by creating awareness of problems and stirring their imagination to create high-quality solutions.
- *Integrity:* Being honest and credible, acting consistently out of personal conviction, and by following through commitments.[29]

← Attributes of transformational leaders

EMOTIONAL INTELLIGENCE AND LEADERSHIP

The concept of **emotional intelligence,** or "EI" for short, has caught the attention of leadership scholars and consultants.[30] Defined as both the ability to understand emotions in one's self and others and the ability to use that understanding to guide behavior, EI is now recognized as an important contributor to leadership success. Research reported by Daniel Goleman indicates that EI may be more important that technical and cognitive skills in creating performance excellence. When high performing leaders and average performers were compared, he found that almost 90% of the difference could be accounted for by differences in emotional intelligence.[31] Goleman goes on to suggest that EI gains importance in leadership as one moves into higher levels of management responsibility.

From Goleman's perspective, technical or knowledge-based skills and cognitive or analytical skills are "threshold capabilities" for leadership.[32] They are baseline or entry-level requirements for performing in a leadership capacity. The achievement of true excellence in leadership, however, depends additionally on the presence of EI. In this sense emotional intelligence is not an option or a "nice to have" leadership component; it is a necessity. Someone low in emotional intelligence, for example, may fail to spot signs of excessive stress or burnout in members of a work team. Without this awareness and the ability to act on it, the team leader may push too hard to meet performance expectations

- **Emotional intelligence** is the ability to understand and deal well with emotions at work.

and find members responding with anger, job avoidance and/or poor performance. By contrast, a leader high in EI would have the interpersonal insight and sensitivity to recognize that emotions are running high. He or she would also have the confidence and expertise to take actions that help team members balance work demands and find relief for stressful conditions.

One of the important implications of research on EI is the notion that it can be learned. This means that a person can make the improvement of emotional intelligence an important component in any leadership development agenda. *Manager's Notepad 11.2* identifies five components of emotional intelligence at work.[33] By consciously and persistently seeking to acquire and develop these skills, the implication is that anyone can improve upon their leadership effectiveness. Important in the present context is the fact that these components of EI are all addressed in the chapters that follow on motivation, communication, interpersonal skills, teamwork, and change leadership.

GENDER AND LEADERSHIP

A leadership theme of continuing interest deals with the question of how and if gender influences leadership. Sara Levinson, president of NFL Properties, Inc. of New York, for example, explored the question directly in a conversation with the all-male members of her management team. "Is my leadership style different from a man's?" she asked. "Yes," they replied, suggesting that the very fact that she was asking the question helped to demonstrate the difference. They also indicated that her leadership style emphasized communication and the gathering of ideas and opinions from others. When Levinson probed further by asking the team members, "Is this a distinctly 'female' trait?," they said that they thought it was.[34]

MANAGER'S NOTEPAD 11.2

FIVE COMPONENTS OF EMOTIONAL INTELLIGENCE

1. *Self-awareness*—the ability to understand one's moods, emotions, drives, and how they affect others.
2. *Self-regulation*—the ability to think before acting and to control disruptive impulses or moods.
3. *Motivation*—the ability to work for more than money or status, and to work with perseverence and high energy.
4. *Empathy*—the ability to understand emotions of others and deal with them according to their emotional states.
5. *Social skill*—the ability to manage relationships, build interpersonal networks, and establish social rapport.

The evidence clearly supports that both women and men can be effective leaders. As suggested by the prior example, however, they may tend toward somewhat different styles.[35] Women may be more prone to behaviors typically considered democratic and participative—such as showing respect for others, caring for others, and sharing power and information with others. This style is sometimes referred to as *interactive leadership*, focusing on the building of consensus and good interpersonal relations through communication and involvement. It also has qualities in common with the transformational leadership just discussed.[36] Men, by contrast, may be more transactional in their leadership tendencies—tending toward more directive and assertive behaviors, and toward using authority in a traditional "command and control" sense.

Given the emphasis on shared power, communication, cooperation, and participation in the new-form organizations of today, these results are provocative. Gender issues aside, the interactive leadership style seems to be an excellent fit with the demands of a diverse workforce and the new workplace. Regardless of whether the relevant behaviors are displayed by women or men, it seems clear that future leadership success will rest more often on one's capacity to lead through positive relationships and empowerment than through aloofness and formal authority.

LEADERSHIP ANCHORS IN DYNAMIC TIMES

In the quest for leadership success it is important to remember the fundamentals of leadership responsibility. These are the leadership "anchors" that apply anywhere and everywhere that one accepts the opportunity to lead. One anchor point deals with the everyday hard work of being a leader—what Peter Drucker calls the essentials of "good old-fashioned leadership." A second anchor point rests in the ethical and social responsibility demands of leadership—what John Gardner calls the "moral aspects of leadership."

"GOOD OLD-FASHIONED" LEADERSHIP

The noted scholar and consultant Peter Drucker describes a pragmatic approach to leadership in the new workplace. It is based on what he refers to as a "good old-fashioned" view of the plain hard work it takes to be a successful leader. Consider his description of a telephone conversation with a potential consulting client who was the human resources vice president of a big bank. "We'd want you to run a seminar for us on how one acquires charisma," she said. Drucker advised her to tell the VP that there's more to leadership than the popular emphasis on personal qualities that offer a sense of personal "dash" to charisma. In fact, he said that "leadership . . . is work."[37]

Drucker went on to describe the work of a leader in these three essentials. First, the foundation of effective leadership is *defining and establishing a sense of mission*. A good leader sets the goals, priorities, and standards. A good leader keeps them all clear and visible and maintains them. Second, leadership entails *accepting leadership as a responsibility rather than a rank*. Good leaders surround

Management Across Functions

LOGISTICS AND DISTRIBUTION

Teamwork Builds Internet-Based Customer Service

Visionary leadership today has to embrace technology and tap the power of the Internet. Although GE has been tagged a late-comer to the Internet by some, it's now seeking Internet opportunities with a vengeance. Special cross-functional "dby.com" (destroyyourbusiness.com) teams search throughout the firm for ways to tap the Internet for new business initiatives. Other teams of "Web fanatics" are dedicated to putting existing operations on the Web. The firm's chief information officer, Gary M. Reimer, says that any resulting proposals must "enhance value to the customer and reduce total cost." At GE's Polymerland subsidiary, a Web site now helps with logistics and distribution of plastics to its customers. Special sensors in storage silos of some customers send automatic Internet orders when supplies drop to a certain point. The Web site has increased efficiency in customer service as well. When it was first introduced cost savings and service went right up. Staffing in customer services went from 70 employees to just over 50, and telephone inquiries dropped by 1,000 per week, or some 25%. Peter N. Foss, the unit's president says: "You can't just sit there and let this thing go by. All I am is a service provider. If I'm not providing the best service out there, GE should smack me." [38]

themselves with talented people. They are not afraid to develop strong and capable subordinates. And they do not blame others when things go wrong. Third, great leaders understand the importance of *earning and keeping the trust of others.* This is an issue of personal integrity. The followers of good leaders trust them. They believe the leader means what he or she says and that his or her actions will be consistent with what is said. "Effective leadership . . . is not based on being clever," says Drucker, "it is based primarily on being consistent."

MORAL LEADERSHIP

● **Moral leadership** sets high ethical standards for others to follow.

Firmly embedded in the concept of leadership "integrity" is the leader's honesty, credibility, and consistency in putting values into action. Leaders have an undeniable responsibility to set high ethical standards to guide the behavior of followers. The ethical aspects of leadership are important and everyday concerns. They are captured in the notion of **moral leadership**—that is leadership that by actions and personal example sets high ethical standards for others to follow.

Concerned about what he perceives as a lack of momentum in organizational life, leadership theorist John Gardner further notes that part of a leader's moral obligation is to supply the necessary spark to awaken the potential of each individual—to urge each person "to take the initiative in performing leader-like acts." [39] Moral leaders, accordingly, should instill ownership by being both highly ethical and truly willing to let others do their best.[40] Returning once again to the Herman Miller example that opened the chapter, the words of Max DePree provide a useful final reminder: "Nobody is common," he says, "Everybody has a right to be an insider." [41]

SUMMARY

What Is Leadership?

- Leadership is the process of inspiring others to work hard to accomplish important tasks.

- Visionary leaders are able to communicate their vision to others and build the commitments needed to perform the required work.

- Power, the ability to get others to do what you want them to do, is an essential ingredient of effective leadership.

- Sources of position power include rewards, coercion, and legitimacy or formal authority; sources of personal power include expertise and reference.

- Effective leaders empower others—that is, they help and allow others to take action and make job-related decisions on their own.

What Are the Important Leadership Models and Theories?

- Traits that seem to have a positive impact on leadership include drive, integrity, and self-confidence, among others.

- A suggestion of leader–behavior researchers is that effective leaders will be good at team-based or participative leadership that is high in both task and people concerns.

- Contigency leadership approaches point out that no one leadership style always works best; rather, the best style is one that properly matches the demands of each unique situation.

- Fiedler's contingency theory describes how situational differences in task structure, position power, and leader–member relations may influence which leadership style works best.

- The Hersey-Blanchard situational model recommends using task-oriented and people-oriented behaviors, depending on the "maturity" of the group a manager is attempting to lead.

- House's path-goal theory points out that leaders should add value to situations by responding with supportive, directive, achievement-oriented, and/or participative styles as needed.

What Are Current Issues in Leadership Development?

- Transformational leaders use charisma and related qualities to inspire extraordinary efforts in support of innovation and large-scale change.

- Successful leaders are high in emotional intelligence, and are able to both understand and deal well with emotions at work.

- The interactive leadership style seems consistent with the demands of the new workplace and the emphasis on communication, involvement, and interpersonal respect.

What Are the Leadership "Anchors" for Changing Times?

- All leadership is "hard work" that always requires a personal commitment to meeting the high performance standards and consistent, trustworthy behavior.
- There is no substitute for moral leadership that sets high ethical standards for others to follow.

KEY TERMS

Charismatic leader (p. 180)

Coercive power (p. 172)

Emotional intelligence (p. 181)

Expert power (p. 173)

Leadership (p. 171)

Leadership style (p. 175)

Legitimate power (p. 172)

Moral leadership (p. 184)

Power (p. 172)

Referent power (p. 173)

Reward power (p. 172)

Substitutes for leadership (p. 180)

Transactional leadership (p. 180)

Transformational leadership (p. 180)

Vision (p. 171)

SELF-TEST Take the interactive Self-Test for this chapter on the Schermerhorn Web Site

Chapter Twelve

Motivation and Job Design

PLANNING AHEAD—
Chapter 12 Study Questions

■ How do needs influence motivation?
■ What do the process theories say about motivation?
■ How can motivating jobs be designed?
■ How can motivating work schedules be arranged?

VALUE DIVERSITY AND INDIVIDUAL DIFFERENCES

WHY DO SOME PEOPLE outperform others in their work? What can be done to help everyone achieve high performance? These questions are asked by managers everywhere. Good answers to them will rest on a foundation of true respect for people, with all of their talents and diversity. The best managers already know this; their leadership approaches reflect an awareness that "productivity through people" is a key and irreplaceable ingredient for long-term success. The corporate philosophy of Dana Corporation is a classic example: "People. . . . We are dedicated to the belief that our people are our most important asset. We will encourage all of them to contribute and to grow to the limit of their desire and ability. We believe people respond to recognition, freedom to contribute, opportunity to grow, and to fair compensation."[1]

Human nature is always both fascinating and complex, and all of its intricate facets come into play in the workplace. At a packaging plant in California, for example, senior executive Kevin Kelley learned that a supervisor was starting to retire on the job.[2] The man had worked his 20 years and felt it was time to slow down. He was unresponsive to gentle "nudging" from co-workers and managers. Kelley politely confronted him with the facts, saying: "We need your talent, your knowledge of those machines." The supervisor responded with new vigor in his work and earned the praise of his peers. For his part, Kelley believes in employee involvement and claims that one of the best motivators is information on the firm's competitive environment.

● **Motivation** accounts for the level, direction, and persistence of effort expended at work.

The term **motivation** is used in management theory to describe forces within the individual that account for the level, direction, and persistence of effort expended at work. Simply put, a highly motivated person works hard at a job; an unmotivated person does not. A manager who leads through motivation creates conditions under which other people feel continually inspired to work hard and perform to the best of their abilities.

MOTIVATION AND HUMAN NEEDS

Needs are the unfulfilled physiological or psychological desires of an individual. Some theories of motivation use individual needs to explain the behaviors and attitudes of people at work. Although each discusses a slightly different set of needs, all agree that needs cause tensions that influence attitudes and behavior. Good managers and leaders establish conditions in which people can satisfy important needs through their work. They also take action to eliminate things that can block the satisfaction of important needs.

HIERARCHY OF NEEDS THEORY

Abraham Maslow's theory of human needs provides an important foundation for management thinking. He views people as seeking the satisfaction of the five levels of needs shown in *Figure 12.1*. The **lower order needs** include physiological, safety, and social concerns, and the **higher order needs** include esteem and self-actualization concerns.[3]

● **Lower order needs** are physiological, safety, and social needs in Maslow's hierarchy.

● **Higher order needs** are esteem and self-actualization needs in Maslow's hierarchy.

Two principles are central to Maslow's theory. The *deficit principle* holds that a satisfied need is not a motivator of behavior. People are expected to act in ways that satisfy deprived needs—that is, needs for which a "deficit" exists. The *progression principle* holds that a need at one level does not become activated until the next lower level need is already satisfied. People are expected to advance step by step up the hierarchy in their search for need satisfactions. At the level of self-actualization, the more these needs are satisfied, the stronger they are supposed to grow. According to Maslow, a person should continue to be motivated by opportunities for self-fulfillment as long as the other needs remain satisfied.

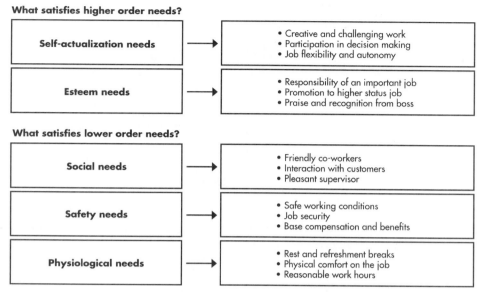

What satisfies higher order needs?

Self-actualization needs	→	• Creative and challenging work • Participation in decision making • Job flexibility and autonomy
Esteem needs	→	• Responsibility of an important job • Promotion to higher status job • Praise and recognition from boss

What satisfies lower order needs?

Social needs	→	• Friendly co-workers • Interaction with customers • Pleasant supervisor
Safety needs	→	• Safe working conditions • Job security • Base compensation and benefits
Physiological needs	→	• Rest and refreshment breaks • Physical comfort on the job • Reasonable work hours

Figure 12.1   Opportunities for work motivation in Maslow's hierarchy of human needs.

Maslow's theory advises managers to recognize that blocked or deprived needs may negatively influence work attitudes and behaviors. By the same token, providing opportunities for need satisfaction may have positive motivational consequences. *Figure 12.1* gives some examples of how managers can use Maslow's ideas to better meet the needs of people at work.

TWO-FACTOR THEORY

Frederick Herzberg's two-factor theory offers another framework for understanding motivation in the work place.[4] The theory was developed from a pattern identified in the responses of almost 4,000 people to questions he asked about their work. When questioned about what "turned them on," they tended to identify things relating to the nature of the job itself. Herzberg calls these **satisfier factors.** When questioned about what "turned them off," they tended to identify things relating more to the work setting. Herzberg calls these **hygiene factors.**

As shown in *Figure 12.2*, the two-factor theory associates hygiene factors, or sources of job *dis*satisfaction, with aspects of job context. That is, "dissatisfiers" are considered more likely to be a part of the work setting than of the nature of the work itself. The hygiene factors include such things as working conditions, interpersonal relations, organizational policies and administration, technical quality of supervision, and base wage or salary. Herzberg's two-factor theory would argue that improving the hygiene factors, such as by adding piped-in music or implementing a no-smoking policy, can make people less dissatisfied with these aspects of their work. But they would not in themselves contribute to increases in satisfaction.

● A **satisfier factor** is found in job content, such as a sense of achievement, recognition, responsibility, advancement, or personal growth.

● A **hygiene factor** is found in the job context, such as working conditions, interpersonal relations, organizational policies, and salary.

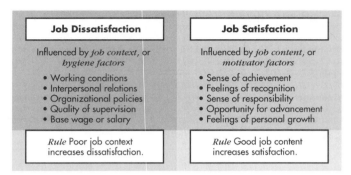

Figure 12.2 Key elements in Herzberg's two-factor theory.

To really improve motivation, Herzberg advises managers to give proper attention to the satisfier factors. As part of job content, the satisfier factors deal with what people actually do in their work. By making improvements in what people are asked to do in their jobs, Herzberg suggests that job satisfaction and performance can be raised. The important satisfier factors include such things as a sense of achievement, feelings of recognition, a sense of responsibility, the opportunity for advancement, and feelings of personal growth.

Scholars have criticized Herzberg's theory as being method-bound and difficult to replicate.[5] Yet, the two-factor theory remains a useful reminder that there are two important aspects of all jobs: *job content*—what people do in terms of job tasks, and *job context*—the work setting in which they do it. Furthermore, Herzberg's advice to managers is still timely: (1) Always correct poor context to eliminate actual or potential sources of job dissatisfaction; and (2) be sure to build satisfier factors into job content to maximize opportunities for job satisfaction.

ACQUIRED NEEDS THEORY

● **Need for Achievement** is the desire to do something better, to solve problems, or to master complex tasks.

● **Need for Power** is the desire to control, influence, or be responsible for other people.

● **Need for Affiliation** is the desire to establish and maintain good relations with people.

David McClelland, offers another motivation theory based on individual needs.[6] **Need for Achievement** (*nAch*) is the desire to do something better or more efficiently, to solve problems, or to master complex tasks. **Need for Power** (*nPower*) is the desire to control other people, to influence their behavior, or to be responsible for them. **Need for Affiliation** (*nAff*) is the desire to establish and maintain friendly and warm relations with other people.

According to McClelland, people acquire or develop these needs over time as a result of individual life experiences. In addition, each need carries a distinct set of work preferences. Managers are encouraged to recognize the strength of each need in themselves and in other people. Attempts can then be made to create work environments responsive to them. People high in the need for achievement, for example, like to put their competencies to work, they take moderate risks in competitive situations, and they are willing to work alone. As a result, the work preferences of high need achievers include individual responsibility for results, achievable but challenging goals, and feedback on performance.

PROCESS THEORIES OF MOTIVATION

Although the details vary, each of the need theories just described can help managers understand individual differences and deal positively with workforce diversity. A set of process theories, adds further to this understanding. The equity, expectancy, and goal-setting theories each offer advice and insight on how people actually make choices to work hard or not, based on their individual preferences, the available rewards, and possible work outcomes.

EQUITY THEORY

The equity theory of motivation is known best through the work of J. Stacy Adams.[7] The essence of the theory is that perceived inequity is a motivating state. That is, when people believe that they have been inequitably treated in comparison to others the theory suggests they will try to eliminate the discomfort and restore a sense of equity to the situation.

Figure 12.3 shows the equity comparison. It typically occurs whenever managers allocate extrinsic rewards, especially monetary incentives or pay increases. Inequities occur whenever people feel that the rewards received for their work are unfair given the rewards other persons appear to be getting. The comparison points may be co-workers in the group, workers elsewhere in the organization, and even persons employed by other organizations. Adams predicts that the ways people deal with perceived inequity include the following:

- Change their work inputs by putting less effort into their jobs.
- Change the rewards received by asking for better treatment.
- Change the comparison points by finding ways to make things seem better.
- Change the situation by transferring or quitting the job.

Possible responses to perceived inequity

The research of Adams and others has largely been accomplished in the laboratory. It is most conclusive with respect to perceived negative inequity, a condition that most managers would want to avoid. People who feel underpaid and perceive negative inequity, for example, tend to reduce their work efforts to compensate for the missing rewards. They are less motivated to work hard in the future. People who feel overpaid and perceive positive inequity, by contrast,

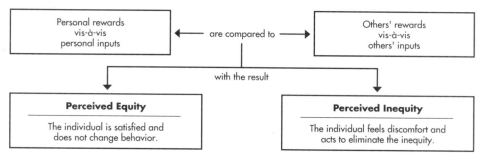

Figure 12.3 Equity theory and the role of social comparison.

have been found to increase the quantity or quality of their work. However, many questions involving this particular issue remain to be answered.

Informed managers anticipate perceived negative inequities whenever especially visible rewards such as pay or promotions are allocated. Instead of letting equity concerns get out of hand, they carefully communicate the intended value of rewards being given, clarify the performance appraisals upon which they are based, and suggest appropriate comparison points.

EXPECTANCY THEORY

Victor Vroom introduced to the management literature an expectancy theory of motivation that asks a central question: What determines the willingness of an individual to work hard at tasks important to the organization?[8] In response, expectancy theory suggests that "people will do what they can do when they want to do it." More specifically, Vroom suggests that the motivation to work depends on the relationships among the *three expectancy factors* listed here and also in *Figure 12.4:*

● **Expectancy** is a person's belief that working hard will result in high task performance.

● **Instrumentality** is a person's belief that various outcomes will occur as a result of task performance.

● **Valence** is the value a person assigns to work-related outcomes.

● **Expectancy:** A person's belief that working hard will result in a desired level of task performance being achieved (this is sometimes called *effort-performance expectancy*).

● **Instrumentality:** A person's belief that successful performance will be followed by rewards and other potential outcomes (this is sometimes called *performance-outcome expectancy*).

● **Valence:** The value a person assigns to the possible rewards and other work-related outcomes.

Expectancy theory posits that motivation (M), expectancy (E), instrumentality (I), and valence (V) are related to one another in a multiplicative fashion: $M = E \times I \times V$. In other words, motivation is determined by expectancy times instrumentality times valence. The multiplier effect has important managerial implications. Mathematically speaking, a zero at any location on the right side of the equation (that is, for E, I, or V) will result in zero motivation.

For example, a typical assumption is that people will be motivated to work hard to earn a promotion. But is this necessarily true? *If expectancy is low, moti-*

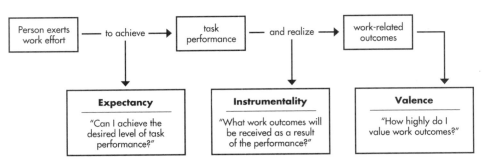

Figure 12.4 Elements in the expectancy theory of motivation.

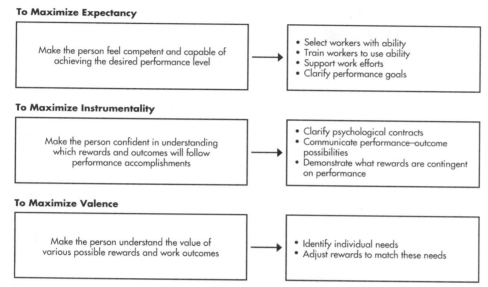

To Maximize Expectancy

Make the person feel competent and capable of achieving the desired performance level →
- Select workers with ability
- Train workers to use ability
- Support work efforts
- Clarify performance goals

To Maximize Instrumentality

Make the person confident in understanding which rewards and outcomes will follow performance accomplishments →
- Clarify psychological contracts
- Communicate performance–outcome possibilities
- Demonstrate what rewards are contingent on performance

To Maximize Valence

Make the person understand the value of various possible rewards and work outcomes →
- Identify individual needs
- Adjust rewards to match these needs

Figure 12.5 Managerial implications of expectancy theory.

vation will suffer. The person may feel that he or she cannot achieve the performance level necessary to get promoted. So why try? *If instrumentality is low, motivation will suffer.* The person may lack confidence that a high level of task performance will result in being promoted. So why try? *If valence is low, motivation will suffer.* The person may place little value on receiving a promotion. It simply isn't much of a reward. So, once again, why try?

As shown in *Figure 12.5*, the management implications of expectancy theory include being willing to work with each individual and try to maximize his or her expectancies, instrumentalities, and valences in ways that support organizational objectives. Stated a bit differently, a manager can apply the insights of expectancy theory by clearly linking effort and performance, linking performance to work outcomes, and choosing work outcomes valued by the individual.

GOAL-SETTING THEORY

Task goals, in the form of clear and desirable performance targets, form the basis of Edwin Locke's goal-setting theory.[9] The theory's basic premise is that task goals can be highly motivating—*if* they are properly set and *if* they are well managed. Goals give direction to people in their work. Goals clarify the performance expectations between a supervisor and subordinate, between co-workers, and across subunits in an organization. Goals establish a frame of reference for task feedback. Goals also provide a foundation for behavioral self-management.[10] In these and related ways, Locke believes goal setting can enhance individual work performance and job satisfaction.

To achieve these benefits, however, research by Locke and his associates indicates that managers and team leaders must work with others to set

● **Task goals** are performance targets for individuals or groups.

MANAGER'S NOTEPAD 12.1

HOW TO MAKE GOAL SETTING WORK FOR YOU

- *Set specific goals:* They lead to higher performance than more generally stated ones, such as "Do your best."
- *Set challenging goals:* As long as they are viewed as realistic and attainable, more difficult goals lead to higher performance than do easy goals.
- *Build goal acceptance and commitment:* People work harder for goals that they accept and believe in; they tend to resist goals forced on them.
- *Clarify goal priorities:* Make sure that expectations are clear as to which goals should be accomplished first and why.
- *Reward goal accomplishment:* Don't let positive accomplishments pass unnoticed; reward people for doing what they set out to do.

the right goals in the right ways. The key issues and principles in managing this goal-setting process are described in *Manager's Notepad 12.1*, and "participation" is an important element. The degree to which the person expected to do the work is involved in setting the performance goals can influence his or her satisfaction and performance. Research indicates that a positive impact is most likely to occur when the participation (1) allows for increased understanding of specific and difficult goals and (2) provides for greater acceptance and commitment to them. The concept of *management by objectives* (described in Chapter 7) is a good illustration of such a participative approach to goal setting.

MOTIVATION AND JOB DESIGN

● **Job design** is the allocation of specific work tasks to individuals and groups.

The process of **job design** is one of creating or defining jobs by assigning specific work tasks to individuals and groups. It should contribute to the accomplishment of two major goals—job performance and job satisfaction. One without the other is simply insufficient to meet the high standards expected of today's workplace.

WHAT IS A GOOD JOB?

● **Job performance** is the quantity and quality of task accomplishment by an individual or group.

Job performance is the quantity and quality of tasks accomplished by an individual or group at work. Performance, as is commonly said, is the "bottom line" for people at work. It is a cornerstone of productivity, and it should contribute to the accomplishment of organizational objectives. Indeed, a *value-added criterion* is being used in more and more organizations to evaluate the worthwhileness of jobs and/or jobholders. The performance of every job should add value to the organization's production of useful goods and/or services.

In addition to its performance potential, any job should also provide opportunities for **job satisfaction.** This indicator of quality of work life is defined as the degree to which a person feels positively or negatively about various aspects of a job.[11] The *Wall Street Journal* reports the following levels of job satisfaction in a poll of American workers: completely satisfied–37%, somewhat satisfied–47%, somewhat dissatisfied–10%, completely dissatisfied–4%, not sure–2%.[12] Wouldn't it be ideal if the majority of workers in this sample, and workers anywhere, could say that they were "completely satisfied" with their jobs? An important goal in job design should always be to create jobs rich with potential satisfaction. This means that such things as pay, tasks, supervision, coworkers, work setting, and advancement opportunities must be considered. These are all facets of job satisfaction that can be addressed by employers in the attempt to improve attitudes and raise the quality of work life.

● **Job satisfaction** is the degree to which an individual feels positively or negatively about a job.

The consulting firm Hewitt Associates does employee-satisfaction surveys for clients. In one 6,000-worker credit card processing company, a survey revealed that workers had concerns about the quality of their work lives and didn't feel valued by their employer. They liked the employer's good benefits but disliked the lack of privacy at their workstations and the poor relationships with managers. In response to the consultant's report, company executives provided more private workstations, gave more attention to management training and selection, and reemphasized teamwork. An evaluation of the changes reported a decrease in employee turnover from 35 percent to 15 percent, making it well worth the consulting costs.[13]

Job design in many ways is an exercise in "fit." A good job provides a fit between the needs and capabilities of workers and tasks so that both job performance and satisfaction are high. Common job design alternatives are job simplification, job enlargement and rotation, and job enrichment.

JOB SIMPLIFICATION

Job simplification involves standardizing work procedures so that people work in well-defined and highly specialized tasks. Simplified jobs are narrow in job scope—that is, the number and variety of different tasks a person performs. The logic is straightforward: Because the jobs don't require complex skills, workers should be easier and quicker to train, less difficult to supervise, and easy to replace if they leave. Furthermore, because tasks are precisely and narrowly defined workers should become good at doing the same tasks over and

● **Job simplification** employs people in clearly defined and very specialized tasks.

Browser

Go to: http://www.wiley.com/college/schermerhorn

 THE WALL STREET JOURNAL.

WILEY

IN PRACTICE

Motivation can be described as a "person's willingness to expend effort." High performance organizations depend on motivated individuals to execute their business plans. The problem becomes, not only how you motivate employees, but also how do you sustain that high level of performance over time?

The two areas of compensation and benefits receive most of the attention in the business press. Select **Careers** in the **Other wsj.com Sites** section of the left-hand menu.

Select **Salaries and Profiles** to inspect salary levels for professionals in careers in which you are interested.

The area of employee benefits, including medical, family, and retirement attract increasing attention each year. Under the **Career Columnists** link, there are numerous articles concerning benefit packages and compensation issues.

Returning to the Interactive Journal **Front Section,** use the **Search** feature to investigate arti-

cles on "merit pay," "stock options," and "incentive pay." More and more firms are moving toward a pay-for-performance incentive package for both managers and employees.

In the area of Job Design, corporate reengineering dominated much of the early 1990s. Process redesign, spurred by technology and computers, has resulted in faster, better, and cheaper products and services. Old industries are being reshaped by new processes borrowed from computer and high technology companies from around the globe.

Try the **Search** feature with "reengineering" and "downsizing," two catch phrases for corporate reorganization.

Go back to the **Careers** site and select **HR ISSUES.** Look for the **Manager's Journal** hyperlink. There are a variety of articles concerning work and work processes under this heading.

ADDITIONAL SITES

Pratt & Whitney provides a host of compensation benefits

for its employees at http://www.pratt-whitney.com/careers/. Click on the benefits link to view the nature of their flexible benefits program.

SHRM link to benefits pages on the web at http://www.shrm.org/hrlinks/comp.htm.

DELIVERABLES:

Make a list of outcomes that serve to energize you as an individual.

DISCUSSION QUESTIONS:

1. What salary range are you anticipating in your career search? Back this up with statistics for actual salaries in your career field.

2. Utilizing the **Glossary** link under **Resources** in the left-hand menu, make sure you understand the following:

- 401
- ESOP—Employee Stock Ownership Plan
- Keogh
- SEP—Simplified Employee Pension

3. How would you change the motivation factors in your undergraduate program to increase levels of effort?

 *Note: The underscored words/phrases in the Interactive Journal feature indicate Internet links provided in the online versions. See the *Introducing Management* Web site at www.wiley.com/college/schermerhorn.

over again. But as you might expect, things don't always work out this well in highly simplified jobs. Productivity can suffer as unhappy workers drive up costs through absenteeism and turnover and through poor performance caused by boredom and alienation. The most extreme form of job simplification is **automation,** or the total mechanization of a job.

- **Automation** is the total mechanization of a job.

JOB ROTATION AND JOB ENLARGEMENT

One way to move beyond job simplification is to expand job scope by increasing the number and variety of tasks involved in a job. This can be done by **job rotation** that increases task variety by periodically shifting workers between jobs involving different task assignments. It can also be done by **job enlargement** that increases task variety by combining two or more tasks that were previously assigned to separate workers. Often these are tasks done immediately before or after the work performed in the original job.

- **Job rotation** increases task variety by periodically shifting workers between jobs involving different tasks.

- **Job enlargement** increases task variety by combining into one job two or more tasks previously assigned to separate workers.

JOB ENRICHMENT

Frederick Herzberg, whose two-factor theory of motivation was discussed earlier, questions the true value of the job rotation and job enlargement. "Why," he asks, "should a worker become motivated when one or more meaningless tasks are added to previously existing ones or when work assignments are rotated among equally meaningless tasks?" By contrast, he says: "If you want people to do a good job, give them a good job to do."[14] He recommends **job enrichment** that builds more opportunities for satisfaction into a job by expanding not just job scope but also job depth—that is, the extent to which task planning and evaluating duties are performed by the individual worker rather than the supervisor. Herzberg's recommendations for enriching jobs through vertical loading are found in *Manager's Notepad 12.2.*

- **Job enrichment** increases job depth by adding work planning and evaluating duties normally performed by the supervisor.

MANAGER'S NOTEPAD 12.2

JOB ENRICHMENT CHECKLIST

Check 1: Remove controls that limit people's discretion in their work.

Check 2: Grant people authority to make decisions about their work.

Check 3: Make people understand their accountability for results.

Check 4: Allow people to do "whole" tasks or complete units of work.

Check 5: Make performance feedback available to those doing the work.

CORE CHARACTERISTICS MODEL

Modern management theory adopts a contingency perspective and recognizes that job enrichment may not be best for everyone. The core characteristics model developed by Richard Hackman and his associates offers a way for managers to create jobs, enriched or otherwise, that best fit the needs of people and organizations.[15] The model, described in *Figure 12.6*, identifies five core job characteristics.

Five core job characteristics

- *Skill variety:* The degree to which a job requires a variety of different activities to carry out the work and involves the use of a number of different skills and talents of the individual.

- *Task identity:* The degree to which the job requires completion of a "whole" and identifiable piece of work, that is, one that involves doing a job from beginning to end with a visible outcome.

- *Task significance:* The degree to which the job has a substantial impact on the lives or work of other people elsewhere in the organization or in the external environment.

- *Autonomy:* The degree to which the job gives the individual substantial freedom, independence, and discretion in scheduling the work and in determining the procedures to be used in carrying it out.

- *Feedback from the job itself:* The degree to which carrying out the work activities required by the job results in the individual obtaining direct and clear information on the results of his or her performance.

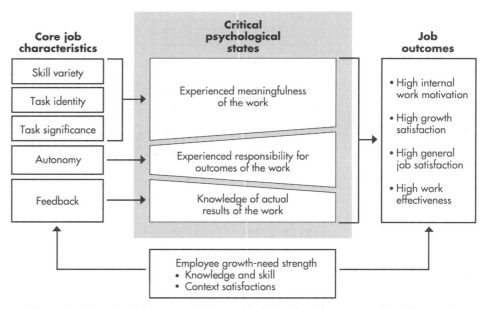

Figure 12.6 Core job characteristics and individual work outcomes in a diagnostic model of job design. *Source:* Reprinted by permission from J. Richard Hackman and Greg R. Oldham, *Work Redesign* (Reading, MA: Addison-Wesley, 1980), p. 90.

A job that is high in the core characteristics is considered enriched; the lower a job scores on the core characteristics, the less enriched it is. In true contingency fashion, however, the core characteristics will not affect all people in the same way. Generally speaking, people who respond most favorably to enriched jobs will have strong higher-order needs and appropriate job knowledge and skills. They will also be otherwise satisfied with job context.

When job enrichment is a good job design choice, Hackman and his colleagues recommend five ways to improve the core characteristics. First, you can *form natural units of work*. Make sure that the tasks people perform are logically related to one another and provide a clear and meaningful task identity. Second, try to *combine tasks*. Expand job responsibilities by pulling together into one larger job a number of smaller tasks previously done by others. Third, *establish client relationships*. Put people in contact with others who, as clients inside and/or outside the organization, use the results of their work. Fourth, *open feedback channels*. Provide opportunities for people to receive performance feedback as they work and to learn how performance changes over time. Fifth, *practice vertical loading*. Give people more control over their work by increasing their authority to perform the planning and controlling previously done by supervisors.

At Boeing Company, technology and people are keys to the development of new planes to compete successfully with Europe's Airbus Industries. Designs for the 777 airplane utilized the latest computer-assisted techniques and were largely paperless. Engineers worked out problems on powerful computers, including all the coordinating details of over 130,000 engineered parts and more than 3 million rivets, screws, and fasteners. But technology doesn't stand alone; people count too. A team structure of cross-functional "design-build" teams includes representatives from all areas. Design and manufacturing problems are to be solved by the teams *before* production starts.

ALTERNATIVE WORK ARRANGEMENTS

Not only is the content of jobs changing for individuals and groups in today's workplace, but the context is changing too. Work–life balance is increasingly at issue for a diverse workforce, and the information economy is bringing new employment opportunities.[16] Among the more significant developments is the emergence of a number of alternative ways for people to schedule their time to balance work and personal/family needs.[17]

COMPRESSED WORKWEEK

A **compressed workweek** is any work schedule that allows a full-time job to be completed in less than the standard 5 days of 8-hour shifts. Its most common

* A **compressed workweek** allows a full-time, 40-hour-per-week job to be completed in less than 5 days.

form is the "4–40," that is, accomplishing 40 hours of work in four 10-hour days. One advantage of the 4–40 schedule is that the employee receives 3 consecutive days off from work each week. This benefits the individual through more leisure time and lower commuting costs. The organization should also benefit through lower absenteeism and any improved performance that may result. Potential disadvantages include increased fatigue and family adjustment problems for the individual, as well as increased scheduling problems, possible customer complaints, and possible union objections.

FLEXIBLE WORKING HOURS

● **Flexible working hours** give employees some choice in the pattern of daily work hours.

The term **flexible working hours,** also called *flexitime* or *flextime*, describes any work schedule that gives employees some choice in the pattern of their daily work hours. Some may choose to come in earlier and leave earlier, while still completing an 8-hour day; others may choose to start later in the morning and leave later. In between these extremes are opportunities to attend to personal affairs, such as dental appointments, home emergencies, visits to children's schools, and so on. The advantages are especially important to members of a diverse workforce. Flexibility is important to many dual-career couples who face the complications of managing careers and other responsibilities, including parenting. Single parents with young children and employees with elder-care responsibilities also find it very attractive to have the option of adjusting work schedules to allow for other obligations to be met. The added discretion flextime provides may also encourage workers to have more positive attitudes toward the organization.

JOB SHARING

● **Job sharing** splits one job between two people.

Another important development for today's workforce is **job sharing,** whereby one full-time job is split between two or more persons. Job sharing often involves each person working one-half day, but it can also be done on weekly or monthly sharing arrangements. When it is feasible for jobs to be split and shared, organizations can benefit by employing talented people who would otherwise be unable to work. The qualified specialist who is also a parent may be unable to stay away from home for a full workday but may be able to work a half day. Job sharing allows two such persons to be employed as one. Although there are sometimes adjustment problems, the arrangement can be good for all concerned.

TELECOMMUTING

Another significant development in our high-tech economy is the growing popularity of ways for people to work away from a fixed office location.

Management Across Functions

HUMAN RESOURCES

Workers Value Control Over Time

When Brock Holmes gave up his job as marketing director for a telephone company he wasn't complaining about his paycheck, stock options or work team. He liked all of them. But he valued his time more. He traded in 10+ hour workdays to become an independent contractor moving from project to project for different employers. He typically sets two days a week aside for his family, gets great performance reviews, and has plenty of work. Progressive employers are recognizing that high-pressure work schedules take their toll and that time is increasingly valuable to employees. To attract and maintain quality workers they are offering more vacation time for fewer years employment and better time-off options during the work year. "Paid-time-off banks" are increasingly popular. They combine personal and sick days and allow workers to use them as desired with the supervisor's approval. Other employers are making special time off a performance incentive, offering "balance days" to high performing workers so that they can catch up with personal and family matters. Giving workers more control over their time can have positive results. An American Management Association survey of 352 employers found time off more important than money in employee retention. Smart employers have learned to value workers' time—time for themselves and time for their families. At First Union Bank in Charlotte, N.C., where paid-time-off banks are popular, assistant vice president Angela Mull says: "We wanted to empower employees to own their time off and schedule it." [18]

Telecommuting, sometimes called *flexiplace* or *cyber-commuting*, is a work arrangement that allows at least a portion of scheduled work hours to be completed outside of the office, facilitated by various forms of electronic communication and computer-mediated linkages to clients or customers and a central office.

Telecommuting frees the jobholder from the normal constraints of commuting, fixed hours, and special work attire. It is popular among computer programmers and is found increasingly in such diverse areas as marketing, financial analysis, and administrative services. The new vocabulary of telecommuting practices includes *hoteling*—where telecommuters come to the central office and use temporary office facilities, and *virtual offices* that include everything from an office at home to mobile workspace in automobiles.

These options offer both advantages and disadvantages from a job design and management perspective. On the positive side are the freedom to be your own boss and the benefit of having more time for yourself. On the negative side are the possibilities of working too much, difficulty separating work and personal life, feelings of isolation and loss of visibility for promotion.

● **Telecommuting** involves working at home or other places using computer links to the office.

Managers, in turn, may be required to change their routines and procedures to accommodate the challenges of supervising people from a distance.

INDEPENDENT CONTRACTING AND PART-TIME WORK

● **Independent contracting** engages outsiders to complete special tasks or projects.

Among the developments in more flexible work arrangements is a growing use of **independent contracting,** where specific tasks or projects are assigned to outsiders rather than full-time workers. When the project is completed, the contractor moves on to another assignment elsewhere. This benefits the organization by allowing for the hiring of special talents and expertise "as needed" and without the need to engage in a long-term employment relationship. For the independent contractors, it can allow flexibility and variety in their jobs while providing opportunities for personal choice in work–life balance.

● **Contingency workers** are employed on a part-time and temporary basis to supplement a permanent workforce.

Independent contractors are examples of the growing number of American workers who work on a part-time basis. In fact, employers are increasingly reliant on **contingency workers,** or *permatemps*, who supplement the full-time workforce and often do so on a long-term basis. Because part-time or contingency workers can be easily hired, contracted with, and/or terminated in response to changing needs, many employers like the flexibility they offer in controlling labor costs and dealing with cyclical demand.[19] On the other hand, some worry that temporaries lack the commitment of permanent workers and may lower productivity.

Perhaps the most controversial issue of the part-time work trend relates to the different treatment part-timers may receive from employers. They may be paid less than their full-time counterparts, and they often fail to receive important benefits, such as health care, life insurance, pension plans, and paid vacations. The social and economic implications of the growing role of part-time and contingent employment are fast gaining the attention of concerned policymakers.[20]

SUMMARY

How Do Individual Needs Influence Motivation?

- Maslow's hierarchy of human needs suggests a progression from lower order physiological, safety, and social needs to higher order ego and self-actualization needs.
- Herzberg's two-factor theory points out the importance of both job content and job context factors in satisfying human needs.
- McClelland's acquired needs theory identifies the needs for achievement, affiliation, and power, all of which may influence what a person desires from work.

What Do the Process Theories Say About Motivation?

- Adams's equity theory recognizes that people who feel inequitably treated are motivated to act in ways that reduce the sense of inequity; perceived *negative* inequity may result in someone working less hard in the future.

- Vroom's expectancy theory states that Motivation = Expectancy $\times$ Instrumentality $\times$ Valence; the theory encourages managers to make sure that any rewards offered for motivational purposes are both achievable and individually valued.

- Locke's goal-setting theory emphasizes the motivational power of goals; people tend to be highly motivated when task goals are specific rather than ambiguous, difficult but achievable, and set through participatory means.

How Can Motivating Jobs Be Designed?

- Jobs should be designed so that workers enjoy high levels of both job performance and job satisfaction.

- Job simplification creates narrow and repetitive jobs consisting of well-defined tasks with many routine operations, such as the typical assembly-line job.

- Job enlargement allows individuals to perform a broader range of simplified tasks; job rotation allows individuals to transfer between different jobs of similar skill levels on a rotating basis.

- Job enrichment results in more meaningful jobs that involve more autonomy in decision making and broader task responsibilities.

- The diagnostic approach to job enrichment involves analyzing jobs according to five core characteristics: skill variety, task identity, task significance, autonomy, and feedback.

How Can Motivating Work Schedules Be Arranged?

- Alternative work schedules can make work hours less inconvenient and enable organizations to respond better to individual needs and personal responsibilities.

- The compressed workweek allows 40 hours of work to be completed in only 4 days' time.

- Flexible working hours allow people to adjust the starting and ending times of their daily schedules.

- Job sharing allows two or more people to share one job.

- Telecommuting allows people to work at home or in mobile offices through computer links with their employers and/or customers.

- An increasing number of people work as independent contractors; more and more organizations are employing part-timers or contingency workers.

KEY TERMS

Automation (p. 197)

Compressed workweek (p. 199)

Contingency workers (p. 202)

Expectancy (p. 192)

Flexible working hours (p. 200)

Higher order needs (p. 188)

Hygiene factors (p. 189)

Independent contractors (p. 202)

Instrumentality (p. 192)

Job design (p. 194)

Job enlargement (p. 197)

Job enrichment (p. 197)

Job performance (p. 194)

Job rotation (p. 197)

Job satisfaction (p. 195)

Job sharing (p. 200)

Job simplification (p. 195)

SELF-TEST

Take the interactive Self-Test for this chapter on the Schermerhorn Web Site

Chapter Thirteen

Communication and Interpersonal Skills

PLANNING AHEAD—
Chapter 13 Study Questions

- What is the communication process?
- How can communication be improved?
- How can conflict be dealt with positively?
- How can negotiation be successfully accomplished?

WHEN IN DOUBT, COMMUNICATE

SOME 30 PERCENT OR more of managers report difficulties in dealing with communication and interpersonal relations. Helping them to do something about such problems is what the Center for Creative Leadership, a well-known management training center, is all about. Richard S. Herlich came to the Center after being promoted to director of marketing for his firm. "I thought I had the perfect style," he said. He learned through role-playing that others viewed him as an aloof and poor communicator. Back on the job, Herlich became more involved in others' work projects. Another participant, Robert Siddall, received feedback that he was too domineering. Center instructors worked with him to develop more positive relationships and a "coaching" style of management. Siddall's relationships with co-workers improved. He says, "If I start screaming and yelling, they say—'Old Bob, old Bob.'" [1]

The ability to communicate well, both orally and in writing, is a critical leadership skill.[2] Through communication people exchange and share information with one another, and influence one another's attitudes, behaviors, and understandings. Communication allows one to establish and maintain interpersonal relationships, listen to others, and gain information. No manager can handle conflict, negotiate successfully, and succeed at leadership without being a good communicator. It is no wonder that "communication skills" often top the list of attributes employers look for in job candidates.

THE COMMUNICATION PROCESS

● **Communication** is the process of sending and receiving symbols with meanings attached.

Formally defined, **communication** is an interpersonal process of sending and receiving symbols with messages attached to them. The key elements in the communication process are shown in *Figure 13.1*. They include a *sender*, who is responsible for encoding an intended *message* into meaningful symbols, both verbal and nonverbal. The message is sent through a *communication channel* to a *receiver*, who then decodes or interprets its meaning. This interpretation, importantly, may or may not match the sender's original intentions. *Feedback*, when present, reverses the process and conveys the receiver's response back to the sender. Another way to view the communication process is as a series of questions. "Who?" (sender) "says what?" (message) "in what way?" (channel) "to whom?" (receiver) "with what result?" (interpreted meaning).

● In **effective communication** the intended meaning of the source and the perceived meaning of the receiver are identical.

WHAT IS EFFECTIVE COMMUNICATION?

Effective communication occurs when the intended message of the sender and the interpreted meaning of the receiver are one and the same. Although this should be the goal in any communication attempt, it is not always achieved. **Efficient communication** occurs at minimum cost in terms of resources expended, such as the amount of time involved. Efficiency is one reason

● **Efficient communication** occurs at minimum cost.

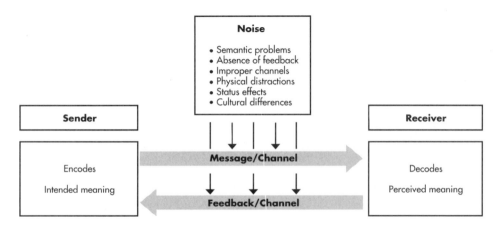

Figure 13.1   The process of interpersonal communication.

why we often leave voice mail messages and interact by e-mail, rather than visit others personally to communicate a message.

Efficient communication is not always effective. A low-cost approach such as an e-mail note to a distribution list may save time, but it does not always result in everyone getting the same meaning from the message. Without opportunities to ask questions and clarify the message, erroneous interpretations are possible. By the same token, an effective communication may not always be efficient. If a work team leader visits each team member individually to explain a new change in procedures, this may guarantee that everyone truly understands the change. But it may also be very costly in the demands it makes on the leader's time. A team meeting would be more efficient. In these and other ways, potential tradeoffs between effectiveness and efficiency must be recognized in communication.

COMMUNICATION BARRIERS

Communication is a two-way process that requires effort and skill on the part of both the sender and the receiver. **Noise,** as *Figure 13.1* shows, is anything that interferes with the effectiveness of the communication process. Common sources of noise include poor choice of channels, poor written or oral expression, failure to recognize nonverbal signals, physical distractions, and status effects.

● **Noise** is anything that interferes with communication effectiveness.

Poor Choice of Channels

A **communication channel** is the medium through which a message is conveyed from sender to receiver.[3] In general, written channels are acceptable for simple messages that are easy to convey and for those that require extensive dissemination quickly. They are also important, at least as follow-up communications, when formal policy or authoritative directives are being conveyed. Oral channels work best for messages that are complex and difficult to convey, where immediate feedback to the sender is valuable. They are also more personal and can create a supportive, even inspirational, emotional climate.

● A **communication channel** is the medium through which a message is sent.

The late Sam Walton, Wal-Mart's founder, was a master communicator. Stopping once to visit a Memphis store, he called everyone to the front, saying, "Northeast Memphis, you're the largest store in Memphis, and you must have the best floor-cleaning crew in America. This floor is so clean, let's sit down on it." Kneeling casually and wearing his Wal-Mart baseball cap, Walton congratulated them on their fine work. "I thank you," he said. "The company is so proud of you we can hardly stand it," he said reminding them of bonus checks recently given out. "But," he added, "you know that confounded Kmart is getting better, and so is Target. So what's our challenge?" Walton asked. "Customer service," he replied in answer to his own question. Walton's quality message was clear to everyone.[4]

Poor Written or Oral Expression

Communication will be effective only to the extent that the sender expresses a message in a way that can be clearly understood by the receiver. Words must be well chosen and properly used to express the sender's intentions. Consider the following "bafflegab" found among some executive communications. *The report said:* "Consumer elements are continuing to stress the fundamental necessity of a stabilization of the price structure at a lower level than exists at the present time." (*Translation:* Consumers keep saying that prices must go down and stay down.) *The manager said:* "Substantial economies were effected in this division by increasing the time interval between distribution of data-eliciting forms to business entities." (*Translation:* The division was saving money by sending fewer questionnaires to suppliers.)

Both written and oral communication require skill. It isn't easy, for example, to write a concise letter or to express one's thoughts in a computer e-mail report. Any such message can easily be misunderstood. It takes practice and hard work to express yourself well. The same holds true for oral communication that takes place via the spoken word in telephone calls, face-to-face meetings, formal briefings, video conferences, and the like. *Manager's Notepad 13.1* identifies guidelines for a common and important oral communication situation faced by managers—the executive briefing or formal presentation.

Failure to Recognize Nonverbal Signals

● **Nonverbal communication** takes place through gestures and body language.

Nonverbal communication takes place through such things as hand movements, facial expressions, body posture, eye contact, and the use of interpersonal space. It can be a powerful means of transmitting messages. Eye contact or voice intonation can be used intentionally to accent special parts of an oral communication. The astute observer notes the "body language" that may be "talking" for us even as we otherwise maintain silence. And when we do speak, a **mixed message** may occur as words communicate one message while actions, body language, appearance, or situational use of interpersonal space communicate something else. For example, watch how people behave in a meeting. A person who feels under attack may move back in a chair or lean away from the presumed antagonist, even while expressing verbal agreement. All of this is done quite unconsciously, but it sends a message to those alert enough to pick it up.

● A **mixed message** results when words communicate one message while actions, body language, or appearance communicate something else.

Physical Distractions

Any number of physical distractions can interfere with the effectiveness of communication. Some, such as telephone interruptions, drop-in visitors, and lack of privacy, are evident in the following conversation between an employee, George, and his manager. The obvious problems could have been easily avoided, given proper attention by the manager.

Okay, George, let's hear your problem [phone rings, boss picks it up, promises to deliver a report "just as soon as I can get it done"]. Uh, now, where were we—oh, you're having a problem with your technician. She's [manager's secretary brings in some papers that need his immediate signature; secretary leaves] . . . you say she's overstressed lately, wants to leave. . . . I tell you what, George, why don't you [phone rings again, lunch partner drops by] . . . uh, take a stab at handling it yourself. . . . I've got to go now.[5]

MANAGER'S NOTEPAD 13.1

How to Make a Successful Presentation

- *Be prepared:* Know what you want to say; know how you want to say it; and rehearse saying it.
- *Set the right tone:* Act audience centered; make eye contact; be pleasant and confident.
- *Sequence points:* State your purpose; make important points; follow with details; then summarize.
- *Support your points:* Give specific reasons for your points; state them in understandable terms.
- *Accent the presentation:* Use good visual aids and provide supporting "handouts" when possible.
- *Add the right amount of polish:* Attend to details; have the room, materials, and other arrangements ready to go.
- *Check your technology:* Check everything ahead of time; make sure it works and know how to use it.
- *Don't bet on the Internet:* Beware of plans to make real-time Internet visits; save your sites on a disk and then use a browser to open the file.
- *Be professional:* Be on time; wear appropriate attire; and act organized, confident, and enthusiastic.

Status Effects

"Criticize my boss? I don't have the right to." "I'd get fired." "It's her company, not mine." These comments show how the hierarchy of authority creates another potential barrier to effective communications. Simply put, people often find it difficult to communicate with bosses and others of higher organizational status. **Filtering** is the intentional distortion of information to make it appear favorable to the recipient. It most often involves someone "telling the boss what he or she wants to hear." Whether the reason behind this is a fear of retribution for bringing bad news, an unwillingness to identify personal mistakes, or just a general desire to please, the end result is the same. The person receiving filtered communications can end up making poor decisions because of a biased and inaccurate information base.

- **Filtering** is the intentional distortion of information to make it appear most favorable to the recipient.

PERCEPTION AND COMMUNICATION

Communication is also influenced by the way people receive and interpret information from the environment, a process called **perception**.[6] As shown in *Figure 13.2*, perception acts as a screen or filter through which information must pass

- **Perception** is the process through which people receive, organize, and interpret information from the environment.

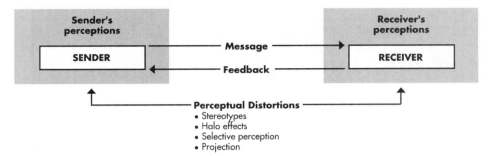

Figure 13.2 How perception influences communication.

in interpersonal communication. The results of this screening process vary because individual perceptions are influenced by such things as values, cultural background, and other circumstances of the moment. Because people can and do perceive the same things or situations very differently, perception can be an important influence on communication and interpersonal relations. In particular, a variety of tendencies toward perceptual distortions must be recognized for their impact on communication. They include the use of stereotypes, halo effects, selectivity, and projection as we deal with and judge other people.

Stereotypes

● A **stereotype** is when attributes commonly associated with a group are assigned to an individual.

A **stereotype** occurs when someone is identified with a group or category, and then oversimplified attributes associated with the group or category are linked back to the individual. Common stereotypes are those of young people, old people, teachers, students, union members, males, and females, among others. The phenomenon in each case is the same: A person is classified into a group on the basis of one piece of information, such as age or gender. Characteristics commonly associated with the group are then assigned to the individual. What is generalized about the group (e.g., "Young people dislike authority") may or may not be true about the individual. Stereotypes based on such factors as gender, age, and race can, and unfortunately still do, bias perceptions in some work settings. Consider this example of *gender stereotypes:* "*He's* talking with co-workers." (*Interpretation:* He's discussing a new deal.); "*She's* talking with co-workers." (*Interpretation:* She's gossiping.)[7]

Halo Effects

● A **halo effect** occurs when one attribute is used to develop an overall impression of a person or situation.

A **halo effect** occurs when one attribute is used to develop an overall impression of a person or situation. When meeting someone new, for example, the halo effect may cause one trait, such as a pleasant smile, to result in a positive first impression. By contrast, a particular hairstyle or manner of dressing may create a negative reaction. Halo effects, like stereotypes, cause individual differences to become obscured. This is especially significant in communication regarding someone's work performance. One factor, such as a person's punctuality, may become the "halo" for a positive overall performance evaluation. But even though the general conclusion seems to make sense, it may or may not be true in a given circumstance.

Selectivity

Selective perception is the tendency to single out for attention those aspects of a situation or person that reinforce or appear consistent with one's existing beliefs, values, or needs.[8] What this often means in an organization is that people from different departments or functions—such as marketing and manufacturing—tend to see things from their own points of view and fail to recognize or listen to other points of view. One way to reduce its impact is to actively gather inputs from a variety of people and perspectives.

- **Selective perception** is the tendency to define problems from one's own point of view.

Projection

Projection is the assignment of personal attributes to other individuals. A classic projection error is to assume that other persons share our needs, desires, and values. Suppose, for example, that you enjoy a lot of responsibility and challenge in your work. Suppose, too, that you are the newly appointed leader for a team whose work you consider dull and routine. You might move quickly to start a program of job enrichment to help members experience more responsibility and challenge. This may or may not be a good decision. Instead of designing jobs to best fit *their* needs, you have designed their jobs to fit *yours*. In fact, team members may be quite satisfied with jobs that, to you, seem routine. Projection errors can be minimized by self-awareness and a willingness to communicate and empathize with others, that is, to try to see things through their eyes.

- **Projection** is the assignment of personal attributes to other individuals.

IMPROVING COMMUNICATION

A number of things can be done to overcome barriers, minimize perceptual distortions, and improve the process of communication. They include active listening, constructive feedback, open communication channels, the use of space and technology, and valuing diversity.

ACTIVE LISTENING

When people "talk," they are trying to communicate something. That "something" may or may not be what they are saying. **Active listening** is the process of helping the source of a message say exactly what he or she really means.[9] The five rules for active listening are:

1. *Listen for message content*—try to hear exactly what content is being conveyed in the message.
2. *Listen for feelings*—try to identify how the source feels about the content in the message.
3. *Respond to feelings*—let the source know that her or his feelings are being recognized.
4. *Note all cues*—be sensitive to nonverbal and verbal messages; be alert for mixed messages.
5. *Paraphrase and restate*—state back to the source what you think you are hearing.

- **Active listening** helps the source of a message say what he or she really means.

← Rules for active listening

MANAGER'S NOTEPAD 13.2

TEN STEPS TO GOOD LISTENING

1. Stop talking.
2. Put the other person at ease.
3. Show that you want to listen.
4. Remove any potential distractions.
5. Empathize with the other person.
6. Don't respond too quickly; be patient.
7. Don't get mad; hold your temper.
8. Go easy on argument and criticism.
9. Ask questions.
10. Stop talking.

Consider the following conversations. Question 1: "Don't you think employees should be promoted on the basis of seniority?" *Passive listener's response:* "No, I don't!" *Active listener's response:* "It seems to you that they should, I take it?" Question 2: "What does the supervisor expect us to do about these out-of-date computers?" *Passive listener's response:* "Do the best you can, I guess." *Active listener's response:* "You're pretty disgusted with those machines, aren't you?"

The two examples show how active listening can facilitate and encourage communication in difficult circumstances, rather than discourage it. *Manager's Notepad 13.2* offers additional guidelines for good listening. Note that both the first and last steps are the same—stop talking!

CONSTRUCTIVE FEEDBACK

● **Feedback** is the process of telling someone else how you feel about something that person did or said.

The process of telling other people how you feel about something they did or said, or about the situation in general, is called **feedback.** The art of giving feedback is an indispensable skill, particularly for those who must regularly give performance feedback to others. When poorly done, such feedback can be threatening and cause resentment. When well done, feedback—even performance criticism—is listened to, accepted, and used to good advantage by the receiver.[10] Guidelines for giving "constructive" feedback include:[11]

Constructive feedback guidelines →

● Give feedback directly and with real feeling, based on trust between you and the receiver.

● Make sure that feedback is specific rather than general; use good, clear, and preferably recent examples to make your points.

● Give feedback at a time when the receiver seems most willing or able to accept it.

- Make sure the feedback is valid and limit it to things the receiver can be expected to do something about.
- Give feedback in small doses; never give more than the receiver can handle at any particular time.

OPEN CHANNELS

There are many ways to keep communication channels open. An approach called **managment by wandering around,** or **MBWA,** involves regularly spending time walking around and talking with others about a variety of work-related matters. It involves managers and leaders finding out for themselves what is going on in their organizations. For example, for Patricia Gallup, CEO of PC Connection, MBWA is clearly part of her style. She spends as much time as possible out of her office and on the floor where she can be close to workers in the various departments.[12] She also makes herself available by e-mail and greets employees by name as she walks the hallways.

Another communication approach that helps to make "bosses" more aware of the feelings and perceptions of other people with whom they work closely is

 In **management by wandering around (MBWA)** workers at all levels talk with bosses about a variety of work-related matters.

 Management Across Functions

MARKETING

Tell Employees How Good They Are

It's all too often that the underperformer gets a manager's attention while the star goes without recognition. But a psychologist working for BankOne warns: "Sure you want to encourage self reliance, but those high-achieving perfectionist people need and want daily feedback." Changes in today's organizations—flatter structures, wider spans of control, more telecommuting, and globalization, can make it harder for managers to stay in touch. But technology can also help close the gap. After all, positive feedback can be only an e-mail or voice-mail message away. Mark Dowley's job at MCCann Erickson's Momentum marketing unit often involves international travel. But he makes extra efforts to encourage his direct reports to call him as needed while he visits customers worldwide. "Everyone wants time to talk," he says, "and that's more difficult when you are trying to take care of customers and growing quickly." At Foote, Cone & Belding, a Chicago advertising firm, Julie Danis benefits from a manager who is quick to offer praise. Her boss "announces that I have done a good job in front of others and tells me when she's complimented me to the chairman." All organizations run on talent and none can afford to lose high-performing employees. In this age of information technology there's also fewer excuses for not staying in touch with the people who count the most—those who work for you. Who wouldn't enjoy a workday rich with praise, recognition and a strong dose of appreciation?[15]

● **360-degree feedback** involves upward appraisals from subordinates as well as additional feedback from peers, internal and external customers, and higher managers.

360-degree feedback. This technique involves gathering performance feedback from a manager's subordinates, as well as from peers, bosses, and others. A self-assessment is also part of the process. The goal of 360 feedback is to gain awareness and information that can be used for constructive improvement. Managers who have participated in the process often express surprise at what they learn. True success with 360 feedback, however, requires a commitment to make the changes needed to improve communication and work relationships in the future.

USE OF SPACE

● **Proxemics** is the use of interpersonal space.

An important but sometimes neglected aspect of communication is **proxemics**, or the use of interpersonal space.[13] The distance between people suggests varying intentions in terms of intimacy, openness, and status. And the proxemics or physical layout of an office is an often overlooked form of nonverbal communication. Check it out. Offices with two or more chairs available for side-by-side seating, for example, convey a different message than having the manager's chair behind the desk and those for visitors directly in front.

Office or workspace architecture is becoming increasingly valued. If you visit Sun Microsystems in San Jose, California, for example, you will see many public spaces designed to encourage communication among persons from different departments. At the firm's Sunsoft Experimental Space on the research campus you can't get to a private office without passing through a public space. Most meeting areas have no walls and most of the walls that exist are glass. Importantly, the Sun project involved not only the assistance of expert architectural consultants, but also extensive inputs and suggestions from the employees themselves. The results seem to justify the effort. A senior technical writer, Terry Davidson says: "This is the most productive workspace I have ever been in." [14]

USE OF TECHNOLOGY

Communication in organizations can benefit greatly from advancements in information technology. The new age of communication is one of e-mail, voice mail, videoconferencing, computer-mediated meetings, and more. An important development is the use of in-house intranets to provide opportunities for increased communication and collaboration. Intranet sites allow employees to easily share ideas and opinions. The purpose is to encourage freewheeling communication, share information and help one another solve problems. Such information-rich work environments are characteristic of the current emphasis on organizational learning and knowledge management.

VALUING CULTURE AND DIVERSITY

For years, cultural challenges in communication have been recognized by international travelers and executives.[16] But as we know, you don't have to travel abroad to come fact to face with diversity. Just going to work today is like a cross-cultural journey. The workplace abounds with subcultures based on gender, age, ethnicity, race, and other factors. As a result, the importance of cross-cultural communication skills applies at home just as well as it does in a foreign country. Cultural skills are gained by reaching out, crossing cultural boundaries, and embracing and respecting differences. And, they include an awareness of *ethnocentrism*—the tendency to consider one's culture superior to any and all others. Ethnocentrism can adversely affect communication in at least three major ways: (1) it may cause someone to *not* listen well to what others have to say; (2) it may cause someone to address or speak with others in ways that alienate them; and (3) it may lead to the use of inappropriate stereotypes when dealing with persons from another culture.

When Hyatt chairman Darryl Hartley-Leonard speaks to the firm's employees, to industry groups, and to other businesspeople, his message communicates a common theme: Value diversity and fulfill your social responsibilities. Says Hartley-Leonard, "No longer can we hide from the social, educational, and cultural challenges taking place in this country." Hyatt encourages employees to take up to 4 days leave per year for volunteer services. The firm works in Chicago with inner-city schools to help train students for careers in the hotel industry. This is part of business today, says Hartley-Leonard: "We all need to accept the fact that there is no longer a difference between what's good for society and what's good for business."[17]

COMMUNICATION AND CONFLICT MANAGEMENT

Among the essential communication skills, the ability to deal with interpersonal conflicts is critical. **Conflict** is a disagreement between people on substantive or emotional issues.[18] Managers and leaders spend a lot of time dealing with conflicts of various forms. *Substantive conflicts* involve disagreements over such things as goals; the allocation of resources; the distribution of rewards, policies and procedures; and job assignments. *Emotional conflicts* result from feelings of anger, distrust, dislike, fear, and resentment, as well as from personality clashes.

● **Conflict** is a disagreement over issues of substance and/or an emotional antagonism.

FUNCTIONAL AND DYSFUNCTIONAL CONFLICT

Conflict in organizations has two "faces"—one positive and one negative. *Figure 13.3* shows that conflict of moderate intensity can be good for performance. This *functional conflict* stimulates people toward greater work efforts, cooperation, and creativity. At very low or very high intensities *dysfunctional conflict* occurs. Too much conflict is distracting and interferes with other more task-relevant activities; too little conflict may promote complacency and the loss of a creative, high-performance edge. For example, this negative side of conflict can occur when two team members are unable to work together because of interpersonal hostilities (an emotional conflict) or when members of a committee can't agree on common goals (a substantive conflict).

Browser

Go to: http://www.wiley.com/college/schermerhorn

 THE WALL STREET JOURNAL.

WILEY

IN PRACTICE

Communication exists as one of the fundamental skills required of all managers. Interpersonal skills acts as one of the three major categories of managerial roles described by Mintzberg in Chapter 1.

The impact of technology, and in particular the Internet, on the communication process for managers is enormous. E-mail, pagers, cell phones, videoconferencing—they all have a profound effect on the ways managers interact.

The ability for managers to access online news, as it happens, increases the level of dynamism in the environment for many industries. Financial services, banking, e-commerce and others have felt this increased speed and focus on customer satisfaction.

Check out some additional on-line news sources, including:

- CNNfn at http://cnnfn.com/
- Smart Money at http://www.smartmoney.com/
- The Washington Post at http://www.washingtonpost.com/

- Barron's Online at http://interactive.wsj.com/pages/barrons.htm

More and more communication takes on a pronounced high-technology component. The concept of the "virtual office" allows individuals to locate great distances from the home office and still stay in touch with co-workers.

Check out this site for work on digital communications:

http://www.duke.edu/~ mccann/q-work.htm

Look here for information on Reinventing the Workplace

If the digital revolution is reengineering the work for managers, then technology understanding and mastery are two goals for which all managers must strive.

CONFLICT

A study on conflict made the following findings:

1. 20% of managers' time is spent handling conflict
2. Conflict management is rated

higher in importance than planning, communication, and decision making.

The Interactive Journal regularly contains articles highlighting disputes and conflict among upper-level managers in organizations. In addition, conflict and negotiations between unions and management are also covered. Try using the **Search** feature to check for articles on "labor unions." Also search for "labor strikes."

DELIVERABLES:

Take the Conflict Management Styles assessment online at the Web site. After scoring yourself, compare this with others around you. How would you change your conflict handling style?

DISCUSSION QUESTIONS:

1. Discuss how technology has changed the way you communicate with friends and family (i.e., e-mail, chat rooms).
2. Identify some examples of conflict in your student associations and how you reacted.
3. What conflict resolution technique mentioned in the text do you most depend on to resolve conflict?

 *Note: The underscored words/phrases in the Interactive Journal feature indicate Internet links provided in the online versions. See the *Introducing Management* Web site at www.wiley.com/college/schermerhorn.

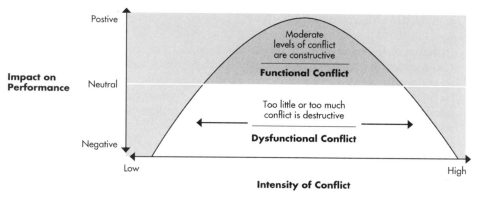

Figure 13.3 The positive and negative relationship between conflict and performance.

CONFLICT RESOLUTION

Conflicts can either be "resolved" in the sense that their causes are corrected, or they can be "suppressed," in that the causes remain but the conflict is controlled for a period of time. Suppressed conflicts run the risk of recurring at a later time. True **conflict resolution,** by contrast, eliminates the underlying causes of conflict and reduces the potential for similar conflicts in the future.

There are ways that work situations can be restructured to resolve conflicts. An *appeal to superordinate goals* can focus the attention of conflicting parties on one mutually-desirable objective. It offers them a common frame of reference against which to analyze and reconcile disagreements. Conflicts whose antecedents lie in competition for scarce resources can be resolved by *expanding the resources available* to everyone. By *altering one or more human variables*—that is, by replacing or transferring one or more of the conflicting parties—conflicts caused by poor interpersonal relationships can be eliminated. The same holds true if one can *alter the physical environment* by rearranging facilities, workspace, or workflows to decrease opportunities for conflict.

The *use of integrating devices* such as liaison personnel, special task forces, and cross-functional teams, and even the matrix form of organization, can change communication patterns and assist in conflict resolution. *Changes in reward systems* may reduce the competition between individuals and groups for rewards. Creating systems that reward cooperation can encourage teamwork and keep conflict within constructive limits. *Policies and procedures* may be created to direct behavior in ways that minimize the likelihood of negative conflict situations.

Finally, *training* can help prepare people to communicate and work more effectively in situations that are conflict prone. For example, differences in cultural styles were evident when IBM participated in a multicultural task force in an ambitious project to develop a 21st-century computer chip. Team members from America, Germany, and Japan had to learn how to work with each other. Before leaving home, the Germans were advised on what was called the American "hamburger style of management." When it comes to giving criticism, their trainer said, Americans start soft (the top of the bun), then criticize (the meat), and then end with encouragement (the bottom of the bun). Germans only give the meat and the Japanese only give the bun—you have to "smell" the meat.[19]

● **Conflict resolution** is the removal of the substantial and/or emotional reasons for a conflict.

CONFLICT MANAGEMENT STYLES

In terms of interpersonal styles, people respond to conflict in different ways.[20] *Cooperativeness* is the desire to satisfy another party's needs and concerns; *assertiveness* is the desire to satisfy one's own needs and concerns. *Figure 13.4* shows five interpersonal styles of conflict management that result from various combinations of the two. Briefly stated, these conflict management styles involve the following behaviors:

- **Avoidance** pretends conflict doesn't exist.

- **Accommodation** plays down differences to reduce conflict.

- **Competition** uses force or superior skill to "win" a conflict.

- **Compromise** occurs when each party gives up something of value to the other.

- **Collaboration** involves working out differences and solving problems so everyone wins.

- **Avoidance:** Being uncooperative and unassertive; downplaying disagreement, withdrawing from the situation, and/or staying neutral at all costs.

- **Accommodation,** or *smoothing:* Being cooperative but unassertive; letting the wishes of others rule; smoothing over or overlooking differences to maintain harmony.

- **Competition,** or *authoritative command:* Being uncooperative but assertive; working against the wishes of the other party, engaging in win-lose competition, and/or forcing through the exercise of authority.

- **Compromise:** Being moderately cooperative and assertive, bargaining for "acceptable" solutions in which each party wins a bit and loses a bit.

- **Collaboration** or *problem solving:* Being both cooperative and assertive; trying to satisfy everyone's concerns fully by working through differences; finding and solving problems so that everyone gains.[21]

These conflict management styles can have quite different outcomes.[22] Conflict management by avoidance or accommodation often creates a *lose-lose conflict*. No one achieves her or his true desires, and the underlying reasons for conflict often remain unaffected. Although a lose-lose conflict may appear settled or may even disappear for a while, it tends to recur in the future. Competition and compromise tend to create *win-lose conflict*. Here, each party strives to gain at the other's expense. In extreme cases, one party achieves its desires to the complete exclusion of the other party's desires. Because win-lose methods

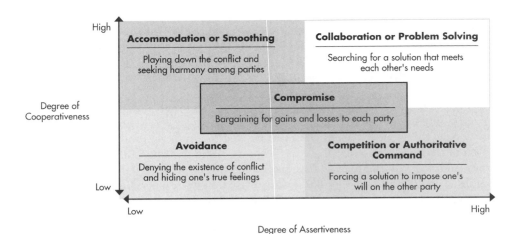

Figure 13.4 Alternative conflict management styles.

fail to address the root causes of conflict, future conflicts of the same or a similar nature are likely to occur.

Collaboration uses problem solving to reconcile underlying differences and is often the most effective conflict management style. It creates *win-win conflict* whereby issues are resolved to the mutual benefit of all conflicting parties. This is typically achieved by openly confronting the issues and through the willingness of those involved to recognize that something is wrong and needs attention. Win-win methods are preferred approaches to conflict management.

COMMUNICATION AND NEGOTIATION

How would you behave, and what would you do if: (1) You have been offered a promotion and would really like to take it, but the pay raise offered is less than you hoped? (2) You have enough money to order one new computer for your department, but you have requests for two new machines? These are but two examples of the many work situations that involve **negotiation,** the process of making joint decisions when the parties involved have different preferences. People negotiate over such diverse matters as salary, merit raises and performance evaluations, job assignments, work schedules, work locations, special privileges, and many other considerations. All such situations are susceptible to conflict and require exceptional communication skills.

● **Negotiation** is the process of making joint decisions when the parties involved have different preferences.

NEGOTIATION APPROACHES

There are two important goals in negotiation. *Substance goals* are concerned with outcomes; they are tied to the "content" issues of the negotiation. *Relationship goals* are concerned with processes; they are tied to the way people work together while negotiating and how they (and any constituencies they represent) will be able to work together again in the future. Negotiation can be considered successful when issues of substance are resolved and working relationships among the negotiating parties are maintained or even improved.[23]

The way each party approaches a negotiation can have a major impact on its outcomes.[24] In **distributive negotiation** each party makes "claims" for certain preferred results. This is a competitive "win-lose" approach in which one party can gain only if the other loses. Relationships are often sacrificed as the negotiating parties focus only on their respective self-interests. By contrast, in **principled negotiation** a "win-win" orientation operates.[25] The interests of all parties are considered and the goal is to base the final outcome on the merits of individual claims. Everyone look for ways for all claims to be satisfied if possible, with no one "losing" in the process.

● **Distributive negotiation** focuses on "win-lose" claims made by each party.

● **Principled negotiation** uses a "win-win" orientation to reach solutions acceptable to each party.

RULES FOR PRINCIPLED NEGOTIATION

In their popular book *Getting to Yes*, Roger Fisher and William Ury argue in favor of principled negotiation that results in truly integrative agreements. The recommended approach involves the following four negotiation rules.[26]

Four rules of principled
negotiation →

- Separate the people from the problem.
- Focus on interests, not on positions.
- Generate many alternatives before deciding what to do.
- Insist that results are based on some objective standard.

Proper attitudes, good information, and effective communication are important foundations for integrative agreements. Each negotiating party must be willing to trust, share information with, and ask reasonable questions of the other party. Each must know what is really important to them and communicate it well. By the same token each must find out what is really important to the other party.

NEGOTIATION PITFALLS

The negotiation process is admittedly complex, and negotiators must guard against common mistakes. There are many obstacles that can stand in the way of success in gaining integrative agreements. Pitfalls such as the following can all too easily create distributive "win-lose" conditions.[27]

The first pitfall is the tendency of *falling prey to the myth of the "fixed pie."* This involves acting on the distributive assumption that in order for you to gain, the other person must give something up. Negotiating this way fails to recognize the integrative assumption that the "pie" can sometimes be expanded and/or utilized to everyone's advantage. A second pitfall is the *nonrational escalation of conflict.* The negotiator in this case becomes committed to previously stated "demands" and allows concerns for "ego" and "face saving" to increase the perceived importance of satisfying these demands. The third pitfall is *overconfidence and ignoring the other's needs.* The error here is becoming overconfident that your position is the only correct one and failing to see the needs of the other party and the merits in its position. The fourth pitfall is the tendency to do *too much "telling" and too little "hearing."* When committing the "telling" problem, parties to a negotiation don't really make themselves understood to each other. When committing the "hearing" problem, they don't "listen" sufficiently to understand what the other is saying.

It may not always be possible to achieve integrative agreements. When negotiations reach the point of impasse, dispute resolution through mediation and arbitration can be useful. *Mediation* involves a neutral third party who tries to improve communication between negotiating parties and keep them focused on relevant issues. This mediator does not issue a ruling or make a decision, but can take an active role in discussions. This may include making suggestions in an attempt to move the parties toward agreement. *Arbitration*, such as salary arbitration in professional sports, is a stronger form of dispute resolution. It involves a neutral third party, the arbitrator, who acts as a "judge" and issues a binding decision. This usually includes a formal hearing in which the arbitrator listens to both sides and reviews all facets of the case before making a ruling.

SUMMARY

What Is the Communication Process?

- Communication is the interpersonal process of sending and receiving symbols with messages attached to them.

- Effective communication occurs when both the sender and the receiver of a message interpret it in the same way; efficient communication occurs when the message is sent at low cost for the sender.

- Noise is anything that interferes with the effectiveness of communication, including poor use of channels, poor expression, physical distractions, and status effects, among other possibilities.

- Perception acts as a filter through which all communication passes as it travels from one person to the next.

- Because people tend to perceive things differently, the same message may be interpreted quite differently by different people.

- Common perceptual distortions that may reduce communication effectiveness include stereotypes, projections, halo effects, and selective perception.

How Can Communication Be Improved?

- Active listening, through reflecting back and paraphrasing, can help overcome communication barriers.

- The act of giving performance feedback can be difficult for the sender and threatening to the receiver; care must be taken to keep such feedback constructive.

- Upward communication may be improved through such techniques MBWA—management by wandering around—and by 360-degree feedback.

- Space can be used and designed to improve opportunities for communication in organizations, as can the appropriate use of information technology, such as e-mail and intranets.

- Greater cross-cultural awareness and sensitivity can help reduce the difficulties of communication and diversity.

How Can Managers Deal Positively With Conflict?

- Conflict occurs as disagreements over substantive or emotional issues.

- Managers should support functional conflict that facilitates a high-performance edge and creativity; they should avoid the harmful effects of too little or too much conflict that becomes dysfunctional.

- Conflict may be managed through structural approaches that involve changing people, goals, resources, or work arrangements.

- Personal conflict management "styles" include avoidance, accommodation, compromise, competition, and collaboration.

- True conflict resolution involves problem solving through a win-win collaborative approach.

How Can Negotiation Be Successfully Accomplished?

- Negotiation is the process of making decisions in situations in which the participants have different preferences.
- Both substance goals, those concerned with outcomes, and relationship goals, those concerned with processes, are important in successful negotiation.
- Effective negotiation occurs when issues of substance are resolved and the process results in good working relationships.
- Distributive approaches to negotiation emphasize win-lose outcomes and are usually harmful to relationships.
- Principled approaches to negotiation emphasize integrative win-win outcomes and the interests of all parties.

KEY TERMS

Accommodation
(p. 218)

Active listening (p. 211)

Avoidance (p. 218)

Collaboration (p. 218)

Communication (p. 206)

Communication channel
(p. 207)

Competition (p. 218)

Compromise (p. 218)

Conflict (p. 215)

Conflict resolution
(p. 217)

Distributive negotiation
(p. 219)

Effective communication
(p. 206)

Efficient communication
(p. 206)

Feedback (p. 212)

Filtering (p. 209)

Halo effect (p. 210)

MBWA (p. 213)

Mixed message (p. 208)

Negotiation (p. 219)

Noise (p. 207)

Nonverbal
communication (p. 208)

Perception (p. 209)

Principled negotiation
(p. 219)

Projection (p. 211)

Proxemics (p. 214)

Selective perception
(p. 211)

Stereotype (p. 210)

360-degree feedback
(p. 214)

SELF-TEST

Take the interactive Self-Test for this chapter on the Schermerhorn Web Site

Chapter Fourteen

Teams and Teamwork

PLANNING AHEAD—
Chapter 14 Study Questions

- How do teams help organizations?
- How do teams work?
- How do teams make decisions?
- How can leaders build high-performance teams?

TEAMS ARE WORTH THE HARD WORK

A BOY SCOUT CAMP in central Ohio found a new purpose in life. In addition to its traditional work with the scouts, Camp Lazarus hosts team-building exercises for corporations. On a fall day, for example, a team of employees from American Electric Power (AEP) worked to solve the problem of how to get six members through a spider-web maze of bungee cords strung 2 feet above the ground. When her colleagues lifted Judy Gallo into their hands to pass her over the obstacle, she was nervous. But a trainer told the team this was just like solving a problem together at the office. The spider web was just another performance constraint like difficult policies or financial limits they might face at work. After swapping "high-fives" for making it through the web, Judy's team went on to jump tree stumps together, pass hula hoops while holding hands, and more. Says one team trainer, "We throw clients into situations to try and bring out the traits of a good team." [1]

Just the words *group* and *team* elicit both positive and negative reactions in the minds of many people. Although it is said that "two heads are better than one," we are also warned that "too many cooks spoil the broth." The true skeptic can be heard to say, "A camel is a horse put together by a committee." But against this somewhat humorous background lies a most important point: Teams and teamwork are indispensable to the new workplace. The new organizational designs and cultures require it, as does a comprehensive commitment to empowerment and employee involvement.[2]

TEAMS IN ORGANIZATIONS

● A **team** is a collection of people who regularly interact to pursue common goals.

● **Teamwork** is the process of people actively working together to accomplish common goals.

Formally defined, a **team** is a small group of people with complementary skills, who work together to achieve a shared purpose, and hold themselves mutually accountable for its accomplishment.[3] **Teamwork** is the process of people working together to accomplish these goals. The ability to lead through teamwork requires a special understanding of how teams operate and the commitment to use that understanding to help them achieve high levels of task performance and membership satisfaction.

A special benefit of teamwork is *synergy*—the creation of a whole that is greater than the sum of its parts. It occurs when teams use their resources to the fullest and achieve through collective performance far more than is otherwise possible. This is obviously an important advantage, but teams are also useful in other ways. Being part of a team can have a strong influence on individual attitudes and behaviors. Working in and being part of a team can satisfy important individual needs and can also improve performance. Teams, simply put, can be very good for both organizations and their members. The usefulness of teams includes:[4]

How teams help organizations

- Increasing resources for problem solving.
- Fostering creativity and innovation.
- Improving the quality of decision making.
- Enhancing members' commitments to tasks.
- Raising motivation through collective action.
- Helping control and discipline members.
- Satisfying individual needs as organizations grow in size.

● **Social loafing** is the tendency of some people to avoid responsibility by "free-riding" in groups.

There is no guarantee that teams will always be successful. Who hasn't encountered **social loafing,** that is, the presence of "free-riders" who slack off because responsibility is diffused in teams and others are present to do the work?[5] And who hasn't heard people complain about having to attend what they consider to be another "time-wasting" meeting?[6]

Things don't have to be this way. In fact, they must not be if teams are to make their best contributions to organizations. The time we spend in groups can be productive and satisfying, but to make it so we must understand the complex nature of groups and their internal dynamics. An important part of a manager's job, in particular, is knowing *when* a team is the best choice for a task. The second is to know *how* to work with and lead the team to best accomplish that task.

COMMITTEES AND TASK FORCES

Two common types of teams in organizations are "committees" and "task forces." Each brings people together outside of their daily job assignments to work in small teams for a specific purpose. They are typically led by a designated head or chairperson who, in turn, is held accountable for committee or task force results. A **committee** usually operates with a continuing purpose while its membership may change over time. A **task force** is more temporary, and its official tasks are very specific and time defined. Once its stated purpose has been accomplished, the task force disbands. Like committees, task forces are increasingly used to bring together people from various parts of an organization to work on common problems, such as a new product development project. But to achieve the desired results, any task force must be carefully established and then well run. Some task force management guidelines are found in the accompanying *Manager's Notepad 14.1.*

- A **committee** is a formal team designated to work on a special task on a continuing basis.

- A **task force** is a formal team convened for a specific purpose and expected to disband when that purpose is achieved.

CROSS-FUNCTIONAL TEAMS

Organizational design today emphasizes horizontal integration, problem solving and information sharing. It also tries to eliminate the tendency of workers to remain within their functions and restrict communication with other parts of an organization. The members of a **cross-functional team** come together from different functional units to work on a specific problem or task, and to do so

- Members of **cross-functional teams** come from different functional units.

MANAGER'S NOTEPAD 14.1

GUIDELINES FOR LEADING A TASK FORCE

- *Select appropriate task force members* who will be challenged by the assignment, who have the right skills, and who seem able to work well together.

- *Clearly define the purpose of the task force* to ensure that members and important outsiders know what is expected, why, and on what timetable.

- *Carefully select a task force leader* who has good interpersonal skills, can respect the ideas of others, and is willing to do what needs to be done.

- *Periodically review progress* to ensure that all task force members feel collectively accountable for results and that they receive performance feedback.

Management Across Functions

RESEARCH AND DEVELOPMENT

Virtual Teams Bridge Distance and Cultures

Take the task—design the most complex product Lucent Technologies has ever developed, add 500 engineers, spread them all over the world, and what do you get? For one thing, a new fiberoptic telephone switch with a selling price of $1 million plus. For another, major lessons in teamwork. Team leaders Cill Klinger and Frank Polito learned the lessons while wrestling with the challenges and opportunities of the 18-month project. But the difficulties of leading a team whose members worked on three continents and 13 time zones were substantial. Says Klinger: "You lose informal interaction—going to lunch, to the water cooler. You can never discount how many issues get solved that way." The team faced immense time pressures of a competitive marketplace. They had the support of the best communication technologies. But the members had very different personalities and cultural as well as professional backgrounds. Good old-fashioned team development helped bridge some of the gaps. At one point technical managers participated in special team-building exercises, scaling walls and solving puzzles together. Subgroups also met regularly in alternating cities, to socialize as well as work. Says a German team member: "Going into another culture is the only way to understand it. If you don't have a common understanding it's much more expensive to correct it later." Voice mail, conference calls, e-mail and the intranet filled in other gaps. This combination of face-to-face and electronic teamwork paid off for Kliner, Polito and the Lucent team. They met the deadline with a top quality product. And, from very challenging and complicated foundations, they built a team in the process.[7]

with the needs of the whole organization in mind. They are expected to share information, explore new ideas, seek creative solutions, meet project deadlines, and importantly, not to be limited in performance by purely functional concerns and demands. Rather, the team members collectively and individually are to think and act cross-functionally and in the best interests of the total system.

EMPLOYEE INVOLVEMENT TEAMS

● An **employee involvement team** meets on a regular basis to use its talents to help solve problems and achieve continuous improvement.

Many organizations now utilize functional or cross-functional **employee involvement teams.** These are groups of workers who meet on a regular basis outside of their formal assignments, with the goal of applying their expertise and attention to continuous improvement. Using a problem-solving framework, the teams try to bring the benefits of employee participation to bear on a wide variety of performance issues and concerns. A popular form of employee involvement team is the

quality circle, a group of workers that meets regularly to discuss and plan specific ways to improve work quality.[8] Usually, it consists of 6 to 12 members from a work area. After receiving special training in problem solving, team processes, and quality issues, members of the quality circle try to come up with suggestions that can be implemented to raise productivity through quality improvements.

● A **quality circle** is a team of employees who meet periodically to discuss ways of improving work quality.

Recycling car parts is the goal of the RAT pack at Ford Motor Company. The firm's Recycle Action Team meets once a week to find new ways to use recycled materials and to recycle as much as possible of the firm's products. Take scrap tires, for example. Ford vehicles now are incorporating parts made from recycled tires, soda bottles, and even used carpeting from homes. A special project of Ford's environmental outreach and strategy program, RAT is a good example of using team creativity and initiative to solve important problems.[9]

VIRTUAL TEAMS

The use of intranets and special software support for computerized meetings has given rise to **virtual teams.** They are teams whose members work together and solve problems through largely computer-mediated rather than face-to-face interactions.[10] Potential advantages of virtual teams make them increasingly important. Team members from widely dispersed locations can deal collectively with issues in a time-efficient fashion and without some of the interpersonal difficulties that might otherwise occur—especially when the issues are controversial. Such electronic team meetings can cause problems, however, particularly when members' working relationships are depersonalized and some of the advantages of face-to-face interaction are lost.[11]

● Members of a **virtual team** work together and solve problems through computer based interactions.

SELF-MANAGING WORK TEAMS

In a growing number of organizations the functional team consisting of a first-level supervisor and his or her immediate subordinates is disappearing. It is being replaced with **self-managing work teams.** These are teams of workers whose jobs have been redesigned to create a high degree of task interdependence and who have been given authority to make many decisions about how they go about doing the required work.[12] The expected advantages include better performance, decreased costs, and higher morale.

● Members of a **self-managing work team** have the authority to make decisions about how they share and complete their work.

Self-managing teams operate with participative decision making, shared tasks, and responsibility for many of the managerial tasks performed by supervisors in more traditional settings. The "self-management" responsibilities include planning and scheduling work, training members in various tasks, sharing tasks, meeting performance goals, ensuring high quality, and solving day-to-day operating problems. In some settings, the team's authority may even extend to "hiring" and "firing" its members when necessary. A key feature is *multitasking*, in which team members each have the skills to perform several different jobs.

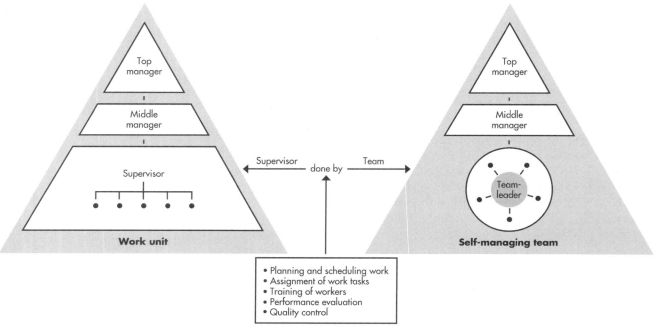

Figure 14.1   Organizational and management implications of self-managing work teams.

The implications of self-managing teams are depicted in *Figure 14.1*. Members of a self-managing team report to higher management through a team leader rather than a formal supervisor, making the traditional role of first-line supervisor unnecessary. This is an important change in organizational structure, since each self-managing team handles the supervisory duties on its own. Within a self-managing team, furthermore, the emphasis is always on participation. The leader and members are expected to work together not only to do the required work, but also to make the decisions that determine how it gets done. A true self-managing team operates with these characteristics.

Characteristics of self-managing teams

●   Members are held collectively accountable for performance results.
●   Members have discretion in distributing tasks within the team.
●   Members have discretion in scheduling work within the team.
●   Members are able to perform more than one job on the team.
●   Members train one another to develop multiple job skills.
●   Members evaluate one another's performance contributions.
●   Members are responsible for the total quality of team products.

HOW TEAMS WORK

The model in *Figure 14.2* shows how teams work as open systems that transform resource inputs (such as people and ideas) into product outputs (such as a finished good or service, or a special report or action recommendation).[13] On the output side, *task performance* is a concrete result that should add value to the organization. Also on the output side, *member satisfaction* is essential. Unless team members are satisfied with their accomplishments and with their experiences working together, the team is unlikely to retain long-term performance viability.

TEAM EFFECTIVENESS

An **effective team** is one that achieves and maintains high levels of both task performance and member satisfaction. As shown in the figure, a team's ability to be effective depends on the strength of its internal operations and the quality of its inputs.

The way the members of any team actually work together as they transform inputs into outputs is called the **group process.** It includes how well team members communicate with one another, make decisions, and handle conflicts, among other things. When the group process breaks down and the internal dynamics fail in any way, team effectiveness can suffer.

Although good process is essential to team effectiveness, it does not guarantee success. Any team must have available to it the resource inputs needed to deal best with the task at hand. Among the input factors, the *organizational setting* can affect how team members relate to one another and apply their skills. A key issue is the available support in terms of information, material resources, technology, spatial arrangements, organization structures, and rewards. The *nature of the task* is also important. It affects how well a team can focus its efforts and how intense the group process needs to be. Clearly defined tasks make it easier to focus work efforts; complex tasks require more information exchange and intense interactions.

- An **effective team** achieves high levels of both task performance and membership satisfaction.

- **Group process** is the way team members work together to accomplish tasks.

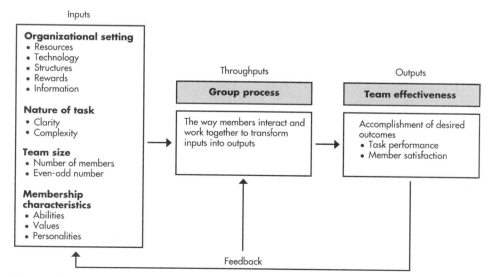

Figure 14.2 An open-systems model of work team effectiveness.

Team size affects how members work together, handle disagreements, and reach agreements. The number and complexity of interactions can make teams larger than six or seven members difficult to manage. When voting is required, teams with odd numbers of members are often preferred so as to prevent "ties."

Membership characteristics are also important, particularly the blend of competencies, skills and personalities. Whereas heterogeneity in the mix of skills, values, and personalities broadens the resource base of a team, it also adds complexity to members' interpersonal relationships.[14] Research suggests, for example, that culturally diverse work teams have more difficulty learning how to work well together than do culturally homogeneous ones. This is true, even though the diverse teams often prove more creative than the homogeneous ones.[15]

STAGES OF TEAM DEVELOPMENT

A synthesis of research on small groups suggests that there are five distinct phases in the life cycle of any team: forming, storming, norming, performing and adjourning.[16]

Forming Stage

The forming stage involves the initial entry of individual members into a team. This is a stage of initial task orientation and interpersonal testing. As individuals come together for the first time or two, they ask a number of questions: "What can or does the team offer me?" "What will I be asked to contribute?" "Can my needs be met while my efforts serve the task needs of the team?"

In the forming stage, people begin to identify with other members and with the team itself. They are concerned about getting acquainted, establishing interpersonal relationships, discovering what is considered acceptable behavior, and learning how others perceive the team's task. This may also be a time when some members rely on or become temporarily dependent on another member who appears "powerful" or especially "knowledgeable." Such things as prior experience with team members in other contexts and individual impressions of organization philosophies, goals, and policies may also affect member relationships in new work teams. Difficulties in the forming stage tend to be greater in more culturally and demographically diverse teams.

Storming Stage

The storming stage of team development is a period of high emotionality. Tension often emerges between members over tasks and interpersonal concerns. There may be periods of outright hostility and infighting. Coalitions or cliques may form around personalities or interests. Subteams form around areas of agreement and disagreement involving group tasks and/or the manner of operations. Conflict may develop as individuals compete to impose their preferences on others and to become influential in the group's status structure.

Important changes occur in the storming stage as task agendas become clarified and members begin to understand one another's interpersonal styles. Here attention begins to shift toward obstacles that may stand in the way of task accomplishment. Efforts are made to find ways to meet team goals while

Browser

Go to: http://www.wiley.com/college/schermerhorn

 THE WALL STREET JOURNAL.

WILEY

IN PRACTICE

The use of teams and teamwork in business environments is pervasive. Consequently, it becomes important for students to improve their group skills as they enter the business arena.

The Interactive Journal is on the cutting edge of new team processes. From virtual offices to distributed work places, the Interactive Journal covers all the changes in our definition of "teams."

Using the drop-down **Search Articles** button in the upper right-hand corner, select terms such as "teamwork" and "virtual teams" to look for recent articles. What best practices do leading edge companies appear to be utilizing in the quest for more efficient and effective work teams?

Under the **More Dow Jones Sites,** click on dowjones.com and search for information on teams. This search vehicle looks for relevant news articles in many Dow Jones publications, Web pages, and company press releases.

Increasingly, top managers are sharing the leadership role as top management teams take precedence. Check out http://

public.wsj.com/careers/ resources/documents/ 1999016-hymowitz.htm for an article on this phenomenon.

Consider joining a discussion in the upper right hand of the Front Section window. See if any discussions focus on teams and teamwork (e.g.: Idea Sharing Systems was a recent discussion topic).

ADDITIONAL SITES

Look at the University of Arizona's Center for the Management of Information for the latest news on distributed teams at http://www.cmi.arizona.edu/ frame java.html.

The Web site at http://rampages. onramp.net/ ~ bodwell/home. htm provides useful information on individuals and groups who wish to harness the power of high performance teams.

This site http://webreview.com/ pub/97/09/26/hour/index.html supports virtual tours of a large number of museums from around the world.

This Web Review http://web review.com/wr/pub site supports cross-training for Web teams and its article http://webreview.com/ pub/1999/01/01/arch/index.

html supplies information about virtual "chunking," a byproduct of the virtual environment.

Observe how the authors of this text attempt to utilize the Internet to facilitate the classroom experience for their students. See Schermerhorn at http://oak.cats.ohiou.edu/ ~ schermer and Chappell at http://oak.cats.ohiou. edu/ ~ chappell.

DELIVERABLES:

Prepare a list of 10 criteria that you would like to see in your group's members. Things such as "shows up to all meetings," "possesses excellent computer skills," and others should be considered. Once you have created the list, compare it with others. Looking back on your team experiences, how has your team membership compared?

DISCUSSION QUESTIONS:

1. How satisfied have you been with teamwork you have experienced in your college career?

2. What did you do to attempt to correct behavioral problems in your group members?

3. How will the Internet impact your group interaction in the future?

 *Note: The underscored words/phrases in the Interactive Journal feature indicate Internet links provided in the online versions. See the *Introducing Management* Web site at www.wiley.com/college/schermerhorn.

also satisfying individual needs. Failure in the storming stage can be a lasting liability, whereas success in the storming stage can set a strong foundation for later team effectiveness.

Norming Stage

Cooperation is an important theme for teams in the norming stage. At this point, members of the team begin to become coordinated as a working unit and tend to operate with shared rules of conduct. The team feels a sense of leadership, with each member starting to play useful roles. Most interpersonal hostilities give way to a precarious balancing of forces as norming builds initial integration. Harmony is emphasized, but minority viewpoints may be discouraged.

In the norming stage, members are likely to develop initial feelings of closeness, a division of labor, and a sense of shared expectations. This helps protect the team from disintegration. Holding the team together may become even more important than successful task accomplishment.

Performing Stage

Teams in the performing stage are more mature, organized, and well functioning. This is a stage of total integration in which team members are able to deal in creative ways with both complex tasks and any interpersonal conflicts. The team operates with a clear and stable structure, and members are motivated by team goals.

The primary challenges of teams in the performing stage is to continue refining the operations and relationships essential to working together as an integrated unit. Such teams need to remain coordinated with the larger organization and adapt successfully to changing conditions over time.

Adjourning Stage

The final stage of team development is one in which team members prepare to disband. It is especially common for temporary groups that operate in the form of committees, task forces, and projects. Ideally, the team disbands with a sense that important goals have been accomplished. Members are acknowledged for their contributions and the group's overall success.

The adjourning stage may be an emotional time. For members who have worked together intensely for a period of time, breaking up the close relationships may be painful. The ideal is for a team to disband with members feeling they would like to work with one another again in the future, should the need or opportunity arise.

NORMS AND COHESIVENESS

● A **norm** is a behavior, rule, or standard expected to be followed by team members.

A **norm** is a behavior expected of team members.[17] It is a "rule" or "standard" that guides their behavior. When violated, a norm may be enforced with reprimands and other sanctions. In the extreme, violation of a norm can result in a member being expelled from a team or socially ostracized by other members. The *performance norm*, which defines the level of work effort and performance that team members are expected to contribute, is extremely important. It can have positive or negative implications for team performance and organizational productivity. In general, work groups and teams with positive performance norms are more successful in accomplishing task objectives than are teams with negative performance norms. Other important norms relate to such things as helpfulness, participation, timeliness, and innovation.

A team spirit rallies workers at Motorola's Penang, Malaysia, plant. In one year they submitted 41,000 suggestions for improvement and saved the firm some $2 million. Motorola actively tries to capture the same team spirit elsewhere. New applicants at a Florida plant are carefully screened for their attitudes toward teamwork. A quality team there suggested ways to streamline workflow and increased output by 150 percent. Still, the Malaysian plant sets a high benchmark. Says one manager who spent three years working there, "The whole plant in Penang had this craving for learning." [18]

Because a team's norms are largely determined by the collective will of its members, it is difficult for a manager or designated leader simply to dictate which norms will be adopted. Instead, supportive team members must be helped and encouraged to develop positive norms. Leadership guidelines for building positive norms include:

- Act as a role model.
- Reinforce the desired behaviors with rewards.
- Control results by performance reviews and regular feedback.
- Train and orient new members to adopt desired behaviors.
- Recruit and select new members who exhibit the desired behaviors.
- Hold regular meetings to discuss progress and ways of improving.
- Use team decision-making methods to reach agreement. [19]

◄ How to build positive norms

The degree of conformity to norms is largely determined by **cohesiveness,** the degree to which members are attracted to and motivated to remain part of a team. Persons in a highly cohesive team value their membership and strive to maintain positive relationships with other team members. They experience satisfaction from identifying and working with the team.

Look at *Figure 14.3*. When the performance norm of a team is positive and cohesion is high, a "best-case" scenario results. Competent team members

● **Cohesiveness** is the degree to which members are attracted to and motivated to remain part of a team.

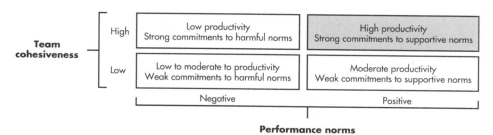

Figure 14.3 Productivity and the relationship between team cohesiveness and performance norms.

work hard and reinforce one another's task accomplishments while experiencing satisfaction with the team. But when the performance norm is negative in a highly cohesive team, conformity to the negative norm results in a "worst-case" scenario—low productivity and restricted work efforts. Between these two extremes are mixed situations of moderate to low productivity.

Managers and team leaders should build and maintain teams with both positive performance norms and high cohesiveness. Guidelines on how to increase cohesion include:

How to increase team cohesiveness

- Induce agreement on team goals.
- Increase membership homogeneity.
- Increase interactions among members.
- Decrease team size.
- Introduce competition with other teams.
- Reward team rather than individual results.
- Provide physical isolation from other teams.

TASK AND MAINTENANCE NEEDS

- A **task activity** is an action taken by a team member that contributes directly to the group's performance purpose.

- A **maintenance activity** is an action taken by a team member that supports the emotional life of the group.

Two types of activities are essential if team members are to work well together over time.[20] **Task activities** contribute directly to the team's performance purpose, while **maintenance activities** support the emotional life of the team as an ongoing social system. The responsibility for both should be shared and distributed among all team members. In this sense, any member can help lead a team by taking actions that satisfy its task and maintenance needs. This concept of *distributed leadership in teams* is explained further by *Figure 14.4*.

Leading through task activities involves such behavior as initiating agendas, sharing information, and summarizing. Leading through maintenance activities involves such things as gatekeeping, encouraging others and reducing tensions. Both task and maintenance activities stand in distinct contrast to the dysfunctional activities also described in the figure. Self-serving activities such

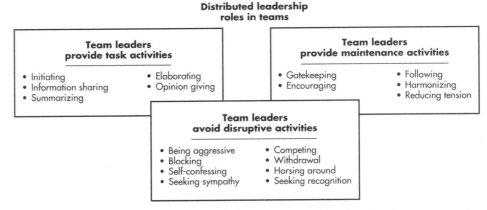

Figure 14.4 Distributed leadership helps a team meet its task and maintenance needs.

as withdrawing and horsing around detract from, rather than enhance, team effectiveness.

COMMUNICATION NETWORKS

Figure 14.5 shows three interaction patterns and communication networks used by teams.[21] As expected, the best teams use communication networks in the right ways, at the right times, and for the right tasks. In **centralized communication network,** sometimes called a wheel or chain structure, activities are coordinated and results pooled by a central point of control. Most communication flows back and forth between individual members and the hub or center point. Centralized networks tend to work best on simple tasks that require little creativity, information processing, and problem solving.

In a **decentralized communication network,** sometimes called the all-channel or star, all members communicate directly with one another. The decentralized networks work best for more complex tasks since they are able to support more intense interactions and information sharing.

When teams are composed of subgroups experiencing issue-specific disagreements, such as a temporary debate over the best means to achieve a goal, the resulting interaction pattern involves a *restricted communication network.*

- In a **centralized communication network,** communication flows only between individual members and a hub or center point.

- A **decentralized communication network** allows all members to communicate directly with one another.

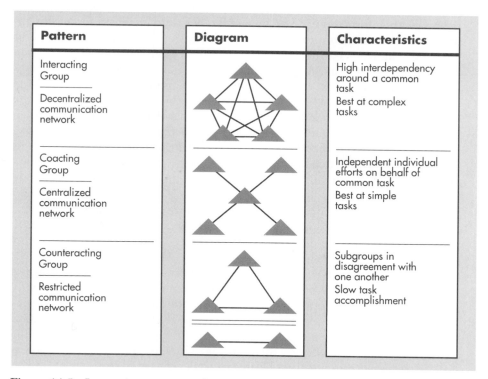

Pattern	Diagram	Characteristics
Interacting Group — Decentralized communication network		High interdependency around a common task — Best at complex tasks
Coacting Group — Centralized communication network		Independent individual efforts on behalf of common task — Best at simple tasks
Counteracting Group — Restricted communication network		Subgroups in disagreement with one another — Slow task accomplishment

Figure 14.5 Interaction patterns and communication networks in teams. *Source:* John R. Schermerhorn, Jr., James G. Hunt, and Richard N. Osborn, *Organizational Behavior,* Sixth Edition (New York: John Wiley & Sons, 1997), p. 351. Used by permission.

Here, the polarized subgroups engage in contests and even antagonistic relations. Communication between the subgroups is often limited and biased, with the result that problems can easily occur.

DECISION MAKING IN TEAMS

Decision making is one of the most important group processes, and decisions in teams can be made in several different ways. Edgar Schein, a respected scholar and consultant, notes that teams make decisions by at least six methods: lack of response, authority rule, minority rule, majority rule, consensus, and unanimity.[22]

METHODS FOR TEAM DECISIONS

In *decision by lack of response*, one idea after another is suggested without any discussion taking place. When the team finally accepts an idea, all others have been bypassed and discarded by simple lack of response rather than by critical evaluation. In *decision by authority rule*, the leader, manager, committee head, or some other authority figure makes a decision for the team. This can be done with or without discussion and is very time efficient. Whether the decision is a good one or a bad one, however, depends on whether the authority figure has the necessary information and on how well other team members accept this approach. In *decision by minority rule*, two or three people are able to dominate or "railroad" the team into making a mutually agreeable decision. This is often done by providing a suggestion and then forcing quick agreement by challenging the team with such statements as "Does anyone object? . . . Let's go ahead then."

One of the most common ways teams make decisions, especially when early signs of disagreement arise, is *decision by majority rule*. Here, formal voting may take place, or members may be polled to find the majority viewpoint. This method parallels the democratic political system and is often used without awareness of its potential problems. The very process of voting can create coalitions; that is, some people will be "winners" and others will be "losers" when the final vote is tallied. Those in the minority—the "losers"—may feel left out or discarded without having had a fair say. They may be unenthusiastic about implementing the decision of the "majority," and lingering resentments may impair team effectiveness in the future.

Another alternative is *decision by consensus*. Formally defined, consensus is a state of affairs whereby discussion leads to one alternative being favored by most members and the other members agreeing to support it. When a consensus is reached, even those who may have opposed the chosen course of action know that they have been heard and have had an opportunity to influence the decision outcome. Consensus, therefore, does not require unanimity. But it does require that team members be able to argue, engage in reasonable conflict, and yet still get along with and respect one another.[23] And, it requires that there be the opportunity for any dissenting members to feel they have been able to speak—and that they have been listened to.

A *decision by unanimity* may be the ideal state of affairs. Here, all team members agree on the course of action to be taken. This is a "logically perfect" method for decision making in teams, but it is also extremely difficult to attain in actual practice. One of the reasons that teams sometimes turn to authority decisions, majority voting, or even minority decisions, in fact, is the difficulty of managing the team process to achieve consensus or unanimity.

ASSETS AND LIABILITIES OF TEAM DECISIONS

The best teams don't limit themselves to just one decision-making method. Instead, they change methods to best fit the problems at hand. An important team leadership skill is helping a team choose the "right" decision method— one that provides for a timely and quality decision to which the members are highly committed.[24] To do this well, however, team leaders must understand both the potential assets and potential liabilities of team-based decisions.[25]

Team decisions are highly desirable whenever time and other circumstances permit. They bring greater amounts of information, knowledge, and expertise to bear on problems. They expand the number of action alternatives that are examined, and they help to avoid tunnel vision and consideration of only limited options. Team decisions increase the understanding and acceptance of outcomes by members. And importantly, they increase the commitments of members to work hard to implement final plans.

The potential disadvantages of team decision making trace largely to possible difficulties in group process. In a team decision there may be social pressure to conform. Individual members may feel intimidated or compelled to go along with the apparent wishes of others. There may be minority domination, where some members feel forced or "railroaded" to accept a decision advocated by one vocal individual or small coalition. Also, the time required to make team decisions can sometimes be a disadvantage. As more people are involved in the dialogue and discussion, decision making takes longer. This added time may be costly, even prohibitively so, in some circumstances.

GROUPTHINK

Among the risks of team decision making is a phenomenon called **groupthink,** the tendency for highly cohesive groups to lose their critical evaluative capabilities.[26] Members of very cohesive teams may publicly agree with actual or suggested courses of action while privately having serious doubts about them. Strong feelings of team loyalty can make it hard for members to criticize and evaluate one another's ideas and suggestions. Desires to hold the team together and avoid disagreements may result in poor decisions.

Listed below are symptoms that indicate when groupthink may be occurring during team decision making. When and if you encounter groupthink, preventive actions can be taken along the lines shown in *Manager's Notepad 14.2.*[27]

- *Illusions of invulnerability:* members assume the team is too good for criticism or beyond attack.

● **Groupthink** is a tendency for highly cohesive teams to lose their evaluative capabilities.

◄──────

Symptoms of groupthink

MANAGER'S NOTEPAD 14.2

How To Avoid Groupthink

- Assign the role of critical evaluator to each team member; encourage a sharing of viewpoints.
- Don't, as a leader, seem partial to one course of action; do absent yourself from meetings at times to allow free discussion.
- Create subteams to work on the same problems and then share their proposed solutions.
- Have team members discuss issues with outsiders and report back on their reactions.
- Invite outside experts to observe team activities and react to team processes and decisions.
- Assign one member to play a "devil's advocate" role at each team meeting.
- Hold a "second-chance" meeting after consensus is apparently achieved to review the decision.

- *Rationalizing unpleasant and disconfirming data:* members refuse to accept contradictory data or to consider alternatives thoroughly.
- *Belief in inherent group morality:* members act as though the group is inherently right and above reproach.
- *Stereotyping competitors as weak, evil, and stupid:* members refuse to look realistically at other groups.
- *Applying direct pressure to deviants to conform to group wishes:* members refuse to tolerate anyone who suggests the team may be wrong.
- *Self-censorship by members:* members refuse to communicate personal concerns to the whole team.
- *Illusions of unanimity:* members accept consensus prematurely, without testing its completeness.
- *Mind guarding:* members protect the team from hearing disturbing ideas or outside viewpoints.

LEADERSHIP AND HIGH-PERFORMANCE TEAMS

When we think of the word "team", sporting teams often come to mind, and they certainly have their share of problems. Members slack off or become disgruntled; even world champion teams have losing streaks; and the most highly talented players sometimes lose motivation, quibble with other team members, and lapse into performance slumps. When these things happen, the owners, managers, and players are apt to take corrective action to "rebuild the team" and restore what we have called team effectiveness. Work teams are teams in a similar sense. And even the most mature work team is likely to experience problems over time. When such difficulties arise, "team building" can help.

THE TEAM-BUILDING PROCESS

Team building is a sequence of planned activities used to gather and analyze data on the functioning of a team and to implement constructive changes to increase its operating effectiveness.[28] Most systematic approaches to team building follow the steps described in *Figure 14.6*. The cycle begins with the awareness that a problem may exist or may develop within the team. Members then work together to gather and analyze data so that the problem is finally understood. Action plans are made by members and collectively implemented. Results are evaluated in similar fashion by team members working together. Any difficulties or new problems that are discovered serve to recycle the team-building process.

The ultimate goal of team building is to create more and better teamwork among group members. This is accomplished as members work together to conduct careful and collaborative assessments of the team's inputs, processes and results. It is also accomplished as they collectively decide to take action to resolve and/or prevent problems that interfere with team effectiveness.

● **Team building** is a sequence of collaborative activities to gather and analyze data on a team and make changes to increase its effectiveness.

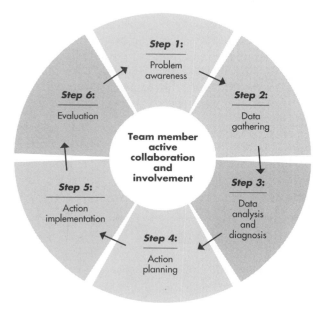

Figure 14.6 Collaboration and involvement in the team-building process.

CHALLENGES OF TEAM LEADERSHIP

Among the many developments in today's workplace, continuing efforts to refine and apply creative team concepts are at the forefront of progressive action.[29] But harnessing the full potential of teams involves special leadership challenges. We know, for example, that high-performance teams generally share common characteristics. These include a clear and elevating goal, a task driven and results-oriented structure, competent and committed members who work hard, a collaborative climate, high standards of excellence, external support and recognition, and strong and principled leadership.[30]

The last point on this list, the need for strong and principled leadership, may be the key to them all. In their book *Teamwork: What Can Go Right/What Can Go Wrong*, Carl Larson and Frank LaFasto state: "The right person in a leadership role can add tremendous value to any collective effort, even to the point of sparking the outcome with an intangible kind of magic."[31]

High performing teams are built with the efforts of strong and principled leadership. The best team leaders *establish a clear vision of the future*. This vision serves as a goal that inspires hard work and the quest for performance excellence; it creates a sense of shared purpose. The best team leaders help to *create change*. They are dissatisfied with the status quo, influence team members toward similar dissatisfaction, and infuse the team with the motivation to change in order to become better. The best team leaders *unleash talent*. They make sure the team is staffed with members who have the right skills and abilities. And they make sure these people are highly motivated to use their talents to achieve the group's performance objectives.

Clearly, you don't get a high-performing team by just bringing a group of people together and giving them a shared name or title. Leaders of high-performance teams create supportive climates in which team members know what to expect from the leader and each other, and know what the leader expects from them. The best team leaders empower team members. By personal example, they demonstrate the importance of setting aside self-interests to support the team's goals. And they use team building on a relatively continuous basis, viewing it as an ongoing leadership responsibility.

There is no doubt that teams take hard work. But, they are worth it![32] That's part of any manager's leadership challenge.

SUMMARY

How Do Teams Help Organizations?

- A team is a collection of people who work together to accomplish a common goal.
- Teams help organizations through synergy in task performance, the creation of a whole that is greater than the sum of its parts.
- Teams help satisfy important needs for their members, providing various types of support and social satisfactions.

- Committees and task forces are used to facilitate operations and allow special projects to be completed with creativity.
- Cross-functional teams bring members together from different departments and help improve lateral relations and integration in organizations.
- Employee involvement teams, such as the quality circle, allow employees to provide important insights into daily problem solving.
- New developments in information technology are also making virtual teams, or computer-mediated teams, more commonplace.
- Self-managing teams are changing organizations by allowing team members to perform many tasks previously reserved for their supervisors.

How Do Teams Work?

- An effective team achieves high levels of both task performance and member satisfaction.
- Important team input factors include the organizational setting, nature of the task, size, and membership characteristics.
- A team matures through various stages of development, including forming, storming, norming, performing, and adjourning.
- Norms are the standards or rules of conduct that influence the behavior of team members; cohesion is the attractiveness of the team to its members.
- In highly cohesive teams, members tend to conform to norms; the best situation for a manager or leader is a team with positive performance norms and high cohesiveness.
- Distributed leadership in serving a team's task and maintenance needs helps in achieving long-term effectiveness.
- Effective teams make use of alternative communication networks to best complete tasks.

How Do Teams Make Decisions?

- Teams can make decisions by lack of response, authority rule, minority rule, majority rule, consensus, and unanimity.
- The potential advantages of team decision making include having more information available and generating more understanding and commitment.
- The potential liabilities to team decision making include social pressures to conform and greater time requirements.
- Groupthink is a tendency of members of highly cohesive teams to lose their critical evaluative capabilities and make poor decisions.

How Can Leaders Build High-Performance Teams?

- Team building helps team members develop action plans for improving the way they work together and the results they accomplish.
- The team-building process should be data based and collaborative, involving a high level of participation by all team members.
- High-performance work teams have supportive leaders who create a clear and shared sense of purpose as well as strong internal commitments to its accomplishment.

KEY TERMS

Centralized communication network (p. 235)

Cohesiveness (p. 233)

Committee (p. 225)

Cross-functional teams (p. 225)

Decentralized communication network (p. 235)

Effective team (p. 229)

Employee involvement team (p. 226)

Group process (p. 229)

Groupthink (p. 237)

Maintenance activity (p. 234)

Norm (p. 232)

Quality circle (p. 227)

Self-managing work teams (p. 227)

Social loafing (p. 224)

Task force (p. 225)

Team (p. 224)

Team building (p. 239)

Teamwork (p. 224)

Virtual team (p. 227)

SELF-TEST Take the interactive Self-Test for this chapter on the Schermerhorn Web Site

Chapter Fifteen

Innovation and Change Leadership

PLANNING AHEAD—
Chapter 15 Study Questions

- ■ What is innovation?
- ■ What are the challenges of organizational change?
- ■ How can one lead the change process?
- ■ What are the challenges of organization development?

INNOVATION = COMPETITIVE ADVANTAGE

WHEN A GROUP OF Japanese students drove out of Tokyo one day, the event wouldn't have seemed remarkable to bystanders. But when they arrived some 900 kilometers later on the northern island of Hokkaido, Mitsubishi's president was sure pleased. The students' car, powered by a new Gasoline Direct Engine (GDI) technology, had made the trip without refueling! In fact, there was fuel to spare in the gas tank. The engine and its success were an important breakthrough for the company. Says President Takemune Kimura, "For many years engineers knew it would be technically possible, but they didn't know how. . . . Our computers finally found the answer." Mitsubishi's push for engine innovation is part of its commitment to safeguarding the environment. It also helps in its quest for advantage in a highly competitive global industry.[1]

● A **learning organization** utilizes people, values, and systems to continuously change and improve its performance.

Learning was obviously an important part of the process through which Mitsubishi developed the GDI engine. Indeed, this is the age of the **learning organization,** one that by virtue of people, values, and systems is able to continuously change and improve its performance based on the lessons of experience."[2] And in this age the watchwords are *change, change* and *change*. In his book *The Circle of Innovation*, consultant Tom Peters argues that we must refocus the attention away from past accomplishments and toward innovation as the primary source of competitive advantage.[3] In this final chapter of the book the future is the issue, and our inquiry is into innovation and the dynamics of organizational change leadership.

THE NATURE OF INNOVATION

Organizations and their managers must continually innovate and adapt to new situations if they are to survive and prosper over the long run. Max DePree, CEO of Herman Miller Company, and noted for his leadership accomplishments, says it well: "You have to have an environment where the body of people are really amenable to change and can deal with the conflicts that arise out of change and innovation."[4] Consultant Peter Senge further describes this environment as one in which managers stimulate and lead change in order to create learning organizations with the following characteristics—everyone sets aside old ways of thinking, everyone becomes self-aware and open to others, everyone learns how the whole organization works, everyone understands and agrees to a plan of action, and everyone works together to accomplish the plan.[5]

THE INNOVATION PROCESS

● **Innovation** is the process of taking a new idea and putting it into practice.

Innovation is the process of creating new ideas and putting them into practice.[6] It is the act of converting new concepts into usable applications. In

---

MANAGER'S NOTEPAD 15.1

TEN WAYS TO INCREASE CREATIVITY

1. Look for more than one "right" answer or "one best way."
2. Avoid being too logical; let your thinking roam.
3. Challenge rules; ask "why"; don't settle for the status quo.
4. Ask "what if" questions.
5. Let ambiguity help you and others see things differently.
6. Don't be afraid of error; let trial and error be a path to success.
7. Take time for play and experiment as paths to discovery.
8. Open up to other viewpoints and perspectives.
9. Support nonconformity; let differences exist.
10. Believe in creativity; make it a self-fulfilling prophecy.

organizations these applications occur as *process innovations*—which result in better ways of doing things, and as *product innovations*—which result in the creation of new or improved goods and services.

The management of both process and product innovations involves supporting both *invention*—the act of discovery, and *application*—the act of use.[7] Invention relates to creativity (see *Manager's Notepad 15.1*) and the development of new ideas. Today's organizations must be work environments that stimulate creativity and an ongoing stream of new ideas. Application, on the other hand, deals with the utilization of inventions to take the best advantage of ideas. This requires managers that actually make sure that good ideas for new or modified work processes are actually implemented. They must also make sure that the commercial potential of ideas for new products or services is fully realized.

Figure 15.1 uses the example of new product development to highlight the business significance of *commercializing innovations*. This is the process of turning new ideas into products or processes that can make a difference in sales, profits, and/or costs. As illustrated, four steps in the product innovation process are:

1. *Idea creation:* New knowledge forms around basic discoveries, extensions of existing understanding, or spontaneous creativity made possible by individual ingenuity and communication with others.

    ← Four steps in product innovation

2. *Initial experimentation:* Ideas are initially tested in concept by discussions with others; referrals to customers, clients, or technical experts; and/or in the form of prototypes or samples.

3. *Feasibility determination:* Practicality and financial value are examined in formal feasibility studies, which also identify potential costs and benefits as well as potential markets or applications.

4. *Final application:* A new product is finally commercialized or put on sale in the open market, or a new process is implemented as part of normal operating routines.

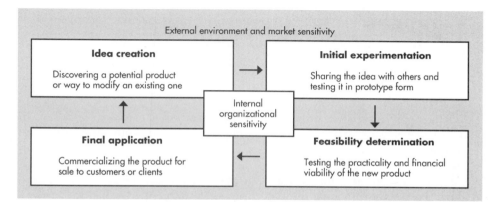

Figure 15.1 Process of innovation in organizations: the case of new product development.

CHARACTERISTICS OF INNOVATIVE ORGANIZATIONS

Innovative organizations are focused on supporting creativity and entrepreneurship, and their managers take active roles in leading the process.[8] In highly innovative organizations, *the corporate strategy and culture support innovation.* The strategies of the organization, the visions and values of senior management, and the framework of policies and expectations emphasize an entrepreneurial spirit. Innovation is expected, failure is accepted, and the organization is willing to take risks. For example, Johnson & Johnson CEO James Burke has said, "I try to give people the feeling that it's okay to fail, that it's important to fail."[9] The key here is for managers to eliminate risk-averse climates and replace them with organizational cultures that expect innovation and tolerate failure.

In highly innovative organizations, *organization structures support innovation.* More and more large organizations are trying to capture the structural flexibility of smaller ones. That is, they are striving for more organic operations, with a strong emphasis on lateral communications and cross-functional teams and task forces. In particular, research and development, historically a separate and isolated function, is being integrated into a team setting. As Peter Drucker points out, "Successful innovations . . . are now being turned out by cross-functional teams with people from marketing, manufacturing, and finance participating in research work from the very beginning."[10] Innovative organizations are also reorganizing to create many smaller divisions that allow creative teams or "skunk works" to operate and to encourage intrapreneurial new ventures.

In highly innovative organizations, *staffing supports innovation.* Organizations need different kinds of people to succeed in all stages of the innovation process. The critical innovation roles to be filled include the following:

Innovation roles in organizations

- *Idea generators:* People who create new insights from internal discovery or external awareness, or both.
- *Information gatekeepers:* People who serve as links between people and groups within the organization and with external sources.
- *Product champions:* People who advocate and push for change and innovation in general and for the adoption of specific product or process ideas in particular.
- *Project managers:* People who perform the technical functions needed to keep an innovative project on track with all the necessary resource support.
- *Innovation leaders:* People who encourage, sponsor, and coach others to keep the innovation values and goals in place and channel energies in the right directions.[11]

In highly innovative organizations, *top management supports innovation.* In the case of 3M, for example, many top managers have been the innovators and product champions of the company's past. They understand the innovation process, are tolerant of criticisms and differences of opinion, and take all possible steps to keep the goals clear and the pressure on. The key, once again, is to allow the creative potential of people to operate fully. As Max DePree of Herman Miller again states, "If you want the best things to happen in corporate life, you have to find ways to be hospitable to the unusual person."[12] Finally, an

MANAGER'S NOTEPAD 15.2

SPOTTING BARRIERS TO INNOVATION

- *Top management isolation* fosters misunderstandings and contributes to a "risk-averse" climate.
- *Intolerance of differences* denies uniqueness, creates homogeneity, and brands as "troublemakers" those who question the status quo.
- *Vested interests* focus on the "parts" rather than the "whole" and emphasize the defense of one's "turf" against inroads by outsiders.
- *Short time horizons* emphasizes short-term goals rather than the potential for new ideas to generate long-term gains.
- *Overly rational thinking* tries to make creativity a systematic process and emphasizes schedules over results.
- *Inappropriate incentives* use rewards and controls to reinforce routines; they discourage surprises and differences linked to innovation.
- *Excessive bureaucracy* gives allegiance to rules, procedures, and efficiency that frustrate creativity and innovation.

enlightened top management helps break down the possible barriers to innovation listed in *Manager's Notepad 15.2.*[13]

The Toro Company is a global manufacturer of outdoor landscape products, services, and systems. When a new molding technique didn't work, Toro lost mower sales. Members of the engineering team responsible for the technique were called to CEO Kendrick Melrose's office. Instead of "pink slips," they were met with a party that included balloons and a cake. The celebration was in honor of the risk they had taken. Later, it was found that the technique could be used successfully in the production of other Toro products.[14]

CHALLENGES OF ORGANIZATIONAL CHANGE

"Change" is an essential part of the processes of organizational creativity and innovation. Especially today, many people say that change is inevitable and a way of life. But is it? Rockport CEO Angel Martinez says that "the one constant factor in business today is that we live in a perpetual hurricane season." Yet when as a new CEO Martinez sought to change traditional ways in his company, he encountered resistance from those he said "gave lip service to my ideas and hoped I'd go away."[15]

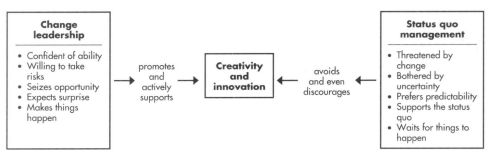

Figure 15.2 Change leadership versus status quo management.

CHANGE LEADERSHIP

● A **change leader** actively sponsors and leads the processes of change.

A **change leader** is a person or group who takes leadership responsibility for changing the existing pattern of behavior of another person or social system. A key part of every manager's job is to lead change in the work setting. This requires being alert to situations or to people needing change, being open to good ideas, and being able to support the implementation of new ideas in actual practice. *Figure 15.2* contrasts, for example, a change leader with a status quo manager. The change leader is forward-looking, proactive and embraces new ideas. The status quo manager is backward-looking, reactive, and comfortable with habit. Obviously, the new workplace demands change leadership.

In the last chapter on teams and teamwork, we discussed the concept of distributed leadership in groups. The point was that everyone in a team has the potential to lead by serving group needs for task and maintenance activities. The same notion applies when it comes to leading change in organizations—the responsibilities for change leadership are ideally distributed and shared from top to bottom.

In *top-down change*, strategic and comprehensive changes are initiated with the goal of comprehensive impact on the organization and its performance capabilities. But change that is driven from the top runs the risk of being perceived as insensitive to the needs of lower level personnel. It can easily fail if implementation suffers from excessive resistance and insufficient commitments to change. The success of top-down change is usually determined by the willingness of middle- and lower-level workers to actively support top-management initiatives.

Bottom-up change is also important. Here, the initiatives for change come from persons throughout an organization and are supported by the efforts of middle- and lower-level managers acting as change agents. Bottom-up change is essential to organizational innovation and is very useful in terms of adapting operations and technologies to the changing requirements of work. It is made possible by empowerment, involvement, and participation, as discussed in earlier chapters.

FORCES AND TARGETS FOR CHANGE

● **Planned change** occurs as a result of specific efforts by a change leader.

We are particularly interested in **planned change** that occurs as a result of the specific efforts of a change leader. Planned change is a direct response to a person's perception of a *performance gap*, or a discrepancy between the desired and actual state of affairs. Performance gaps may represent problems to be resolved or opportunities to be explored.

Performance gaps and the impetus for change can arise from a variety of external forces.[16] These include the global economy and market competition, local economic conditions, government laws and regulations, technological developments, market trends, and social forces. As an organization's general and specific environments develop and change over time, the organization must adapt as well.

Internal forces for change are important too. Indeed, any change in one part of the organization as a complex system—perhaps a change initiated in response to one or more of the external forces just identified—can often create the need for change in another part of the system. The internal or organizational targets for change are highly interrelated and include:[17]

- *Tasks:* The nature of work as represented by organizational mission, objectives, and strategy and the job designs for individuals and groups.

- *People:* The attitudes and competencies of the employees and the human resource systems that support them.

- *Culture:* The value system for the organization as a whole and the norms guiding individual and group behavior.

- *Technology:* The operations and information technology used to support job designs, arrange workflows, and integrate people and machines in systems.

- *Structure:* The configuration of the organization as a complex system, including its design features and lines of authority and communications.

← Organizational targets for change

LEADING CHANGE

People tend to act habitually and in stable ways over time. They may not want to change even when circumstances require it. Any manager and change leader will need to recognize and deal with such tendencies and their implications.

PHASES OF PLANNED CHANGE

Kurt Lewin, a noted psychologist, recommends that any planned-change effort be viewed as the three-phase process shown in *Figure 15.3*.[18] These phases of planned change are (1) *unfreezing*—preparing a system for change; (2) *changing*—making actual changes in the system; and (3) *refreezing*—stabilizing the system after change.

Unfreezing

In order for change to be successful, people must be ready for it. Planned change has little chance for long-term success unless people are open to doing things differently. **Unfreezing** is the stage in which a situation is prepared for change and felt needs for change are developed. It can be facilitated in several ways: through environmental pressures for change, declining performance, the recognition that problems or opportunities exist, and through the observation of behavioral models that display alternative approaches. When handled well,

- **Unfreezing** is the phase during which a situation is prepared for change.

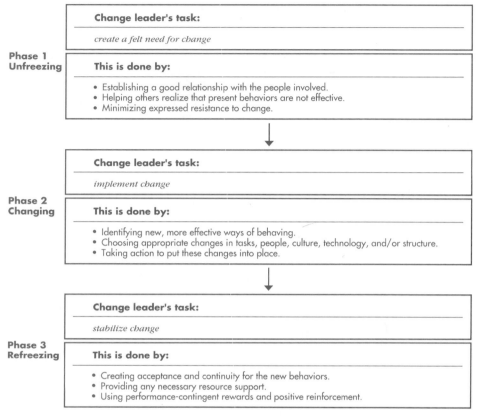

**Phase 1
Unfreezing**

Change leader's task:

create a felt need for change

This is done by:

- Establishing a good relationship with the people involved.
- Helping others realize that present behaviors are not effective.
- Minimizing expressed resistance to change.

**Phase 2
Changing**

Change leader's task:

implement change

This is done by:

- Identifying new, more effective ways of behaving.
- Choosing appropriate changes in tasks, people, culture, technology, and/or structure.
- Taking action to put these changes into place.

**Phase 3
Refreezing**

Change leader's task:

stabilize change

This is done by:

- Creating acceptance and continuity for the new behaviors.
- Providing any necessary resource support.
- Using performance-contingent rewards and positive reinforcement.

Figure 15.3 Lewin's three phases of planned organizational change: unfreezing, changing, and refreezing.

conflict can be an important unfreezing force in organizations. It often helps people break old habits and recognize alternative ways of thinking about or doing things.

Changing

● **Changing** is the phase where a planned change actually takes place.

In the **changing** phase, something new takes place in a system, and change is actually implemented. This is the point at which managers initiate changes in such organizational targets as tasks, people, culture, technology, and structure. Ideally, all change is done in response to a good diagnosis of a problem and a careful examination of alternatives. However, Lewin believes that many change agents enter the changing phase prematurely, are too quick to change things, and therefore end up creating resistance to change. When managers implement change before people feel a need for it, there is an increased likelihood of failure.

Refreezing

● **Refreezing** is the phase at which change is stabilized.

The final stage in the planned-change process is **refreezing.** Here, the manager is concerned about stabilizing the change and creating the conditions for its long-term continuity. Refreezing is accomplished by appropriate rewards for performance, positive reinforcement, and providing necessary resource support. It is also important to evaluate results carefully, provide feedback to the people involved, and make any required modifications in the original change. When refreezing is done poorly, changes are too easily forgotten or abandoned with the passage of time. When it is done well, change can be more long lasting.

CHANGE STRATEGIES

Change leaders use various approaches when trying to get others to adopt a desired change. *Figure 15.4* summarizes three common change strategies known as force-coercion, rational persuasion, and shared power.[19]

Force-Coercion Strategies

A **force-coercion strategy** uses the power bases of legitimacy, rewards, and punishments as the primary inducements to change. As *Figure 15.4* shows, the likely outcomes of force-coercion are immediate compliance but little commitment.

● A **force-coercion strategy** pursues change through formal authority and/or the use of rewards or punishments.

Force-coercion can be pursued in at least two ways, both of which can be commonly observed in organizations. In a *direct forcing* strategy, the change agent takes direct and unilateral action to "command" that change take place. This involves the exercise of formal authority or legitimate power, offering special rewards, and/or threatening punishment. In *political maneuvering*, the change agent works indirectly to gain special advantage over other persons and thereby make them change. This involves bargaining, obtaining control of important resources, or granting small favors.

In both versions, the force-coercion strategy produces limited results. Although it can be implemented rather quickly, most people respond to this strategy out of fear of punishment or hope for a reward. This usually results in only

Change Strategy	Power Bases	Managerial Behavior	Likely Results
Force–Coercion Using position power to create change by decree and formal authority	Legitimacy Rewards Punishments	*Direct forcing and unilateral action* *Political maneuvering and indirect action*	Fast → Temporary compliance
Rational Persuasion Creating change through rational persuasion and empirical argument	Expertise	*Informational efforts using credible knowledge, demonstrated facts, and logical argument*	
Shared power Developing support for change through personal values and commitments	Reference	*Participative efforts to share power and involve others in planning and implementing change*	Slow → Longer term Internalization

Figure 15.4 Alternative change strategies and their managerial implications.

temporary compliance with the change agent's desires. The new behavior continues only so long as the opportunity for rewards and punishments is present. For this reason, force-coercion is most useful as an unfreezing device that helps people break old patterns of behavior and gain initial impetus to try new ones.

A change agent that seeks to create change through force-coercion believes that people who run things are basically motivated by self-interest and by what the situation offers in terms of potential personal gains or losses. This change agent believes that people change only in response to such motives, tries to find out where their vested interests lie, and then puts the pressure on. If the change agent has formal authority, she or he uses it along with whatever rewards and punishments are available. Once a weakness is found, it is exploited. This change agent is always quick to work "politically" by building supporting alliances wherever possible.[20]

Rational Persuasion Strategies

● A **rational persuasion strategy** pursues change through empirical data and rational argument.

Change agents using a **rational persuasion strategy** attempt to bring about change through persuasion backed by special knowledge, empirical data, and rational argument. The likely outcome is eventual compliance with reasonable commitment. This is an informational strategy that assumes that rational people will be guided by facts, reason, and self-interest when deciding whether or not to support a change.

A manager using rational persuasion must convince others that the cost-benefit value of a planned change is high and that it will leave them better off than before. Accomplishing this depends to a large extent on the presence of expert power. This can come directly from the change agent if she or he has personal credibility as an "expert." If not, it can be obtained in the form of consultants and other outside experts or from credible demonstration projects. When successful, a rational persuasion strategy helps unfreeze and refreeze a change situation. Although slower than force-coercion, it tends to result in longer lasting and more internalized change.

A change agent following this strategy believes that people are inherently rational and are guided by reason in their actions and decision making. Once a specific course of action is demonstrated to be in a person's self-interest, the change agent assumes that reason and rationality will cause the person to adopt it. Thus, he or she uses information and facts to communicate the essential desirability of change. If the logic is sound, the change agent is confident that the person will adopt and support the proposed change.

Shared Power Strategies

● A **shared power strategy** pursues change by participation in assessing values, needs, and goals.

A **shared power strategy** engages people in a collaborative process of identifying values, assumptions, and goals from which support for change will naturally emerge. The process is slow, but it is likely to yield high commitment. Sometimes called a *normative-reeducative strategy*, this approach is based on empowerment and is highly participative in nature. It relies on involving others in examining personal needs and values, group norms, and operating goals as they relate to the issues at hand. Power is shared by the change agent and other persons as they work together to develop a new consensus to support needed change.

Browser

Go to: http://www.wiley.com/college/schermerhorn

 THE WALL STREET JOURNAL.

WILEY

IN PRACTICE

Perhaps more than at anytime in history, change and innovation are sweeping the business landscape. Many are heralding the Internet age as more dynamic than the industrial revolution in its impact on our lives.

While some companies founder in this environment, many firms recognize that change brings both threats and opportunities. Those companies that can successfully MANAGE change have a greater chance to benefit from it.

The Interactive Journal itself represents tremendous change. It remains as one of the most successful online newspaper sites in the world. Late-breaking news items, frequent updates, and expanded services are a few of the innovations it brings to the paper edition of the WSJ.

Look over the headlines on the **Front Section** any day and changes, ranging from mergers to technical inventions, highlight the news.

Using the **Article Search** feature in the right-hand corner of the screen, try "change management" and "innovation" as search terms.

In the **Front Section**, look under **Resources** in the left-hand menu, and select **Special Reports.** Many of these address change and innovation in different industries. Look for telecommunications or other high tech industries for news articles.

ENTREPRENEURSHIP /INTRAPRENEURSHIP

This new dynamism offers particular opportunities for entrepreneurial thinkers located both outside and inside firms. Check out these sites for entrepreneurial assistance:

Business Owners Toolkit at http://www.toolkit.cch.com/

American Express Small Business Exchange at http://www6. americanexpress.com/ smallbusiness/.

ADDITIONAL SITES

Check out the Change Management web site at http://www. change-management.org/ for books and articles on the subject.

A prior edition of the WSJ ran an article titled "Web Sites Made of Steel" concerning Internet auction sites for surplus steel. Look under http:// metalsite.net/ and http://www. esteel.com for examples.

DELIVERABLES:

Many firms are using the Internet in ways few dreamed of even ten years ago. Inspect some of the employment sections of

- PriceWaterhouseCoopers at http://www.pwcglobal.com and click on Careers

- CollegeHire at http://www. Collegehire.com/

- Aetna collects its hiring data under http://www.aetna. com/working/college.htm

How much do you anticipate online recruiting will impact your job search?

DISCUSSION QUESTIONS:

1. Identify the three largest factors that have impacted you personally regarding change in the last year.

2. How would you describe your ability to handle change?

3. Discuss the meaning of "Value-Added" performance. How much value do you personally add to your work assignments?

 *Note: The underscored words/phrases in the Interactive Journal feature indicate Internet links provided in the online versions. See the *Introducing Management* Web site at www.wiley.com/college/schermerhorn.

Managers using shared power as an approach to planned change need reference power and the skills to work effectively with other people in group situations. They must be comfortable allowing others to participate in making decisions that affect the planned change and the way it is implemented. Because it entails a high level of involvement, a normative-reeducative strategy is often quite time consuming. But it is also likely to result in long lasting and internalized change.

A change agent who shares power begins by recognizing that people have varied needs and complex motivations. He or she believes people behave as they do because of sociocultural norms and commitments to the expectations of others. Changes in organizations are understood to inevitably involve changes in attitudes, values, skills, and significant relationships, not just changes in knowledge, information, or intellectual rationales for action and practice. Thus, when seeking to change others, this change agent is sensitive to the way group pressures can support or inhibit change. In working with people, every attempt is made to gather their opinions, identify their feelings and expectations, and incorporate them fully into the change process.

RESISTANCE TO CHANGE

Change typically brings with it resistance. When people resist change, furthermore, they are defending something that is important and that appears to them as threatened by the attempted change. Resistance is often viewed by change leaders and managers as something that must be "overcome" in order for change to be successful. This is not always correct or helpful. Resistance is best viewed as feedback that indicates something can be done to achieve a better "fit" between the planned change, the situation, and the people involved.

There are any number of reasons why people in organizations may resist planned change. Some of the more common ones are shown in *Manager's Notepad 15.3*. Once resistance to change is recognized and understood, it can be dealt with in various ways. Among the alternatives for effectively managing resistance, the *education and communication* approach uses discussions, presentations, and demonstrations to educate people beforehand about a change. *Participation and involvement* allows others to contribute ideas and help design and implement the change. The *facilitation and support* approach involves providing encouragement and training, actively listening to problems and complaints, and helping to overcome performance pressures. *Facilitation and agreement* provides incentives that appeal to those who are actively resisting or ready to resist. This approach makes tradeoffs in exchange for assurances that change will not be blocked. *Manipulation and co-optation* tries to influence others covertly by providing information selectively and structuring events in favor of the desired change. *Explicit and implicit coercion* forces people to accept change by threatening resistors with a variety of undesirable consequences if they do not go along as planned.[21] Obviously, the last two approaches carry great risk and potential for negative side effects.

TECHNOLOGICAL CHANGE

Technological change is common in today's organizations, but it also brings special challenges to change leaders. For the full advantages of new technolo-

MANAGER'S NOTEPAD 15.3

WHY PEOPLE MAY RESIST CHANGE

- *Fear of the unknown:* Not understanding what is happening or what comes next.
- *Disrupted habits:* Feeling upset when old ways of doing things can't be followed.
- *Loss of confidence:* Feeling incapable of performing well under the new ways of doing things.
- *Loss of control:* Feeling that things are being done "to" you rather than "by" or "with" you.
- *Poor timing:* Feeling overwhelmed by the situation or that things are moving too fast.
- *Work overload:* Not having the physical or psychic energy to commit to the change.
- *Loss of face:* Feeling inadequate or humiliated because it appears that the "old" ways weren't "good" ways.
- *Lack of purpose:* Not seeing a reason for the change and/or not understanding its benefits.

gies to be realized, a good fit must be achieved with work needs, practices, and people. This, in turn, requires a special sensitivity to resistance. It also requires continual gathering of information so that appropriate adjustments can be made all during the time a new technology is being implemented. In this sense, the demands of managing technological change can be described in this historical analogy of Trukese and European navigators.[22]

The European navigator works from a plan, relates all moves during a voyage to the plan, and tries to always stay "on course." When something unexpected happens, the plan is revised systematically, and the new plan followed again until the navigator finds the ship to be off course. The Trukese navigator, by contrast, starts with an objective and moves off in its general direction. Always alert to information from waves, clouds, winds, etc., the navigator senses subtle changes in conditions and steers and alters the ship's course continually to reach the ultimate objective.

Like the Trukese navigator, technological change may best be approached as an ongoing process that will inevitably require improvisation as things are being implemented. New technologies are often designed external to the organization in which they are to be used. The implications of such a technology for a local application may be difficult to anticipate and plan for ahead of time. A technology that is attractive in concept may appear complicated to the new users; the full extent of its benefits and/or inadequacies may not become known until it is tried. This, in turn, means that the change leader and manager should be alert to resistance, should continually gather and process information relating to the change, and should be willing to customize the new technology to best meet the needs of the local situation.

DEVELOPING ORGANIZATIONS

● **Organization development** is a comprehensive effort to improve an organization's ability to deal with its environment and solve problems.

Among consulting professionals **organization development,** or *OD* for short, is known as a comprehensive approach to planned organizational change that involves the application of behavioral science in a systematic and long-range effort to improve organizational effectiveness.[23] Organization development is supposed to help organizations cope with environmental and other pressures for change while also improving their internal problem-solving capabilities. OD, in this sense, brings the quest for continuous improvement to the planned change process.

GOALS AND PROCESSES OF ORGANIZATION DEVELOPMENT

In organization development two goals are pursued simultaneously. The *outcome goals of OD* focus on task accomplishments, while the *process goals of OD* focus on the way people work together. It is this second goal that strongly differentiates OD from more general attempts at planned change in organizations. You may think of OD as a form of "planned change plus," with the "plus" meaning that change is accomplished in such a way that organization members develop a capacity for continued self-renewal. That is, OD tries to achieve change while helping organization members become more active and self-reliant in their ability to continue changing in the future. What also makes OD unique is its commitment to strong humanistic values and established principles of behavioral science. OD is committed to improving organizations through freedom of choice, shared power and self-reliance, and by taking the best advantage of what we know about human behavior in organizations.

Figure 15.5 presents a general model of OD and shows its relationship to Lewin's three phases of planned change. To begin the OD process successfully, any consultant or facilitator must *establish a change relationship* with members of

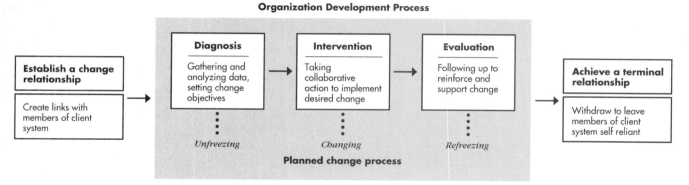

Figure 15.5 Organization development and the planned change process.

the client system. The next step is *diagnosis*—gathering and analyzing data to assess the situation and set appropriate change objectives. This helps with unfreezing as well as pinpointing appropriate directions for action. Diagnosis leads to active *intervention*, wherein change objectives are pursued through a variety of specific interventions, a number of which will be discussed shortly.

Essential to any OD effort is *evaluation*. This is the examination of the process to determine if things are proceeding as desired and if further action is needed. Eventually, the OD consultant or facilitator should *achieve a terminal relationship* that leaves the client able to function on its own. If OD has been done well, the system and its members should be better prepared to manage their ongoing need for self-renewal and development.

ORGANIZATION DEVELOPMENT INTERVENTIONS

The foundations of organization development include respect for people and a commitment to their full participation in self-directed change processes. It is employee involvement in action. OD rallies an organization's human resources through teamwork and in support of constructive change. This process is evident in the variety of **OD interventions** or activities that are initiated to directly facilitate the change processes. Importantly, these interventions are linked to concepts and ideas that are discussed elsewhere in this book and that are well represented in the practices and approaches of the new workplace.

● An **OD intervention** is a structured activity that helps create change in organization development.

Organizationwide Interventions

At the level of the total organization, OD practitioners operate on the premise that any changes in one part of the system will also affect other parts. The organization's culture is considered to have an important impact on member attitudes and morale. And it is believed that structures and jobs can be designed to bring together people, technology, and systems in highly productive and satisfying working combinations. Some of the OD interventions often applied with an emphasis on organizational effectiveness include the following:

● *Survey feedback:* Comprehensive and systematic data collection to identify attitudes and needs, analyze results, and plan for constructive action.

Organization-wide OD interventions

● *Confrontation meeting:* One-day intensive, structured meetings to gather data on workplace problems and plan for constructive actions.

● *Structural redesign:* Realigning the organization structure to meet the needs of environmental and contextual forces.

● *Management by objectives (MBO):* Formalizing MBO throughout the organization to link individual, group, and organizational objectives.

Hyatt Corporation operates more than 190 hotels and resorts worldwide. The firm has used surveys for many years to examine organizational climate and effectiveness. Questionnaires distributed annually to all employees include items like: "Tell us what you think of management." A General Morale Index is closely watched by senior management, and a computer program compares the results from various operating locations.[24]

Management Across Functions

BUSINESS LAW

The Corporate Soul Sometimes Needs Searching

It only takes a lawsuit to remind corporate leaders of the importance of attending to business ethics. Not just for themselves mind you, but for all members of their organizations. Sears Roebuck & Co., for example, was charged in court with charging customers of some of its auto service centers for services that had not been performed. While denying the charges, Sears' leadership heard the message. The firm now works with Steve Priest, a graduate of Harvard's Divinity School, and founder of Ethical Leadership Group. He and his firm provide consulting services to help companies and their employees understand the demands of ethical workplace behavior. Says Priest about Sears and the problems of managing ethics among a 300,000 member workforce: "Any town that size is going to have some bad apples. The task is to find them and root them out." Motorola sent Priest to Malaysia to help workers understand the firm's new code of conduct. He helped Sara Lee Corp. develop a brochure to communicate its code of conduct. And, Boeing hired him to discuss business ethics with corporate officers. Consultants like Priest have gotten a boost for their businesses since the U.S. government clarified required fines and sentencing guidelines for corporate wrongdoing. The laws allow leniency for companies that have solid programs for finding and eliminating illegal practices. Priest's approach to moral development for organizations is strict but forgiving. He says: "Human beings are subject to temptation. You just have to set up the environment for people to follow their conscience." [25]

Team Interventions

The team plays a very important role in organization development. OD practitioners recognize two principles in this respect. First, teams are viewed as important vehicles for helping people satisfy important needs. Second, it is believed that improved collaboration within and among teams can improve organizational performance. Selected OD interventions designed to improve team effectiveness include the following:

Team OD interventions

- *Team building:* Structured experiences to help team members set goals, improve interpersonal relations, and become a better functioning team.
- *Process consultation:* Third-party observation and advice on critical team processes (e.g., communication, conflict, and decision making).
- *Intergroup team building:* Structured experiences to help two or more teams set shared goals, improve intergroup relations, and become better coordinated.

Individual Interventions

Concerning individuals, organization development practitioners generally recognize that the need for personal growth and development is most likely to be satisfied in a supportive and challenging work environment. They also accept the premise that most people are capable of assuming responsibility for their own actions and of making positive contributions to organizational performance. Based on these principles, some of the more popular *OD* interventions designed to help improve individual effectiveness include the following:

- *Sensitivity training (T-groups):* Unstructured group sessions where participants learn interpersonal skills and increased sensitivity to other people.
- *Management training:* Structured educational opportunities for developing important managerial skills and competencies.
- *Role negotiation:* Structured interactions to clarify and negotiate role expectations among people who work together.
- *Job redesign:* Realigning task components to better fit the needs and capabilities of the individual.
- *Career planning:* Structured advice and discussion sessions to help individuals plan career paths and programs of personal development.

← Individual OD interventions

FINAL ADVICE: CHANGE AND CAREER READINESS

The world of work as described here and throughout this book is dynamic and ever challenging. The career demands and pressures of this environment are as unrelenting as they are stimulating. With the challenges of change come special responsibilities to build and maintain career readiness. And when it comes to career success during changing times, one thing is without a doubt true—what happens is up to you.

The best early career advice returns again and again to the same message—what happens is up to you. Don't let yourself down. Step forward and take charge of your learning. Begin building what author and consultant Tom Peters refers to as the "brand called 'you.'"[26] Peters advises each of us to continually work hard to create and maintain a unique and timely package of skills and capabilities with career potential. In Peters' words, your personal brand should be "remarkable, measurable, distinguished, and distinctive" relative to the competition—others like you.[27]

In times of great change, the career challenge is even more dramatic. Like organizations that must innovate and adapt to achieve competitive advantage, you and your brand must also be flexible and change with the times. According to another noted author and consultant, Stephen Covey, this means that you must be prepared to step forward in a career and always (1) behave like an entrepreneur, (2) seek feedback on your performance continually, (3) set up your own mentoring systems, (4) get comfortable with teamwork, (5) take risks to gain experience and learn new skills, (6) be a problem solver, and (7) keep your life in balance.[28]

Introducing Management has been rich with insights into the new workplace, the nature of leadership and management, and the great challenges organizations face in a highly competitive global economy. As you move forward in this exciting world of opportunity, you must continue the process of personal brand building and continue to strengthen your potential for satisfying lifelong career advancement. Don't be afraid of change, and don't ever forget that what you do with your career is up to you. Many foundations for career success have been set during this introductory study of management. Remember to always build on these foundations in your commitment to life-long learning and continued personal development.

SUMMARY

What Is Innovation?

- A learning organization is one in which people, values, and systems support innovation and continuous change based on the lessons of experience.

- Innovation allows creative ideas to be turned into products and/or processes that benefit organizations and their customers.

- Highly innovative organizations tend to have supportive cultures, strategies, structures, staffing, and top management.

- The possible barriers to innovation in organizations include a lack of top management support, excessive bureaucracy, short time horizons, and vested interests.

What Are the Challenges of Organizational Change?

- A change agent is someone who takes leadership responsibility for helping to change the behavior of people and organizational systems.

- Managers should be able to spot change opportunities and lead the process of planned change in their areas of work responsibilities.

- Although organizational change can proceed with a top-down emphasis, inputs from all levels of responsibility are essential to achieve successful implementation.

- The many possible targets for change include organizational tasks, people, cultures, technologies, and structures.

How Can One Lead the Change Process?

- Lewin identified three phases of planned change: unfreezing—preparing a system for change; changing—making a change; and refreezing—stabilizing the system with a new change in place.

- Good change agents understand the nature of force-coercion, rational persuasion, and shared power change strategies.

- People resist change for a variety of reasons, including fear of the unknown and force of habit.

- Good change agents deal with resistance positively and in a variety of ways, including education, participation, facilitation, manipulation, and coercion.

What Are the Challenges of Organization and Career Development in Change Environments?

- Organization development (OD) is a comprehensive approach to planned organization change that uses principles of behavioral science to improve organizational effectiveness over the long term.

- OD has both outcome goals, with a focus on improved task accomplishment, and process goals, with a focus on improvements in the way people work together to accomplish important tasks.

- OD interventions are structured activities that are used to help people work together to accomplish change; they may be implemented at the individual, group, and/or organizational levels.

KEY TERMS

Change leader (p. 248)

Changing (p. 250)

Force-coercion strategy (p. 251)

Innovation (p. 244)

Learning organization (p. 244)

OD interventions (p. 257)

Organization development (OD) (p. 256)

Planned change (p. 248)

Rational persuasion strategy (p. 252)

Refreezing (p. 250)

Shared power strategy (p. 252)

Unfreezing (p. 249)

SELF-TEST Take the interactive Self-Test for this chapter on the Schermerhorn Web Site

Module

Historical Foundations of Management

I N *The Evolution of Management Thought*, Daniel Wren traces management as far back as 5000 B.C., when the ancient Sumerians used written records to assist in governmental and commercial activities.[1] Management was important to the construction of the Egyptian pyramids, the rise of the Roman Empire, and the commercial success of 14th-century Venice. By the time of the Industrial Revolution in the 1700s great social changes helped prompt a great leap forward in the manufacture of basic staples and consumer goods. Industrial change was accelerated by Adam Smith's ideas of mass production through specialized tasks and the division of labor. By the turn of the 20th century, Henry Ford and others were making mass production a mainstay of the modern economy. Since then, the science and practices of management have been on a rapid and continuing path of development. The legacies of this rich history of management can be understood in the following framework:

- The *classical approaches* that focus on developing universal principles for use in various management situations.
- The *human resource approaches* that focus on human needs, the work group, and the role of social factors in the workplace.
- The *modern approaches* that focus on the systems view of organizations and contingency thinking in a dynamic and complex environment.

Major schools of management thought

CLASSICAL APPROACHES

The three branches of the classical approach to management are (1) scientific management, (2) administrative principles, and (3) bureaucratic organization. The classical approaches generally assume that people at work act in a rational manner that is primarily driven by economic concerns. Workers are expected to rationally consider opportunities made available to them and do whatever is necessary to achieve the greatest personal and monetary gain.[2]

SCIENTIFIC MANAGEMENT

In 1911 Frederick W. Taylor published *The Principles of Scientific Management*, in which he makes the following statement: "The principal object of management should be to secure maximum prosperity for the employer, coupled with the maximum prosperity for the employee."[3] Taylor, often called the "father of scientific management," noticed that many workers did their jobs their own way and without clear and uniform specifications. He believed that this caused them to lose efficiency and perform below their true capacities. He also believed that this problem could be corrected if workers were taught and then helped by supervisors to always perform their jobs in the right way.

Taylor used the concept of "time study" to analyze the motions and tasks required in any job and to develop the most efficient ways to perform them. He then linked these job requirements with both training for the worker and a systematic management approach in which supervisors offered proper direction, support, and monetary incentives. Taylor's four principles of **scientific management** are the following: (1) Develop for every job a "science" that includes

- **Scientific management** involves a job science that includes careful selection and training of workers, and proper supervisory support.

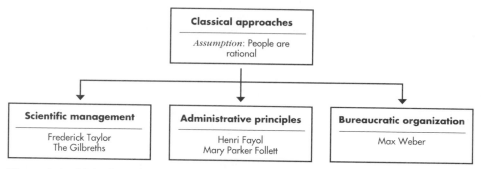

Figure A.1   Major branches in the classical approach to management.

rules of motion, standardized work implements, and proper working conditions. (2) Carefully select workers with the right abilities for the job. (3) Carefully train workers to do the job and give them the proper incentives to cooperate with the job "science." (4) Support workers by carefully planning their work and by smoothing the way as they go about their jobs.

Taylor tried to use scientific techniques to improve the productivity of people at work. The implications of his efforts, if not his exact scientific management principles, are found in many management settings today. These include the following practical lessons:

Lessons of scientific management

- Make results-based compensation a performance incentive.
- Carefully design jobs with efficient work methods.
- Carefully select workers with the abilities to do these jobs.
- Train workers to perform jobs to the best of their abilities.
- Train supervisors to support workers so they can perform jobs to the best of their abilities.

- **Motion study** is the science of reducing a task to its basic physical motions.

Mentioned in Taylor's first principle, **motion study** is the science of reducing a job or task to its basic physical motions. As contemporaries of Taylor, Frank and Lillian Gilbreth pioneered motion studies as a management tool. In one famous study, they reduced the number of motions used by bricklayers and tripled their productivity.[4] The Gilbreths' work established the foundation for later advances in the areas of job simplification, work standards, and incentive wage plans—all techniques still used in the modern workplace.

ADMINISTRATIVE PRINCIPLES

A second classical approach to management is based on attempts to document and understand the experiences of successful managers. Two prominent writers in the school of thought are Henri Fayol and Mary Parker Follett.

Henri Fayol

The early work of Henri Fayol, a career executive, scholar, and writer, represents the "administrative principles" school of thought. In 1916, after a career in French industry, Fayol published *Administration Industrielle et Générale*.[5] The book outlines his views on the proper management of organizations and the people within them. It identifies the following five "rules" or "duties" of management, which closely resemble the four functions of management that we talk about today—planning, organizing, leading, and controlling.

Fayol's rules of management

- *Foresight:* To complete a plan of action for the future.
- *Organization:* To provide and mobilize resources to implement the plan.
- *Command:* To lead, select, and evaluate workers to get the best work toward the plan.
- *Coordination:* To fit diverse efforts together and ensure that information is shared and problems solved.

- *Control:* To make sure things happen according to plan and to take necessary corrective action.

Most importantly, Fayol believed that management could be taught. He was very concerned about improving the quality of management and set forth a number of "principles" to guide managerial action. A number of them are still part of the management vocabulary. They include the *scalar chain principle*—there should be a clear and unbroken line of communication from the top to the bottom in the organization; the *unity of command principle*—each person should receive orders from only one boss; and, the *unity of direction principle*—one person should be in charge of all activities that have the same performance objective.

Mary Parker Follett

Another contributor to the administrative principles school was Mary Parker Follett, who was eulogized at her death in 1933 as "one of the most important women America has yet produced in the fields of civics and sociology."[6] In her writings about businesses and other organizations Follett displayed an understanding of groups and a deep commitment to human cooperation—ideas that are highly relevant today. For her, groups were mechanisms through which diverse individuals could combine their talents for a greater good. She viewed organizations as "communities" in which managers and workers should labor in harmony, without one party dominating the other and with the freedom to talk over and truly reconcile conflicts and differences. She believed it was the manager's job to help people in organizations cooperate with one another and achieve an integration of interests.

A review of *Dynamic Administration: The Collected Papers of Mary Parker Follett* helps to illustrate the modern applications of her management insights.[7] Follett believed that making every employee an owner in the business would create feelings of collective responsibility. Today we address the same issues under such labels as "employee ownership," "profit sharing," and "gain-sharing plans." Follett believed that business problems involve a wide variety of factors that must be considered in relationship to one another. Today we talk about "systems" when describing the same phenomenon. Follett believed that businesses were services and that private profits should always be considered vis-à-vis the public good. Today, we pursue the same issues under the labels of "managerial ethics" and "corporate social responsibility."

BUREAUCRATIC ORGANIZATION

Max Weber was a late 19th-century German intellectual whose ideas have had a major impact on the field of management and the sociology of organizations. His ideas developed somewhat in reaction to what he considered to be performance deficiencies in the organizations of his day. Among other things, Weber was concerned that people were in positions of authority, not because of their job-related capabilities, but because of their social standing or "privileged" status in German society. For this and other reasons he believed that organizations largely failed to reach their performance potential.

● **Bureaucracy** is a rational and efficient form of organization founded on logic, order, and legitimate authority.

Characteristics of Weber's bureaucracy

At the heart of Weber's thinking was a specific form of organization he believed could correct the problems just described—a **bureaucracy.**[8] This is an ideal, intentionally rational, and very efficient form of organization founded on principles of logic, order, and legitimate authority. The defining characteristics of Weber's bureaucratic organization are as follows:

● *Clear division of labor:* Jobs are well defined, and workers become highly skilled at performing them.
● *Clear hierarchy of authority:* Authority and responsibility are well defined for each position, and each position reports to a higher level one.
● *Formal rules and procedures:* Written guidelines direct behavior and decisions in jobs, and written files are kept for historical record.
● *Impersonality:* Rules and procedures are impartially and uniformly applied with no one receiving preferential treatment.
● *Careers based on merit:* Workers are selected and promoted on ability and performance, and managers are career employees of the organization.

Weber believed that organizations would perform well as bureaucracies. They would have the advantages of efficiency in utilizing resources and of fairness or equity in the treatment of employees and clients.

This is the ideal side of bureaucracy. However, the terms "bureaucracy" and "bureaucrat" are now often used with negative connotations. The possible disadvantages of bureaucracy include excessive paperwork or "red tape," slowness in handling problems, rigidity in the face of shifting customer or client needs, resistance to change, and employee apathy. These disadvantages are most likely to cause problems for organizations that must be flexible and quick in adapting to changing circumstances—a characteristic of challenges in today's dynamic organizational environments. As discussed in Chapters 8 and 9 on organizational structures and design, researchers now try to determine when and under what conditions bureaucratic features work best. They also want to identify alternatives to the bureaucratic form. Current trends in management include many innovative organizational forms that seek the same goals as Weber but with different approaches to how organizations can be structured.

HUMAN RESOURCE APPROACHES

During the 1920s, an emphasis on the human side of the workplace began to establish its influence on management thinking. Major branches that emerged in this tradition include the famous Hawthorne studies and Maslow's theory of human needs, as well as theories generated from these foundations by Douglas McGregor and others. These human resource approaches maintain that people are social and self-actualizing. People at work are assumed to seek satisfying social relationships, respond to group pressures, and search for personal fulfillment.

HAWTHORNE STUDIES

In 1924, the Western Electric Company (predecessor to today's Lucent Technologies) commissioned a research program to study individual productivity at

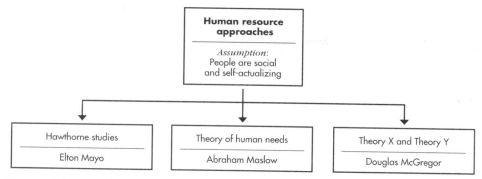

Figure A.2 Foundations in the human resource approach to management.

the Hawthorne Works of the firm's Chicago plant.[9] The initial "Hawthorne studies" had a scientific management perspective and sought to determine how economic incentives and the physical conditions of the workplace affected the output of workers. An initial focus was on the level of illumination in the manufacturing facilities; it seemed reasonable to expect that better lighting would improve performance. After failing to find this relationship, however, the researchers concluded that unforeseen "psychological factors" somehow interfered with their illumination experiments. This finding and later Hawthorne studies directed attention toward human interactions in the workplace and ultimately had a major influence on the field of management.

In 1927, a team led by Harvard's Elton Mayo began more research to examine the effect of worker fatigue on output. Care was taken to design a scientific test that would be free of the psychological effects thought to have confounded the earlier illumination studies. Six workers who assembled relays were isolated for intensive study in a special test room. They were given various rest pauses, and workdays and workweeks of various lengths, and production was regularly measured. Once again, researchers failed to find any direct relationship between changes in physical working conditions and output. Productivity increased regardless of the changes made.

Mayo and his colleagues concluded that the new "social setting" created for workers in the test room accounted for the increased productivity. Two factors were singled out as having special importance. One was the *group atmosphere*. The workers shared pleasant social relations with one another and wanted to do a good job. The other was more *participative supervision*. Test-room workers were made to feel important, were given a lot of information, and were frequently asked for their opinions. This was not the case in their, or in the other workers', regular jobs elsewhere in the plant.

Mayo's studies continued to examine these factors until the worsening economic conditions of the Depression forced their termination in 1932. Until then, interest focused on employee attitudes, interpersonal relations, and group relations. In one study, over 21,000 employees were interviewed to learn what they liked and disliked about their work environment. "Complex" and "baffling" results led the researchers to conclude that the same things (e.g., work conditions or wages) could be sources of satisfaction for some workers and of dissatisfaction for others. The final Hawthorne study was conducted in the bank wiring room and centered on the role of the work group. A surprise finding here was that people would restrict their output in order to avoid the displeasure of the group, even if it meant sacrificing pay that could otherwise be earned by increasing output. Thus, it was recognized that groups can have strong negative, as well as positive, influences on individual productivity.

As scholars now look back, they criticize the Hawthorne studies for poor research design, weak empirical support for the conclusions drawn, and the tendency of researchers to overgeneralize their findings.[10] Yet these studies remain a turning point in the evolution of management thought. The Hawthorne studies helped shift the attention of managers and management researchers away from the technical and structural concerns of the classical approach and toward social and human concerns as keys to productivity. They showed that people's feelings, attitudes, and relationships with co-workers should be important to management, and they recognized the importance of the work group. They also identified the **Hawthorne effect**—the tendency of people who are singled out for special attention to perform as anticipated merely because of expectations created by the situation.

● **The Hawthorne effect** is the tendency of persons singled out for special attention to perform as expected.

HUMAN RELATIONS MOVEMENT

The Hawthorne studies contributed to the emergence of the **human relations movement** as an important influence on management thought during the 1950s and 1960s. This movement was largely based on the viewpoint that managers who used good human relations in the workplace would achieve productivity. Furthermore, the insights of the human relations movement set the stage for what has now evolved as the field of **organizational behavior,** the study of individuals and groups in organizations.

● The **human relations movement** suggests that managers using good human relations will achieve productivity.

● **Organizational behavior** is the study of individuals and groups in organizations.

MASLOW'S THEORY OF HUMAN NEEDS

Among the insights of the human relations movement, Abraham Maslow's work in the area of human "needs" is a key foundation. A **need** is a physiological or psychological deficiency a person feels the compulsion to satisfy. This is a significant concept for managers because needs create tensions that can influence a person's work attitudes and behaviors.

● A **need** is a physiological or psychological deficiency that a person wants to satisfy.

Maslow identified five levels of human needs arranged in a hierarchy: physiological, safety, social, esteem, and self-actualization. His theory is based on two underlying principles.[11] The first is the *deficit principle*—a satisfied need is not a motivator of behavior. People act to satisfy "deprived" needs, those for which a satisfaction "deficit" exists. The second is the *progression principle*—the five needs exist in a hierarchy of "prepotency." A need at any level only becomes activated once the next lower level need has been satisfied.

Maslow suggested that people try to satisfy the five needs in sequence. They progress step by step from the lowest level in the hierarchy to the highest. Along the way, a deprived need dominates individual attention and determines behavior until it is satisfied. Then, the next higher level need is activated and progression up the hierarchy occurs. At the level of self-actualization, the deficit and progression principles cease to operate. The more this need is satisfied, the stronger it grows.

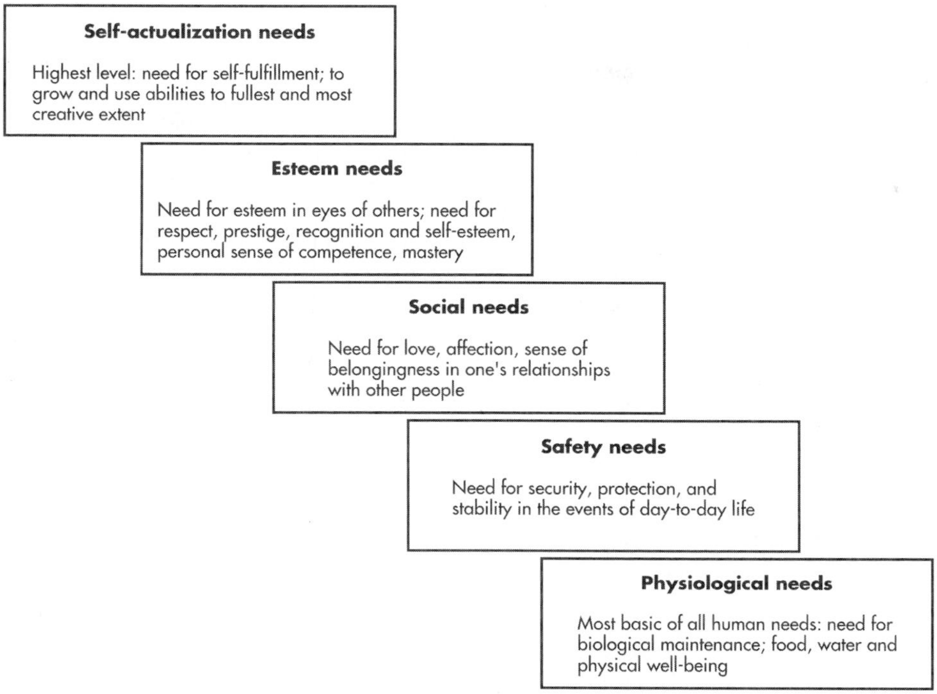

Figure A.3 Maslow's hierarchy of human needs.

Consistent with the human relations thinking. Maslow's theory implies that managers who can help people satisfy their important needs at work will achieve productivity. Although scholars now recognize that things are more complicated than this, as was discussed in Chapter 12 on motivation, Maslow's ideas are still relevant to everyday management.

MCGREGOR'S THEORY X AND THEORY Y

Douglas McGregor was heavily influenced by both the Hawthorne studies and Maslow. His classic book *The Human Side of Enterprise* advances the thesis that managers should give more attention to the social and self-actualizing needs of people at work.[12] McGregor called upon managers to shift their view of human nature away from a set of assumptions he called "Theory X" and toward ones he called "Theory Y." Managers holding **Theory X** assumptions approach their jobs believing that those who work for them generally dislike work, lack ambition, are irresponsible, are resistant to change, and prefer to be led rather than to lead. McGregor considers such thinking inappropriate. He argues instead for the value of **Theory Y** assumptions in which the manager believes people are willing to work, are capable of self-control, are willing to accept responsibility, are imaginative and creative, and are capable of self-direction.

An important aspect of McGregor's ideas is his belief that managers who hold either set of assumptions can create **self-fulfilling prophecies**—that is, through their behavior they create situations where subordinates act in ways

- **Theory X** assumes that people dislike work, lack ambition, are irresponsible and resistant to change, and prefer to be led.

- **Theory Y** assumes that people are willing to work, accept responsibility, and are capable of self-direction and creativity.

- A **self-fulfilling prophecy** occurs when a person acts in ways in order to confirm another's expectations.

that confirm the original expectations. Managers with Theory X assumptions act in a very directive "command-and-control" fashion that gives people little personal say over their work. These supervisory behaviors often create passive, dependent, and reluctant subordinates who tend to do only what they are told to or required to do. This reinforces the original Theory X viewpoint. In contrast, managers with Theory Y perspectives behave in "participative" ways that allow subordinates more job involvement, freedom, and responsibility. This creates opportunities to satisfy esteem and self-actualization needs and causes workers to perform as expected with initiative and high performance. This time the self-fulfilling prophecy is a positive one.

Theory Y thinking is very consistent with developments in the new workplace and its emphasis on valuing workforce diversity. It is also central to the popular notions of employee participation, involvement, empowerment, and self-management.

MODERN MANAGEMENT APPROACHES

Modern approaches to management respect the classical and human resource schools, but they also recognize that no one model applies universally in all situations. People are considered to have multiple and varied needs that can change over time. They possess a range of talents and capabilities that can be developed. Organizations and managers, therefore, must respond to the individual differences with a wide variety of strategies and practices.

SYSTEMS THINKING

● An **open system** interacts with its environment and transforms resource inputs into outputs.

Organizations can be viewed as **open systems** that interact with their environments in the continual process of transforming resource inputs into product outputs (finished goods and/or services).[13] The external environment is a critical element in the open-systems view of organizations. It is a source of both resources and customer feedback, and it can have a significant impact on operations and outcomes. Feedback from the environment tells an organization how well it is meeting the needs of customers and of society at large. Without customer willingness to use the organization's products, it is difficult to operate or stay in business over the long run. The open-systems view of organizations, therefore, helps to keep the spotlight on the all-important customer.

Internally, the organization is a collection of interrelated parts or subsystems that must function together to achieve a common purpose. Consider, for example, the case of a regional electric utility. All elements in the organization's complex network of subsystems must work together so that the firm can produce and sell electric power to its customers. It is the job of the president, vice president for operations, and the respective subsystems managers to make this coordinated action possible. They must ensure not only that the necessary subsystem tasks are accomplished (such as purchasing, power generation, distribution, and accounting) but that they get done in an integrated fashion. The ultimate goal is for all subsystems to perform in ways that facilitate high productivity for the entire enterprise.

CONTINGENCY THINKING

Contingency thinking tries to match managerial responses with the problems and opportunities unique to different situations, particularly those posed by individual and environmental differences. The modern management approach does not try to find the "one best way" to manage in all circumstances. Rather, the contingency perspective tries to help managers understand situational differences and respond to them in appropriate ways.[14]

Contingency thinking is an important theme in management today, and its implications extend to all of the management functions. For example, consider again Weber's concept of bureaucracy. From a contingency perspective the strict bureaucratic form is only one possible way of organizing things. What turns out to be the "best" structure in any given situation will depend on many factors, including environmental uncertainty, an organization's primary technology, and the strategy being pursued. Only when the environment is relatively stable and operations are predictable does the bureaucracy work best; in other situations, alternative structures may be needed. Contingency thinking also recognizes that what is a good structure for one organization may not work well for another, and what works well at one time may not work as well in the future as circumstances change.[15]

- **Contingency thinking** maintains that there is no one best way to manage; what is best depends on the situation.

CONTINUING MANAGEMENT THEMES

This history and its many accumulating insights have set strong foundation for important continuing developments in management thought. Among the most important is recognition that we live and work in a dynamic and ever-changing environment that puts unique and never-ending competitive pressures on organizations. Key themes considered throughout this book and highly relevant as we move into the 21st century include continuing pressures for quality and performance excellence, ethics and social responsibility, an expanding global awareness, and the importance of leadership, knowledge workers, information technology and the new management. Management is a dynamic and evolving discipline, and in its richness offers valuable insight to all those committed to organizational and career excellence.

Glossary

A

Accommodation or **smoothing** plays down differences and highlights similarities to reduce conflict.

An **accommodative strategy** accepts social responsibilities and tries to satisfy prevailing economic, legal, and ethical performance criteria.

Accountability is the requirement to show performance results to a supervisor.

Active listening involves taking action to help the source of a message say what he or she really means.

An **adaptive organization** operates with a minimum of bureaucratic features and encourages worker empowerment and teamwork.

In **arbitration** a neutral third party issues a binding decision to resolve a dispute.

An **assessment center** is a selection technique that engages job candidates in a series of experimental activities over a 1- or 2-day period.

Authority is the right to assign tasks and direct the activities of subordinates in ways that support accomplishment of the organization's purpose.

An **authority decision** is a decision made by the leader and then communicated to the group.

Automation is the total mechanization of a job.

Avoidance involves pretending that a conflict doesn't really exists or hoping that a conflict will simply go away.

B

The **BCG matrix** ties strategy formulation to an analysis of business opportunities according to market growth rate and market share.

A **behaviorally anchored rating scale (BARS)** is a performance appraisal method that uses specific descriptions of actual behaviors to rate various levels of performance.

Benchmarking is a process of comparing operations and performance with other organizations known for excellence.

A **budget** is a plan that commits resources to projects or programs; a formalized way of allocating resources to specific activities.

Bureaucracy is a rational and efficient form of organization founded on logic, order, and legitimate authority.

A **business plan** describes the direction for a new business and the financing needed to operate it.

A **business strategy** identifies the intentions of a division or strategic business unit to compete in its special product and/or service domain.

C

A **career portfolio** documents academic and personal accomplishments for external review.

Centralization is the concentration of authority for most decisions at the top level of an organization.

In a **centralized communication network** communication flows only between individual members and a hub or center point.

A **certain environment** offers complete information on possible action alternatives and their consequences.

A **change leader** takes leadership responsibility for changing the existing pattern of behavior of another person or social system.

Changing is the central phase in the planned-change process in which a planned change actually takes place.

A **charismatic leader** is a leader who develops special leader-follower relationships and inspires followers in extraordinary ways.

Coaching is the communication of specific technical advice to an individual.

A **code of ethics** is a written document that states values and ethical standards intended to guide the behavior of employees.

Coercive power is the capacity to punish or withhold positive outcomes as a means of influencing other people.

Cohesiveness is the degree to which members are attracted to and motivated to remain part of a team.

Collaboration or **problem solving** involves working through conflict differences and solving problems so everyone wins.

Collective bargaining is the process of negotiating, administering, and interpreting a labor contract.

A **combination strategy** involves stability, growth, and retrenchment in one or more combinations.

A **committee** is a formal team designated to work on a special task on a continuing basis.

Communication is the process of sending and receiving symbols with meanings attached.

A **communication channel** is the medium through which a message is sent.

Comparative management is the study of how management practices differ systematically from one country and/or culture to the next.

Competition or **authoritative command** uses force, superior skill, or domination to "win" a conflict.

A **competitive advantage** is a special edge that allows an organization to deal with market and environmental forces better than its competitors.

A **compressed workweek** is any work schedule that allows a full-time job to be completed in less than the standard 5 days of 8-hour shifts.

Compromise occurs when each party to the conflict gives up something of value to the other.

A **conceptual skill** is the ability to think analytically and solve complex problems to the benefit of everyone involved.

A **concurrent control** or **steering control** is a control that acts in anticipation of problems and focuses primarily on what happens during the work process.

Conflict is a disagreement over issues of substance and/or an emotional antagonism.

Conflict resolution is the removal of the reasons—substantial and/or emtional—for a conflict.

A **consultative decision** is a decision made by a leader after receiving information, advice, or opinions from group members.

Contingency planning identifies alternative courses of action that can be taken if and when circumstances change with time.

Contingency thinking maintains that there is no one best way to manage; what is best depends on the situation.

Contingency workers are employed on a part-time and temporary basis to supplement a permanent workforce.

Continuous improvement involves always searching for new ways to improve operations quality and performance.

Controlling is the process of measuring performance and taking action to ensure desired results.

A **control process** is the process of establishing performance objectives and standards, measuring actual performance, comparing actual performance with objectives and standards, and taking necessary action.

A **core competency** is a special strength that gives an organization a competitive advantage.

Core values are underlying beliefs shared by members of the organization and that influence their behavior.

Corporate culture is the predominant value system for the organization as a whole.

Corporate governance is the system of control and performance monitoring of top management.

Corporate social responsibility is an obligation of an organization to act in ways that serve both its own interests and the interests of its many external publics.

A **corporate strategy** sets long-term direction for the total enterprise.

A **cost leadership strategy** is a corporate competitive strategy that seeks to achieve lower costs than competitors by improving efficiency of production, distribution, and other organizational systems.

Cost-benefit analysis involves comparing the costs and benefits of each potential course of action.

Creativity is ingenuity and imagination that results in a novel solution to a problem.

A **crisis problem** is an unexpected problem that can lead to disaster if not resolved quickly and appropriately.

A **critical incident technique** is a performance appraisal method that involves a running log of effective and ineffective job behaviors.

A **cross-functional team** is a team structure in which members from different functional departments work together as needed to solve problems and explore opportunities.

Cultural relativism suggests there is no one right way to behave; ethical behavior is determined by its cultural context.

Culture is a shared set of beliefs, values, and patterns of behavior common to a group of people.

Culture shock is the confusion and discomfort a person experiences when in an unfamiliar culture.

D

Decentralization is the dispersion of authority to make decisions throughout all levels of the organization.

A **decentralized communication network** allows all members to communicate directly with one another.

A **decision** is a choice among alternative courses of action for dealing with a "problem."

Decision making involves the identification of a problem and the choice of preferred problem-solving alternatives.

A **defensive strategy of social responsibility** seeks to protect the organization by doing the minimum legally required to satisfy social expectations.

Delegation is the process of distributing and entrusting work to other persons.

Departmentalization is the process of grouping together people and jobs under common supervisors to form various work units or departments.

Differentiation is the degree of differences that exists among people, departments, or other internal components of an organization.

A **differentiation strategy** is a corporate strategy that seeks competitive advantage through uniqueness, by developing goods and/or services that are clearly different from those offered by the competition.

Discipline is the act of influencing behavior through reprimand.

Discrimination is an active form of prejudice that disadvantages people by denying them full benefits of organizational membership.

A **distinctive competence** is a special strength that gives an organization a competitive advantage in its operating domain.

Distributive negotiation focuses on "win-lose" claims made by each party for certain preferred outcomes.

A **divisional structure** groups together people who work on the same product, work with similar customers, or who work in the same area or processes.

Dysfunctional conflict is destructive and hurts task performance.

E

The **economic order quantity (EOQ)** method orders a fixed number of items every time an inventory level falls to a predetermined point.

Effective communication occurs when the intended meaning of the source and the perceived meaning of the receiver are identical.

An **effective group** is a group that achieves and maintains high levels of both task performance and membership satisfaction over time.

An **effective team** achieves high levels of both task performance and membership satisfaction.

Efficient communication is communication that occurs at minimum cost in terms of resources expended.

Electronic commerce or *e-business* uses information technology to support online commercial transactions.

Emotional conflict results from feelings of anger, distrust, dislike, fear, and resentment as well as from personality clashes.

Emotional Intelligence is the ability to understand and deal well with emotions at work.

An **employee involvement team** meets on a regular basis to use its talents to help solve problems and achieve continuous improvement.

An **entrepreneur** is willing to pursue opportunities in situations others view as problems or threats.

Entrepreneurship is dynamic, risk taking, creative, and growth oriented behavior.

Equal employment opportunity (EEO) is the right to employment and advancement without regard to race, sex, religion, color, or national origin.

Escalating commitment is the tendency to continue to pursue a course of action, even though it is not working.

Ethical behavior is accepted as "right" or "good" in the context of a governing moral code.

An **ethical dilemma** is a situation with a potential course of action that, although offering potential benefit or gain, is also unethical.

The attempt to externally impose one's ethical standards on other cultures is criticized as a form of **ethical imperialism.**

Ethics form the code of morals that set standards as to what is good or bad, or right or wrong in one's conduct.

Ethics training seeks to help people better understand the ethical aspects of decision making and to incorporate high ethical standards into their daily behavior.

Ethnocentrism is the tendency to consider one's culture as superior to all others.

An **expatriate** lives and works in a foreign country.

Expectancy is a person's belief that working hard will result in high task performance.

Expert power is the capability to influence other people because of specialized knowledge.

Exporting is the process of producing products locally and selling them abroad in foreign markets.

External control is control that occurs through direct supervision or administrative systems, such as rules and procedures.

Extranets are computer networks that use the public Internet for communication between the organization and its environment.

F

Feedback is the process of telling someone else how you feel about something that person did or said or about the situation in general.

A **feedback control** or **postaction control** is a control that takes place after an action is completed.

A **feedforward control** or **preliminary control** ensures that proper directions are set and that the right resources are available to accomplish them before the work activity begins.

A **flexible benefits program** allows employees to choose from a range of benefit options within certain dollar limits.

A **flexible budget** allows the allocation of resources to vary in proportion with various levels of activity.

Flexible working hours are work schedules that give employees some choice in the pattern of daily work hours.

A **focus strategy** is a corporate competitive strategy that concentrates attention on a special market segment to serve its needs better than the competition.

A **force-coercion strategy** attempts to bring about change through formal authority and/or the use of rewards or punishments.

A **forecast** is an attempt to predict outcomes; it is a projection into the future based on historical data combined in some scientific manner.

Formal structure is the structure of the organization in its pure or ideal state.

Fringe benefits are additional nonmonetary forms of compensation (e.g., health plans, retirement plans) provided to an organization's workforce.

The **functional chimneys problem** is a lack of communication and coordination across functions.

Functional conflict is constructive and helps task performance.

A **functional strategy** guides activities within one specific area of operations.

A **functional structure** is an organizational structure that groups together people with similar skills who perform similar tasks.

G

The **general environment** is comprised of the cultural, economic, legal–political, and educational conditions in the locality in which an organization operates.

General managers are responsible for complex organizational units that include many areas of functional activity.

A **geographical structure** is a divisional structure that groups together jobs and activities being performed in the same location or geographical region.

The **glass ceiling effect** is an invisible barrier that limits the advancement of women and minorities to higher level responsibilities in organizations.

The **global economy** is an economic perspective based on worldwide interdependence of resource supplies, product markets, and business competition.

A **global manager** works successfully across international boundaries.

Global sourcing is a process of purchasing materials or components in various parts of the world and then assembling them at home into a final product.

A **graphic rating scale** is a performance appraisal method that uses a checklist of traits or characteristics thought to be related to high-performance outcomes in a given job.

A **group** is a collection of people who regularly interact with one another over time in respect to the pursuit of one or more common goals.

Group dynamics are forces operating in groups that affect task performance and membership satisfaction.

Group process is the way team members work together to accomplish tasks.

Groupthink is a tendency for highly cohesive teams to lose their evaluative capabilities.

A **growth strategy** involves expansion of the organization's current operations.

H

A **halo effect** occurs when one attribute is used to develop an overall impression of a person or situation.

The **Hawthorne effect** is the tendency of persons singled out for special attention to perform as expected.

Heuristics are strategies for simplifying decision making.

Higher order needs, in Maslow's hierarchy, are esteem and self-actualization needs.

The **human relations movement** is based on the viewpoint that managers who use good human relations in the workplace will achieve productivity.

Human resource management is the process of attracting, developing, and maintaining a talented and energetic workforce.

Human resource planning is the process of analyzing staffing needs and identifying actions to fill those needs over time.

Human resources are the people, individuals, and groups that help organizations produce goods or services.

A **human skill** is the ability to work well in cooperation with other people.

A **hygiene factor** is a factor in the work setting, such as working conditions, interpersonal relations, organizational policies, and administration, supervision, and salary.

I

Importing is the process of acquiring products abroad and selling them in domestic markets.

An **individual decision** is made when a manager chooses a preferred course of action without consulting others.

The **individualism view** is a view of ethical behavior based on the belief that one's primary commitment is to the advancement of long-term self-interests.

Informal structure is the undocumented and officially unrecognized structure that coexists with the formal structure of an organization.

An **information system** collects, organizes, and distributes data regarding activities occurring inside and outside an organization.

Innovation is the process of taking a new idea and putting it into practice as part of the organization's normal operating routines.

An **input standard** is a standard that measures work efforts that go into a performance task.

Instrumentality is a person's belief that various work-related outcomes will occur as a result of task performance.

Integration is the level of coordination achieved among subsystems in an organization.

Intellectual capital is the collective brainpower or shared knowledge of a workforce.

Internal control is self-control that occurs through self-discipline and the personal exercise of individual or group responsibility.

An **internal customer** is someone who uses or depends on the work of another person or group within the organization.

An **international business** conducts commercial transactions across national boundaries.

International management involves the conduct of business or other operations in foreign countries.

Intranets are computer networks that allow persons within an organization to share databases and communicate electronically.

Intrapreneurship is entrepreneurial behavior displayed by people or subunits within large organizations.

An **intrinsic** or **natural reward** is a reward that occurs naturally as a person performs a task or job.

Intuitive thinking occurs when someone approaches problems in a flexible and spontaneous fashion.

Inventory consists of materials or products kept in storage.

ISO 9000 certification is granted by the International Standards Organization to indicate that a business meets a rigorous set of quality standards.

J

A **job** is the collection of tasks a person performs in support of organizational objectives.

Job analysis is an orderly study of job requirements and facets that can influence performance results.

A **job description** is a written statement that details the duties and responsibilities of any person holding a particular job.

Job design is the allocation of specific work tasks to individuals and groups.

Job enlargement is a job-design strategy that increases task variety by combining into one job two or more tasks that were previously assigned to separate workers.

Job enrichment is a job-design strategy that increases job depth by adding to a job some of the planning and evaluating duties normally performed by the supervisor.

Job performance is the quantity and quality of task accomplishment by an individual or group.

Job rotation is a job-design strategy that increases task variety by periodically shifting workers among jobs involving different tasks.

Job satisfaction is the degree to which an individual feels positively or negatively about various aspects of the job, including assigned tasks, work setting, and relationships with coworkers.

Job scope is the number and combination of tasks an individual or group is asked to perform.

Job sharing is an arrangement that splits one job between two people.

Job simplification is a job-design strategy that involves standardizing work procedures and employing people in clearly defined and very specialized tasks.

A **job specification** is a list of the qualifications required of any job occupant.

A **joint venture** is a form of international business that establishes operations in a foreign country through joint ownership with local partners.

The **justice view** considers ethical behavior as that which treats people impartially and fairly according to guiding rules and standards.

Just-in-time scheduling (JIT) schedules materials to arrive at a work station or facility "just in time" to be used.

K

Knowledge management is the processes utilizing organizational knowledge to achieve competitive advantage.

L

A **labor contract** is a formal agreement between a union and the employing organization that specifies the rights and obligations of each party with respect to wages, work hours, work rules, and other conditions of employment.

A **labor union** is an organization to which workers belong and that deals with employers on their collective behalf.

Leadership is the process of inspiring others to work hard to accomplish important tasks.

Leading is the process of arousing enthusiasm and directing human-resource efforts toward organizational goals.

Learning is any change in behavior that occurs as a result of experience.

A **learning organization** utilizes people, values, and systems to continuously change and improve its performance based on the lessons of experience.

Legitimate power is the capability to influence other people by virtue of formal authority or the rights of office.

A **licensing agreement** occurs when a firm pays a fee for the rights to make or sell another company's products.

In **lose-lose conflict** no one achieves his or her true desires and the underlying reasons for conflict remain unaffected.

Lower order needs, in Maslow's hierarchy, are physiological, safety, and social needs.

M

A **maintenance activity** is an action taken by a team member that supports the emotional life of the group.

Management is the process of planning, organizing, leading, and controlling the use of resources to accomplish performance goals.

Management by exception focuses managerial attention on substantial differences between actual and desired performance.

Management by objectives (MBO) is a process of joint objective setting between a superior and subordinate.

In **management by wandering around (MBWA)** workers at all levels talk with bosses about a variety of work-related matters.

Management development is training to improve knowledge and skills in the fundamentals of management.

A **management information system (MIS)** collects, organizes, and distributes data in such a way that the information meets managers' needs.

A **manager** is a person in an organization who is responsible for the work performance of one or more other persons.

Managerial competency is a skill or personal characteristic that contributes to high performance in a management job.

A **matrix structure** is an organizational form that combines functional and divisional departmentation to take best advantage of each.

A **mechanistic design** is highly bureaucratic, with centralized authority, many rules and procedures, a clearcut division of labor, narrow spans of controls, and formal coordination.

In **mediation** a neutral party engages in substantive discussions with conflicting parties in the hope that the dispute can be resolved.

Mentoring is the act of sharing experiences and insights between a seasoned and a junior manager.

Merit pay is a system of awarding pay increases in proportion to performance contributions.

The **mission** of an organization is its reason for existing as a supplier of goods and/or services to society.

A **mixed message** results when a person's words communicate one message while actions, body language, or appearance communicate something else.

Modeling demonstrates through personal behavior that which is expected of others.

In a **monochronic culture** people tend to do one thing at a time.

The **moral-rights view** is a view of ethical behavior that seeks to respect and protect the fundamental rights of people.

Motion study is the science of reducing a task to its basic physical motions.

Motivation is a term used in management theory to describe forces within the individual that account for the level, direction, and persistence of effort expended at work.

A **multicultural organization** is based on pluralism and operates with respect for diversity in the workplace.

Multiculturalism involves pluralism and respect for diversity in the workplace.

A **multinational corporation (MNC)** is a business firm with extensive international operations in more than one foreign country.

A **multiperson comparison** is a performance appraisal method that involves comparing one person's performance with that of one or more persons.

N

A **narrative approach** to performance appraisal method uses a written essay description of a person's job performance.

A **need** is a physiological or psychological deficiency a person feels the compulsion to satisfy.

Need for Achievement (nAch) is the desire to do something better or more efficiently, to solve problems, or to master complex tasks.

Need for Affiliation (nAff) is the desire to establish and maintain good relations with people.

Need for Power (nPower) is the desire to control, influence, or be responsible for other people.

Negotiation is the process of making joint decisions when the parties involved have different preferences.

A **network** is a system of computers that are linked together to allow users to easily transfer and share information.

A **network structure** is an organizational structure that consists of a central core with "networks" of outside suppliers of essential business services.

Noise is anything that interferes with the effectiveness of the communication process.

A **nonprogrammed decision** is unique and specifically tailored to a problem at hand.

Nonverbal communication is communication that takes place through channels such as body language and the use of interpersonal space.

A **norm** is a behavior, rule, or standard expected to be followed by team members.

O

Objectives are the specific results or desired end states that one wishes to achieve.

An **OD intervention** is a structured activity initiated by consultants or managers that directly assists in a comprehensive organizational development program.

An **open system** interacts with its environment and transforms resource inputs into outputs.

Operating objectives are specific results that organizations try to accomplish.

An **operational plan** is a plan of limited scope that addresses those activities and resources required to implement strategic plans.

Operations management is a branch of management theory that studies how organizations transform resource inputs into product and service outputs.

An **optimizing decision** results when a manager chooses an alternative that gives the absolute best solution to a problem.

An **organic design** is decentralized with fewer rules and procedures, more open divisions of labor, wide spans of control, and more personal coordination.

An **organization** is a collection of people working together in a division of labor to achieve a common purpose.

An **organization chart** is a diagram that describes the basic arrangement of work positions within an organization.

Organizational design is the process of creating structures that best organize resources to serve mission and objectives.

Organization development (OD) is the application of behavioral science knowledge in a long-range effort to improve an organization's ability to cope with change in its external environment and increase its internal problem-solving capabilities.

Organization structure is the system of tasks, reporting relationships, and communication that links people and groups together to accomplish tasks that serve the organizational purpose.

Organizational behavior is the study of individuals and groups in organizations.

Organizational communication is the process through which information is exchanged through interactions among people inside an organization.

Organizational culture is the system of shared beliefs and values that develops within an organization and guides the behavior of its members.

Organizational design is the process of creating structures that best organize resources to serve mission and objectives.

Organizing is the process of arranging people and resources to work toward a common purpose.

Orientation consists of activities through which new employees are made familiar with their jobs, their co-workers, and the policies, rules, objectives, and services of the organization as a whole.

An **output standard** is a standard that measures performance results in terms of quantity, quality, cost, or time.

Outside-in planning uses analysis of the external environment and makes plans to take advantage of opportunities and avoid problems.

P

Participative planning is the inclusion in the planning process of as many people as possible from among those who will be affected by plans and/or asked to help implement them.

Part-time work is work done on a basis that classifies the employee as "temporary" and requires less than the standard 40-hour workweek.

Perception is the process through which people receive, organize, and interpret information from the environment.

Performance appraisal is a process of formally evaluating performance and providing feedback on which performance adjustments can be made.

Performance effectiveness is an output measure of a task or goal accomplishment.

Performance efficiency is a measure of the resource cost associated with goal accomplishment.

A **performance gap** is a discrepancy between the desired and actual state of affairs.

A **plan** is a statement of intended means for accomplishing a desired result.

Planned change occurs as a result of specific efforts in its behalf by a change agent.

Planning is the process of setting objectives and determining what should be done to accomplish them.

A **policy** is a standing plan that communicates broad guidelines for making decisions and taking action.

Political risk is the possible loss of investment or control over a foreign asset because of political changes in the host country.

In a **polychronic culture** time is used to accomplish many different things at once.

A **portfolio planning** approach seeks the best mix of investments among alternative business opportunities.

Power is the ability to get someone else to do something you want done or to make things happen the way you want.

Prejudice is the holding of negative, irrational attitudes toward individuals because of their group identity.

Principled negotiation or **integrative negotiation** uses a "win-win" orientation to reach solutions acceptable to each party.

Privatization is the selling of state-owned enterprises into private ownership.

A **proactive strategy** meets all the criteria of social responsibility, including discretionary performance.

A **problem** is a difference between an actual situation and a desired situation.

Problem solving is the process of identifying a discrepancy between an actual and desired state of affairs and then taking action to resolve it.

Procedural justice concerns the degree to which policies and rules are fairly administered.

A **procedure** or **rule** is a standing plan that precisely describes what actions are to be taken in specific situations.

A **process** is a group of related tasks creating something of value to a customer.

Process reengineering systematically analyzes work processes to design new and better ones.

A **process structure** groups jobs and activities that are part of the same processes.

Process value analysis identifies and evaluates core processes for their performance contributions.

Product life cycle is the series of stages a product or service goes through in the "life" of its marketability.

A **product structure** is an organizational structure that groups together jobs and activities working on a single product or service.

Productivity is a summary measure of the quantity and quality of work performance with resource utilization considered.

The **program evaluation and review technique (PERT)** is a means for identifying and controlling the many separate events involved in the completion of projects.

A **programmed decision** applies a solution from past experience to the problem at hand.

Progressive discipline is the process of tying reprimands in the form of penalties or punishments to the severity of the employee's infractions.

Project management is the responsibility for making sure that all activities in a project are completed on time, in the order specified, and with high quality.

A **project schedule** is a single-use plan for accomplishing a specific set of tasks.

Projection is the assignment of personal attributes to other individuals.

Proxemics is the use of interpersonal space, such as in the process of interpersonal communication.

Punishment discourages a behavior by making an unpleasant consequence contingent on the occurrence of that behavior.

Q

Quality is a degree of excellence, often defined as the ability to meet customer needs 100 percent of the time.

A **quality circle** is a group of employees who meet periodically to discuss ways of improving the quality of their products or services.

Quality control involves checking processes, material, products, or services to ensure that they meet high standards.

Quality of work life (QWL) is the overall quality of human experiences in the workplace.

R

A **rational persuasion strategy** attempts to bring about change through persuasion backed by special knowledge, empirical data, and rational argument.

Realistic job previews are attempts by the job interviewer to provide the job candidate with all pertinent information about a prospective job and the employing organization, without distortion and before a job offer is accepted.

Recruitment is a set of activities designed to attract a qualified pool of job applicants to an organization.

Referent power is the capability to influence other people because of their desires to identify personally and positively with the power source.

Refreezing is the final stage in the planned-change process during which the manager is concerned with stabilizing the change and creating the conditions for its long-term continuity.

Reliability refers to the ability of an employment test to yield the same result over time if taken by the same person.

Replacement is the management of promotions, transfers, terminations, layoffs, and retirements.

A **retrenchment strategy** involves slowing down, cutting back, and seeking performance improvement through greater efficiencies in operations.

A **reward** is a work outcome of positive value to the individual.

Reward power is the capability to offer something of value—a positive outcome—as a means of influencing other people.

A **risk environment** is a problem environment in which information is lacking, but some sense of the "probabilities" associated with action alternatives and their consequences exists.

A **role** is a set of activities expected of a person in a particular job or position within the organization.

Role ambiguity occurs when a person in a role is uncertain about what others expect in terms of his or her behavior.

Role conflict occurs when the person in a role is unable to respond to the expectations held by one or more others.

Role overload occurs when too many role expectations are being communicated to a person at a given time.

Role underload occurs when a person is underutilized or asked to do too little and/or to do things that fail to challenge her or his talents and capabilities.

S

Satisficing involves choosing the first satisfactory alternative that comes to your attention.

A **satisfier factor** is a factor in job content, such as a sense of achievement, recognition, responsibility, advancement, or personal growth, experienced as a result of task performance.

Scenario planning identifies alternative future "scenarios" and makes plans to deal with each.

Scientific management involves developing a science for every job, including rules of motion and standardized work instruments, careful selection and training of workers, and proper supervisory support for workers.

Selection is the process of choosing from a pool of applicants the person or persons who best meet job specifications

Selective perception is the tendency to define problems from one's own point of view or to single out for attention things consistent with one's existing beliefs, values, or needs.

A **self-fulfilling prophecy** occurs when a person acts in ways in order to confirm another's expectations.

A **self-managing work team,** sometimes called an autonomous work group, is a group of workers whose jobs have been redesigned to create a high degree of task interdependence and who have been given authority to make decisions about how they go about the required work.

Semantic barriers are verbal and nonverbal symbols that are poorly chosen and expressed, creating barriers to successful communication.

A **shared power strategy** is a participative change strategy that relies on involving others to examine values, needs, and goals in relationship to an issue at hand.

A **simultaneous structure** involves the co-existence of mechanistic and organic structures within an organization in the attempt to accomplish both production efficiency and innovation.

A **single-use plan** is used only once.

A **skill** is the ability to translate knowledge into action that results in the desired performance.

A **social audit** is a systematic assessment and reporting of an organization's commitments and accomplishments in areas of social responsibility.

Social loafing is the tendency of some people to avoid responsibility by "free-riding" in groups.

Socialization is the process of systematically changing the expectations, behavior, and attitudes of a new employee in a manner considered desirable by the organization.

Span of control is the number of subordinates reporting directly to a manager.

A **specific environment** is comprised of the actual organizations and persons with whom the focal organization must interact in order to survive and prosper.

A **stability strategy** maintains the present course of action.

Stakeholders are the persons, groups, and institutions directly affected by an organization's performance.

A **standing plan** is used more than once.

A **stereotype** results when an individual is assigned to a group or category and then the attributes commonly associated with the group or category are assigned to the individual in question.

A **strategic business unit (SBU)** is a separate operating division that represents a major business area and operates with some autonomy vis-à-vis other similar units in the organization.

A **strategic constituencies analysis** is the review and analysis of the interests of external stakeholders of an organization.

Strategic human resource planning analyzes staffing needs and identifies actions to fill those needs.

Strategic management is the managerial responsibility for leading the process of formulating and implementing strategies that lead to longer term organizational success.

A **strategic plan** is comprehensive and addresses longer term needs and directions of the organization.

A **strategy** is a comprehensive plan or action orientation that sets critical direction and guides the allocation of resources for an organization to achieve long-term objectives.

A **structured problem** is familiar, straightforward, and clear in its information requirements.

Substitutes for leadership are factors in the work setting that move work efforts toward organizational objectives without the direct involvement of a leader.

A **SWOT analysis** sets the stage for strategy formulation by analyzing organizational strengths and weaknesses and environmental opportunities and threats.

A **symbolic manager** uses symbols to establish and maintain a desired organizational culture.

Synergy is the creation of a whole that is greater than the sum of its individual parts.

T

A **task activity** is an action taken by a group member that contributes directly to the group's performance purpose.

A **task force** is a formal team convened for a specific purpose and expected to disband when that purpose is achieved.

A **team** is a collection of people who regularly interact to pursue common goals.

Team building is a sequence of collaborative activities to gather and analyze data on a team and make changes to increase its effectiveness.

A **team structure** is an organizational structure through which permanent and temporary teams are created to improve lateral relations and solve problems throughout an organization.

Teamwork is the process of people working together in groups to accomplish common goals.

A **technical skill** is the ability to use a special proficiency or expertise in one's work.

Technology is the combination of equipment, knowledge, and work methods that allows an organization to transform inputs into outputs.

Telecommuting or **flexiplace** involves working at home or other places using computer links to the office.

Theory X is a set of managerial assumptions that people in general dislike work, lack ambition, are irresponsible and resistant to change, and prefer to be led than to lead.

Theory Y is a set of managerial assumptions that people in general are willing to work and accept responsibility and are capable of self-direction, self-control, and creativity.

Top-down planning begins with broad objectives set by top management.

Total quality management (TQM) is managing with an organization-wide commitment to continuous work improvement, product quality, and meeting customer needs completely.

Training involves a set of activities that provide learning opportunities through which people can acquire and improve job-related skills.

A **trait** is a relatively stable and enduring personal characteristic of an individual.

Transactional leadership is leadership that orchestrates and directs the efforts of others through tasks, rewards, and structures.

Transformational leadership is the ability of a leader to get people to do more than they originally expected to do in support of large-scale innovation and change.

A **transnational corporation** is an MNC that operates worldwide on a borderless basis.

360-degree feedback is an upward communication approach that involves upward appraisals done by a manager's subordinates, as well as additional feedback from peers, internal and external customers, and higher ups.

U

An **uncertain environment** is a problem environment in which information is so poor that it is difficult even to assign probabilities to the likely outcomes of known alternatives.

Unfreezing is the initial phase in the planned-change process during which the manager prepares a situation for change.

An **unstructured problem** involves ambiguities and information deficiencies.

The **utilitarian view** considers ethical behavior as that which delivers the greatest good to the greatest number of people.

V

Valence is the value a person assigns to work-related outcomes.

Validity refers to the ability of an employment test to measure exactly what it is intended to relative to the job specification.

Values are broad beliefs about what is or is not appropriate behavior.

A **virtual team** is a group of people who work together and solve problems through computer-based rather than face-to-face interactions.

Vision is a term used to describe a clear sense of the future.

W

A **whistleblower** exposes the misdeeds of others in organizations.

A **wholly owned subsidiary** is a local operation completely owned by a foreign firm.

A **win-lose conflict** occurs when one party achieves its desires at the expense and exclusion of the other party's desires.

A **win-win conflict** occurs when conflict is resolved to the mutual benefit of all concerned parties.

A **work process** is a related group of tasks that together create a value for the customer.

Workflow is the movement of work from one point to another in a system.

Workforce diversity is a term used to describe demographic differences (age, gender, race and ethnicity, and able-bodiedness) among members of the workforce.

Work-life balance involves balancing career demands with personal and family needs.

Z

A **zero-based budget** allocates resources to a project or activity as if it were brand new.

Notes

Chapter 1 Notes

[1] Information from the *Fast Company* web site, <http://www.fast-company.com/partners/mission.htm>

[2] *Fortune*, February 10, 1992, pp. 40–70. See also Johnson & Johnson home page at http://www.johnsonandjohnson.com/.

[3] Information from Thomas A. Stewart, "Brain Power," *Fortune* (March 17, 1997), p. 107; John A. Byrne, "Jack: A Close-Up Look at How America's #1 Manager Runs GE," *Business Week* (June 8, 1998), pp. 91–111.

[4] See Dave Ulrich, "Intellectual Capital = Competence × Commitment," *Sloan Management Review* (Winter 1998), pp. 15–26.

[5] Max DePree, "It Begins with a Belief in People," *New York Times*, September 10, 1989, p. 2F; *Fortune*, February 10, 1992, pp. 40–70; and Herman Miller's home page at <http://www.hermanmiller.com/company/blueprint.html>.

[6] Based on Jay A. Conger, *Winning 'em Over: A New Model for Managing in the Age of Persuasion* (New York: Simon & Schuster, 1998), pp. 180–181; Stewart D. Friedman, Perry Christensen and Jessica DeGroot, "Work and Life: The End of the Zero-Sum Game, *Harvard Business Review* (November–December, 1998), pp. 119–129; and, Argyris, C., "Empowerment: The emperor's new clothes," *Harvard Business Review* (May–June, 1998), pp. 98–105.

[7] Henry Mintzberg, "The Manager's Job: Folklore and Fact," *Harvard Business Review*, vol. 53 (July–August 1975): 61.

[8] For a perspective on the first-level manager's job, see Leonard A. Schlesinger and Janice A. Klein, "The First-Line Supervisor: Past, Present and Future," pp. 370–82, in Jay W. Lorsch (editor), *Handbook of Organizational Behavior* (Englewood Cliffs, N.J.: Prentice-Hall, 1987).

[9] Hal Lancaster, "Middle Managers Are Back—But Now They're 'High-Impact' Players," *Wall Street Journal*, April 14, 1998, p. B1.

[10] R. Roosevelt Thomas Jr., "From Affirmative Action to Affirming Diversity," *Harvard Business Review* (March–April 1990), pp. 107–17; see also Mary Gentile (editor), *Differences That Work: Organizational Excellence through Diversity* (Boston: Harvard Business School Press, 1996).

[11] Taylor Cox Jr., "The Multicultural Organization," *Academy of Management Executives* vol. 5 (1991), pp. 34–47, and *Cultural Diversity in Organizations: Theory, Research and Practice* (San Francisco: Berrett-Koehler, 1993).

[12] Quotation from *Business Week*, August 8, 1990, p. 50, emphasis added.

[13] Information from Alexis D. Coleman, "Diversity: The question is, are we going to recognize it and LIVE it for a select few or for EVERYONE?" Unpublished manuscript personally communicated to the author, Emmanuel University (July 8, 1999).

[14] Ann M. Morrison, Randall P. White, and Ellen Van Velso, *Breaking the Glass Ceiling* (Reading, MA: Addison-Wesley, 1987).

[15] Information on this series of examples from "Accountants Have Lives, Too, You Know," *Business Week*, February 23, 1998, pp. 88–90.

[16] Henry Mintzberg, *The Nature of Managerial Work* (New York: Harper & Row, 1973), p. 30.

[17] John R. Veiga and Kathleen Dechant, "Wired World Woes: www.help," *Academy of Management Executive*, vol. 11 (August 1997): 73–79.

[18] Mintzberg, op. cit., p. 30.

[19] Morgan W. McCall Jr., Ann M. Morrison, and Robert L. Hannan, *Studies of Managerial Work: Results and Methods.* Technical Report #9 (Greensboro, NC: Center for Creative Leadership, 1978), pp. 7–9. See also John P. Kotter, "What Effective General Managers Really Do," *Harvard Business Review*, (March–April, 1999): 5–12.

[20] Mintzberg, op. cit., p. 46. For a related discussion see also Henry Mintzberg, "Covert Leadership: Notes on Managing Professionals," *Harvard Business Review* (November–December, 1998), pp. 140–147.

[21] John P. Kotter, *The General Managers* (New York: The Free Press, 1982), p. 164. See also research by David Barry, Catherine Durnell Crampton, and Stephen J. Carroll, "Navigating the Garbage Can: How Agendas Help Managers Cope with Job Realities," *Academy of Management Executive*, vol. 11 (May 1997): 43–56.

[22] Robert L. Katz, "Skills of an Effective Administrator," *Harvard Business Review*, vol. 52 (September–October 1974), p. 94.

[23] Richard E. Boyatzis, *The Competent Manager: A Model for Effective Performance* (New York: Wiley, 1982). See also Edward A. Powers, "Enhancing Managerial Competence: The American Management Association Competency Program," *Journal of Management Development*, vol. 6 (1987): 7–18.

[24] Kenichi Ohmae, *The Borderless World: Power and Strategy in the Interlinked Economy* (New York: Harper, 1989) and *The End of the Nation State* (New York: The Free Press, 1996).

[25] See for example, Michael A. Cusumano and David B. Yoffie, *Competing on Internet Time* (New York: The Free Press, 1998).

[26] Peter F. Drucker, "Looking Ahead: Implications of the Present," *Harvard Business Review* (September–October, 1997), pp. 18–32.

[27] See Richard W. Judy and Carol D'Amico (editors), *Workforce 2020* (Indianapolis: Hudson Institute, 1997); *Opportunity 2000: Creative Affirmative Action Strategies for a Changing Workforce* (Indianapolis: Hudson Institute, 1988); and, *Workforce 2000: Work and Workers for the 21st Century* (Indianapolis: Towers Perrin/Hudson Institute, 1987).

[28] Information from Jason Fry, "eToys Story," *The Wall Street Journal* (July 12, 1999), p. R38.

[29] *Handbook of the Business Revolution* (New York: Fast Company, Inc., 1997).

[30] Charles Handy, *The Age of Unreason* (Cambridge, MA: Harvard Business School Press, 1990) and *Beyond Certainty: The Changing Worlds of Organizations* (Cambridge, MA: Harvard Business School Press, 1997).

[31] Quotation from "Is Your Job Your Calling," *Fast Company*, no. 13, p. 108, taken from <http://www.fastcompany.com/13/hbrplus.htm>.

[32] This material is provided courtesy of Ronald Larimer and is used with his permission.

Chapter 2 Notes

[1] "Virtual Campuses Offer Compelling Reasons for Business Schools to Improve their Distance Vision," *AACSB Newsline*, spring, 1998, pp. 2–10.

[2] Thomas A. Stewart, *Intellectual Capital: The Wealth of Organizations* (New York: Doubleday, 1997).

[3] Peter F. Drucker, "Looking Ahead: Implications of the Present," *Harvard Business Review*, September–October 1997, pp. 18–32.

[4] *The New Blue: 1997 IBM Annual Report*, p. 8.

[5] See Michael E. Porter, *Competitive Strategy: Techniques for Analyzing Industries and Competitors* (New York: Free Press, 1980) and *Competitive Advantage: Creating and Sustaining Superior Performance* (New York: Free Press, 1986); also, Richard A. D'Aveni, *Hyper-Competition: Managing the Dynamics of Strategic Maneuvering* (New York: The Free Press, 1994).

[6] Information from *The Vermont Teddy Bear Company Gazette*, vol. 4 (summer 1993), and the company web site at www.vtbears.com.

[7] Michael Porter, *The Competitive Advantage of Nations* (New York: Free Press, 1989).

[8] Quotation from Richard J. Shonberger and Edward M. Knod Jr., *Operations Management: Serving the Customer*, 3d ed. (Plano, TX: Business Publications, 1988), p. 4.

[9] *The Vermont Teddy Bear Company Gazette*, op cit.

[10] Rosabeth Moss Kanter, "Transcending Business Boundaries: 12,000 World Managers View Change," *Harvard Business Review*, May–June 1991, pp. 151–64.

[11] Reported in Jennifer Steinhauer, "The Undercover Shoppers," *New York Times*, February 4, 1998, pp. C1, C2.

[12] For a classic discussion see Wickham Skinner, "Manufacturing—Missing Link in Corporate Strategy," *Harvard Business Review*, May–June 1969, pp. 136–45, and *Manufacturing in the Corporate Strategy* (New York: Wiley, 1978). For current thinking, see Richard J. Schonberger, *World Class Manufacturing—The Next Decade: Building Power, Strength, and Value* (New York: The Free Press, 1996) and Robert H. Hayes, Gary P. Pisano, and David M. Upton, *Strategic Operations: Competing through Capabilities* (New York: The Free Press, 1996).

[13] See Joseph M. Juran, *Quality Control Handbook*, 3d ed. (New York: McGraw-Hill, 1979) and "The Quality Trilogy: A Universal Approach to Managing for Quality," in H. Costin (editor), *Total Quality Management* (New York: Dryden, 1994); W. Edwards Deming, *Out of Crisis* (Cambridge, MA: MIT Press, 1986) and "Deming's Quality Manifesto," *Best of Business Quarterly*, vol. 12 (winter 1990–1991): 6–10. See also Howard S. Gitlow and Shelly J. Gitlow, *The Deming Guide to Quality and Competitive Position* (Englewood Cliffs, NJ: Prentice-Hall, 1987); Juran, "Made in U.S.A."

[14] "Does the Baldrige Award Really Work?" *Harvard Business Review*, January–February 1992, pp. 126–47; see also the Baldrige website at www.baldrige.org.

[15] Rafael Aguay, *Dr. Deming: The American Who Taught the Japanese about Quality* (New York: The Free Press, 1997). Points adapted from W. Edwards Deming, *Out of Crisis*.

[16] For a description of the technical elements of electronic commerce see Turban, McClean, and Wetherbe, *Information Technology for Management*, 2d ed. (New York: John Wiley & Sons, 1998).

[17] Information from "What Is an E-Business? And Why Should You Be One? *Far Eastern Economic Review*, May 14, 1998, p. 43.

[18] Drucker, "Looking Ahead," 1997, p. 22.

[19] Mary J. Cronin, "Ford's Intranet Success," *Fortune*, March 30, 1998, p. 158; and Steven V. Brull, "Networks That do New Tricks," *Business Week*, April 6, 1998, p. 100.

[20] Peter F. Drucker, *Management Challenges for the 21st Century* (New York: Harper, 1999); Peter F. Drucker, "An Age of Social Transformation," *Atlantic Monthly* (November 1994), pp. 53–80; Peter F. Drucker, "The Future That has Already Happened," *Harvard Business Review*, vol. 75 (September–October 1997): 20–24; Peter F. Drucker, Esther Dyson, Charles Handy, Paul Daffo, and Peter M. Senge, "Looking Ahead: Implications of the Present," *Harvard Business Review*, vol. 75 (September–October, 1997); Robert B. Reich, "The Company of the Future," *Fast Company* (November 1998), pp. 124+.

[21] Information from Scott Thurn, "What Do You Know?" *The Wall Street Journal* (June 21, 1999), pp. R10, R19.

[22] Steven E. Prokesch, "Unleashing the Power of Learning," *Harvard Business Review* September–October 1997, pp. 147–68.

[23] Peter Senge, *The Fifth Discipline* (New York: Harper, 1990); Allan M. Weber, "Learning for a Change: An Interview with Peter Senge," *Fast Company* (May 1999), pp. 178+.

[24] Senge, *The Fifth Discipline*, op. cit.

[25] Prokesch, op. cit., 1997.

[26] Richard Waters, "Own Words: Jack Welch, General Electric," *Financial Times*, October 1, 1997.

[27] See, for example, Thomas H. Davenport and Laurence Prusak,

Working Knowledge: How Organizations Manage What They Know (Cambridge, MA: Harvard Business School Press, 1997).

[28] Thomas A. Stewart, "Is This Job Really Necessary?" *Fortune* (January 12, 1998), pp. 154–155.

Chapter 3 Notes

[1] See, for example, Hal Lancaster, "Learning to Manage in a Global Marketplace," *The Wall Street Journal* (June 2, 1998), p. B1.

[2] See Kenichi Ohmae, *The Evolving Global Economy* (Cambridge, Mass.: Harvard Business School Press, 1995).

[3] Rosabeth Moss Kanter, *World Class: Thinking Locally in the Global Economy* (New York: Simon & Schuster, 1995), preface.

[4] Information from Dana Milbank, "New Competitor: East Europe Industry Is Raising Its Quality and Taking on West," *Wall Street Journal*, September 21, 1994, pp. 1, A4.

[5] A monthly publication that covers the *maquiladora* industries is the *Twin Plant News* (El Paso, Texas).

[6] Scott Shuster, "The Business Future of the Americas," *Business Week*, April 27, 1998, special advertising section; and Kerry Capell, "What a 'Euro' Could Do for the Latins," *Business Week*, April 13, 1998, p. 100.

[7] "Special Report: The Growing Power of Asia," *Fortune*, October 7, 1991, pp. 118–60; "Special Report: Asia—The Next Era of Growth," *Business Week*, November 11, 1991, pp. 56–68. See also Jim Rohwer, *Asia Rising: Why America Will Prosper as Asia's Economies Boom*, (New York: Simon & Schuster, 1995); and John Frankenstein, special report, "The Business of Business: Values and Outlook," *Far Eastern Economic Review*, August 7, 1997; "Asian Crisis Offers Unexpected Opportunities," *Wall Street Journal*, April 23, 1998, p. B17.

[8] Mike Pramik, "Salient's Dealings in China Illustrate Need to Prepare for Differing Practices," *Columbus Dispatch*, May 4, 1998, p. 3.

[9] James A. Austin and John G. McLean, "Pathways to Business Success in Sub-Saharan Africa," *Journal of African Finance and Economic Development*, Vol. 2 (1996), pp. 57–76.

[10] Information from "International Business: Consider Africa," *Harvard Business Review*, Vol. 76 (January–February 1998), pp. 16–18.

[11] Paul Magnusson and Dean Foust, "Don't Waste a Huge Opportunity on Africa," *Business Week*, April 6, 1998, p. 37.

[12] "Best Practices for Global Competitiveness," *Fortune*, March 30, 1998, pp. S1–S3, special advertising section.

[13] Reports are published annually by *Fortune*, *Business Week* and other business periodicals.

[14] Peter F. Drucker, "The Global Economy and the Nation-State," *Foreign Affairs*, vol. 76 (September–October 1997): 159–71.

[15] Information from Michelle M. Phillips, "Globalization Comes to a Southern Town," *Wall Street Journal* (February 12, 1998), p. A2.

[16] See www.nike.com for a full description and news releases.

[17] Based on Barbara Benedict Bunker, "Appreciating Diversity and Modifying Organizational Cultures: Men and Women at Work," in Suresh Srivastva, David L. Cooperrider, *Appreciative Management and Leadership: The Power of Positive Thought and Action in Organizations* (San Francisco: Jossey-Bass, 1990), pp. 127–49.

[18] Edward T. Hall, *The Silent Language* (New York: Doubleday, 1959).

[19] For a good overview of the practical issues, see Philip R. Harris and Robert T. Moran, *Managing Cultural Differences*, 2d ed. (Houston: Gulf Publishing, 1987); and Martin J. Gannon, *Understanding Global Cultures* (Thousand Oaks, CA: Sage, 1994).

[20] Edward T. Hall, *Hidden Differences* (New York: Doubleday, 1990).

[21] Edward T. Hall, *The Hidden Dimension* (New York: Doubleday, 1969).

[22] Hall, op. cit., 1990.

[23] Geert Hofstede's research is summarized in the article, "Motivation, Leadership, and Organization: Do American Theories Apply Abroad?" *Organizational Dynamics*, vol. 9 (summer 1980): p. 43. It is presented in detail in his book *Culture's Consequences* (Beverly Hills: Sage, 1984). Hofstede and Michael H. Bond further explore Eastern and Western perspectives on national culture in their article "The Confucius Connection: From Cultural Roots to Economic Growth," *Organizational Dynamics*, vol. 16 (1988): pp. 4–21, which presents comparative data from Bond's "Chinese Values Survey."

[24] See John E. Rehfeld, *Alchemy of a Leader* (New York: John Wiley & Sons, 1994).

[25] Fons Trompenaars, *Riding the Waves of Culture: Understanding Cultural Diversity in Business* (London: Nicholas Brealey Publishing, 1993).

[26] "Going International: Willett Systems Limited," *Fortune*, February 16, 1998, p. S6, special advertising section.

[27] For information on Compaq and Digital see www.digital.com.

[28] Geert Hofstede, "Motivation, Leadership, and Organization," p. 43. See also Hofstede's "Cultural Constraints in Management Theories," *Academy of Management Review*, vol. 7 (1993): 81–94.

[29] Information from Jonathan Karp, "Sri Lanka Keeps Victoria's Secret," *The Wall Street Journal* (July 13, 1999), pp. B1, B4.

[30] J. Bernard Keys, Luther Tray Denton, and Thomas R. Miller, "The Japanese Management Theory Jungle—Revisited," *Journal of Management*, vol. 20 (1994): 373–402.

[31] Quote from Kenichi Ohmae, "Japan's Admiration for U.S. Methods Is an Open Book," *Wall Street Journal*, October 10, 1983, p. 21. See also his book *The Borderless World: Power and Strategy in the Interlinked Economy* (New York: Harper, 1999).

[32] Geert Hofstede, "A Reply to Goodstein and Hunt," *Organizational Dynamics*, vol. 10 (summer 1981): 68.

Chapter 4 Notes

[1] See Joel Makower, *Beyond the Bottom Line: Putting Social Responsibility to Work for your Business and the World* (New York: Simon & Schuster, 1994).

[2] "Quad/Graphics's Environmental Philosophy," corporate document, Pewaukee, WI: Quad/Graphics, 1998; Larry Reynolds, "When Green Begets Green," *Business Week*, November 10, 1997, pp. 98–99.

[3] Michael J. McCarthy, "An Ex-Divinity Student Works on Searching the Corporate Soul," *The Wall Street Journal* (June 18, 1999), p. B1.

[4] Desmond Tutu, "Do More Than Win," *Fortune*, December 30, 1991, p. 59.

[5] For an overview, see Francis Joseph Aguilar, *Managing Corporate Ethics: Learning from America's Ethical Companies How to Supercharge*

Business Performance (New York: Oxford, 1994); and Linda K. Trevino and Katherine A. Nelson, *Managing Business Ethics* (New York: John Wiley & Sons, 1995).

[6] Tom Chappell, *The Soul of a Business: Managing for Profit and for the Common Good* (New York: Bantam Books, 1993) and *Managing Upside Down* (New York: Harper, 1999).

[7] See Trevino and Nelson, op. cit., 1995.

[8] Raymond L. Hilgert, "What Ever Happened to Ethics in Business and in Business Schools," *The Diary of Alpha Kappa Psi*, April 1989, pp. 4–8.

[9] Robert D. Haas, "Ethics—A Global Business Challenge," *Vital Speeches of the Day*, June 1, 1996, pp. 506–9.

[10] Thomas Donaldson, "Values in Tension: Ethics Away from Home," *Harvard Business Review*, vol. 74 (September–October 1996): 48–62.

[11] Thomas Donaldson and Thomas W. Dunfee, "Towards a Unified Conception of Business Ethics: Integrative Social Contracts Theory," *Academy of Management Review*, vol. 19 (1994): 252–85; and Thomas Donaldson and Thomas W. Dunfee, *Ties that Bind* (Boston, MA.: Harvard Business School Press, 1999).

[12] Reported in Barbara Ley Toffler, "Tough Choices: Managers Talk Ethics," *New Management*, vol. 4 (1987): 34–39. See also Barbara Ley Toffler, *Tough Choices: Managers Talk Ethics* (New York: Wiley, 1986).

[13] The case and subsequent discussion are developed from Steven N. Brenner and Earl A. Mollander, "Is the Ethics of Business Changing?" *Harvard Business Review*, vol. 55 (January–February 1977): 57.

[14] Saul W. Gellerman, "Why 'Good' Managers Make Bad Ethical Choices," *Harvard Business Review*, vol. 64 (July–August, 1986): 85–90.

[15] Information from Thomas Teal, "Not a Fool, Not a Saint," *Fortune*, November 11, 1996, pp. 201–4.

[16] Information on this case from William M. Carley, "Antitrust Chief Says CEOs Should Tape all Phone Calls to Each Other," *Wall Street Journal*, February 15, 1983, p. 23; "American Air, Chief End Antitrust Suit, Agree Not to Discuss Fares with Rivals," *Wall Street Journal* (July 15, 1985), p. 4; "American Airlines Loses Its Pilot," *Economist*, April 18, 1998, p. 58.

[17] Alan L. Otten, "Ethics on the Job: Companies Alert Employees to Potential Dilemmas," *Wall Street Journal*, July 14, 1986, p. 17; and "The Business Ethics Debate," *Newsweek*, May 25, 1987, p. 36.

[18] See McCarthy, op. cit., 1999.

[19] Timothy L. O'Brien, "Rabid Infighting Brings Dog Days to ASPCA," *Wall Street Journal*, August 3, 1994, pp. B1, B8. See also "Whistle-Blowers on Trial," *Business Week*, March 24, 1997, pp. 172–78; "NLRB Judge Rules for Massachusetts Nurses in Whistle-Blowing Case," *American Nurse*, January–February 1998, p. 7.

[20] For a review of whistleblowing, see Marcia P. Micelli and Janet P. Near, *Blowing the Whistle* (Lexington, MA: Lexington Books, 1992); see also Micelli and Near, "Whistleblowing: Reaping the Benefits," *Academy of Management Executive*, vol. 8 (August 1994): 65–72.

[21] Daniel Wesman, *Whistleblowing: The Law of Retaliatory Discharge* (New York: BNA Books); and see "Blowing the Whistle without Paying the Piper"; Daniel Wesman, *Whistleblowing*.

[22] James A. Waters, "Catch 20.5: Mortality as an Organizational Phenomenon," *Organizational Dynamics*, vol. 6 (spring 1978): 3–15. Robert D. Gilbreath, "The Hollow Executive," *New Management*, vol. 4 (1987): 24–28.

[23] All reported in Charles D. Pringle and Justin G. Longnecker, "The Ethics of MBO," *Academy of Management Review*, vol. 7 (April 1982); 309. See also Barry Z. Posner and Warren H. Schmidt, "Values and the American Manager: An Update," *California Management Review*, vol. 26 (spring 1984): 202–16.

[24] Developed from a discussion in Makower, *Beyond the Bottom Line*, pp. 17–18.

[25] "Tom's of Maine: Company Overview," Kennebunk, Maine: Tom's of Maine, 1998.

[26] See Makower, op cit., 1994, pp. 71–75; and Sandra A. Waddock and Samuel B. Graves, "The Corporate Social Performance-Financial Performance Link," *Strategic Management Journal* (1997), pp. 303–319.

[27] Information from "Global Ethics Codes Gain Importance as a Tool to Avoid Litigation and Fines," *The Wall Street Journal* (August 19, 1999), p. 1.

[28] Archie B. Carroll, "A Three-Dimensional Model of Corporate Performance," *Academy of Management Review*, vol. 4 (1979): 497–505.

[29] See Jane Palley Katz, *Levi Strauss & Co.: Global Sourcing (A)* (Boston, MA.: Harvard Business School Publishing, 1996).

Chapter 5 Notes

[1] Information from T. J. Rodgers, with William Taylor and Rick Foreman, "No Excuses Management," *World Executive's Digest*, May 1994, pp. 26–30.

[2] Ibid.

[3] Henry Mintzberg, "The Manager's Job: Folklore and Fact," *Harvard Business Review*, vol. 53 (July–August 1975): 54–67; Henry Mintzberg, "Planning on the Left Side and Managing on the Right," *Harvard Business Review*, vol. 54 (July–August 1976).

[4] Information from *Business Week* (October 13, 1997), pp. ENT 20–22.

[5] Stephen Covey and Roger Merrill, "New Ways to Get Organized at Work," *USA Weekend*, February 6–8, 1998, p. 18.

[6] William Oncken Jr. and Donald L. Wass, "Management Time: Who's Got the Monkey?" *Harvard Business Review*, vol. 65 (March–April 1987).

[7] Shelly Branch, "So Much Work, So Little Time," *Fortune*, February 3, 1997, pp. 115–17.

[8] See Romuald A. Stone, "AIDS in the Workplace: An Executive Update," *Academy of Management Executive*, vol. 8 (August 1994): 52–64.

[9] See George P. Huber, *Managerial Decision Making* (Glenview, IL: Scott, Foresman 1975). For a comparison, see the steps in Xerox's problem-solving process as described in "David A. Garvin, "Building a Learning Organization," *Harvard Business Review*, July–August 1993, pp. 78–91.

[10] For classic treatments of decision making see Herbert A. Simon, *Administrative Behavior* (New York: Free Press, 1947); James G. March and Herbert A. Simon, *Organizations* (New York: Wiley, 1958); Herbert A. Simon, *The New Science of Management Decision*

(New York: Harper, 1960); Simon, ("Making Management Decisions,") 1987.

[11] Barry M. Staw, "The Escalation of Commitment to a Course of Action," *Academy of Management Review*, vol. 6 (1981): 577–87; Barry M. Staw and Jerry Ross, "Knowing When to Pull the Plug," *Harvard Business Review*, vol. 65 (March–April 1987): 68–74.

[12] Information from, "Mexico Builds a Home-Appliance Bonanza," *The Wall Street Journal* (August 23, 1999), p. A12.

[13] For scholarly reviews, see Dean Tjosvold, "Effects of Crisis Orientation on Managers' Approach to Controversy in Decision Making," *Academy of Management Journal*, vol. 27 (1984): 130–38; Ian I. Mitroff, Paul Shrivastava, and Firdaus E. Udwadia, "Effective Crisis Management," *Academy of Management Executive*, vol. 1 (1987): 283–92.

[14] See Hugh Courtney, Jane Kirkland, and Patrick Viguerie, "Strategy Under Uncertainty," *Harvard Business Review*, November–December 1997, pp. 67–79.

[15] For a thorough review of forecasting, see J. Scott Armstrong, *Long-Range Forecasting*, 2d ed. (New York: Wiley, 1985).

[16] The scenario-planning approach is described in Peter Schwartz, *The Art of the Long View* (New York: Doubleday/Currency, 1991); and Arie de Geus, *The Living Company: Habits for Survival in a Turbulent Business Environment* (Boston, MA: Harvard Business School Press, 1997).

Chapter 6 Notes

[1] Quote from Louise Lee and Cacilie Rohwedder, "Wal-Mart to Acquire German Retailer, Moving into Europe for the First Time, *Wall Street Journal*, December 19, 1997, pp. A2, A10.

[2] Gary Hamel and C. K. Prahalad, "Strategic Intent," *Harvard Business Review*, May–June, 1989, pp. 63–76.

[3] See Michael E. Porter, *Competitive Strategy: Techniques for Analyzing Industries and Competitors* (New York: The Free Press, 1980), and *Competitive Advantage: Creating and Sustaining Superior Performance* (New York: The Free Press, 1986); and Richard A. D'Aveni, *Hyper-Competition: Managing the Dynamics of Strategic Maneuvering* (New York: The Free Press, 1994).

[4] Peter F. Drucker, "Five Questions," *Executive Excellence*, November 6, 1994, pp. 6–7.

[5] Peter F. Drucker, *Management: Tasks, Responsibilities, Practices* (New York: Harper & Row, 1973), p. 122.

[6] See Laura Nash, "Mission Statements—Mirrors and Windows," *Harvard Business Review*, (March–April 1988), pp. 155–56; and James C. Collins and Jerry I. Porras, *Built to Last: Successful Habits of Visionary Companies* (New York: Harper, 1994).

[7] See Collins and Porras, op. cit.; Collins and Porras, "Building Your Company's Vision," *Harvard Business Review*, September–October, 1996, pp. 65–77.

[8] Terrence E. Deal and Allen A. Kennedy, *Corporate Cultures: The Rites and Rituals of Corporate Life* (Reading, MA: Addison-Wesley, 1982), p. 22. See also Ralph H. Killmann, M. J. Saxon, and R. Serpa (eds.), *Managing Corporate Cultures* (San Francisco: Jossey-Bass, 1985); and, Collins and Porras, op. cit., 1994, 1996.

[9] Peter F. Drucker's views on organizational objectives are expressed in his classic books, *The Practice of Management* (New York: Harper & Row, 1954); and *Management: Tasks, Responsibilities, Practices*

(New York: Harper & Row, 1973). For a more recent commentary, see his article, "Management: The Problems of Success," *Academy of Management Executive*, vol. 1 (1987): 13–19.

[10] C. K. Prahalad and Gary Hamel, "The Core Competencies of the Corporation," *Harvard Business Review*, May–June 1990, pp. 79–91.

[11] See Howard Schultz and Dori Jones Yang, *Pour Your Heart Into It* (San Francisco: Hyperion, 1997); and, Starbucks Company Fact Sheet, Seattle, WA: Starbucks, 1998.

[12] D'Aveni, *Hyper-Competition*, pp. 13–16, 21–24.

[13] D' Aveni, *Hyper-Competition*.

[14] Richard G. Hammermesh, "Making Planning Strategic," *Harvard Business Review*, vol. 64 (July–August 1986): 115–120.

[15] See Gerald B. Allan, "A Note on the Boston Consulting Group Concept of Competitive Analysis and Corporate Strategy," Harvard Business School, Intercollegiate Case Clearing House, ICCH9-175-175 (Boston: Harvard Business School, June 1976).

[16] For a discussion of Michael Porter's approach to strategic planning, see his books *Competitive Strategy, and Competitive Advantage*; op. cit., 1980 and 1986.

[17] Information from Suzanne Steel, "Quality in Bloom," *Business Today*, August 22, 1994, pp. 1–2.

[18] See George V. Potts, "Exploit Your Product's Life Cycle," *Harvard Business Review*, September–October 1988, pp. 32–36.

[19] James Brian Quinn, "Strategic Change: Logical Incrementalism," *Sloan Management Review*, vol. 20 (fall 1978): 7–21.

[20] Henry Mintzberg, *The Nature of Managerial Work* (New York: Harper & Row, 1973); John R. P. Kotter, *The General Managers* (New York: The Free Press, 1982).

[21] Henry Mintzberg, "Planning on the Left Side and Managing on the Right," *Harvard Business Review*, vol. 54 (July–August 1976): 46–55; Henry Mintzberg and James A. Waters, "Of Strategies, Deliberate and Emergent," *Strategic Management Journal*, vol. 6 (1985): 257–72; Henry Mintzberg, "Crafting Strategy," *Harvard Business Review*, vol. 65 (July–August 1987): 66–75.

[22] Developed from Dick Levin, *The Executive's Illustrated Primer of Long-Range Planning* (Englewood Cliffs, N.J.: Prentice-Hall, 1981) and David A. Aaker, "How to Select a Business Strategy," *California Management Review*, vol. 26 (spring 1984): 167–75.

[23] See Daniel H. Gray, "Uses and Misuses of Strategic Planning," *Harvard Business Review*, vol. 64 (January–February 1986): 89–97.

[24] Jon R. Katzenbach, "The Myth of the Top Management Team," *Harvard Business Review*, November–December 1997, pp. 82–91.

[25] For a discussion of corporate governance issues, see Hugh Sherman and Rajeswararao Chaganti, *Corporate Governance and the Timeliness of Change* (Westport, CT: Quorum Books, 1998).

[26] See for example Robert D. Hisrich and Michael P. Peters, *Entrepreneurship* (New York: McGraw-Hill, 1998).

[27] See *The State of Small Business: A Report of the President* (Washington, D.C.: U.S. Government Printing Office, 1988); and *The Small Business Forum* (Winter 1991).

[28] See, for example, William A. Sahlman, "How to Write a Good Business Plan," *Harvard Business Review* (July–August 1997), pp. 98–108.

[29] Information from Dan Morse, "Many Small Businesses Don't

Devote Time to Planning," *The Wall Street Journal* (September 7, 1999), p. B2.

[30] Christopher Farrell, "When Bureaucrats Are a Boon," *Business Week*, Enterprise issue (September 1, 1997), pp. ENT4–6.

[31] Gifford Pinchot III, *Intrapreneuring, or Why You Don't Have to Leave the Corporation to Become an Entrepreneur* (New York: Harper & Row, 1985).

Chapter 7 Notes

[1] Information from Thomas Petzinger Jr., "How a Ski Maker on a Slippery Slope Regained Control," *Wall Street Journal*, October 3, 1997, p. 3.

[2] Information from Raju Narisetti, "For IBM, a Groundbreaking Sales Chief," *Wall Street Journal*, January 19, 1998, pp. B1, B5.

[3] See, for example, Robert C. Camp, *Business Process Benchmarking* (Milwaukee: ASQ Quality Press 1994); Michael J. Spendolini, *The Benchmarking Book* (New York: AMACOM, 1992); and Christopher E. Bogan and Michael J. English, *Benchmarking for Best Practices; Winning through Innovative Adaptation* (New York: McGraw-Hill, 1994).

[4] Adapted from Harold Koontz and Cyril O'Donnell, *Essentials of Management* (New York: McGraw-Hill, 1974), pp. 362–365.

[5] Toddi Gutner, "Better Your Business: Benchmark It," *Business Week*, Enterprise issue (April 27, 1998), pp. ENT4–6.

[6] See William Newman, *Constructive Control: Design and Use of Control Systems* (Englewood Cliffs, NJ: Prentice-Hall, 1975).

[7] See John F. Love, *McDonald's: Behind the Arches* (New York: Bantam Books, 1986; and William McGurn, "Burger Boom," *Far Eastern Economic Review*, November 20, 1997, pp. 66–69.

[8] Douglas McGregor, *The Human Side of Enterprise* (New York: McGraw-Hill, 1960).

[9] Information from "ISO 9000 Update," *Fortune*, September 30, 1996, p. 134.

[10] The "hot stove rules" are developed from R. Bruch McAfee and William Poffenberger, *Productivity Strategies: Enhancing Employee Job Performance* (Englewood Cliffs, NJ: Prentice-Hall, 1982), pp. 54–55. They are originally attributed to Douglas McGregor, "Hot Stove Rules of Discipline," in *Personnel: The Human Problems of Management*, G. Strauss and L. Sayles, eds. (Englewood Cliffs, NJ: Prentice-Hall, 1967).

[11] Information from Nikhil Deogun, James R. Hagerty, Steve Stecklow and Laura Johannes, *The Wall Street Journal* (June 29, 1999), pp. A1, A6.

[12] Shawn Tully, "Purchasing's New Muscle," *Fortune*, February 20, 1995, p. 75.

[13] See Dale D. McConkey, *How to Manage by Results*, 3d ed. (New York: AMACOM, 1976); Stephen J. Carroll Jr. and Henry J. Tosi Jr., *Management by Objectives: Applications and Research* (New York: Macmillan, 1973); and Anthony P. Raia, *Managing by Objectives* (Glenview, IL: Scott, Foresman, 1974).

[14] For a discussion of research, see Carroll and Tosi, *Management by Objectives*; Raia, *Managing by Objectives*; 1974; Steven Kerr, "Overcoming the Dysfunctions of MBO," *Management by Objectives* 5, no. 1 (1976).

[15] See Douglas McGregor, *The Human Side of Enterprise* (New York: McGraw-Hill, 1960). The work on goal setting and motivation is summarized in Edwin A. Locke and Gary P. Latham, *Goal Setting: A Motivational Technique That Works!* (Englewood Cliffs, NJ: Prentice-Hall, 1984).

Chapter 8 Notes

[1] Information from Richard Teitelbaum, "The Wal-Mart of Wall Street," *Fortune*, October 13, 1997, pp. 128–30.

[2] The classic work is Alfred D. Chandler, *Strategy and Structure* (Cambridge, MA: MIT Press, 1962).

[3] See Alfred D. Chandler Jr., "Origins of the Organization Chart," *Harvard Business Review*, March–April 1988, pp. 156–57.

[4] See David Krackhardt and Jeffrey R. Hanson, "Informal Networks: The Company behind the Chart," *Harvard Business Review*, July–August 1993, pp. 104–11.

[5] Maggie Jackson, "Work's Lessons Occurring in Unexpected Places," *Rockland Journal-News*, January 7, 1998, pp. 4A, 4E.

[6] Kenneth Noble, "A Clash of Styles: Japanese Companies in the U.S.," *New York Times*, January 25, 1988, p. 7.

[7] For a discussion of departmentalization, see H. I. Ansoff and R. G. Bradenburg, "A Language for Organization Design," *Management Science*, vol. 17 (August 1971): B705–B731; Mariann Jelinek, "Organization Structure: The Basic Conformations," in *Organizations by Design: Theory and Practice*, Mariann Jelinek, Joseph A. Litterer, and Raymond E. Miles, eds. (Plano, TX: Business Publications, 1981), pp. 293–302; Henry Mintzberg, "The Structuring of Organizations," in *The Strategy Process: Concepts, Contexts, and Cases*, James Brian Quinn, Henry Mintzberg, and Robert M. James, eds. (Englewood Cliffs, NJ: Prentice-Hall, 1988), pp. 276–304.

[8] These alternatives are well described by Mintzberg, "The Structuring of Organizations."

[9] Excellent reviews of matrix concepts are found in Stanley M. Davis and Paul R. Lawrence, *Matrix* (Reading, MA: Addison-Wesley, 1977); Paul R. Lawrence, Harvey F. Kolodny, and Stanley M. Davis, "The Human Side of the Matrix," *Organizational Dynamics*, vol. 6 (1977): 43–61; Harvey F. Kolodny, "Evolution to a Matrix Organization," *Academy of Management Review*, vol. 4 (1979): 543–53.

[10] Susan Albers Mohrman, Susan G. Cohen, and Allan M. Mohrman Jr., *Designing Team-Based Organizations* (San Francisco: Jossey-Bass, 1996).

[11] See Jon R. Katzenbach and Douglas K. Smith, "The Discipline of Teams," *Harvard Business Review*, March–April 1993, pp. 111–20; and, Glenn M. Parker, *Cross-Functional Teams* (San Francisco: Jossey-Bass, 1995).

[12] See Ron Ashkenas, Dave Ulrich, Todd Jick, Steve Kerr, *The Boundaryless Organization: Breaking the Chains of Organizational Structure* (San Francisco: Jossey-Bass, 1996); Rupert F. Chisholm, *Developing Network Organizations: Learning from Practice and Theory* (Reading, MA: Addison Wesley, 1998).

[13] See, for example, Johnathon Rosenoer, Douglas Armstrong, J. Russell Gates, *The Clickable Corporation* (New York: The Free Press, 1999).

[14] Information from Thomas Petzinger Jr., "June Holley Brings a Touch of Italy to Appalachian Effort," *The Wall Street Journal* (October 24, 1997), p. B1.

[15] David Van Fleet, "Span of Management Research and Issues," *Academy of Management Journal*, vol. 26 (1983): 546–52.

[16] Developed from Roger Fritz, *Rate Your Executive Potential* (New York: Wiley, 1988), pp. 185–86; Roy J. Lewicki, Donald D. Bowen, Douglas T. Hall, and Francine S. Hall, *Experiences in Management and Organizational Behavior*, 3d ed. (New York: Wiley, 1988), p. 144.

[17] Information from "The Internet Transforms the Jobs in Human-Resources Departments," *The Wall Street Journal* (August 31, 1999), p. A1.

[18] See George P. Huber, "A Theory of Effects of Advanced Information Technologies on Organizational Design, Intelligence, and Decision Making," *Academy of Management Review*, vol. 15 (1990): 67–71.

Chapter 9 Notes

[1] Quote from Carla Rapoport, "Nestle's Brand Building Machine," *Fortune*, September 19, 1994, pp. 147–56.

[2] Tom Peters, *The Circle of Innovation* (New York: Alfred A. Knopf, 1997).

[3] For a discussion of organization theory and design, see W. Richard Scott, *Organizations: Rational, Natural, and Open Systems*, 4th ed. (Upper Saddle River, NJ: Prentice-Hall, 1998).

[4] Edgar H. Schein, "Organizational Culture," *American Psychologist*, vol. 45 (1990): 109–19. See also Schein's *Organizational Culture and Leadership*, 2d ed. (Reading, MA: Addison-Wesley, 1997).

[5] James Collins and Jerry Porras, *Built to Last* (New York: Harper Business, 1994).

[6] Terrence E. Deal and Alan A. Kennedy, *Corporate Cultures: The Rites and Rituals of Corporate Life* (Reading, MA: Addison-Wesley, 1982); Ralph Kilmann, *Beyond the Quick Fix* (San Francisco: Jossey-Bass, 1984); Schein, 1997.

[7] In their book *Corporate Culture and Performance* (New York: MacMillan, 1992), John P. Kotter and James L. Heskett make the point that strong cultures have desired long-term effects only if they encourage adaptation to a changing environment. See also Collins and Porras, *Built to Last* 1994.

[8] This is based on Schein, *Organizational Culture*, op. cit., 1997.

[9] Deal and Kennedy *Corporate Cultures*, op. cit., 1982.

[10] James C. Collins and Jerry I. Porras, "Building Your Company's Vision," *Harvard Business Review*, September–October 1996, pp. 65–77.

[11] Ralph H. Kilmann, Mary J. Saxton, and Roy Serpa, "Issues in Understanding and Changing Culture," *California Management Review*, vol. 28 (1986): 87–94.

[12] Information from Hal Lancaster, "Herb Kelleher has One Main Strategy: Treat Employees Well," *The Wall Street Journal* (August 31, 1999), p. B1.

[13] Information from Nina Munk, "The New Organization Man," *Fortune*, March 16, 1998, pp. 62–74.

[14] Collins and Porras, op. cit., 1994 and 1996.

[15] Roosevelt Thomas, "From 'Affirmative Action' to 'Affirming Diversity,'" *Harvard Business Review*, November–December 1990, pp. 107–17; Taylor Cox Jr., *Cultural Diversity in Organizations* (San Francisco: Berrett-Koehler Publishers, Inc., 1994).

[16] John B. Cullen, Bart Victor, and Carroll Stephens, "An Ethical Weather Report: Assessing the Organization's Ethical Climate," *Organizational Dynamics*, winter 1990, pp. 50–63.

[17] Information from "Great Performances," *Fortune* (February 16, 1998), p. 51.

[18] See Jay R. Galbraith, *Organizational Design* (Reading, MA: Addison Wesley, 1977).

[19] Max Weber, *The Theory of Social and Economic Organization*, A. M. Henderson trans. and H. T. Parsons (New York: The Free Press, 1947).

[20] For classic treatments of bureaucracy, see Alvin Gouldner, *Patterns of Industrial Bureaucracy* (New York: The Free Press, 1954); Robert K. Merton, *Social Theory and Social Structure* (New York: The Free Press, 1957).

[21] Tom Burns and George M. Stalker, *The Management of Innovation* (London: Tavistock, 1961, republished by Oxford University Press, London, 1994.)

[22] See Henry Mintzberg, *Structure in Fives: Designing Effective Organizations* (Englewood Cliffs, NJ: Prentice-Hall, 1983). This discussion is based on Henry Mintzberg, "The Structuring of Organizations," in *The Strategy Process: Concepts, Contexts, and Cases*, James Brian Quinn, Henry Mintzberg, and Robert M. James, eds. (Englewood Cliffs, NJ: Prentice-Hall, 1988), pp. 276–304.

[23] See Rosabeth Moss Kanter, *The Changing Masters* (New York: Simon & Schuster, 1983).

[24] See Jay R. Galbraith, Edward E. Lawler III, and Associates, *Organizing for the Future* (San Francisco: Jossey-Bass Publishers, 1993).

[25] "The Rebirth of IBM," *The Economist* (June 6, 1998), pp. 65–68.

[26] Alfred D. Chandler Jr., *Strategy and Structure: Chapter in the History of American Industrial Enterprise* (Cambridge, MA: MIT Press, 1962).

[27] A classic treatment of environment and organizational design is found in James D. Thompson, *Organizations in Action* (New York: McGraw-Hill, 1967). See also Scott, *Organizations*, pp. 264–69.

[28] See Peter M. Blau and Richard A. Schoennerr, *The Structure of Organizations* (New York: Basic Books, 1971); and Scott, *Organizations*, pp. 259–63; and John R. Kimberly, Robert H. Miles, *The Organizational Life Cycle* (San Francisco: Jossey-Bass, 1980).

[29] Paul R. Lawrence and Jay W. Lorsch, *Organizations and Environment* (Boston: The Division of Research, Graduate School of Business Administration, Harvard University, 1967).

[30] See Jay R. Galbraith, *Organizational Design* (Reading, MA: Addison-Wesley, 1977); and, Susan Albers Mohrman, "Integrating Roles and Structure in the Lateral Organization," chapter 5 in Galbraith, Lawler and Associates, op. cit., 1993.

[31] Michael Hammer, *Beyond Reengineering* (New York: Harper Business, 1997).

[32] Michael Hammer and James Champy, *Reengineering the Corporation: A Manifesto for Business Revolution* (New York: Harper Business, 1993).

[33] Ronni T. Marshak, "Workflow Business Process Reengineering," special advertising section, *Fortune*, 1997; and www.psggroup.com.

[34] Ibid.

[35] Example in Hammer, *Beyond Reengineering*, pp. 28–30.

Chapter 10 Notes

[1] Information from "Coopers & Lybrand: Weaving Diversity into the Fabric of Business," *Fortune*, June 23, 1997, special advertising section.

[2] See, for example, "Rethinking Work," special report, *Business Week*, October 17, 1994, pp. 74–87.

[3] Nancy J. Perry, "The Workers of the Future," *Fortune*, "The New American Century" (special issue) (spring–summer 1991), pp. 68–72.

[4] Quote from William Bridges, "The End of the Job," *Fortune*, September 19, 1994, p. 68.

[5] See Boris Yavitz, "Human Resources in Strategic Planning," in *Executive Talent: Developing and Keeping the Best People*, Eli Ginzberg (ed.)(New York: Wiley, 1988), p. 34.

[6] See John P. Wanous, *Organizational Entry: Recruitment, Selection, and Socialization of Newcomers* (Reading, MA: Addison-Wesley, 1980), pp. 34–44.

[7] Information from Justin Martin, "Mercedes: Made in Alabama," *Fortune*, July 7, 1997, pp. 150–58.

[8] "Would You Hire This Person Again?" *Business Week*, Enterprise issue, June 9, 1997, pp. ENT32.

[9] Information from William M. Bulkeley, "Replaced by Technology: Job Interviews," *Wall Street Journal*, August 22, 1994, pp. B1, B4.

[10] For a scholarly review, see John Van Maanen and Edgar H. Schein, "Toward a Theory of Socialization," in *Research in Organizational Behavior*, vol. 1, Barry M. Staw, ed. (Greenwich, CT: JAI Press, 1979), pp. 209–64; for a practitioner's view, see Richard Pascale, "Fitting New Employees into the Company Culture," *Fortune*, May 28, 1984, pp. 28–42.

[11] This involves the social information processing concept as discussed in Gerald R. Salancik and Jeffrey Pfeffer, "A Social Information Processing Approach to Job Attitudes and Task Design," *Administrative Science Quarterly*, vol. 23 (June 1978): 224–53.

[12] Larry L. Cummings and Donald P. Schwab, *Performance in Organizations: Determinants and Appraisal* (Glenview, IL: Scott, Foresman, 1973).

[13] Charles Handy, *The Age of Unreason* (Cambridge, MA.: Harvard Business School Press, 1990), p. 55.

[14] See Betty Friedan, *Beyond Gender: The New Politics of Work and the Family* (Washington, DC: Woodrow Wilson Center Press, 1997) and James A. Levine, *Working Fathers: New Strategies for Balancing Work and Family* (Reading, MA: Addison-Wesley, 1997).

[15] Information from David Coburn, "Balancing Home, Work Still Big Concern," *Columbus Dispatch*, February 16, 1998, pp. 8, 9.

[16] Information from Jeffrey Ball, "DaimlerChrysler's Transfer Woes," *The Wall Street Journal* (August 24, 1999), p. B1.

[17] For a good review, see Richard B. Freeman and James L. Medoff, *What Do Unions Do?* (New York: Basic Books, 1984); and Charles C. Heckscher, *The New Unionism* (New York: Basic Books, 1988).

[18] "Trade Union Membership," *Economist*, December 6, 1997, p. 114.

[19] See "Reinventing Labor: An Interview with Union President Lynn Williams," *Harvard Business Review*, July–August 1993, pp. 115–25.

Chapter 11 Notes

[1] Max DePree, "An Old Pro's Wisdom: It Begins with a Belief in People," *New York Times*, September 10, 1989, p. F2; Max DePree, *Leadership Is an Art* (New York: Doubleday, 1989); David Woodruff, "Herman Miller: How Green Is My Factory," *Business Week*, September 16, 1991, pp. 54–56; Max DePree, *Leadership Jazz* (New York: Doubleday, 1992).

[2] DePree, op. cit., 1989 & 1992.

[3] Abraham Zaleznick, "Leaders and Managers: Are They Different?" *Harvard Business Review*, May–June, 1977, pp. 67–78.

[4] James M. Kouzes and Barry Z. Posner, "The Leadership Challenge," *Success*, April 1988, p. 68. See also their book, *The Leadership Challenge: How to Get Extraordinary Things Done in Organizations* (San Francisco: Jossey-Bass, 1987), and James M. Kouzes and Barry Z. Posner, *Credibility: How Leaders Gain and Lose It; Why People Demand It* (San Francisco: Jossey-Bass, 1996).

[5] Quotation from General Electric Company annual report 1997, p. 5.

[6] See Kouzes and Posner, "The Leadership Challenge," *The Leadership Challenge: How to Get Extraordinary Things Done in Organizations*. See also James C. Collins and Jerry I. Porras, "Building Your Company's Vision," *Harvard Business Review*, September–October 1996, pp. 65–77.

[7] Rosabeth Moss Kanter, "Power Failure in Management Circuits," *Harvard Business Review*, vol. 47 (July–August 1979): 65–75.

[8] For a good managerial discussion of power, see David C. McClelland and David H. Burnham, "Power Is the Great Motivator," *Harvard Business Review*, vol. 54 (March–April 1976): 100–110.

[9] See John R. P. French Jr. and Bertram Raven, "The Bases of Social Power," in *Group Dynamics: Research and Theory* Darwin Cartwright, ed. (Evanston, IL: Row, Peterson, 1962), pp. 607–13. For managerial applications of this basic framework, see Gary Yukl and Tom Taber, "The Effective Use of Managerial Power," *Personnel*, vol. 60 (1983): 37–49; Robert C. Benfari, Harry E. Wilkinson, and Charles D. Orth, "The Effective Use of Power," *Business Horizons*, vol. 29 (1986): pp. 12–16.

[10] Gary A. Yukl, *Leadership in Organizations*, 4th ed. (Englewood Cliffs, NJ: Prentice-Hall, 1998), includes "information" as a separate, but related, power source.

[11] Jay A. Conger, "Leadership: The Art of Empowering Others," *Academy of Management Executive*, vol. 3 (1989): 17–24.

[12] Esther Wachs Book, "Leadership for the Millennium," *Working Woman*, March 1998, pp. 29–34.

[13] Conger, op. cit.

[14] DePree, "An Old Pro's Wisdom," op cit.

[15] The early work on leader traits is well represented in Ralph M. Stogdill, "Personal Factors Associated with Leadership: A Survey of the Literature," *Journal of Psychology*, vol. 25 (1948): 35–71. See also Edwin E. Ghiselli, *Explorations in Management Talent* (Santa Monica, CA: Goodyear, 1971), and Shirley A. Kirkpatrick and Edwin A. Locke, "Leadership: Do Traits Really Matter?" *Academy of Management Executive* (1991): 48–60.

[16] See also John W. Gardner's article, "The Context and Attributes of Leadership," *New Management*, vol. 5 (1988): 18–22; John P. Kotter, *The Leadership Factor* (New York: The Free Press, 1988); and Bernard M. Bass, *Stogdill's Handbook of Leadership* (New York: The Free Press, 1990).

[17] See Bass, *Stogdill's Handbook of Leadership*.

[18] Joseph Weber, "Meet DuPont's In-house Conscience," *Business Week*, June 24, 1991, pp. 62–65; Sue Shellenbarger, "Executives

Reflect on Past Choices Made for Family and Jobs," *Wall Street Journal*, December 31, 1997, p. B1.

[19] Robert R. Blake and Jane Srygley Mouton, *The New Managerial Grid III* (Houston: Gulf Publishing, 1985).

[20] For a good discussion of this theory, see Fred E. Fiedler, Martin M. Chemers, and Linda Mahar, *The Leadership Match Concept* (New York: Wiley, 1978); Fiedler's current contingency research with the cognitive resource theory is summarized in Fred E. Fiedler and Joseph E. Garcia, *New Approaches to Effective Leadership* (New York: Wiley, 1987).

[21] Paul Hersey and Kenneth H. Blanchard, *Management and Organizational Behavior* (Englewood Cliffs, NJ: Prentice-Hall, 1988). For an interview with Paul Hersey on the origins of the model, see John R. Schermerhorn Jr., "Situational Leadership: Conversations with Paul Hersey," *Mid-American Journal of Business*, fall 1997, pp. 5–12.

[22] See, for example, Robert J. House, "A Path-Goal Theory of Leader Effectiveness," *Administrative Sciences Quarterly*, vol. 16 (1971): 321–38; Robert J. House and Terrence R. Mitchell, "Path-Goal Theory of Leadership," *Journal of Contemporary Business*, autumn 1974, pp. 81–97; the path-goal theory is reviewed by Bernard M. Bass in *Stogdill's Handbook of Leadership*, and Yukl in *Leadership in Organizations*. A supportive review of research is offered in Julie Indvik, "Path-Goal Theory of Leadership; A Meta-Analysis," in *Academy of Management Best Paper Proceedings 1986*, John A. Pearce II and Richard B. Robinson Jr., eds. pp. 189–92.

[23] See Steven Kerr and John Jermier, "Substitutes for Leadership: Their Meaning and Measurement," *Organizational Behavior and Human Performance*, vol. 22 (1978): 375–403; Jon P. Howell and Peter W. Dorfman, "Leadership and Substitutes for Leadership among Professional and Nonprofessional Workers," *Journal of Applied Behavioral Science*, vol. 22 (1986): 29–46.

[24] For a review see Yukl, *Leadership in Organizations*, 1998.

[25] For additional thoughts, see Warren Bennis, *Why Leaders Can't Lead* (San Francisco: Jossey-Bass, 1996).

[26] Among the popular books addressing this point of view are Warren Bennis and Burt Nanus, *Leaders* (New York: Harper & Row, 1985); Max DePree, *Leadership Is an Art* (Lansing: Michigan State University Press, 1987); Kotter, *The Leadership Factor*; The Leadership Challenge Kouzes and Posner, op. cit. A number of the issues are well summarized in James O'Toole, ed., "Special Section on Leadership," *New Management: The Magazine for Innovative Managers*, vol. 5 (1988): 2–31.

[27] See, for example, Jay A. Conger, "Inspiring Others: The Language of Leadership," *Academy of Management Executive*, vol. 5 (1991): 31–45.

[28] The distinction was originally made by James McGregor Burns, *Leadership* (New York: Harper & Row, 1978) and was further developed by Bernard Bass, *Leadership and Performance beyond Expectations* (New York: The Free Press, 1985) and Bernard M. Bass, "Leadership: Good, Better, Best," *Organizational Dynamics*, vol. 13 (winter 1985): 26–40.

[29] This list is based on Kouzes and Posner, op. cit.; Gardner, op. cit.

[30] See Daniel Goleman, *Emotional Intelligence* (New York: Bantam Books, 1995) and *Working with Emotional Intelligence* (New York: Bantam Books, 1998).

[31] Daniel Goleman, "What Makes a Leader?" *Harvard Business Review* (November–December, 1998), pp. 93–102.

[32] Ibid.

[33] Ibid., p. 95.

[34] Information from "Women and Men, Work and Power," *Fast Company*, Issue 13 (1998), p. 71.

[35] Research on gender issues in leadership is reported in Sally Helgesen, *The Female Advantage: Women's Ways of Leadership* (New York: Doubleday, 1990); Judith B. Rosener, "Ways Women Lead," *Harvard Business Review* (November–December 1990), pp. 150–60; and Alice H. Eagly, Steven J. Karau, and Blair T. Johnson, "Gender and Leadership Style among School Principals: A Meta Analysis," *Administrative Science Quarterly*, vol. 27 (1992): 76–102. See also Harriet Rubin, *Machiavelli for Women* (New York: Doubleday, 1997).

[36] For debate on whether some transformational leadership qualities tend to be associated more with female than male leaders, see Judy B. Rosener, "Ways Women Lead," *Harvard Business Review*, November–December 1990, pp. 119–25; "Debate: Ways Women and Men Lead," *Harvard Business Review*, January–February 1991, pp. 150–60.

[37] Peter F. Drucker, "Leadership: More Doing than Dash," *Wall Street Journal*, January 6, 1988, p. 16. For a compendium of writings on leadership sponsored by the Drucker Foundation, see Frances Hesselbein, Marshall Goldsmith, and Richard Beckhard, *Leader of the Future* (San Francisco: Jossey-Bass, 1997).

[38] Information from Matt Murray, "Late to the Web, GE Now Views Internet as Key to New Growth," *The Wall Street Journal* (June 22, 1999), pp. B1, B6.

[39] Gardner, "The Context and Attributes of Leadership," op. cit., 1988.

[40] For a view of the "spiritual" aspects of leadership, see Lee G. Bolman and Terrence E. Deal, *Leading With Soul* (San Francisco: Jossey-Bass, 1995). See also Steven R. Covey, *Principle-Centered Leadership* (New York: The Free Press, 1992).

[41] De Pree, "An Old Pro's Wisdom."

Chapter 12 Notes

[1] Thomas J. Peters and Robert H. Waterman Jr., *In Search of Excellence* (New York: Warner books, 1982); "Global Business Sets Its Goals," *Fortune*, August 4, 1997, p. S5.

[2] Example taken from Kevin Kelley, "I'm the Boss, That's Why," *Business Week*, Enterprise issue, June 9, 1997, p. ENT 32.

[3] See Abraham H. Maslow, *Eupsychian Management* (Homewood, IL: Richard D. Irwin, 1965); Abraham H. Maslow, *Motivation and Personality*, 2d ed. (New York: Harper & Row, 1970). For a research perspective, see Mahmoud A. Wahba and Lawrence G. Bridwell, "Maslow Reconsidered: A Review of Research on the Need Hierarchy," *Organizational Behavior and Human Performance*, vol. 16 (1976): 212–40.

[4] The complete two-factor theory is in Frederick Herzberg, Bernard Mausner, and Barbara Block Snyderman, *The Motivation to Work*, 2d ed. (New York: Wiley, 1967); Frederick Herzberg, "One More Time: How Do You Motivate Employees?" *Harvard Business Review*, vol. 47 (January–February 1968): 53–62, and reprinted as an *HBR* classic in vol. 65, September–October 1987, pp. 109–20.

[5] Critical reviews are provided by Robert J. House and Lawrence A.

Wigdor, "Herzberg's Dual-Factor Theory of Job Satisfaction and Motivation: A Review of the Evidence and a Criticism," *Personnel Psychology*, vol. 20 (winter 1967): 369–89; Steven Kerr, Anne Harlan, and Ralph Stogdill, "Preference for Motivator and Hygiene Factors in a Hypothetical Interview Situation," *Personnel Psychology*, vol. 27 (winter 1974): 109–24.

[6] For a collection of McClelland's work, see David C. McClelland, *The Achieving Society* (New York: Van Nostrand, 1961); "Business Drive and National Achievement," *Harvard Business Review*, vol. 40 (July–August 1962): 99–112; David C. McClelland and David H. Burnham, "Power Is the Great Motivator," *Harvard Business Review*, vol. 54 (March–April 1976): 100–10; David C. McClelland, *Human Motivation* (Glenview, IL: Scott, Foresman, 1985); David C. McClelland and Richard E. Boyatsis, "The Leadership Motive Pattern and Long-Term Success in Management," *Journal of Applied Psychology*, vol. 67 (1982): 737–43.

[7] See, for example, J. Stacy Adams, "Toward an Understanding of Inequity," *Journal of Abnormal and Social Psychology*, vol. 67 (1963): 422–36; J. Stacy Adams, "Inequity in Social Exchange," in *Advances in Experimental Social Psychology*, vol. 2, L. Berkowitz, ed. (New York: Academic Press, 1965), pp. 267–300.

[8] Victor H. Vroom, *Work and Motivation* (New York: Wiley, 1964, republished by Jossey-Bass, 1994).

[9] The work on goal-setting theory is well summarized in Edwin A. Locke and Gary P. Latham, *Goal Setting: A Motivational Technique That Works!* (Englewood Cliffs, NJ: Prentice-Hall, 1984). See also Edwin A. Locke, Kenneth N. Shaw, Lisa A. Saari, and Gary P. Latham, "Goal Setting and Task Performance 1969–1980," *Psychological Bulletin*, vol. 90 (1981): 125–52; Mark E. Tubbs, "Goal Setting: A Meta-Analytic Examination of the Empirical Evidence," *Journal of Applied Psychology*, vol. 71 (1986): 474–83.

[10] Gary P. Latham and Edwin A. Locke, "Self-Regulation through Goal Setting," *Organizational Behavior and Human Decision Processes*, vol. 50 (1991): 212–47.

[11] For an overview, see Paul E. Spector, *Job Satisfaction* (Thousand Oaks, CA: Sage, 1997).

[12] Linda Grant, "Happy Workers, High Returns," *Fortune*, January 12, 1998, p. 81.

[13] "Nine to Five: How Workers Feel," *Wall Street Journal*, September 19, 1997, p. R4.

[14] Herzberg, op cit., 1987, pp. 109–20.

[15] For a complete description of the job characteristics model, see J. Richard Hackman and Greg R. Oldham, *Work Redesign* (Reading, MA: Addison-Wesley, 1980); additional descriptions of directions in job design research and practice are available in Ramon J. Aldag and Arthur P. Brief, *Task Design and Employee Motivation* (Glenview, IL: Scott, Foresman, 1979); and Ricky W. Griffin, *Task Design: An Integrative Approach* (Glenview, IL: Scott, Foresman, 1982).

[16] See Michelle Conlin, "9 to 5 Isn't Working Anymore," *Business Week* (September 20, 1999), p. 94.

[17] A good overview is Allen R. Cohen and Herman Gadon, *Alternative Work Schedules: Integrating Individual and Organizational Needs* (Reading, MA: Addison-Wesley, 1978).

[18] Information from Sue Schellenbarger, "Employees Who Value Time as Much as Money Now Get Their Reward," *The Wall Street Journal* (September 22, 1999), p. B1.

[19] Daniel Eisenberg, "Rise of the Permatemp," *Business Week* (July 12, 1999), p. 48.

[20] "A Leg Up for the Lowly Temp," *Business Week* (June 21, 1999), pp. 102–103.

Chapter 13 Notes

[1] These case examples are reported in *Business Week*, July 8, 1991, pp. 60–61. For more information on the Center for Creative Leadership, Greensboro, North Carolina, see:<http:>

[2] For a description of the centrality of communication to managerial roles see Henry Mintzberg, *The Nature of Managerial Work* (New York: Harper & Row, 1973).

[3] See Robert H. Lengel and Richard L. Daft, "The Selection of Communication Media as an Executive Skill," *Academy of Management Executive*, vol. 2 (August 1988): 225–32.

[4] Quotations from John Huey, "America's Most Successful Merchant," *Fortune*, September 23, 1991, pp. 46–59.

[5] Adapted from Richard V. Farace, Peter R. Monge, and Hamish M. Russell, *Communicating and Organizing* (Reading, MA: Addison-Wesley, 1977), pp. 97–98.

[6] See H. R. Schiffman, *Sensation and Perception: An Integrated Approach*, 3d ed. (New York: John Wiley, 1990).

[7] These examples are from Natasha Josefowitz, *Paths to Power* (Reading, MA: Addison-Wesley, 1980), p. 60.

[8] The classic work is Dewitt C. Dearborn and Herbert A. Simon, "Selective Perception: A Note on the Departmental Identification of Executives," *Sociometry*, vol. 21 (1958): 140–44. See also, J. P. Walsh, "Selectivity and Selective Perception: Belief Structures and Information Processing," *Academy of Management Journal* vol. 24 (1988): 453–70.

[9] This discussion is based on Carl R. Rogers and Richard E. Farson, "Active Listening" (Chicago: Industrial Relations Center of the University of Chicago), n.d.

[10] A useful source of guidelines is John J. Gabarro and Linda A. Hill, "Managing Performance," Note 9-96-022, Harvard Business School Publishing, Boston, MA.

[11] Developed from John Anderson, "Giving and Receiving Feedback," in Paul R. Lawrence, Louis B. Barnes, and Jay W. Lorsch, *Organizational Behavior and Administration*, 3d ed. (Homewood, IL: Richard D. Irwin, 1976), p. 109.

[12] Information from "How'm I Doing" No, Really," *Business Week*, Enterprise Issue, September 1, 1997, pp. ENT10–12.

[13] A classic work on proxemics is Edward T. Hall's book *The Hidden Dimension* (Garden City, NY: Doubleday, 1986).

[14] Mirand Wewll, "Alternative Spaces Spawning Desk-Free Zones," *Columbus Dispatch*, May 18, 1998, pp. 10–11.

[15] Information from Carol Hymowitz, "Criticism is a Cinch: Try Telling Employees How Good They Are," *The Wall Street Journal* (July 6, 1999), p. A17.

[16] See Edward T. Hall, *The Silent Language* (New York: Doubleday, 1973).

[17] Information from "Corporate Community Service: Seeking America's Leaders," *Fortune*, October 17, 1994, special insert.

[18] Richard E. Walton, *Interpersonal Peacemaking: Confrontations and Third-Party Consultation* (Reading, MA: Addison-Wesley, 1969), p. 2.

[19] Information from E. S. Browning, "Chip Project Brings Rivals Together, but Cultures Clash," *The Asian Wall Street Journal* (May 5, 1994), pp. 1, 7.

[20] See Kenneth W. Thomas, "Conflict and Conflict Management," in *Handbook of Industrial and Organizational Behavior*, M. D. Dunnett, ed. (Chicago: Rand McNally, 1976), pp. 889–935.

[21] See Robert R. Blake and Jane Strygley Mouton, "The Fifth Achievement," *Journal of Applied Behavioral Science*, vol. 6 (1970), pp. 413–427; Alan C. Filley, *Interpersonal Conflict Resolution* (Glenview, IL: Scott Foresman, 1975).

[22] This discussion is based on Filley, op. cit.; and, Vincent L. Ferraro and Sheila A. Adams, "Interdepartmental Conflict: Practical Ways to Prevent and Reduce It," *Personnel*, vol. 61 (1984), pp. 12–23.

[23] Roger Fisher and William Ury, *Getting to Yes: Negotiating Agreement without Giving in* (New York: Penguin, 1983); and William L. Ury, Jeanne M. Brett, and Stephen B. Goldberg, *Getting Disputes Resolved* (San Francisco: Jossey-Bass, 1997).

[24] Fisher and Ury, *Getting to Yes*; see also James A. Wall Jr., *Negotiation: Theory and Practice* (Glenview, Il: Scott Foresman, 1985).

[25] Ibid.

[26] Ibid.

[27] Developed from Max H. Bazerman, *Judgment in Managerial Decision Making*, 3d ed. (New York: Wiley, 1994), chap. 7; and Fisher and Ury, *Getting to Yes*, pp. 10–14.

Chapter 14 Notes

[1] Information from Jennifer Scott, "Working Better Together Is the Challenge," *Columbus Dispatch*, November 3, 1997, pp. 10–11.

[2] See, for example, Edward E. Lawler III, Susan Albers Mohrman, and Gerald E. Ledford Jr., *Employee Involvement and Total Quality Management: Practices and Results in Fortune 1000 Companies* (San Francisco: Jossey-Bass, 1992); Frank Ostroff, *The Horizontal Organization* (New York: Oxford University Press, 1999); Jean Lipman-Blumens and Harold J. Leavitt, *Hot Groups* (New York: Oxford University Press, 1999).

[3] Jon R. Katzenbach and Douglas K. Smith, *The Wisdom of Teams: Creating the High Performance Organization* (Boston: Harvard Business School Press, 1993).

[4] See Marvin E. Shaw, *Group Dynamics: The Psychology of Small Group Behavior*, 2d ed. (New York: McGraw-Hill, 1976); Harold J. Leavitt, "Suppose We Took Groups More Seriously," in *Man and Work in Society* Eugene L. Cass and Frederick G. Zimmer, eds. (New York: Van Nostrand Reinhold, 1975), pp. 67–77.

[5] See W. Jack Duncan, "Why Some People Loaf in Groups While Others Loaf Alone," *Academy of Management Review*, vol. 8 (1004): 79–80.

[6] For insights on how to run an effective meeting see Mary A. De Vries, *How to Run a Meeting* (New York: Penguin, 1994).

[7] Information from Thomas Pefzinger, Jr., "With the Stakes High, A Lucent Duo Conquers Distance and Culture," *The Wall Street Journal* (April 23, 1999), p. B1.

[8] For a good discussion of quality circles, see Edward E. Lawler III and Susan A. Mohrman, "Quality Circles after the Fad," *Harvard Business Review*, vol. 63 (January–February 1985): 65–71; Gerald E. Ledford Jr., Edward E. Lawler III, and Susan A. Mohrman, "The Quality Circle and Its Variations," chapter 10 in John R. Campbell, Richard J. Campbell and *Productivity in Organizations* (San Francisco: Jossey-Bass, 1988); and Lawler, Mohrman, and Ledford, 1992, *Employee Involvement*.

[9] Information from "Ford Team Find Ways to Recycle Car Parts," special from *Chicago Tribune*, as reported in *Columbus Dispatch*, December 20, 1997, p. G1.

[10] Wanda J. Orlikowski and J. Debra Hofman, "An Improvisational Model for Change Management: The Case of Groupware Technologies," *Sloan Management Review*, fall 1993, pp. 27–36.

[11] R. Brent Gallupe and William H. Cooper, "Brainstorming Electronically," *Sloan Management Review*, winter 1997, pp. 11–21.

[12] See, for example, Paul S. Goodman, Rukmini Devadas, and Terri L. Griffith Hughson, "Groups and Productivity: Analyzing the Effectiveness of Self-Managing Teams," chapter 11 in John R. Campbell, Richard J. Campbell, *Productivity in Organizations* (San Francisco: Jossey-Bass, 1988); Jack Orsbrun, Linda Moran, Ed Musslewhite, and John H. Zenger, with Craig Perrin, *Self-Directed Work Teams: The New American Challenge* (Homewood, IL: Business One Irwin, 1990); Dale E. Yeatts and Cloyd Hyten, *High Performing Self-Managed Work Teams* (Thousand Oaks, CA: Sage, 1997).

[13] For a review of research on group effectiveness, see J. Richard Hackman, "The Design of Work Teams," in *Handbook of Organizational Behavior* Jay W. Lorsch ed. (Englewood Cliffs, NJ: Prentice-Hall, 1987), pp. 315–42.

[14] See Patricia Doyle Corner and Angelo J. Kinicki, "A Proposed Mediator between Top Team Demography and Financial Performance," *Academy of Management Proceedings '97*, pp. 7–11.

[15] See Warren Watson, "Cultural Diversity's Impact on Interaction Process and Performance," *Academy of Management Journal*, vol. 16 (1993).

[16] Bruce W. Tuckman, "Developmental Sequence in Small Groups," *Psychological Bulletin*, vol. 63 (1965): 384–99; Bruce W. Tuckman and Mary Ann C. Jensen, "Stages of Small-Group Development Revisited," *Group & Organization Studies*, vol. 2 (1977): 419–27. For a slightly different model, see also J. Steven Heinen and Eugene Jacobson, "A Model of Task Group Development in Complex Organizations and a Strategy of Implementation," *Academy of Management Review*, vol. 1 (1976): 98–111.

[17] For a good discussion, see Robert F. Allen and Saul Pilnick, "Confronting the Shadow Organization: How to Detect and Defeat Negative Norms," *Organizational Dynamics*, spring 1973, pp. 13–17.

[18] Information from "Importing Enthusiasm," *Business Week*, special section on "21st Century Capitalism," November 7, 1994.

[19] See Edgar H. Schein, Process Consultation, Volumes I & II, Second Edition (Englewood Cliffs, N.J.: Prentice-Hall, 1988).

[20] A classic work in this area is the 1948 article in the *Journal of Social Issues*, vol. 2: 42–47, by K. Benne and P. Sheets. See also op. cit., 1988.

[21] Research on communication networks is found in Alex Bavelas, "Communication Patterns in Task-Oriented Groups," *Journal of the Accoustical Society of America*, vol. 22 (1950): 725–30; see also Marvin E. Shaw, *Group Dynamics: The Psychology of Small Group Behavior* (New York: McGraw-Hill, 1976).

[22] Schein, op. cit., 1988.

[23] See Kathleen M. Eisenhardt, Jean L. Kahwajy, and L. J. Bourgeois III, "How Management Teams Can Have a Good Fight," *Harvard Business Review*, July–August 1997, pp. 77–85.

[24] Victor H. Vroom and Arthur G. Jago, *The New Leadership: Managing Participation in Organizations* (Englewood Cliffs, NJ: Prentice-Hall, 1988).

[25] Norman F. Maier, "Assets and Liabilities in Group Problem Solving," *Psychological Review*, vol. 74 (1967): 239–49.

[26] See Irving L. Janis, "Groupthink," *Psychology Today*, November 1971, pp. 43–46; *Victims of Groupthink*, 2d ed. (Boston: Houghton Mifflin, 1982).

[27] Both the symptoms and guidelines are from Ibid.

[28] See William D. Dyer, *Team-Building* (Reading, MA: Addison-Wesley, 1977).

[29] See Lynda C. McDermott, Nolan Brawley and William W. Waite, *World-Class Teams* (New York: John Wiley & Sons, 1998).

[30] Katzenbach & Smith, 1993.

[31] From Carl E. Larson and Frank M. J. LaFasto, *Team Work: What Must Go Right/What Can Go Wrong* (Newbury Park, CA: Sage, 1990).

[32] See Katzenbach & Smith, op. cit., 1993; Jon R. Katzenbach, "The Myth of the Top Management Team," *Harvard Business Review*, vol. 75 (November–December 1997): 83–91; and McDermott, et al., op. cit., 1998.

Chapter 15 Notes

[1] Information from "On the Road to Innovation," in special advertising section, "Charting the Course: Global Business Sets Its Goals," *Fortune*, August 4, 1997.

[2] Peter Senge, *The Fifth Discipline* (New York: Harper, 1990); Alan Webber, "Learning for a Change," *Fast Company* (September 1999), pp. 178+.

[3] Tom Peters, *The Circle of Innovation* (New York: Alfred A. Knopf, 1997).

[4] George Melloan, "Herman Miller's Secrets of Creativity," *Wall Street Journal*, May 3, 1988, p. 23.

[5] Senge, *The Fifth Discipline*, see also Brian Dumaine, "Mr. Learning Organization," *Fortune*, October 17, 1994, pp. 147–57.

[6] This discussion is based on Edward B. Roberts, "Managing Invention and Innovation," *Research Technology Management* (January–February 1988): 1–19.

[7] On creativity see Roger von Oech, *A Whack on the Side of the Head* (New York: Warner Books, 1983) and *A Kick in the Seat of the Pants* (New York: Harper & Row, 1986).

[8] This discussion is stimulated by James Brian Quinn, "Managing Innovation Controlled Chaos," *Harvard Business Review*, vol. 63 (May–June 1985). Selected quotations and examples from Kenneth Labich, "The Innovators," *Fortune*, June 6, 1988, pp. 49–64.

[9] Ibid.

[10] Peter F. Drucker, "Best R&D Is Business Driven," *Wall Street Journal*, February 10, 1988, p. 11.

[11] See Roberts, "Managing Invention and Innovation."

[12] *Wall Street Journal*, May 3, 1988, p. 23.

[13] Developed in part from Quinn, "Managing Innovation Controlled Chaos."

[14] Information from *Fortune* (December 1991), pp. 56–62; Toro Company website: www.toro.com.

[15] Carol Hymowitz, "Task of Managing Changes in Workplace Takes a Careful Hand," *The Wall Street Journal* (July 1, 1997), p. B1.

[16] See Edward E. Lawler III, "Strategic Choices for Changing Organizations," chapter 12 in Allan M. Mohrman Jr., Susan Albers Mohrman, Gerald E. Ledford Jr., Thomas G. Cummings, Edward E. Lawler III, and associates, *Large Scale Organizational Change* (San Francisco: Jossey-Bass, 1989).

[17] The classic description of organizations on these terms is by Harold J. Leavitt, "Applied Organizational Change in Industry: Structural, Technological and Humanistic Approaches," in *Handbook of Organizations* James G. March, ed. (Chicago: Rand McNally, 1965), pp. 1144–70. Another timely approach is described by Ralph H. Kilmann in *Beyond the Quick Fix* (San Francisco: Jossey-Bass, 1984).

[18] Kurt Lewin, "Group Decision and Social Change," in *Readings in Social Psychology*, G. E. Swanson, T. M. Newcomb and E. L. Hartley, eds. (New York: Holt Rinehart, 1952), pp. 459–73.

[19] This discussion is based on Robert Chin and Kenneth D. Benne, "General Strategies for Effecting Changes in Human Systems," in eds. *The Planning of Change*, 3d ed., Warren G. Bennis, Kenneth D. Benne, Robert Chin, and Kenneth E. Corey, (New York: Holt, Rinehart, 1969), pp. 22–45; Patrick E. Connor, "Strategies for Managing Technological Change," *Harvard International Review*, vol. 10 (1988): 10–13.

[20] The change strategy examples in this section are developed from an exercise reported in J. William Pfeiffer and John E. Jones, *A Handbook of Structured Experiences for Human Relations Training*, vol. 2 (La Jolla, CA: University Associates, 1973).

[21] John P. Kotter and Leonard A. Schlesinger, "Choosing Strategies for Change," *Harvard Business Review*, vol. 57 (March–April 1979): 109–12.

[22] Wanda J. Orlikowski and J. Debra Hofman, "An Improvisational Model for Change Management: The Case of Groupware Technologies," *Sloan Management Review*, winter 1997, pp. 11–21.

[23] Overviews of organization development are provided by Wendell L. French and Cecil H. Bell Jr., *Organization Development*, 6th ed. (Englewood Cliffs, NJ: Prentice-Hall, 1999).

[24] Information from *Asian Wall Street Journal* (March 10, 1993), p. 20; Hoover's online: www.hoovers.com.

[25] Information from Michael J. McCarthy, "An Ex-Divinity Student Works on Searching the Corporate Soul," *The Wall Street Journal* (June 18, 1999), p. B1.

[26] Tom Peters, "The Brand Called You," *Fast Company*, August-September 1997).

[27] Ibid.

[28] Stephen Covey, "How to Succeed in Today's Workplace," *USA Weekend*, August 29–31, 1997, pp. 4–5.

Module Notes

[1] A thorough review and critique of the history of management thought, including management in ancient civilizations, is provided by Daniel A. Wren, *The Evolution of Management Thought*, 4th ed. (New York: Wiley, 1993); see also Daniel A. Wren and John A.

Pearce II (eds.), *Papers Dedicated to the Development of Modern Management: Celebrating 100 Years of Modern Management* (Mississippi State, Academy of Management, 1986).

[2] For a sample of this work see Henry L. Gantt, *Industrial Leadership* (Easton, MD: Hive, 1921; Hive edition published in 1974); Henry C. Metcalfe and Lyndall Urwick (eds.), *Dynamic Administration: The Collected Papers of Mary Parker Follett* (New York: Harper & Brothers, 1940); James D. Mooney, *The Principles of Administration*, rev. ed. (New York: Harper & Brothers, 1947); Lyndall Urwick, *The Elements of Administration* (New York: Harper & Brothers, 1943) and *The Golden Book of Management* (London: N. Neame, 1956).

[3] References on Taylor's work are from Frederick W. Taylor, *The Principles of Scientific Management* (New York: W. W. Norton, 1967), originally published by Harper & Brothers in 1911. See Charles W. Wrege and Amedeo G. Perroni, "Taylor's Pig-Tale: A Historical Analysis of Frederick W. Taylor's Pig-Iron Experiments," *Academy of Management Journal*, vol. 17 (March 1974): 6–27, for a criticism; see Edwin A. Lock, "The Ideas of Frederick W. Taylor: An Evaluation," *Academy of Management Review*, vol. 7 (1982): p. 14, for an examination of the contemporary significance of Taylor's work. See also the recent biography, Robert Kanigel, *The One Best Way* (New York: Viking, 1997).

[4] See Frank B. Gilbreth, *Motion Study* (New York: Van Nostrand, 1911).

[5] Available in the English language as Henri Fayol, *General and Industrial Administration* (London: Pitman, 1949); subsequent discussion is based on M. B. Brodie, *Fayol on Administration* (London: Pitman, 1949).

[6] M. P. Follett, *Freedom and Coordination* (London: Management Publications Trust, 1949). Discussion developed in part from Judith Garwood, "A Review of Dynamic Administration: The Collected Papers of Mary Parker Follett," New Management, vol. 2 (1984): 61–62; eulogy from Richard C. Cabot, *Encyclopedia of Social Work*, vol. 15, s.v., "Follett, Mary Parker," p. 351.

[7] Garwood, op. cit. *New Management*.

[8] A. M. Henderson and Talcott Parsons (eds. and trans.), *Max Weber: The Theory of Social Economic Organization* (New York: The Free Press, 1947).

[9] The Hawthorne studies are described in detail in F. J. Roethlisberger and William J. Dickson, *Management and the Worker* (Cambridge: Harvard University Press, 1966) and G. Homans, *Fatigue of Workers* (New York: Reinhold, 1941). For an interview with three of the participants in the relay-assembly test-room studies, see R. G. Greenwood, A. A. Bolton, and R. A. Greenwood, "Hawthorne a Half Century Later: "Relay Assembly Participants Remember," *Journal of Management*, vol. 9 (1983): 217–31.

[10] The criticisms of the Hawthorne studies are detailed in Alex Carey, "The Hawthorne Studies: A Radical Criticism," *American Sociological Review*, vol. 32 (1967): 403–16; H. M. Parsons, "What Happened at Hawthorne?" *Science*, vol. 183 (1974): 922–32; B. Rice, "The Hawthorne Defect: Persistence of a Flawed Theory," *Psychology Today*, vol. 16 (1982): 70–74. See also Wren, *Evolution*.

[11] This discussion of Maslow's theory is based on Abraham H. Maslow, *Eupsychian Management* (Homewood, IL: Richard D. Irwin, 1965), and Abraham H. Maslow, *Motivation and Personality*, 2d ed. (New York: Harper & Row, 1970).

[12] Douglas McGregor, *The Human Side of Enterprise* (New York: McGraw-Hill, 1960).

[13] The ideas of Ludwig von Bertalanffy contributed to the emergence of this systems perspective on organizations. See his article, "The History and Status of General Systems Theory," *Academy of Management Journal*, vol. 15 (1972): 407–26. This viewpoint is further developed by Daniel Katz and Robert L. Kahn in their classic book, *The Social Psychology of Organizations* (New York: Wiley, 1978). For an integrated systems view, see Lane Tracy, *The Living Organization* (New York: Quorum Books, 1994). For an overview, see W. Richard Scott, *Organizations: Rational, Natural, and Open Systems*, 4th ed. (Upper Saddle River, NJ: Prentice-Hall, 1998).

[14] For an overview see Scott, *Organizations*.

[15] Jay R. Galbraith, *Organizational Design* (Reading, MA: Addison-Wesley, 1977).

Index

Books are to be returned on or before
the last date below.

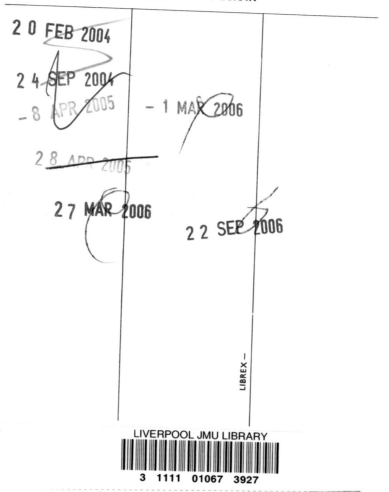

2 0 FEB 2004

2 4 SEP 2004

- 8 APR 2005   - 1 MAR 2006

2 8 APR 2006

2 7 MAR 2006   2 2 SEP 2006

LIBREX —

INTRODUCING MANAGEMENT
Schermerhorn and Chappell
©**John Wiley & Sons, Inc.**
www.wiley.com/college/schermerhorn
For Technical Support: 212-850-6753
techhelp@wiley.com
http://www.wiley.com/techsupport

Step 1: Register to access the **Introducing Management** Web site:

1. Go to *www.wiley.com/college/schermerhorn*
2. Select INTRODUCING MANAGEMENT
3. Select "Student Resources"
4. Click on the Student box under New Users
5. Type the name of your school in the box and press "Find School"
6. Follow on screen instructions
7. This is your registration code:
8. User name _____
9. Password   7100202-96942-1386-8

Step 2: Register to access **wsj.com**

1. Once you've completed **Step 1**, enter the **Introducing Management** Web site and select "**Register for wsj.com**".
2. Your username is:
3. Your password is: s4m00059like68
4. Complete the required fields, and click "I Accept"

* Keep this card to remind you of the password you create!